Contemporary linguistic theories distinguish the principal element of a phrase – the 'head' – from the subordinate elements it dominates. This pervasive grammatical concept has been used to describe and account for linguistic phenomena ranging from agreement and government to word-order universals, but opinions differ widely on its precise definition. A key question is whether the head is not already identified by some other, more basic notion or interacting set of notions in linguistics.

Heads in grammatical theory is the first book devoted to this subject. Providing a clear view of current research on heads, some of the foremost linguists in the field tackle the problems set by the assumptions of particular grammatical theories and offer insights which have relevance across theories. They consider whether there is a theory-neutral definition of head, whether heads have cognitive reality, how to identify the head of a phrase, how many heads a phrase can have, how functional heads behave in head-marking and dependent-marking languages and whether there are any universal correlations between headedness and deletability.

Heads in grammatical theory

Heads in grammatical theory

Edited by

GREVILLE G. CORBETT

*Professor of Linguistics and of Russian Language
Department of Linguistic and International Studies
University of Surrey*

NORMAN M. FRASER

*Logica Cambridge Ltd
and Department of Sociology
University of Surrey*

and

SCOTT McGLASHAN

*Department of Sociology
University of Surrey*

CAMBRIDGE
UNIVERSITY PRESS

Published by the Press Syndicate of the University of Cambridge
The Pitt Building, Trumpington Street, Cambridge CB2 1RP
40 West 20th Street, New York, NY 10011-4211, USA
10 Stamford Road, Oakleigh, Melbourne 3166, Australia

First published 1993

Printed in Great Britain at the University Press, Cambridge

A catalogue record for this book is available from the British Library

Library of Congress cataloguing in publication data

Heads in grammatical theory / edited by Greville G. Corbett, Norman M. Fraser,
and Scott McGlashan.
     p.   cm.
ISBN 0 521 42070 9
1. Grammar, Comparative and general – Noun phrase. I. Corbett, Greville G.
II. Fraser, Norman M. III. McGlashan, Scott.
P271.H35 1993
415 – dc20   92-19986 CIP

ISBN 0 521 42070 9 hardback

TS

Contents

Contributors

ROBERT D. BORSLEY
School of English and Linguistics, University of Wales, Bangor

RONNIE CANN
Department of Linguistics, University of Edinburgh

BERNARD COMRIE
Department of Linguistics, University of Southern California

GREVILLE G. CORBETT
Department of Linguistic and International Studies, University of Surrey

NORMAN M. FRASER
Logica Cambridge Ltd, and Social and Computer Sciences Research Group, Department of Sociology, University of Surrey

JOHN A. HAWKINS
Department of Linguistics, University of Southern California

RICHARD HUDSON
Department of Phonetics and Linguistics, University College London

SCOTT McGLASHAN
Social and Computer Sciences Research Group, Department of Sociology, University of Surrey

JOHANNA NICHOLS
Department of Slavic Languages and Literatures, University of California, Berkeley

JOHN PAYNE
Department of Linguistics, University of Manchester

ANDREW RADFORD
Department of Language and Linguistics, University of Essex

NIGEL VINCENT
Department of Linguistics, University of Manchester

ARNOLD M. ZWICKY
Department of Linguistics, Ohio State University, and Department of Linguistics, Stanford University

1 *Introduction*

NORMAN M. FRASER, GREVILLE G. CORBETT *and*
SCOTT McGLASHAN

1.1 Heads in grammatical theory

The majority of current grammatical theories refer explicitly to the *head* of a phrasal constituent. Yet while the term 'head' has entered the common currency of theoretical linguistics, this does not provide evidence of agreement on what it means. Nor does the term's long and varied career in linguistics guarantee that it identifies a notion which is not already identified by some other, more basic notion or interacting set of notions. The purpose of this volume is twofold: first, it aims to uncover and make explicit the notion (or notions) behind the term 'head'; second, it aims to investigate the status of the notion (or notions) in linguistic theory.

Most linguists would agree with the informal characterization that the head of a phrase is one of its constituents which in some sense dominates and represents the whole phrase. In an important paper published in the *Journal of Linguistics* in 1985, Zwicky drew attention to the fact that use of the term 'head' had been extended from syntax to morphology (for example, by Lieber, 1981; Williams, 1981; and Kiparsky, 1982) in spite of the fact that there was no generally agreed formal definition of the notion in syntax (though an important contribution had already been made by Gazdar and Pullum, 1981 and Gazdar, Pullum and Sag, 1982). Zwicky therefore set out to find a rigorous, generally acceptable definition for 'head'. He proceeded by examining the following eight candidate criteria for the identification of a constituent as a syntactic head.

1 Is the constituent the **semantic argument**, that is, the constituent whose meaning serves as argument to some functor?
2 Is it the **determinant of concord**, that is, the constituent with which co-constituents must agree?
3 Is it the **morphosyntactic locus**, that is, the constituent which bears inflections marking syntactic relations between the whole construct and other syntactic units?

4 Is it the **subcategorizand**, that is, the constituent which is subcategorized with respect to its sisters?

5 Is it the **governor**, that is, the constituent which selects the morphological form of its sisters?

6 Is it the **distributional equivalent**, that is, the constituent whose distribution is identical to that of the whole construct?

7 Is it the **obligatory** constituent, that is, the constituent whose removal forces the whole construct to be recategorized?

8 Is it the **ruler** in dependency theory, that is, the constituent on which others depend in a dependency analysis?

Application of Zwicky's criteria to a range of common syntactic constructions suggests that headedness is distributed amongst the constituents of a phrase: for example, in the construction NP+VP, VP is the morphosyntactic locus, the governor, and the obligatory constituent, but NP is the semantic argument and the determinant of concord. A harmonious solution cannot be achieved simply by discarding some criteria so as to yield a consistent set of results, since the distribution of successful and failed criteria differs between constructions. Zwicky concluded that 'head' should be identified with 'morphosyntactic locus' since this is all that is needed in order to state the very general principle of **percolation** which can be found in various forms in a variety of current grammatical theories. Briefly, percolation requires identity of some feature or features (such as syntactic category) between a head and its mother. Zwicky concluded that since headedness could be identified with a single, simple criterion, heads should not be accorded a privileged place in syntactic theory.

Zwicky also argued that a different generalization is required for the purpose of percolation in morphology, so the supposed relevance of heads to morphology is spurious. This conclusion is supported by Bauer (1990). The chapters in this volume deal with heads in syntax rather than morphology.

In a subsequent paper Hudson, whilst agreeing with the logic of Zwicky's argument, challenged his views on the ways in which constructions should be analysed and head-identification criteria applied (Hudson, 1987). On the basis of a set of assumptions derived from his theory of Word Grammar, Hudson succeeded in producing a harmonious analysis in which Zwicky's criteria uniquely identified a single head for each kind of construction surveyed. This led Hudson to conclude that 'head' is a category which unifies a range of different properties.

The notions of 'head' as this term has been applied in a variety of different theories are not, in fact, as disparate as Zwicky suggests... Different linguists may use the notion 'head' for different purposes – one for percolation, another for government, and so on – but this is to be expected in view of the multiplicity of properties that we have found for heads. (Hudson, 1987: 126)

The number of criteria for the recognition of heads suggested in this exchange (Hudson rejects one of Zwicky's criteria and goes on to offer others which Zwicky does not mention) and the lack of agreement on basic assumptions underlying the analysis of common syntactic constructions should not come as any surprise when it is remembered that the notion 'head' has entered linguistic theory by an unusually diverse set of routes.

The idea that one word may dominate another – that a subordinate word depends on a head word – is the central insight of traditional dependency grammar and its more recent offspring. Early notions of dependency are discernible in the Sanskrit grammar of Pāṇini (between 600 and 300 BC), in the Greek grammar of Apollonius Dyscolus (second century AD) and in the Latin grammar of Priscian (*c.* AD 450) (Robins, 1979). The medieval Arabic grammarians contrasted the governor or head of a phrase with the governed or dependent elements of the phrase. They stipulated amongst other things that a governor could have many dependents but a dependent could have only one governor; dependency relations were necessarily unidirectional; and dependents were required to be adjacent to their governors (Owens, 1988). Most modern dependency grammarians continue to work with these basic assumptions (for example, Robinson, 1970: 260).

Dependency grammar was first formalized by Tesnière (1959) and further developed by Hays (1964), Gaifman (1965) and Robinson (1970). In recent years there has been an upsurge of interest in dependency grammar, and a significant number of dependency theories have been developed (Anderson, 1971, 1977; Hudson, 1976, 1984, 1990; Miller, 1985; Mel'čuk, 1988; Starosta, 1988). Dependency grammar frameworks are assumed in this volume by Hudson and McGlashan.

The term 'head' is also used by Bloomfield in his seminal discussion of endocentric and exocentric constructions (1933: 195). For him, the head of a constituent is the daughter whose distribution is the same as that of the whole constituent (that is, Zwicky's 'distributional equivalent'). The substitutability of heads for larger constituents played an important part in the development of structuralist linguistics (Wells, 1947; Harris, 1951; Hockett, 1958). The introduction of X-bar grammar by Chomsky in 1970 (though Harris sketched a recognizable version in 1951) can be interpreted as a response to Lyons' observation that 'the notions of endocentricity, subordination, etc., have no systematic significance in a "rewrite" grammar' (Lyons, 1968: 235). In an X-bar grammar, a phrasal category must be identical except for bar level to a daughter category. The daughter category may be regarded as the head of the phrase. In their recent detailed examination of X-bar grammar, Kornai and Pullum conclude that 'the key concept is headedness' (1990: 46).

Many different versions of X-bar grammar have been proposed since 1970 (see Muysken, 1982: 58). X-bar theory is one of the subtheories of Government–Binding (GB) theory, which is assumed in the chapters by Cann, Payne, Radford and Vincent. X-bar theory is also basic to Generalized Phrase Structure Grammar (GPSG) (Gazdar *et al.*, 1985), whose Head Feature Convention requires that mothers and head daughters, by default, should bear the same features (with the exception of the **bar** feature). In this way phrase-structure trees become structures for head-to-head feature percolation. Warner (1989) argues within a GPSG framework that certain kinds of phrase are multiply headed, namely those involving co-ordination and certain minor categories. This calls for a reformulation of the Head Feature Convention and of our understanding of the notion 'head'.

Head-driven Phrase Structure Grammar (HPSG) (Pollard and Sag, 1987; Borsley, this volume) places even more importance on heads, since all heads incorporate information about the non-heads with which they combine (in a way inspired by Categorial Grammar). There are very few independent rules other than the basic information-combining rule of unification.

A further strand of research on heads can be found in work on language typology. The word-order universals of Greenberg (1966) and Vennemann (1975), for example, are expressed in terms of categories such as subject, object and verb. However, the dominant serialization orders of languages have been stated more concisely by reference to the more general categories of head and modifier (Hawkins, 1983). This approach appears first in the writings of the medieval Arabic grammarians (Owens, 1988). Thus, for example, it might be said that the dominant order in Japanese is modifier–head, while the dominant order in Welsh is head–modifier. In chapter 11, Hawkins argues against this approach, an argument which is rendered all the more worthy of attention since it attacks the view which

Hawkins himself previously endorsed. Dryer (1992) bases his rejection of generalizations predicated on consistent ordering of heads and dependents upon detailed study of a sample of more than 600 languages.

Another important typological insight is offered by Nichols (1986), who distinguishes head-marking languages from dependent-marking languages. The fact that different languages place morphosyntactic markers of dependency at different ends of the dependency relation is interesting in itself, but the difference also has important consequences, such as the fact that predominantly head-marking languages appear not to have any exocentric constructions. The chapter by Nichols in this volume extends her typological investigation of centricity into new territory. Nichols' (1986) work focused exclusively on major syntactic categories. Vincent (this volume) carries the investigation forward by considering functional categories as well. (For further work on the role of heads in language typology see Giorgi and Longobardi, 1987, and Clements, 1989.)

So far, the Zwicky–Hudson debate on headedness (including subsequent contributions by other authors) has tended to centre on the English language. There is much scope for re-examination of the arguments and issues in the context of other languages. The chapters by Comrie and Corbett begin this process. Amongst the contributors to this volume, only Nichols (this volume) and Payne (personal communication) maintain what might be termed the 'head of construction constancy principle' which requires the head of a given construction to remain constant across languages. Thus, if N is the head of a nominal construction in English, then N must also be the head of nominal constructions in all languages which have them. The other authors are prepared to accept that the head of a given construction may change from language to language, and Cann's theory predicts that this will happen.

Much which has been written on the subject of heads has been devoted to identifying the heads of specific constructions and, in particular, of the noun phrase (or determiner phrase, or whatever it turns out to be). The major issue here – and one which runs through almost every chapter of the volume – is whether or not functional categories can be heads. Not very many years ago, the idea that anything other than the noun should be taken as the head of a nominal construction would not have found sympathy anywhere. More recently, however, just such a position has been advanced by people working in a variety of different frameworks. These include Hudson (1984), Hellan (1986), Abney (1987), Szabolcsi (1987),

Löbel (1989), Olsen (1989) and Pollock (1989). Early intimations can be found in Jackendoff (1972) and Hogg (1977). The chapters by Corbett, Payne and Radford focus primarily on the question of what heads the nominal phrase. The chapters by Cann and Vincent provide more general discussions of the role of functional categories as heads.

Whilst each of the chapters in this collection makes a significant contribution to at least one of the areas of endeavour in which the notion 'head' has been adduced, many of them succeed in bringing together insights from more than one theory or field of research. Furthermore, several of the chapters strike out in new directions, themselves defining new areas for future investigation: for example, Hudson takes the debate into the realm of psycholinguistics with his question *Do we have heads in our minds?*; Vincent blends existing research in typology and functional categories and adds an ingredient which has not previously been considered in the context of heads, namely processes of grammaticalization; Zwicky examines the foundations of grammatical theory and comes up with a new category to set alongside head, namely 'base'.

Each chapter in the collection addresses the subject of heads in grammatical theory from a slightly different perspective. Taken together, the chapters define both the points of agreement in the centre and the points of divergence at the margins. In this respect, at least, it is clear that many heads are better than one. Whether the same can ultimately be said to apply to grammatical constructions remains to be seen.

1.2 Outline of the book

In their examinations of criteria for the identification of heads, Zwicky and Hudson considered data drawn mainly from English. In chapter 2, Greville Corbett uses Russian numeral phrases to test the competing sets of head-identification criteria. Application of Zwicky's criteria suggests that head-like properties are split between numeral and noun. Application of Hudson's re-interpretation of Zwicky's criteria suggests that head-like properties are unambiguously located on the numeral. Taking the investigation one step further, Corbett applies the two sets of head-identification criteria to adjective–noun combinations. Here it is Zwicky's approach which consistently identifies the noun as head, while Hudson's approach distributes head-like properties between the adjective and the noun. Hudson's approach can only be rescued if the adjective is controversially analysed as the ruler in dependency grammar.

In chapter 3, Bernard Comrie offers a criterion for the identification of heads which is quite different from those which have previously featured in the debate. This criterion is discussed in relation to Haruai, a non-Austronesian language of New Guinea, and the results achieved with that language are quite robust. The generalization which drives the criterion is this: in endocentric constructions in Haruai, stress always falls on the dependent rather than the head, in the absence of special pragmatic marking. This generalization is independent of word order. Comrie suggests that searching for language-internal criteria for heads in other languages may be equally successful. Criteria for the identification of heads may belong to two categories: universal or language-particular.

Chapter 4, by Ronnie Cann, reconsiders the criteria discussed by Zwicky and Hudson. Like Hudson, Cann rejects the 'semantic argument' criterion. He also rejects the 'ruler in dependency grammar' criterion. However, unlike Hudson's analysis, Cann's analysis does not find consistent agreement amongst the criteria in their identification of heads. Agreement is obtained where only major categories are involved but not where functional categories are involved. Working within the framework of GB, Cann develops an explanatory account of the variation in distribution of head-like properties across different constructions. This account predicts that distribution will differ between languages as well as between different constructions in the same language.

Chapter 5, by Andrew Radford, and chapter 6, by John Payne, both investigate the number of heads in a nominal phrase. Following distinct lines of argument, the authors reach opposite conclusions. Assuming a GB theoretical framework, Radford argues that a complex nominal like *all these silly theories* should be analysed as a quantifier phrase containing a determiner phrase containing an adjectival phrase containing a noun phrase, and that each of the superordinate phrasal constituents is double-headed (for example, *silly theories* is a constituent whose immediate head is the adjective *silly*, and whose ultimate head is the noun *theories*). Thus, like the Roman god Janus (the mythical guardian of gates and doors, beginnings and ends), complex nominals have two heads (one at the beginning, the other at the end). Payne tests two hypotheses – the single-head hypothesis and the multi-head hypothesis – to see which provides the better account of the facts of incorporation, subcategorization, the position of possessor phrases, appositional noun phrases and agreement and disagreement. *Contra* Radford, he concludes that – unlike the mythical hydra – nominal phrases possess a single head, and this head must be a noun.

Chapter 7, by Nigel Vincent, examines three recent strands of research in syntax and shows some ways in which they shed light on each other. These are: (a) the typological work initiated by Nichols (1986) on head-marking and dependent-marking languages; (b) the increased importance (especially in GB) accorded to functional categories and their projections; and (c) the study of the process of grammaticalization as mechanism of grammatical change. In her 1986 paper, Nichols excluded function words from consideration. Vincent argues that given the recent interest in functional heads, the head-marking/dependent-marking typological research programme should be extended to include them. He further observes that the grammaticalization principle that 'function words are always etymologically derived from lexical words' has implications for the head/dependent status of function words: does grammaticalization lead to category change with or without corresponding change of head/dependent status? These issues are investigated in the context of complement clauses and complementizers.

Chapter 8, by Johanna Nichols, presents a cross-linguistic study of ellipsis in discourse to see whether selection of elements for deletion under ellipsis is governed by universal principles referring to heads. In her sample, Nichols finds evidence for all logical possibilities. That is, she finds languages in which (a) only heads can be removed, (b) only non-heads can be removed, (c) either heads or non-heads can be removed, and (d) neither heads nor non-heads can be removed. In her earlier work on head-marking and dependent-marking languages, Nichols has shown that there is a strong connection between dependent-marking and the presence of the exocentric/endocentric distinction; in languages which are predominantly head-marking, all constituents appear to be endocentric. By contrast, Nichols' chapter in this volume shows that selection of elements to remove under ellipsis is not related to whether the language in question marks heads or dependents. The somewhat surprising conclusion is that deletion of elements under ellipsis is not subject to any universal principles which make use of the notion 'head'. Making this (or any other) cross-linguistic observation requires a constant cross-linguistic definition of what is head in any given construction.

Chapter 9, by Robert Borsley, examines the Head Feature Principle (HFP) of HPSG. This principle requires the value of the HEAD feature in a mother to be identical to the value of the HEAD feature in its head daughter. Unlike GPSG's Head Feature Convention, which supplies default values, HPSG's HFP is absolute and cannot be overridden. Borsley argues that the HFP as currently conceived misses an important generalization. The solution is to cast the HFP as a default principle which assigns values to features unless other values are explicitly introduced by rule. This revision has serious implications for HPSG since it can no longer be the case that the theory is based purely on unification. Borsley shows how his arguments can be extended to GB, and suggests that they are relevant to any constituency-based framework.

In chapter 10, Scott McGlashan develops a unification-based account of the notion 'head'. Drawing on ideas highlighted in the dependency grammar tradition, categories are partitioned into 'head' and 'modifier' features, roughly corresponding to the distinction between 'take' and 'make' features in Categorial Grammar (CG). He argues that this account is superior to that offered by CG in respect of serialization, category constancy and motivation. However, he also presents evidence which undermines simple accounts of category constancy, and especially those which claim that semantic properties of a head are identical to those of its phrase. For example, in *chocolate soldiers*, the 'material property' of the head is not that of the phrase: *chocolate soldiers* are made of chocolate, not flesh.

Chapter 11, by John Hawkins, is the only contribution in the volume which seriously questions the usefulness of the notion 'head', and its place in Universal Grammar. Hawkins' position is particularly noteworthy since he has in the past made extensive use of the head–modifier distinction in his theories of word-order universals (Hawkins, 1983, 1984). More recently, Hawkins has put forward a parsing theory of word-order universals (Hawkins, 1990), in which serialization patterns are related to such things as the appropriate placement of 'Mother Node Constructing Categories' (MNCCs) so as to minimize cognitive load during processing. MNCCs are constituent-peripheral categories which, by virtue of being unique to a particular kind of phrase, allow a unique mother node to be constructed over the MNCC as early as possible: for example, determiners are MNCCs in English. In this volume, Hawkins argues that many of the properties of heads identified in the Zwicky–Hudson debate are, in fact, properties of MNCCs. The fact that these properties appear in clusters is related to the role of MNCCs as clues for on-line processing, and not to the existence of some putative category 'head'.

The position outlined in chapter 12, by Richard Hudson, is diametrically opposed to the one advanced by Hawkins. Hudson argues that it is necessary to refer explicitly to heads both in grammars and in sentence structures. Drawing on descriptive and psycholinguistic evidence, Hudson claims that a number of complex phenomena can be explained only if listeners are able to identify heads in utterances during processing. Thus, at the coarsest level, there are three distinct views on heads: (a) heads do not exist in grammars or in sentence structures; (b) heads exist in grammars but not in sentence structures; (c) heads exist in grammars and in sentence structures.

It is fitting that the final chapter, chapter 13, should be written by Arnold Zwicky, whose 1985 paper has helped to focus so many of the issues discussed in this volume. In his latest contribution, Zwicky proposes three binary features to make distinctions which, he argues, are required in any adequate account of dependency functions. These features are: 'F', ±semantic functor; 'H', ±morphosyntactic locus or head (recall Zwicky's conclusions in his 1985 paper); and a new feature 'B' (Base), ±external representative. All constituents bear these features. An Operator Head has the feature structure $(+F+H+B)$; a Modified Head has the feature structure $(-F+H+B)$; and a Specifier has the feature structure $(+F+H-B)$. This account therefore argues against a single definition of heads in which all criteria always identify a single constituent as head. Rather, it predicts that criteria of headedness will not always agree, but that patterns of disagreement are meaningful and signify distinctions between Operator/Argument, Modified/Modifier and Specifier/Base.

NOTE

Earlier versions of the chapters which make up this collection were presented at the Talking Heads Round Table held at the University of Surrey in March 1991. The editors would like to express their thanks to the Research Committee of the University of Surrey for generous support and to all the contributors for their enthusiastic participation.

2 *The head of Russian numeral expressions*

GREVILLE G. CORBETT

2.1 Introduction

A major focus of the debate on headedness has been the problem of determining the head in different constructions and of establishing acceptable criteria to enable us to do so.[1] The data have been taken mainly from English, and so this account, by contrast, extends the investigation to a language with a much richer morphological system than that of English, namely Russian. We shall concentrate on numeral expressions in Russian, where the head–dependent relation has long been known to be problematic (see, for example, Isačenko, 1962: 529). We shall examine them in the light of the criteria for heads proposed by Zwicky (1985) and by Hudson (1987).[2] At first sight it seems that no single head can be identified for these constructions; rather, the properties of the head appear to be shared between different elements, which would fit with Zwicky's approach. However, given current assumptions about lexical entries and feature distribution, these constructions can be analysed as being rather less exotic than they first appear, and as having a consistent head, as Hudson would predict. While attempting to remain as theory-neutral as possible, we shall develop the analysis to see whether the idea of a single element having all the head properties can be maintained. It is in focusing on the question of headedness that this chapter differs from most previous accounts of Russian numeral phrases. We shall see that there are two consequences. The first is that we still need to recognize that headedness is a gradient notion: a particular element may have head-like characteristics to a greater or lesser degree, and that these may vary according to external factors (notably, case assignment). The second is that the logic of the analysis requires re-assessment of the head–dependent relation elsewhere, namely in adjective–noun constructions, and the price to be paid may be unacceptably high.

2.2 Headedness in numeral expressions in Russian

A great deal has been written on the complex (morpho-)syntax of numeral expressions in Russian, sometimes with comparative data from other Slavonic languages; see, for example, Suprun (1959; 1969), Worth (1959), Corbett (1978c; 1983: 215–40), Mel'čuk (1985), Babby (1987), Miller (1988, 1989) and references there. The simple cardinal numerals show great variety in their behaviour, but there is a clear pattern to the differences: namely that the larger the numeral, the more closely its syntactic behaviour approximates to that of a noun. Thus *odin* 'one' closely follows adjectives in its syntax, agreeing in gender (including the subgender of animacy), case and even number with the quantified noun. *Million* 'million', on the other hand, does not agree with the quantified noun, but has a full paradigm, singular and plural (with the plural denoting more than one million), it imposes genitive case on the quantified noun and may itself, though rarely, take a determiner which agrees fully with it. Numerals in the middle numerical range, such as *pjat'* 'five', fall between these syntactic extremes.[3] In this way Russian provides particularly good evidence for a claimed universal, namely that if there is any variation in the syntactic behaviour of simple cardinal numerals, then the higher numerals will show more noun-like behaviour (Corbett, 1978c: 363; Hurford, 1987: 187–97).

These data create two problems for the notion of head. First, if head is linked to semantic notions (such as argument–functor), then we must assume that the semantic relations in *odin rubl'* 'one rouble' and *million rublej* are similar, yet the syntax is very different. *Odin* agrees fully with the noun (it is nominative singular masculine), while *million* imposes genitive case on the noun *rublej* (genitive plural), even though the phrase as a whole counts as nominative. The second problem is that with some of the intermediate numerals the relations within the noun phrase are complex, so that it appears difficult to establish a single head of the phrase. This should not surprise us too much, since other apparently monolithic notions, such as 'subject', have been found to consist of clusters of properties which may be shared among more than one element (see Keenan, 1976; and Zwicky, this volume).

We shall concentrate on the second problem, by looking at the most complex of the numerals, *dva* 'two', *tri* 'three' and *četyre* 'four'. The syntax of these three is similar; differences will be pointed out at the appropriate points. For reference, table 2.1 gives the morphology of the numeral *dva* 'two'.

Table 2.1   The morphology of *dva* 'two'

Nominative	dva (masculine and neuter) dve (feminine)
Accusative	as nominative or genitive
Genitive	dvux
Dative	dvum
Instrumental	dvumja
Locative	dvux

The accusative is determined by animacy: if the noun is animate, the form of *dva* is *dvux*, and if inanimate it is *dva/dve*. *Tri* 'three' and *četyre* 'four' do not distinguish the feminine from the masculine and neuter; otherwise they make the same morphological distinctions as *dva* 'two', though the actual forms differ. Let us start from the apparently simple phrase *dva žurnala* 'two magazines' and consider the head–dependent relationship. The phrase as given would fit into a sentence slot requiring a nominative or accusative constituent; *dva* 'two' is in the nominative–accusative form, while *žurnala* 'magazine' stands in the genitive singular (the nominative singular is *žurnal*). The full paradigm of *žurnal* 'magazine' is given in table 2.2.

Table 2.2   The paradigm of the noun *žurnal* 'magazine'

	Singular	Plural
Nominative	žurnal	žurnaly
Accusative	žurnal	žurnaly
Genitive	žurnala	žurnalov
Dative	žurnalu	žurnalam
Instrumental	žurnalom	žurnalami
Locative	žurnale	žurnalax

Our phrase *dva žurnala* 'two magazines' makes it clear that the syntax of such expressions is not simply a matter of matching the obvious forms from the two paradigms; the actual forms for the phrase in the six cases are given in table 2.3.

Table 2.3   The forms of the phrase *dva žurnala* 'two magazines'

Nominative	dva žurnala
Accusative	dva žurnala
Genitive	dvux žurnalov
Dative	dvum žurnalam
Instrumental	dvumja žurnalami
Locative	dvux žurnalax

Given this background, we now consider phrases like *dva žurnala* 'two magazines' in the light of the criteria discussed by Zwicky (1985) and Hudson (1987) and presented in chapter 1, section 1.1.[4] These will now be discussed in turn.

2.2.1 *The semantic argument*

This criterion requires us to consider the semantic interpretation of the phrase and to ask which element has the status of argument. While not so obvious as for other types of phrase, when we look at the semantic relation between the two items in the Russian phrase in question, it would appear that the semantic argument is *žurnala* 'magazine(s)', and the functor is *dva* 'two'. For Zwicky this indicates that *žurnala* is the head; for Hudson, however, this shows that *dva*, the functor, is the head.

2.2.2 *The subcategorizand*

The subcategorizand is *dva*; it subcategorizes for a nominal phrase headed by a count noun (though that noun stands in the singular). On Zwicky's and on Hudson's view of this criterion *dva* is the head and the nominal phrase which includes the noun is the dependent. 'Nominal phrase' is a hedging term to denote the noun and its immediate modifiers. The noun may have various such modifiers (for example, *dva novyx žurnala* 'two new magazines') but it is uncommon for demonstratives (like *ètot* 'this') and possessives (like *moi*) to be included – these more commonly occur before the numeral (*moi dva žurnala* 'my two magazines'). This suggests that a phrase like *moi dva novyx žurnala* 'my two new magazines' constitutes a single complex noun phrase: *novyx žurnala* forms a nominal phrase, this phrase forms a larger phrase together with *dva*, and that whole phrase in turn is modified by *moi*: [*moi* [*dva* [*novyx žurnala*]]]. We shall consider these modifiers in more detail in section 2.3.

2.2.3 *The morphosyntactic locus*

Here we must consider which element can bear 'the morphosyntactic marks of syntactic relations between the construct and other syntactic units' (Zwicky, 1985: 6). The morphosyntactic mark in question is that of case, and the stronger contender appears to be *dva* since it stands in the case appropriate to the slot filled by the construct as a whole.

Although *žurnala* appears to be ruled out, since it stands in the genitive singular, there are arguments to be made in its favour. First, if we look at the oblique cases, we find that numeral and noun stand in the same case, for example *o dvux žurnalax* 'concerning two magazines', where numeral and noun are in the locative (note that *žurnalax* is locative plural), governed by the preposition *o*. So the better claim of *dva* rests on the direct cases (nominative, and accusative when identical to the nominative). Even here we could argue that *žurnala* indicates the appropriate case, if we claim that it carries an exceptional marker, say [dual] as suggested by Dingwall (1969: 227–9), and that in the presence of this marker its (genitive singular) form is an indicator of the nominative (and accusative=nominative). There is overwhelming evidence that some sort of exceptional marker is required. First, there are a few nouns which have a special form used just in this construction, for example *dva časá* 'two hours, two o'clock', where the genitive singular has a different stress *čása*. Furthermore, there are occasional examples of the use of the nominative plural, rather than the genitive singular with feminine nouns. (For many feminine nouns the genitive singular and nominative plural are identical; they may differ in stress, and when they do, normally the genitive singular is used; the exceptional cases mentioned here involve use of the nominative plural differentiated by stress from the genitive singular.)[5] Thus nouns bearing the exceptional marker [dual] do not always take the form of the genitive singular, though the majority do. Second, as we shall see, modifiers of nouns bearing this marker do not take genitive singular modifiers, even though the noun stands in what looks like the regular genitive singular. As far as headedness is concerned, even if we accept the argument based on the exceptional feature, the fact remains that the interpretation of the morphological mark of the genitive (for most nouns) as nominative would depend on the numeral being present. On a generous reading this might make the noun as head-like as the numeral, but it could not possibly count as an argument in favour of the noun.

We conclude that the better claim to be the morphosyntactic locus is that of *dva*, though the situation is not absolutely clear-cut. For both Zwicky and Hudson this would imply that *dva* is the head.

2.2.4 The governor

In so far as there is a governor, it is clearly *dva*. As we saw above, it governs the gentitive singular of the noun (provided it is in a direct case itself). For reasons just discussed, it seems that this government consists of imposing an irregular marker [dual] on the noun, which is normally realized as genitive singular. Note that 'dual' is no more than a mnemonic for an irregular marker since *tri* 'three' and *četyre* 'four' are also involved; some prefer to call it 'paucal'. It might be argued that *dva* itself is dual, and so we are dealing with agreement. While historically this was so, it cannot be maintained for the modern language: *žurnala* cannot be used as a free form to mean 'two–four magazines'. We are indeed dealing with government by the numeral. For both Zwicky and Hudson this again suggests that *dva* is the head.

2.2.5 The determinant of concord (agreement controller)

The question of agreement is particularly interesting in these constructions. The agreement controller is clearly the noun, as is evident when we look at accusative case forms. For inanimate nouns like *žurnal*, the accusative is identical to the nominative form already given. If we take an animate noun we find the following form: *dvux studentov* 'two students'. This is identical to the genitive, following the regular syncretism in Russian for the subgender of animacy. Note that it applies to all three genders, and that *studentov* is genitive plural. Thus the noun is the agreement controller and the numeral is the target.

If we look again at the nominative, we find more of interest. The form already given, *dva*, is appropriate for the masculine and the neuter, while for feminine nouns we find *dve*, as in *dve knigi* 'two books'. This situation runs counter to the regular agreement patterns of Russian. The normal situation for adjectives and pronouns is that three genders are distinguished in the singular, but there is no distinction in the plural. *Dva* is odd in having two forms, one for masculine and neuter, and the other for the feminine (this is shared only with *oba/obe* 'both'; *tri* and *četyre* have no distinct gender forms). It is also odd in having gender agreement in the nominative (and nominative=accusative) only.[6] My earlier analysis (Corbett, 1987b: 7) was in process terms, and looked for economy in feature copying. If *dve* is seen as imposing the dual marker (to be realized as genitive singular) on the noun, the noun is 'now' singular and so agreement in gender is possible. Thus we have a negotiation of features: the numeral imposes case and number on the noun, which in turn determines the gender of the numeral. This appears exotic, but largely because it occurs within the noun phrase. A similar situation occurs in subject–predicate relations: Russian verbs normally take subjects in the nominative, with which they 'then' agree, but some, mainly negated, verbs have genitive subjects with which they cannot agree and so have default (neuter singular) agreement forms.

In several current frameworks, however, there is no concern to impose specific restrictions on the feature information available in particular constructions. Since the lexical entry of a noun contains information on gender (whether specified or derivable from other lexical information), this information is considered to be available when the noun is plural, even though such information is not normally required. The oddity of the construction in this regard can be seen as reducing to the extremely unusual lexical entry required for *dva*, which specifies the need for information on the gender of nouns, even though plural; *dva* is, of course, a high-frequency word and so this irregularity is maintained.

We have established that the numeral agrees with the noun, albeit in a highly idiosyncratic way. For Zwicky, this is evidence that the noun is the head. Hudson (1987: 117) proposes to disregard agreement: 'the direction of concord determination has nothing at all to do with the notion "head" '. This seems a step backwards, since there is a degree of consensus on what can agree with what, as reflected, for example, in the Control Agreement Principle of GPSG (Gazdar *et al.*, 1985: 83–4). Moreover, the fact that the agreement controller is not always the head is not necessarily as damaging to Hudson's case as he may have thought. Nichols (1985a) shows that in various languages there are instances of 'upwards' agreement, where heads agree with dependents.

If the verb is taken to be the head of the sentence, and the subject is a dependent with which it agrees, then we could argue that in Russian we expect the agreement target to be the head. Since the numeral agrees with the noun, this suggests it is the head of the phrase. Such a position is logical, though it goes against the tradition of Slavists, for whom the head and agreement controller would, I think, be expected to coincide.[7] Moreover, given the pervasive nature of agreement in Slavonic languages, this criterion would be taken as a fundamental one, and hence many Slavists would be unwilling to consider the possibility of the numeral being the head of the phrase. If, however, the verb is recognized as head of the sentence then the logic is inescapable.

2.2.6 The distributional equivalent

This operational criterion proves difficult to apply. The idea is that the head will be the element that belongs to a category 'with roughly the same distribution as the construct as a whole' (Zwicky, 1985: 11). In one sense, phrases like *dva žurnala* occur in most of the same positions as other nominal phrases and therefore the distributional equivalent would be the noun (see Mel'čuk, 1985: 63–72). In view of his treatment of determiner–noun constructions, Zwicky might well also take the noun to be the head. When applied to Russian, such a view requires us to disregard morphology: thus in subject position phrases quantified by *dva* take either singular or plural verb agreement, while most nominal phrases permit only one form of number agreement. If we take a strict approach – that is, to consider the distributional equivalent to be that element which can be substituted for the whole with no morphological adjustments – then we could not take the noun to be the distributional equivalent and hence head of the phrase. It could be argued that this is over-strict, since we are looking for *roughly* the same distribution. Thus the view consistent with Zwicky's position would be to take the noun as the distributional equivalent.

Hudson (1987: 118) argues that morphology should not be ignored. However, he is happy to consider constructions which are elliptical (claiming this to be irrelevant for identifying distributional equivalence). If elliptical constructions are accepted, then the numeral too can be taken as the distributional equivalent of the phrase (compare Mel'čuk, 1985: 64).

Hudson also makes the point that many people believe that the head should have the same category features as the phrase (1987: 123). This argument can lead in either direction since some treat the phrases we are analysing as some sort of noun phrase, while others treat them as quantifier phrases (QPs).

The distributional equivalence criterion can lend support to each of the contending heads. Judgement on this criterion depends critically on two other assumptions: whether morphology can be disregarded, and whether elliptical constructions are to be taken into account.

2.2.7 The obligatory constituent

Here again, the criterion is not straightforward; this is true in general terms, as Kornai and Pullum (1990: 33–5) show, as well as in the specific circumstances here. As with the last criterion, judgement depends on our assumptions about disregarding morphology and taking account of elliptical constructions. If we disallow adjustments of the morphology, then the obligatory element is the numeral: we cannot omit the *dva* in *dva žurnala* since the genitive singular form of the noun could not occur in most of the contexts where the full phrase would be found. In the oblique cases, however, when both stand in the same case, then an argument could be made in favour of either constituent. But equally, the circumstances in which numerals can stand on their own in Russian are rather limited (Mel'čuk, 1985: 64–5), unless we include examples of ellipsis.[8] Zwicky (1985: 13) suggests we should not take account of such examples, but Hudson (1987: 118) disagrees. If we follow Zwicky, then the noun would be the head, in terms of being the obligatory element, while if we follow Hudson, then the numeral should be recognized as the obligatory element.[9]

2.2.8 *The ruler in dependency grammar*

Zwicky (1985: 14–15) considers the head-like notion which is central to dependency syntax and asks which element dependency grammarians normally select.[10] In our particular case this is easy to establish, since one of the main proponents of dependency syntax, Igor' Mel'čuk, has written specifically on numeral constructions in Russian and has argued at length that the noun is the head (Mel'čuk, 1985: 59–104;[11] Iomdin, 1979: 37, and 1990: 31, agrees with Mel'čuk). Mel'čuk takes the crucial criterion to be distributional equivalence. However, if we adopt the innovations to dependency syntax introduced by Hudson, then following his argument (1987: 128–9) we could well argue that the numeral is the ruler, as is claimed specifically for Russian by Miller (1989); see the latter paper for the technicalities of one way of dealing with the necessary features in a dependency account.

Let us consider the results so far. Table 2.4 shows the element which is head, according to the criteria of Zwicky and Hudson. It should be stressed that this is my interpretation of the criteria they proposed in the papers cited. The results of the investigation so far are revealing. If we apply Zwicky's criteria, then we find that the head-like properties are split between numeral and noun, which is what we might intuitively have expected. If we take Hudson's view of the criteria proposed by Zwicky, then we must conclude that *dva* is the head of phrases like *dva žurnala*. It is remarkable to reach such an unambiguous result and so, if we can maintain Hudson's approach,

Table 2.4   The head element in Russian numeral phrases (*dva žurnala*)

Criterion	Zwicky (1985)	Hudson (1987)
1 Semantic argument (Z) vs functor (H)[a]	noun	numeral
2 Subcategorizand	numeral	numeral
3 Morphosyntactic locus	numeral	numeral
4 Governor	numeral	numeral
5 Determinant of concord (Z) vs (target)	noun	(numeral)[b]
6 Distributional equivalent	noun	numeral
7 Obligatory constituent	noun	numeral
8 Ruler in dependency grammar	noun	numeral

a For Zwicky the argument is head, for Hudson the functor.
b Recall that Hudson rejects this criterion hence the result is in parentheses. It is based on taking the agreement target to be the head.

we should do so. While the application of certain criteria is somewhat strained, this might be expected since the construction is clearly unusual in various respects.

It is worth distinguishing between the element which is the head 'in principle' and the element which actually exhibits head-like behaviour. Thus if agreeing with the dependent is taken as a feature of head-like behaviour, then *dva* 'two' is more head-like than *tri* 'three' because *dva* shows minimal agreement in gender while *tri* does not. Furthermore, and rather surprisingly, the head–dependent relation is influenced by factors outside the phrase. Thus when the phrase is in one of the direct cases, *dva* governs the noun (requiring the irregular dual marker), but in the oblique cases both numeral and noun have the same case imposed from outside. There is no government in the oblique cases, and so the numeral is less head-like than in the direct cases.[12]

If we step back to look at the numeral system more generally, we could argue, if we follow Hudson's reasoning (and if we also reinstate agreement with the dependent as a head-like behaviour for Russian), that the numeral is always the head of phrases consisting of numeral plus nominal phrase (recall that we exclude pre-numeral items). Yet, as I have shown elsewhere (Corbett, 1978c: 356–9) Russian numerals show great diversity in their syntax. The diversity comes largely from the fact that as they become arithmetically larger, so the numerals show ever 'more' government and 'less' agreement. Thus *pjat'* governs the nominal phrase when in the direct cases, but stands in the same case in the oblique cases, and shows no agreement of gender (including animacy); *tysjača* 'thousand' may behave in this way, or may take the genitive case in all instances, while *million* 'million' always takes the genitive case.

2.3 Adjectives within Russian numeral phrases

We have established that if we apply Zwicky's criteria we find that the possible characteristics of head-like behaviour are distributed between the numeral and noun in Russian, and this has some attractions, given the complex nature of the relation between the two elements. But taking Hudson's approach, and allowing for the fact that some criteria are problematic, we find that the head-like properties are firmly attached to the numeral. If it can be maintained, this simpler analysis has much to commend it.

One way of testing the validity of the analyses presented so far is to introduce a third element into the construction. If the head-like properties are indeed shared, then we may expect problems when a third element is added. If, on the other hand, they are clear, then the third element may be expected to fit easily. A first try is to add a demonstrative, to give a phrase such as *èti dve knigi* 'these two books'. Here *èti* 'these' is a nominative plural form; if the case of the numeral is changed, *èti* will remain plural and will take the same case as the numeral. Following Zwicky's approach, we would say that its head is the numeral, while following Hudson's reasoning we would say that the demonstrative is the head of the phrase, with the numeral as its dependent. There are certain complications, but they cast little light on the relations between numeral and noun.

A second try is more successful, namely to add in an adjective. We shall see that the complexities we have seen so far are almost as nothing compared with those which arise when an adjective is added. In a phrase like *dve interesnye knigi* 'two interesting books', *dve* 'two' is in the nominative (or accusative), *interesnye* 'interesting' is nominative plural, though the genitive plural *interesnyx* is also possible, while *knigi* 'book(s)' is genitive singular.[13] Before tackling the questions of why these two forms arise and what factors influence the choice between them, we must first consider more generally how we would expect an attributive adjective to fit into the construction.

It seems natural to suggest that, in a phrase like that just given, we expect the adjective and noun to form a phrase and that this phrase should in turn be in some sort of relation to additional outside elements. What then, in general terms, is the relation between a noun and an attributive modifier? Zwicky and Hudson did not consider

Table 2.5 The head element in Russian adjective–noun combinations

Criterion	Zwicky (1985)	Hudson (1987)
1 Semantic argument (Z) vs functor (H)	noun	adjective
2 Subcategorizand	(neither)	(neither)
3 Morphosyntactic locus	(both)	(both)
4 Governor	(neither)	(neither)
5 Determinant of concord (Z) vs (target)	noun	(adjective?)
6 Distributional equivalent	noun	?
7 Obligatory constituent	noun	?
8 Ruler in dependency grammar	noun	noun

this relation. I have therefore given my interpretation using their criteria in table 2.5.

Table 2.5 shows an interesting reversal of the situation found in table 2.4. Using Zwicky's approach we obtain consistent results and there is little question but that the noun is the head of the adjective in a phrase like *interesnaja kniga* 'interesting book'. Both show the morphosyntactic mark of nominative case, to indicate the phrase's syntactic relation to other sentence elements, so criterion 3 is of no help here; nor is criterion 4, since government is not involved. But the remaining criteria point in the same direction. If we look at Hudson's approach the picture is less clear. The functor (and so the head) is the adjective. Hudson does not accept the relevance of concord, but since we found it consonant with other criteria when considering the numeral, it is worth noting here that the agreement target in this instance is the adjective. Criteria 6 and 7 at first sight suggest that the noun is head; but bearing in mind the different approach Hudson and Zwicky take to ellipsis, it is possible to claim, as Hudson does in the case of determiners, that these criteria do not produce a clear answer and that one can at least make a case for either element being the head.[14] The ruler in dependency syntax – which is the head for Hudson – is the noun: this is made explicit for English in Hudson (1987: 127–8). Thus for adjective–noun phrases we do not get a clear indication of the head in Hudson's approach. This is a disappointment, since the analysis which radically simplifies the account of Russian numerals is undermined if straightforward adjective–noun phrases are problematic. To preserve the elegance of Hudson's approach it appears that the only possibility would be to claim that the adjective is the head in adjective–noun phrases, and thus that the previous dependency analysis was incorrect. Making the adjective the head is a radical suggestion, but so indeed was the analysis which makes the numeral consistently head of the phrase. Furthermore, it is not new, since it has been argued for, in a dependency approach to Russian, by Miller (1989), and much earlier, in relation to English, by Anderson (1976: 86–126);[15] compare Radford (this volume).

Let us therefore analyse phrases like *dve interesnye knigi* 'two interesting books' with two questions in mind. First, recall our original question, which was whether these phrases suggest that the head properties are shared between numeral and noun (as Zwicky's approach suggests) or whether they indicate that the numeral is clearly the head. Second, given the situation summarized in table 2.5, it is worth considering whether they allow an analysis in which *dve* is head of *interesnye*, which is in turn head of *knigi*.

Before going into details, we should outline the areas of difficulty. The choice in respect of case is found only when the numeral is in the nominative or accusative=nominative. In the oblique cases, numeral and noun stand in the same case (as in table 2.3); the adjective is also in the same case and is plural, like the noun. These oblique case forms do not take us further forward. In the direct cases, where the adjective can stand in the nominative or genitive plural, we must first establish why there is a choice at all, and then consider the factors which influence the choice.[16] The use of the nominative plural is the easier to understand. In a phrase such as *dve interesnye knigi* 'two interesting books' we would expect adjective and noun to be in the plural for semantic reasons. But we have seen that the numeral imposes an irregular marker by government, which, when interpreted in the morphology, causes the noun to take the form of the genitive singular (sometimes, as with *knigi* 'books', the form is identical to the nominative plural). This irregular marker does not cause any change in the morphological form of the adjective and so the nominative plural results as expected. This effect does not provide evidence for the competing hypotheses we are considering. In a constituency model, the irregular feature (say [dual]) will be found on the node dominating the adjective and noun and so will be found on each; in the morphological component it is 'disregarded' in the case of the adjective, since there are no special forms for adjectives marked [dual]. In a dependency approach, provided there is a mechanism for feature spreading, the same result will follow, and it makes little difference whether the adjective or noun is head of the phrase dependent on the numeral (except that if the adjective is head, the irregular feature must be 'passed on' by the adjective, on which it has no effect).

How, then, are we to explain the occurrence of the genitive plural in phrases like *dve interesnyx knigi* 'two interesting books'? We can hardly claim this is government by the numeral since that would involve it imposing the features [dual] and [genitive plural]. The appearance of the genitive becomes much clearer if we look at the numeral system as a whole. With numerals like *pjat'* 'five', we always find the genitive plural of the quantified phrase, provided the numeral is in one of the direct cases. With *tysjača* 'thousand' the same holds, and the genitive may be found when the numeral is in an oblique case. Table 2.6 summarizes the position for each of the simple cardinal numerals.

Table 2.6   Use of the genitive plural with the simple cardinal numerals of Russian

	odin 'one'	dva, tri, četyre 'two, three, four'	pjat' 'five'	sto 'hundred'	tysjača 'thousand'	million 'million'
Direct case	no	no/yes	yes	yes	yes	yes
Oblique cases	no	no	no	no	no/yes	yes

It can be seen that as the numeral becomes higher, so the likelihood of the genitive plural being used increases; at the same time it is more likely in the direct cases than in the oblique. There are two points at which a choice occurs. The first is with the oblique cases of *tysjača* 'thousand', where we find both *o tysjače* (locative) *rublej* (genitive plural) 'concerning a thousand roubles' and *o tysjače* (locative) *rubljax* (locative plural). The second is with *dva* and similar numerals, where the genitive plural is not shown on the noun, which has an exceptional marker, but may be shown on the adjective. In an earlier framework, I proposed a rule of 'genitive insertion' to add a genitive case marker in the appropriate circumstances (Corbett, 1978c: 360–1). These 'appropriate circumstances' vary idiosyncratically within and between languages; thus Danish permits *et glas vand* literally 'a glass water' while English requires 'a glass *of* water'. They are not restricted to quantified expressions: English permits *the River Thames*, but not **the town Guildford*. The contrast between direct and oblique cases in Russian has a functional explanation based on the greater syntactic prominence of the direct cases; since these indicate the main arguments of the verb, non-head elements which would otherwise bear one of these cases are marked with the genitive.

The other clear point already noted from table 2.6 is that as the numerals get larger, so the genitive of the dependent phrase becomes more likely. This is an exact reflection of the fact that the numerals become more noun-like as they become larger – as other aspects of their syntax show. Given the limited noun-like qualities of *dva*, *tri* and *četyre*, the use of the genitive plural adjective is optional. The importance of this for our discussion is that it is not an idiosyncratic fact about these three numerals that they may take, but do not require, a genitive plural adjective; rather, it is a consequence of their lying between *odin* 'one', for which the genitive is excluded, and *pjat'* 'five' for which it is obligatory in the direct cases. The imposition of the genitive is thus rather different from the irregular government of the genitive singular of the noun. I suggest that these numerals optionally take the genitive, simply as a consequence of being numerals (given their place on the numerical scale). However we view the relation between noun and adjective in the quantified expression, it will be necessary for the genitive feature to appear on the noun (or on the node dominating it) for reasons we shall come to later. But it will have no effect on the noun, since the irregular feature [dual] will be interpreted in the morphology to give the genitive singular.

Two objections need to be considered. The first is that the [dual] and the [genitive] features seem to present a conflict. This is not a valid objection, since [genitive] is a value of the category case, while [dual] is an irregular marker, to be interpreted in the morphological component as a unique form for some nouns (like *čas* 'hour') or as the regular genitive singular (occasionally nominative plural) for others. It appears, therefore, that we do not here require the rules for resolving case conflicts suggested by Zwicky (1986: 99–102). The second objection is that the marking of the genitive on the quantified phrase represents an 'overwriting' of features, which is something we should avoid for general theoretical reasons (Corbett, 1981: 74). Although we have considered the nominative to be what we would expect to appear, not needing explanation, the fact that it appears when the genitive is not imposed results from a Feature Specification Default (Gazdar *et al.*, 1985: 29–31). Other things being equal, the nominative is used in Russian, as shown, for example, by the fact that it is used as the citation form. Thus the imposition of the genitive does not overwrite a nominative value of the category case, but if the genitive is not imposed then the nominative will appear by default.

Having established how it is that the adjective can stand in the nominative or genitive plural with the numerals *dva*, *tri* and *četyre*, we should now consider the factors which influence the choice. As already mentioned, these are quite numerous and complex. What is important for our consideration of the head–dependent relation is that we can establish clearly a major factor where the numeral is the determining influence and another which is controlled by the noun.

It will be simpler for exposition purposes if we start from the major factor originating with the noun, which is its gender. It is well established that the adjective is more likely to stand in the genitive if the noun is masculine or neuter than if it is feminine. This is confirmed by the data presented in table 2.7.

Table 2.7   Use of the genitive plural with 2–4 in Russian: effect of gender. (Total number of examples in parentheses.)

	Masculine	Feminine	Neuter
Suprun (1957: 73)	85% (132)	31% (87)	94% (17)
Corbett	100% (214)	27% (161)	93% (40)

Suprun extracted his examples from literary texts – mainly modern – but he includes various word orders (forty-three examples are not of the type numeral–adjective–noun). My examples are from thirty-nine prose works (novels, short stories and non-fiction, including four translations) of the period 1970–80, a total of approximately 2.3 million words of running text.[17] The difference between the two sets of figures in table 2.7 stems largely from Suprun's inclusion of examples with word orders where the nominative is favoured. We can see that if we look strictly at the position between numeral and noun, then the modern norm is for the genitive with masculine and neuter nouns,[18] with both cases possible for the feminine.

The position is indeed curious: the case of the attributive adjective depends in part on the gender of the noun. Moreover, this influence is operating on the plural form of the adjective which, as already mentioned, does not differentiate gender. The reason behind the difference according to gender is clear, in that many feminine nouns have identical forms in the genitive singular and nominative plural, so the retention of the nominative plural adjective is understandable. It is rather less clear how this is reflected in a grammar. At first, it seems that the features should be 'gathered' on the adjective and the potential conflict of features originating with the numeral (case) and with the noun (gender) should be resolved there; but, as we shall see in the next section, where we add a further element to the construction, this approach is inadequate. However, we have already seen that the numeral must be marked for gender, to account for the choice of *dva* (masculine/neuter) versus *dve* (feminine) 'two'. Since the numeral is marked in this way (and so, we shall have to assume, are *tri* 'three' and *četyre* 'four', though there is no external indication here), then this gender marking will influence whether or not the genitive case feature is imposed on the phrase dependent on the numeral. Unfortunately, this does not help us any further with the head–dependent relations. The gender feature can be 'passed up' to the head numeral direct from the noun (if that is head), through an intervening node (in a constituency approach) or through the adjective, if the adjective is head.

The factor influencing the choice of case for the adjective which most obviously depends on the numeral is the actual numeral itself. While what we have said so far is true of all three numerals, apart from the agreement in gender of *dva/dve*, the case of the adjective varies in part according to the numeral, as was pointed out by Gallis (1947). The evidence is taken from rather small sets of examples, which is not too surprising since examples occur on average about once in 5,500 words of running text. Nevertheless, the picture which emerges is clear, as table 2.8 shows.

Table 2.8   Use of the genitive plural with 2–4 in Russian: effect of the numeral. (Total number of examples in parentheses.)

	dva/dve 'two'	*tri* 'three'	*četyre* 'four'
Gallis (1947: 70)	56% (64)	66% (30)	85% (13)
Worth (1959: 123) (feminine only)	28% (29)	50% (6)	66% (3)
Suprun (1957: 77)	63% (147)	68% (73)	81% (16)
(feminine only)	18% (55)	48% (27)	80% (5)
Corbett	71% (293)	72% (82)	70% (40)
(feminine only)	22% (109)	38% (32)	40% (20)

These data are not fully comparable. Gallis' examples come from rather disparate sources and include some with *oba* 'both' (under *dva*). Worth used only twentieth-century prose and, given the considerable influence of gender, gives data just for the feminine gender, where the choice of case is most open. Suprun's corpus and mine are as for table 2.7. There are some problems with the data in terms of sample size, and some uncertainty as to other interfering factors since other example types were included in certain cases. And when we look at my data, taken from the largest corpus and including only examples of the type numeral–adjective–noun, then there seems to be no observable effect. This is because of the different numbers of examples with the different numerals. If we look just at examples where the noun is of feminine gender, then overall the picture is clear: the genitive is more likely to be found with *tri* 'three' than with *dva/dve* 'two', and more likely with *četyre* 'four' than with *tri*. In one respect the data fit beautifully with our analysis. Looking back to table 2.6, we see that the likelihood of the genitive being found in numeral phrases increases monotonically as the numerals become larger. Instead of *dva*, *tri* and *četyre* being lumped together, each fits independently at its rightful place (this ranking gains support from predicate agreement; Corbett, 1983: 221). On the other hand, in most current theories the place where the difference between the options must be coded is in the lexical entries of the numerals, and it is not obvious how this regularity can be captured there. Nevertheless, in terms of our main concern, it appears that the major factors which determine the case of the adjective are found on the numeral, either coming from its lexical entry or by agreement from the noun. In those instances where a choice of form is allowed by the factors already discussed, some investigators claim that there is a difference in meaning between the two forms. (This is discussed in note 24 below.)

Let us return to the two questions we asked when adding an adjective to the numeral–noun construction. On the first, which was whether these phrases suggest that the head properties are shared between numeral and noun or whether they indicate that the numeral is the clear head, we must answer that, though the data are complex, there is nothing which prevents us maintaining the analysis which has the numeral as the head in relation to the quantified nominal phrase. The second question was whether, given table 2.5, it was possible not only to treat the numeral as head of the quantified phrase, but to go on and treat the adjective as head of the noun within the quantified phrase. Unfortunately, there is no evidence from the choice of form of the adjective which forces us to adopt a particular head–dependent structure for phrases consisting of adjective plus noun.

2.4 Worth's riddle

We can continue our investigation by further complicating the phrases we are analysing. Indeed, a major test for any analysis of Russian numeral expressions is whether it can handle 'Worth's riddle' (Worth, 1959: 124; Corbett, 1978a), for which we add a fourth element to our phrase, namely a post-nominal adjectival phrase. First we look at phrases with a post-nominal adjectival phrase and no pre-nominal modifier:

(1)   dve puški,   otlitye   v 1590 g.
         two cannon, cast.NOM in 1590
         'two cannon, cast in 1590'   (Ivanov, *Moskovskij Kreml'*)

In almost any account, phrases such as *otlitye v 1590 g.* 'cast in 1590' are dependents and not heads. They are optional elements, marked off intonationally. Certainly, the majority of the criteria indicate that they are dependents (we return in a moment to what they depend on). The fact that they must be analysed differently from normal pre-nominal adjectives makes the case for treating the adjective as the head of its noun appear rather less strong. Let us accept, however, that the post-nominal adjectival phrase is a dependent and see what light such phrases can throw on the rest of the numeral phrase. The adjective, or participle, heading such phrases can stand in the nominative, as in (1), or in the genitive:[19]

(2)   dva trona, soedinennyx meždu soboj
        two thrones connected.GEN between selves
        'two thrones, joined together'

                                      (Aleksandrov, *Po Kremlju: kratkij putevoditel'*)

Given that an adjective within the numeral phrase can stand in the nominative (including accusative identical to the nominative) or in the genitive, and that the adjective heading a post-nominal adjectival phrase can also stand in either case, if we have both present then logically we should expect four possibilities:[20]

A	2–4	ADJ(NOM)	NOUN	ADJ(NOM)
B	2–4	ADJ(GEN)	NOUN	ADJ(NOM)
*C	2–4	ADJ(NOM)	NOUN	ADJ(GEN)
D	2–4	ADJ(GEN)	NOUN	ADJ(GEN)

It was Worth (1959: 124) who noted that type C does not occur.[21] Type A is relatively easy:

(3)   dve belye   rozy, utonuvšie   v krasnoj luže
        two white.NOM   roses drowned.NOM in red   pool
        'two white roses, drowned in the red pool'[22]

                                        (Bulgakov, *Master i Margarita*)

In example (3) the quantified phrase has not gained a genitive case feature, as the pre-nominal adjective shows, and so there is no source for a genitive case for the participle *utonuvšie* 'drowned'. Examples of type D, with two genitives, are also relatively easy:

(4)   dva bol'šix   kuska stekla, obernutyx   v trjapku
        two large.GEN pieces of.glass wrapped.GEN in rag
        'two large pieces of glass, wrapped in a rag'

                                          (Trifonov, *Starik*)

Here the genitive has been imposed on the quantified phrase, and the participle gains this feature from its head, the noun (even though the noun does not itself show the feature, since it is marked [dual]). This will be possible whether the head of the quantified phrase is the (pre-nominal) adjective or the noun. The mixed case type B is more difficult:

(5)   tri   latvijskix   mužika, počti pozabyvšie   rodinu
        three Latvian.GEN peasants almost having.forgotten.NOM homeland
        'three Latvian peasants, who had almost forgotten their homeland'
                                                            (Trifonov, *Starik*)

In (5) the genitive has been imposed on the quantified phrase, as the adjective *latvijskix* shows; how then can *pozabyvšie* stand in the nominative? It is attached at a higher level of structure, if we use a constituency framework; in terms of dependency, it depends directly on the head of the phrase, *tri*, and so is nominative. These two possible types of attachment/dependency for post-nominal adjectival (and participial) phrases are not an *ad hoc* device, since they are found with other numeral phrases where there is no other source of variation:

(6)   pjat' čelovek, postroennye v kolonnu
        five   men.GEN formed.NOM in column
        'five men, formed up into a column'   (Vojnovič)[23]

(7)   dvenadcat' literatorov, sobravšixsja na zasedanie
        twelve   writers.GEN gathered.GEN for meeting
        'twelve writers gathered assembled for a meeting'
                                                    (Bulgakov, *Master i Margarita*)

These examples show that, using dependency terms, post-nominal adjectival phrases may depend directly on the numeral, as in (6), in which case the adjective or participle stands in the nominative. Alternatively, they may depend on the noun, as in (7), in which case the adjective/participle will be in the genitive.[24] With numerals above *četyre* 'four', marking of the noun as genitive is obligatory (see table 2.6), and so there is no further choice here.

    This analysis implies that examples like (1) and (3) above are structurally ambiguous: the adjective is in the nominative, the numeral is 'two', 'three', or 'four', and there is no evidence that the genitive has been imposed by the numeral: if it has not been, then the adjectival phrase may depend on the numeral or on the noun and in either situation the nominative results.

We can now explain why type C constructions do not occur:

(8) *dve belye   rozy, utonuvšix   v krasnoj luže
     two white.NOM roses drowned.GEN in red   pool
     'two white roses, drowned in the red pool'

The form of *belye* 'white' shows that the genitive has not been imposed on the nominal phrase; thus there is no source for genitive marking on *utonuvšix* 'drowned': whether this participle depends on the numeral or on the noun it will acquire nominative case marking. It is the ungrammaticality of examples like (8) which shows that the features cannot be gathered on the adjective and any conflict resolved there. If this procedure were adopted we could not prevent differing results on the two adjectives, which is required for examples like (5) but must be ruled out for those like (8).

It appears therefore that if the numeral is taken as the head, and the quantified phrase as the dependent, our analysis permits an explanation of Worth's riddle. However, the explanation is available whether we take the adjective to be head of the noun, within the quantified phrase, or the noun to be head of the adjective.

2.5 Conclusion

We have presented an analysis of the most difficult of the numeral phrases in Russian, including an account of Worth's riddle. This required the following: first, the use of an irregular feature (which we called [dual]), needed on morphological grounds; second, the claim that the case Feature Specification Default for Russian is nominative (which is amply justified by other evidence); third, the genitive rule (which can also be seen as a type of default in that nominal phrases dependent on other nominal phrases typically take the genitive in Russian); fourth, feature percolation 'up and down', since gender is a lexical property of nouns, but is realized on the numeral by agreement, while conversely the numerals investigated govern the form of the noun (by imposing the [dual] feature); and fifth, two forms of attachment/dependency for adjectival phrases (again something required independently).

However, the main purpose of the analysis was to see what light it could shed on headedness relations. We noted that the criteria adopted in the Zwicky–Hudson debate proved difficult to apply in some instances as the list of constructions investigated was extended. In particular, looking at a language with a rich morphological system means that it becomes crucial whether or not morphology can be disregarded in applying certain criteria.

If our main aim is to find an analysis in which the headedness relations are simple and consistent, then Hudson's interpretation of the criteria at first sight yields a more elegant analysis. In this approach, the numeral has to be taken as the head in Russian constructions consisting of numeral plus nominal phrase, and this allows us to treat all such numeral constructions alike in terms of headedness. We must, however, recognize that headedness is a gradient notion, since case affects the degree to which the head shows head-like properties. When we looked more closely at the relations within a nominal phrase consisting of adjective plus noun the picture became less clear. Our analysis would work with either element as head. If, however, we wish to maintain simplicity and consistency in our assignment of the head relation, then we are forced to claim that the adjective is the head of adjective–noun constructions in Russian. Such an analysis has already been proposed by Miller, but some might consider this step counter-intuitive and too high a price to pay for an elegant analysis.

Taking a more general view, it is surprising that such apparently simple matters as the relations of the basic elements within the noun phrase are open to debate and that the criteria for deciding the issue are far from settled. It is also worth noting that the approach adopted seemed to push us towards a dependency analysis, as giving the simpler account. And yet, while we have seen that there is room for genuine debate about the internal headedness relations of Russian quantified expressions, there seems little doubt that they form constituents. Thus these constructions could be taken as evidence favouring constituency-based rather than dependency-based analyses (compare Dahl, 1980, and Hudson, 1980a, b). However, that debate has moved on, in that those arguing for constituency-based analyses increasingly treat the head–dependent relation within constituents as crucial (as in Gazdar *et al.*, 1985: 50–2, and in Kornai and Pullum, 1990). This means in turn that it is important to continue undertaking detailed analyses of constructions where the head–dependent relations are not clear, and so to sharpen the criteria available for determining which element is the head.

NOTES

1. I am grateful to participants in the Talking Heads Round Table and to members of the EUROTYP Theme Group on Noun Phrase Structure for

helpful discussion of some of the issues raised in this chapter. Special thanks go to Dick Hudson, Jim Miller, Nigel Vincent and my co-editors for comments on an earlier version.

2. An important addition to their debate can be found in Warner (1989).
3. In terms of morphology, *odin* 'one', though irregular, has as many forms as a normal adjective, distinguishing six cases, two numbers and three genders in the singular, but there is considerable syncretism. *Dva* 'two' has many fewer forms (see table 2.1); *pjat'* 'five' has just three forms, one for the nominative and accusative, one for the instrumental and one for the remaining cases. At the other end of the scale *million* 'million' has the paradigm of a regular noun (like *žurnal* in table 2.2).
4. See also Mel'čuk (1985: 326–61), who distinguishes three types of head–dependent relation: morphological, syntactic and semantic, and suggests that they may or may not be parallel to each other.
5. In addition, nouns which decline as adjectives show exceptional behaviour here: for example, *nasekomoe* 'insect' behaves syntactically like a noun, but declines like a neuter adjective. In constructions with numerals like *dva*, such nouns behave like adjectives (see section 2.3 below) and stand in the plural: *dva nasekomyx* (genitive plural) 'two insects' not *dva nasekomogo (genitive singular) 'two insects' (Mel'čuk, 1985: 168).
6. *Oba* 'both' has distinct feminine forms as opposed to masculine and neuter right through the paradigm; however, these survive largely in the written language, while in the spoken language the masculine/neuter forms are used for the feminine in the oblique cases, giving a situation just like that of *dva*.
7. Thus Babby (1987: 101–12) considers which element is the head of Russian quantified expressions (and concludes that it is the noun), but uses only agreement and case assignment as tests.
8. Miller (1989: 4) treats this as a major criterion and takes the numeral to be the head, but the fact that numerals do not readily stand on their own in Russian means an argument based just on this criterion is somewhat weak. In some instances collective numerals are substituted (Mel'čuk, 1985: 379-90).
9. Zemskaja and Kapanadze (1978: 292–5) give numerous examples from colloquial Russian of numeral without a quantified noun in the buying of tickets, for example *dva Zagorsk* 'two Zagorsk (two tickets to Zagorsk'). In other circumstances the numeral *odin* 'one' (but no others) is frequently omitted, for example *čas* '(one) hour, (one) o'clock'.
10. For earlier discussion of the problem, based on a range of languages, see Kibrik (1977).
11. Note that this work was ready for publication in 1977.
12. Neidle (1988: 90–4), discussing numerals like *pjat'* 'five', goes so far as to treat the numeral as head in the direct cases and the noun as head in the oblique, as does Miller (1988).

13. *Kniga* 'book' is one of the type of nouns for which the genitive singular and nominative plural are identical (*knigi*).

14. In a discussion of determiners as heads, Hudson (1984: 91) notes as problematic the fact that lexical nouns are also optional after ordinary adjectives.

15. I am grateful to Frans Plank for bringing this reference to my attention. Anderson maintains his analysis in Anderson (1989a: 20–1).

16. There are many such factors, for which see Gallis (1947: 66–73), Suprun (1957), Worth (1959: 122-5), Bogusławski (1966: 237–40), Mel'čuk (1985: 126-8); for the development of the construction see Iordanskij (1958), and for comparative data from Ukrainian see Šerech (1952: 124-38).

17. Where more than one adjective was found in a given example, I counted each separately, since occasionally the two different cases are found together (see Iordanskij, 1958: 71, for two examples involving *oba* 'both'). However, in my sample, case was consistent in the position under discussion.

18. The nominative forms with neuter gender in my corpus are all unusual, for instance: *vse tri èti Bož'i sozdanija* '(literally) all three these God's creations' (Maksimov, *Karantin*).

19. In the corpus already described, there were twenty-six examples with the nominative case, comparable to (1), and eight examples with the genitive, comparable to (2). Thus the nominative is much more likely in post-nominal position (76 per cent of the examples); in pre-nominal position it was found in 120 examples out of 415 (29 per cent).

20. Note that ADJ covers participles as well as ordinary adjectives and NOM covers accusative=nominative.

21. The relative frequencies in my corpus were: A (NOM–NOM) four examples; B (GEN–NOM) sixteen examples; C (NOM–GEN) no examples; D (GEN–GEN) nine examples.

22. This phrase is in the accusative (identical to the nominative); for simplicity the adjective and participle are glossed as nominative, following note 19, since we are concentrating on the opposition nominative (and accusative=nominative) vs genitive.

23. Vojnovič, *Žizn' i neobyčajnye priključenija soldata Ivana Čonkina.*

24. It is claimed that in some instances, at least, there is a clear semantic difference between the two (see Iomdin, 1979: 37; Mel'čuk, 1985: 448–9). Elsewhere the nominative case can imply definiteness and the genitive indefiniteness. A. E. Kibrik suggests (personal communication) that the same distinction applies to prenominal adjectives too, when the two case forms are available (that is, with feminine nouns) and his view matches that of Iomdin (1990: 100), who offers the following contrast:

(i)   Na stole stojala ogromnaja vaza s   fruktami, i   Senja vzjal
       on table stood huge   bowl with fruit   and Senja took
       dve spelye/spelyx   gruši

two ripe.ACC=NOM/ripe.GEN pears
'There was a huge bowl of fruit on the table, and Senja took two ripe pears.'

According to Iomdin, the accusative=nominative form would be more appropriate if Senja took all the pears (or at least all the ripe ones), while the genitive would be more appropriate if there were other (ripe) pears too. This matches the view that the nominative implies definiteness. However, this interesting distinction, available in this construction only in a very limited set of circumstances, does not help us in determining headedness. It is generally agreed that definiteness is a property of noun phrases, so whatever is head of the noun phrase will gain the feature for definiteness.

3 *The phonology of heads in Haruai*

BERNARD COMRIE

3.1 Introduction

In examining the interrelation between grammatical terms as used in the description of individual languages and in general linguistic theory, it is useful to bear in mind that individual languages often present language-specific criteria for a particular grammatical notion which, while not forming part of the general linguistic definition of that notion, none the less provide a language-internal means of identifying instances of the notion in question and thus solidifying our data-base for study of the grammatical notion in general linguistic theory. For instance, the possibility of forming a comparative *hungrier* shows that English *hungry* is an adjective in *John is hungry*, thus providing an instance of a concept that can be adjectivalized even though in many languages non-adjectival constructions are preferred (such as a noun in French *Jean a faim*, literally 'John has hunger', or a verb in Russian *Vanja xočet est*, literally 'John wants to eat'); note that cross-linguistically, the existence of comparative forms of adjectives is rather rare, so this is very much a language-particular test. In this chapter, I argue that Haruai has a language-internal phonological correlate of the head–dependent relation, namely that, in the absence of other factors (contrastive stress, greater stress associated with focus, that is, essential new information), dependents receive greater stress than their heads.[1] The basic word-stress rule in Haruai is for stress to fall on the first syllabic segment of the word; the only consistent exceptions are negative verb forms, which are stressed on the negative morpheme, for example *n dw-ö̇l-m-a* 'I did not go', literally 'I go-NEG-PAST(-1.SG)-DEC'. Incidentally, while the difference between stressed and unstressed syllables is in general easy to hear, in particular with phrases pronounced in isolation (for instance, as answers to questions), I have not been able to register systematic differences of degrees of stress, so I will have nothing to say about this, although it is, of course, a question of great potential interest.

Throughout this article, the notion 'head' will be understood in a fairly traditional sense, essentially following Tesnière (1959), so that, for instance, nouns are heads of noun phrases. This reflects my view that this defines a significant linguistic notion, whether or not other concepts that have come to be subsumed under the term 'head' also define other significant linguistic notions.

3.2 Noun phrases

The relation between greater stress and dependent status can be seen most clearly in noun phrases, where the main types of dependents are adjectives and genitives. (In principle, relative clauses should also be treated here, but since they are typically long constituents, other factors of phrasing usually intervene, thus masking any consistent relation between dependent status and stress.)

Haruai has a small set of basic adjectives, such as *dyb* 'big', and a larger set of derived adjectives, such as *höd-yöbö* 'old', derived from *höd* 'before, earlier'. Indeed, the set of derived adjectives is in principle open, since adjectives can be formed from most adverbial phrases of place and time, as in *ram yl-yöbö* 'pertaining to in front of the house', literally 'house base-ADJ'. Adjectives may either follow or precede their head noun. However, positioning is in practice largely determined by the length of the adjective or adjectival phrase (Comrie, 1989). Shorter adjectives usually follow their head noun, as in *nöbö dyb* 'big man', literally 'man big', while longer adjectival expressions are more likely to precede, for example, *ram yl-yöbö b̄* 'tree in front of the house', literally 'house base-ADJ tree'.[2] While this is a strong tendency, however, it is not an absolute rule. Whatever the order of adjective and noun, however, the main stress of the phrase falls on the adjective, unless there are particular pragmatic reasons (contrast, focus) for stressing the head noun.[3] It should be noted that the usual post-head positioning of adjectives is virtually the only exception (other than clitics, for which see below) to the general head-final nature of Haruai. (I have no natural examples of the use of non-restrictive adjectives; elicited examples behave just like restrictive adjectives.)

A genitive almost invariably precedes its head in Haruai. The genitive dependent is not itself marked morphologically in any way, and the head noun does not need to be marked morphologically, although if the genitive refers to a salient human entity, then the head can be marked by a pronominal clitic. Thus, 'the man's pig' can be either *nöbö hön*, literally 'man pig', or *nöbö hön-nwŋ^w*, literally 'man pig-his'. In the absence of contrast or focus on the head, the main stress of the noun phrase falls on the genitive dependent.

Pronominal genitives usually behave differently, since they typically occur after the head noun and are cliticized to that head noun, as in *hön-an* 'our pig', literally 'pig-our', although the reverse order *an hön* was judged acceptable under elicitation. This introduces a general limitation on the correlation between stress and dependent status that will recur below: cliticized elements do not have independent stress, and this overrides the correlation between stress and dependent status. Note that although clitics cannot receive independent stress, they can receive the sole stress if this is required for reasons of contrast or focus, so that although *hön-an* will usually be stressed on the *ö*, it can be stressed on the *a* to indicate '*our* pig'. Lest it be thought that the behaviour of clitics renders vacuous the general claim about a correlation between stress and dependent status, it should be noted that clitics form a small well-defined set of items in Haruai: for instance, the only genitive clitics are the personal pronouns. (In isolation, *nwŋ^w* is 'he, she', *an* is 'we'.)

The special behaviour of clitics is, however, relevant to the demonstratives in Haruai. Demonstratives can be used as independent noun phrases, with a three-way opposition, *k* 'this', *ak^w* 'that (near addressee, or in middle distance)', *k^wö* 'that (far from speaker and addressee)'. When used as dependents of a head noun they are simply cliticized after the head noun, thus making them irrelevant for purposes of the correlation between stress and dependent status, as in *nöbö-k* 'this man', *nöb-ak^w*,[4] *nöbö-k^wö* 'that man'.

3.3 Postpositional phrases

Haruai has no prepositions, and even the existence of postpositions is not entirely clear. As translations of English expressions like 'beside/ at the foot of the mountain', Haruai uses phrases of the type *önöŋ yl*, where *önöŋ* is 'mountain'. However, *yl* also exists independently as a noun, meaning 'base, bottom part' (and also, more abstractly, 'cause'), as do other locational items that can fit into this slot, such as *mo* 'under(side)', *möybl* 'midst'. In Haruai, a noun can be used without any overt marking to indicate location, so that *ram* 'house', for instance, can be used to mean 'at the house', as in *nöbö dyb ram md-a* 'the big man is at the house', literally 'man big house stay(-PRES-3.SG)-DEC'. Thus *önöŋ yl* might simply be an instance of a noun phrase used locatively, *önöŋ* being a genitive and *yl* the head. There is one piece of evidence suggesting that such expressions constitute, or are being re-analysed as, a separate class of postpositional phrases, namely that where the head is a personal pronoun, it is normally preposed, rather than being cliticized. Thus for instance, 'among us' is more likely to be *an möybl* than *möybl-an*, although the latter is also possible. The stress in expressions like *önöŋ yl* falls on the non-locational component. If these constructions are special instances of genitive constructions, then this is just a special instance of the generalization of section 3.2, with stress falling on the genitive in genitive–head constructions. If the locational element is to be analysed as a postposition, then again stress falls on the dependent, this time on the noun-phrase complement of the postposition.

There is another element that occurs as a separate word and is probably to be analysed as a postposition, namely *psaŋ* (with variants: *psak, pcaŋ, pcak*), used to express comitativity, as in *n nöbö dyb psaŋ dy-n-a* 'I will go with the big man', literally, 'I man big together go-FUT(-1.SG)-DEC'. The item *psaŋ* can also occur independently as an adverb, as in *psaŋ dy-n-a* 'I'll go along', but this analysis seems implausible for the sentence first cited, which would leave *nöbö dyb* dangling without any syntactic relation with the rest of the clause. Moreover, the sequence *nöbö dyb psaŋ* in this example is pronounced as a single phrase with stress on *dyb*; that is, the stress falls on the noun phrase, readily explicable if this is dependent on a postposition, and within the noun phrase on the (dependent) adjective.

One further item is probably to be classified as a postposition, namely *-yöŋö* 'with (comitative), for (purposive)', as in *n nöbö dyb-yöŋö dy-n-a* 'I will go with the big man', *n röbö-yöŋö dy-n-a* 'I will go for water',[5] literally 'I water-for go-FUT(-1.SG)-DEC'. However, this item is always cliticized to the preceding word, so while it does not receive stress, this is because it is a clitic and does not provide evidence of its being head of a postpositional phrase.

3.4 Clauses

In examining the stress relations between a verb and its dependents, the intervention of the pragmatic factors of contrast and focus is much more widespread than within the noun phrase or postpositional phrase, so that in most instances the particular stress pattern used by the speaker correlates rather with the distribution of new and old information than with the syntactic structure of the clause. My impression is that in answer to a question like 'What will you do?', the answer 'I will kill a pig', where both 'kill' and 'pig' are new information, would most neutrally be answered with stress on *hön* 'pig' in *n hön pay-n-a* 'I pig kill-FUT(-1.SG)-DEC', but validation of this would require testing against a much wider corpus, in particular a corpus of conversational material with its richer pragmatic variety.

There is, however, one class of exceptions to the general problem of pragmatic interference, namely idiomatic expressions where it would make little sense to place contrastive stress on one or other constituent. Although the amount of evidence is relatively slight, here we do find that the stress falls on the dependent and not on the verb. The verb *pl* in isolation is usually taken to mean 'shoot, pierce'. However, it also occurs in a number of idiomatic constructions: for instance, with the noun *ydö* 'seed' as object, it means 'remove seeds', as in *n ydö pl-l-a* 'I remove seeds', literally 'I seed shoot-PRES(-1.SG)-DEC', in which stress falls on the first syllable of *ydö*. An example where the noun phrase in question is subject rather than object is *rwö pl-a* 'it rains', literally 'rain shoot(-PRES-3.SG)-DEC',[6] where stress falls on *rwö*. Consider, finally, the Haruai for 'I am hungry', namely *n kyö pl-a*, literally 'I hunger shoot(-PRES-3.SG)-DEC'. Syntactic tests, in particular verb agreement and switch-reference, suggest that the clause-initial experiencer is not subject of the clause (Comrie, 1987). The constituent *kyö* 'hunger' is probably subject, though it makes no difference to the present argument whether it is analysed as some other kind of dependent. The stress falls on *kyö* in the expression *kyö pl-a*, thus providing another instance of stress falling on the dependent in a construction whose head is a verb.

It will be noted that in all these examples the stressed constituent immediately precedes the verb. It is not an invariant rule of Haruai that stressed sentence constituents must immediately precede the verb, although examples of this kind might suggest that in Haruai the verb forms a constituent together with whatever other material occupies the immediately pre-verbal slot. I have nothing further to say about this here, although it clearly merits further attention.

3.5 Compounds

Haruai makes frequent use of compound nouns. In almost all cases, the structure is Noun + Noun and the last noun is the head, as in *ram-möl* 'room', literally 'house hole'. In all compound nouns with this structure, the stress falls on the first component – indeed, on the first syllabic segment of the first component. (It should be borne in mind that Haruai has initial word stress.) This is in keeping with our generalization that stress falls on the dependent, but unfortunately does not provide independent evidence in favour of this generalization. This is because the initial stress could equally be the result of the general property of word-initial stress, this rule being applied to the compound noun as a whole. This second analysis might even seem mandated by the stress of such compounds as *b̦aj* 'log', literally 'tree tooth'. Phonetically, this is pronounced as a single syllable, with just one syllabic segment *a*, and the stress falls on this syllabic, which is the initial syllabic segment of the word, but does not fall within the dependent constituent of the compound noun. Presumably, however, the dependent constituent of a compound whose dependent constituent happens not to contain any syllabic segment would need in any event to be excluded from stressability.[7] I am aware of one, and only one, compound noun where the dependent follows the head, namely *yw öböŋ* 'bush-knife, machete', literally 'knife bamboo', semantically, this is clearly a kind of knife and not a kind of bamboo (the name presumably derives from its use to cut bamboo). In terms of Haruai derivational morphology this item is quite exceptional, but in terms of stress it provides striking confirmation of our generalization: stress falls here on the second constituent, as predicted by the correlation between stress and dependent status, and contrary to the alternative analysis whereby stress in compounds is regularly assigned to the initial syllabic segment of the compound (which would be *w*, given the pronunciation [yu]).

The identififation of compound verbs is a little more tricky. Haruai makes widespread use of the serial verb construction, in which only the last verb of the series is marked for verbal categories, the others simply appearing in their stem form. Some instances of serial verb constructions exemplify fully productive patterns, and in these stress, if on the verb sequence, normally falls on the last verb, as in *n dw nwg^w-n-a* 'I will go look', literally 'I go see-FUT(1.SG)-DEC', with stress on *nwg^w-n-a*; I take such examples to involve strings of verbs with no dependency relations among them. However, there are also verb sequences that have become lexicalized, thus forming true compound verbs, such as *rag dw* 'take (away)', literally 'bring go'. Here stress normally falls on the first component, if it falls on the verb complex at all, as in *n yw rag dy-n-a* 'I will take the knife away', literally 'I knife bring go-FUT(-1.SG)-DEC'. In these clear examples of compound verbs, we find once again that stress falls on the dependent, though as with compound nouns this is not distinguishable from lexical stress on the first syllabic. In Haruai, the verb-final constraint is very strict, the only exception being that locatives may follow the verb. In finite clauses, the finite verb must be clause-final (apart from a possible following locative), so there is no possibility of having a verb stem after the finite verb in a serial verb construction, that is, no possibility of testing head–dependent order. An extreme example of the fusion of verbs in a serial verb construction is provided by the marking of imperfective aspect in Haruai, with the suffix -md, as in n dw-md-l-a 'I am going', literally 'I go-IPRFV-PRES-DEC'; the suffix -md is clearly relatable etymologically to the verb md 'be located', that is an original serial verb construction where the last verb has been re-interpreted as an affix, with stress, needless to say, on the first syllable of the whole word.

3.6 Conclusions

In endocentric constructions in Haruai, there seems to be a generalization that, in the absence of marked pragmatic conditions, stress falls on the dependent, irrespective of word order; thus stress falls on the indicated constituent of the following constructions: GÉN-N, N-ADJ/ADJ-N, N-N (that is, right-headed compound nouns; the one example I have of a left-headed compound noun is N-N), and some NP–V collocations (though with argument noun phrases in general it is hard to abstract away from pragmatic conditioning of stress). For elements that are not separate phonological words, other principles apply, so that it is not possible to apply this test for headedness to affixes or to clitics (including most instances of postpositions). The applicability of a logically independent phonological test for heads, however, suggests that it would be profitable to look for other such logically independent tests in other languages, especially in instances where there is controversy concerning the headedness of constructions.

NOTES

1. Haruai is a non-Austronesian language spoken in the south-west of Madang Province, Papua New Guinea (see further Comrie, 1988). All information on Haruai presented here is derived from my own field-work, including both elicited examples and natural speech (especially narrative); this material is based upon work supported by the National Science Foundation under Grant BNS-8504293. I am grateful to the Madang Province Research Committee for permission to conduct this

research and to the Summer Institute of Linguistics (Papua New Guinea Branch) for invaluable material aid. I am especially grateful to the Haruai people for their hospitality and enthusiastic support of my work on their language. I would also like to thank participants in the Talking Heads Round Table for comments on an earlier version of this chapter.

The transcription system used for Haruai is a phonemic one. It should be noted in particular that /w/ and /y/ have syllabic and non-syllabic allophones, and that many consonant clusters are broken up by an epenthetic [ɨ]; this vowel may receive stress.

The following abbreviations are used: ADJ–adjective, DEC–declarative, FUT–future, GEN–genitive, IPRFV–imperfective, N–noun, NEG–negative, PRES–present, SG–singular. Morpheme glosses in parentheses are recoverable from the morphological structure of the word but have no separate segmental representation.

2. One item, *köl* 'other', though on other grounds probably assignable to the class of adjectives, usually precedes its head. As far as I can see, this is simply an exception; there are no other items that behave like *köl*.

3. Haruai is not a very numerate society, but to the extent that numerals, in particular the lower numerals (roughly to 'four'), are used they behave like adjectives with respect to stress.

4. The vowel *ö* is dropped before another vowel.

5. *röbö-yöŋö* is usually contracted, by general rule, to *röbeŋö*.

6. In isolation, speakers of Haruai translate *rwö* by Tok Pisin *ren*, 'rain', although it enters into a number of other meteorological expressions which suggest a more general meaning like 'environment, biosphere', for example *rwö öröw-a* 'dawn breaks', literally 'biosphere dawn(-PRES-3.SG)-DEC'.

7. In isolation, *b̃* is pronounced as a syllable, as [b̥ɨ], but before a further vowel within the same word (including a compound word) the epenthesis of [ɨ] does not take place.

4 *Patterns of headedness*

RONNIE CANN

4.1 Patterns of properties

Although the notion of head has a part to play in almost all current syntactic theories, how heads should be identified remains controversial.[1] Many tests for heads have been proposed in the literature, but which tests are appropriate, what their form should be and how they should be applied vary considerably. As discussed in the introduction, Zwicky (1985) informally presents eight such tests, but concludes pessimistically that only the test for the morphosyntactic locus of a phrase is a significant test for headedness. Hudson (1987) takes up this topic and, revising Zwicky's tests, comes to the conclusion that the tests are non-contradictory and together identify the head in some construction. In a discussion of both papers, Cann (1989) reduces the number of Zwicky's tests to six (rejecting semantics and rulership as diagnostics for headedness) and provides set-theoretic definitions of the remaining tests in terms of the category membership and combinatorial properties of grammatical expressions. The definitions proposed there are given informally in (1), where they are divided into three groups according to the similarities in their set-theoretic definitions.

(1)   1 Subcategorization
          Subcategorizand: X subcategorizes for Y in a construction X+Y iff the ability of members of X to appear with expressions in Y properly partitions the expressions in X into two partially disjoint non-null subsets.
      2 Form control
          (a) *Form governor*: X is a governor in X+Y if there is some group of inflectional variants, $x_1, ..., x_n$ in X that all induce the same proper binary partition on the expression-forms of Y according to their morphological form.
          (b) *Concord controller*: X is a concord controller in X+Y if there is some group of inflectional variants, $x_1, ..., x_n$ in X which induce

different binary partitions on expression-forms of Y according to their morphological form.

3 Distribution

(a) *Obligatory constituent*: X is the obligatory constituent in X+Y iff there are no expressions x in X and y in Y such that x+y is in category A and there is an expression z in category Z such that z+x+y is of category B and z+y is also an expression in B.

(b) *Distributional equivalent*: X is the distributional equivalent in X+Y if there are expressions, x of X, y of Y which combine to give an expression, x+y, of category A, then there is some category Z that contains an expression z which combines with x+y to give an expression of category B such that z+x is also in B.

(c) *Morphosyntactic locus*: X is a morphosyntactic locus in X+Y iff. there are expressions, x and x_1 in X and y in Y such that both x_1+y and x+y are both expressions of category A and for some expressions z in Z z+x+y is of category B but z+x_1+y is not.

Table 4.1 lists the results that can be obtained by applying the tests in (1) to the English constructions: V+NP (for example, *shot the penguins*), Aux+VP (*was shooting the penguins*), Det+N (*some/all/we penguins*), Dem+N (*this/that penguin*), A+N (*happy penguin*), Comp+S (*that Rambo shot the penguin*) and WH+S (*who Rambo shot*). It is not my intention to rehearse the arguments for these results here. Cann (1989) provides detailed arguments for the choice of properties for determiner plus noun and complementizer plus sentence and a sketch of the arguments for the properties shown by the other constructions is also given there. More details can also be gleaned by an examination of Zwicky (1985) and Hudson (1987) and further evidence is presented in the theoretical discussion of sections 4.2–4.

Table 4.1 shows that the head-like properties defined in (1) are not conjunctive and do not necessarily select only a single category in particular constructions. One can see from this that Hudson's optimistic conclusion about the harmonic nature of the head-like properties is not supported, nor, however, is Zwicky's pessimism about their coherence. The distribution of the head-like properties in table 4.1 reveals five primary patterns. The first (type 1), exemplified by V+NP, involves a subcategorizing (major) category which form-controls its complement and shows all the distributional properties. The second (type 2), exemplified by Det+N, has a non-subcategorizing functional category which form-governs its complement and the third (type 3), for example Dem+N, has a non-subcategorizing major category controlling the concord of its complement. In both of the

Table 4.1 Head-like properties in seven English constructions

	V	NP	Aux	VP	Det	N	Dem	N	A	N	Comp	S	WH	S
Sb	+	–	+	–	–	–	–	–	–	–	–	–	–	–
FG	+	–	+	–	+	–	–	–	–	–	+	–	–	–
CC	–	–	–	–	–	–	–	+	–	–	–	–	–	+
OC	+	–	+	+	–	+	–	+	–	+	–	–	+	+
DE	+	–	+	+	+	+	+	+	–	+	+	+	+	+
ML	+	+	+	+	+	+	+	+	–	+	+	+	+	+

+ indicates that the element in question shows the property with respect to the construction.
– indicates that the property is not exhibited.

Sb = subcategorizand   OC = obligatory constituent
FG = form governor   DE = distributional equivalent
CC = concord controller   ML = morphosyntactic locus

latter constructions, distributional properties may not all be realized but where they are, they appear on both categories in the construction. In the fourth pattern (type 4), exemplified by the adjective plus noun construction, no subcategorization or form control occurs and the distributional properties are realized on the major category in the construction. A fifth pattern is exemplified by the Aux+VP construction which appears to be a combination of types 1 and 2 with a subcategorizing and form-controlling (functional) head, but distribution of other properties across both categories in the construction. This situation is summarized in table 4.2.

Table 4.2 Patterns of head-like properties

	Type 1		Type 2		Type 3		Type 4		Type 5	
	M	Y	F	Y	M	Y	M	Y	F	Y
Sb	+	−	−	−	−	−	−	−	+	−
FG	+	−	+	−	−	−	−	−	+	−
CC	−	−	−	−	+	−	−	−	−	−
OC	+	−	−	−	−	−	+	−	+	−
DE	+	−	+	+	+	+	+	−	+	+
ML	+	+	+	+	+	+	+	−	+	+

M = Major category (N, V, A, P)
F = Functional category (Det, Dem, Comp, WH, Aux)
Y = Variable over categories

From these patterns, it is possible to identify a number of descriptive generalizations. In the first place, one expression in each construction is more head-like than the other with respect to at least one of the macro-properties of subcategorization, form control or distribution. Secondly, it would appear that where a category is head with respect to subcategorization, it is also head with respect to form control and distribution. Finally, where neither expression is a subcategorizand or form controller, one must uniquely show the distributional properties. The results of applying the tests in (1) to a range of English constructions thus indicates that one of the constituent expressions is more head-like than the other, thus giving credence to headedness as a significant syntactic notion. On the other hand, the tests are neither conjunctive in their applicability nor uniquely identifying. If the patterns of headedness in table 4.2 correctly represent the distribution of head-like syntactic properties across constructions, then the task of a syntactic theory should be to explain why these should occur.

In current transformational grammar, syntactic structure is determined by X-bar theory, which requires every phrase to have a syntactically projected head, and the Projection Principle, which requires lexical selection properties to remain constant throughout a derivation (Chomsky, 1981). Syntactic projection, as determined by the X-bar schemata in (2), is intended to encapsulate the traditional notion of head in structural terms. The head of a phrase in some tree is the X^{n-1} (or X^n) node immediately dominated by X^n, where n is 1 or 2, and the relationship between a head and a satellite is determined by the level at which the latter is attached. The (optional) specifier of the head appears as a sister to X^1 immediately dominated by X^2 and all complements of the head are attached as sisters to X^0 immediately dominated by X^1. (A third place of attachment is also usually recognized for adjuncts, as sisters and daughters of X^1.)

(2)   a. $X^2 \rightarrow$ (Spec) X^1
        b. $X^1 \rightarrow X^0$ Complement*

According to the schemata in (2), only the head of a phrase is obligatory and hence a lexical head, X^0, must be both the obligatory constituent in, and the distributional equivalent of, X^2. Furthermore, under the interpretation that syntactic projections provide a means for transmitting information about morphosyntactic properties between heads and their phrases, X^0 also functions as the morphosyntactic locus in X^2. One of the fundamental differences between a specifier and a complement is that the latter is generally subcategorized for, and may be θ-marked by, the lexical head. Thus, only X^0 may be subcategorizand of its phrase, while the recent introduction of specifier–head co-indexing (Chomsky, 1986a) provides a means of representing concord relations between heads and specifiers, making the lexical head the only potential concord controller of its phrase.

This apparent uniformity of properties imposed on heads by X-bar theory is, however, complicated by recent developments within transformational theory. It is no longer the case, as it was in Chomsky (1970) and Jackendoff (1973), that only the major categories, N, V, A and P, may head syntactic structures. Since Stowell (1981) and Chomsky (1986a), it has been commonplace to define the clause (C^2) as the projection of the functional category Comp and the sentence (I^2) as the projection of Infl. It has also been proposed (in Abney, 1986) that noun phrases are projections of Det rather than N and (in

Pollock, 1989) that the category Infl is decomposable into its independently projecting Agr and Tns features. Tait and Cann (1990) take these steps to their logical conclusion and allow any feature or combination of features (categories in the sense of Gazdar *et al.*, 1985: 20–7) to project according to X-bar principles. This step has the obvious consequence that the generation of structures which are headed by affixes and other functional or minor elements may be a central feature of the grammar. According to the discussion above, however, there are significant differences in the properties shown by constructions containing functional expressions and those containing major ones. The fact that both types of construction are given an identical structural treatment according to X-bar theory means that factors other than simple syntactic projection must be brought into play to determine the properties of headed structures.

It is the purpose of this chapter to explore how an examination of the patterns of headedness shown in table 4.2 may be constructed within a variant of the Principles and Parameters approach to transformational grammar (Chomsky, 1981, 1986a). In particular, a modified X-bar theory, generalized to cover all functional and major categories, will be used to investigate the relation between subcategorization, form control and the distributional properties of equivalence and obligatoriness. The general approach taken here has developed out of a series of unpublished papers that have been presented sporadically over the last eight years and the specific framework has developed from a joint research project with Mary E. Tait.

4.2 Complements and lexical selection

One of the properties associated with the relation between heads and their complements is that of subcategorization. There are a number of different (but related) ways of interpreting this property from a pre-theoretical point of view. As defined in (1.1) above, subcategorization is the ability of one category to partition expressions in the category of the subcategorizand into partially disjoint sets according to the ability of the latter to appear in construction with expressions of the former. For example in $V+NP^2$ constructions, noun phrases partition the set of verbs into partially disjoint (and non-null) subsets of transitive and intransitive verbs (such as *shoot the penguin* versus *laugh the penguin*).[3]

Since subcategorization so defined is an arbitrary and idiosyncratic property of individual expressions in a particular category, it must be represented as part of the lexical information associated with them.

Let us suppose, following Tait (1991), that lexical information of this sort is encoded in the lexicon in the form of lexical trees, like those in (3) below (where V selects for Det not N, according to the so-called DP analysis of English noun phrases).

(3)   a.

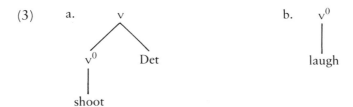

         b.

According to the Projection Principle, lexical properties must be syntactically represented at all levels of structure and we may, therefore, suppose that d-structure is the initial projection of lexical trees like those in (3) into the syntax via the X-bar schemata. X^0 categories are projected to phrase levels and other categories are realized as maximal projections, inducing the relation between schematic lexical trees and their syntactic counterparts shown in (4). This produces schematic trees like those in (5) based on the entries in (3) and the d-structure of a particular sentence is then derived by unifying the schematic trees of all of its lexical items, according to the compatibility of the category of a maximal projection to a lexically projected node (like Det^2 in (5a)). Subcategorization is thus represented as a direct structural relation between an X^0 category, the subcategorizand, and its subcategorized sister, thus entailing that subcategorization is a necessary and sufficient condition for determining the head of a construction and the structural relation between it and its co-constituent.

(4)

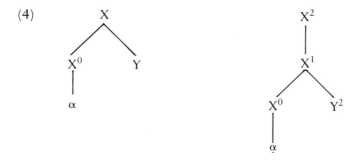

(5) a.

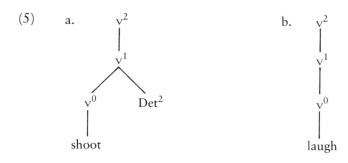

Subcategorization is not the only property that may be lexically represented in this way, nor is the relation between X^0 and its complement always one of subcategorization. One of the head-like properties mentioned in section 4.1 is government in the traditional sense: the determination by one element of the inflectional form of the other: that is, form government. This property can be defined as holding between X and Y in some construction, if varying the inflectional form of Y while keeping X constant leads to ungrammaticality, while varying the form of X and keeping Y constant makes no difference to grammaticality. The classical instance of form government is, of course, case government, and in English, we can show that V form-governs the noun phrase in V+NP because transitive verbs partition pronouns into two sets; with only the accusative forms being able to appear in such positions. Furthermore, this partition holds whatever form an expression of X takes with the same forms of pronouns appearing after participial and third person singular forms (for example, *controls/controlling them* but **controls/ *controlling they*).

Under this interpretation, other types of formal dependency may be recognized as being instances of form government: for example, the traditional wisdom that determiners (excluding demonstratives) do not form-govern their nouns can be shown to be false. The grammaticality patterns in (6) show that the determiners partition nominal expressions according to their grammatical number: *a* partitions N into singular versus plural and unstressed *some* into plural (and mass) versus singular. Furthermore, there is no obvious formal sharing of morphological properties (that is number) between the determiners and their sister nominal (a point made also in Huddleston, 1984: 240, *inter alia*). Neither *the* nor *some* change their form according to the number of the following noun and with the other non-demonstrative determiners there is no formal resemblance at all between those that take the plural and those that take the singular. It follows, therefore, that, contrary to the traditional view, determiners must be analysed as governing the grammatical number of their nominal sisters.

(6)   a. the penguin/penguins
        b. some *penguin/penguins
        c. a penguin/*penguins
        d. every penguin/penguins

Since the determination of number by a determiner is lexically idiosyncratic it can again be assumed that this information is encoded in tree form in the lexicon, yielding lexical trees like those in (7) which are projected into the syntax by the rule in (4).

(7)   a.

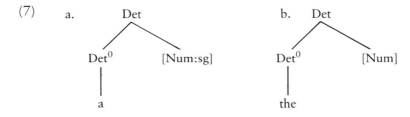

Expressions that form-govern their sisters may be analysed as selecting not the major category of their sister, but only the property that determines their form. Within current transformational theory this difference may be attributed to a difference in θ-marking. Where one expression subcategorizes for another, in the sense of (1.1a), we may analyse this as a case of θ-marking, where the latter is interpreted as the assignment of a specific participant role, not merely as an indication of function–argument structure. Thus, where specific category selection takes place there is θ-marking, but where a formal property is selected there is no θ-marking. In fact, the property of θ-marking (and thus of subcategorization) may be hypothesized to be the defining characteristic of major categories, whilst functional categories do not θ-mark their complements and select only for the formal properties of the latter. If this is so, then the θ-criterion only applies to the instantiation of the complements of major categories, but not to those of minor ones. The obligatoriness of the head in a structure will then depend on the sort of lexical selection that holds between the head and its complement, as can be seen by a consideration of the two structures in (8).

(8)

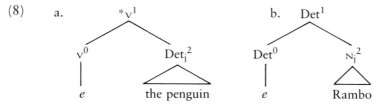

According to θ-theory, the semantic process of determining the properties of an argument, that is, θ-marking, requires the presence of a lexical head. Hence, where that head is not realized, as in (8a), the complement fails to get a θ-role and the functional category Det fails to be properly licensed, violating the θ-criterion. This does not, however, apply to functional heads like Det, since these function semantically as operators, not as constants denoting particular properties or relations. In (8b), therefore, the head is not required to be lexically filled in order to license the major category, as no θ-marking is involved. Hence, major lexical heads are obligatory in head–complement constructions but functional ones are not.

The obligatoriness of the complement, on the other hand, depends on the breadth of the view taken. From the point of view of the wider construction, the complements in both v+NP and Det+N are both optional because of the existence of members of v and Det that do not θ-mark or select for number, that is, intransitive verbs and personal pronouns, respectively. This is the view taken in the construction of table 4.1 (and in Zwicky, 1985; Hudson, 1987). However, with respect to particular instantiations of the construction, complements are generally obligatory, as illustrated in (9).

(9)   a. The penguin laughed
     b. *The penguin kicked
     c. It laughed
     d. *The laughed

Under the hypothesis that functional categories are not θ-markers, the pattern in (9) cannot be attributed to the θ-criterion, since the noun in Det+N constructions does not need to be θ-marked. The obligatoriness of lexically selected complements can, however, be attributed to a principle proposed in Tait and Cann (1990) and Cann and Tait (1989) which requires syntactic projections to be licensed at Phonetic Form (PF). A variant of the Principle of Full Interpretation of Chomsky (1986b: 98), the PF-licensing Principle (PFLP) defined in (10), disallows the postulation of arbitrary elements in the syntax which never receive a PF interpretation.

(10)   α must be PF-licensed, where α is PF-licensed iff the head of α immediately dominates phonetic material or forms part of a PF-licensed chain.

The PFLP constrains what functional categories can be identified, and thus syntactically projected, within a particular language. Where a category has no phonetic realization in a language, it cannot appear in any representation of a sentence in that language, since every node in a tree is required to be PF-licensed, either directly, by having a phonetically realized head, or indirectly, through appearing in a syntactic chain which contains a phonetically realized element. Hence, a category that never has such a phonetic signature can never form part of any well-formed phrase-structure tree. Even where a category does have an overt realization in a language, however, its appearance in particular representations is also constrained by the PFLP. Such a category is only licensed in the syntactic representation of some sentence if it is associated with phonetic material. The principle thus imposes a strong constraint on the appearance of empty heads and it is not possible in this theory to explain syntactic phenomena, like barriers or escape hatches to movement, on the basis of projections that have no phonetic realization.

For the s-structures analysing (9b) and (9d) to be acceptable, therefore, the empty complements, Det^2 and N^2, respectively, must be associated with their lexically filled governing head to satisfy the principle in (10). Lexical selection (L-selection henceforth), however, involves the identification of categorial properties belonging to another expression that are distinct from the head. This difference between a head and its L-selected complement can be incorporated into X-bar theory by adopting the constraint in (11), which requires a head and its L-selected complement to be disjoint in terms of the index that each bears.

(11)   If α L-selects β, then α and β cannot be co-indexed.

Since the PFLP requires an empty category to be co-indexed with some phonetically realized position, the constraint in (11) entails that neither verbs nor determiners co-index their complements. These thus fail to be PF-licensed and hence the trees in (12) are ill-formed as s-structures, as required.

(12) a.

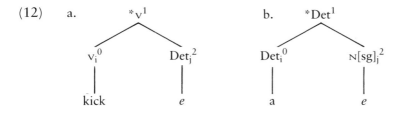

The identification of the distributional equivalents in V+NP and Det+N is also determined by the properties already mentioned. The distributional equivalence of Det with Det+N depends on the delimitation of the class of determiners. If the personal pronouns and the pronominal uses of, for example, *some, each*, etc. are included in the category Det, then it is clear that there are determiners that can appear without complement common noun phrases. In V+NP, the category V, as a whole, is distributionally equivalent because of the existence of intransitive expressions. The distributional equivalence of Det with Det+N and V with V+NP and, in general, of X^0 in X^0+Y^2 constructions, thus depends on the existence of expressions in the head category that are not L-selectors and not on any other properties of the grammar. It cannot, however, always be the case that X^0 is distributionally equivalent to X^2 where X-bar principles are generalized to cover affixal elements, because affixes are not independent morphs and so cannot have the same distribution as a phrase. It seems, therefore, to be a contingent fact that Det and V are distributional equivalents in their respective constructions and nothing to do with grammatical factors. It may be true, however, that non-affixal categories can be defined in terms of this property. In other words, every morphologically independent category contains expressions that have no L-selection properties. This would entail that the head of a non-affixal category would always be identified as the distributional equivalent of its containing projection. What status the generalization in (13) should have in the grammar is, however, not clear and the significance of this definition, apart from ensuring the distributional equivalence of X^0 and X^2 for non-affixal X, will not be further explored here.

(13)   A category, C, is a non-affixal category iff there is some expression α in C which has no L-selection properties.

The complements of major heads are not distributional equivalents of the whole phrase, because they cannot appear without being licensed (θ-marked) by an overt head, as already mentioned. In functional constructions like Det+N, however, the complement does not need to be θ-marked by a lexically filled head, as illustrated in (8b). Proper names, for example, generally appear undetermined in English, although they may take a determiner in certain circumstances (for example, *He's not the Henry I used to know, I know several Henrys*) and in other languages they may be required to appear with some determiner. One may therefore analyse noun phrases consisting only of a name as resulting from the generation of the proper noun as a complement to an empty determiner at d-structure. Where there is no lexical head, we adopt the position that there is free attachment of any category to the complement position. Other principles of the grammar (in particular, co-indexing, categorial compatibility, the θ-criterion and the operation of the PFLP) may be used to determine the restrictions of the categories that may so attach. In the case of empty determiners, the complement must be nominal for reasons that will not be discussed here.

A structure containing an empty determiner with a filled N^2 complement is not a possible s-structure, however, because the determiner position is associated with no phonetic material, thus violating the PFLP. In order to satisfy this principle, some phonetically realized expression must appear in, or be co-indexed with, the determiner position at s-structure. In fact, the structure in (8b) is one in which head movement may occur, where the latter is defined as in (14).

(14)   An expression α immediately dominated by Y^0 may move into a position X^0 that governs its maximal projection, Y^2.

Because Det^0 contains no lexical material to adjoin to, this movement must be an instance of substitution rather than adjunction. For reasons to do with structure preservation, we may adopt the position that substitution operations require categorial compatibility between the category of the moved expression and that of its landing site (see section 4.3). We may further assume that the category of the resulting node at s-structure is determined by that of the moved expression as well as its own d-structure specification. Once the noun has moved into the determiner position, therefore, it is simultaneously analysed as a determiner and a noun and, moreover, the determiner position now contains phonetic material and so is PF-licensed, as required. The N^2 complement position is also licensed via the co-indexing through movement of the head N^0 position with the governing Det^0 position. Because there is no lexical determiner, there is no relation of

L-selection between Det^0 and N^2 and so the structure in (15) does not violate the constraint on co-indexing in (11).[4]

(15)

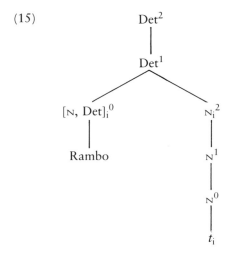

4.3 Specifiers and co-indexing

The properties of specifiers have not in general been well defined. In earlier versions of X-bar theory, the specifier position was given over to hosting the functional categories (like Det, Comp and so on). Recently, interest has been focused on the properties of this position as a θ-position or a landing site (see Stowell, 1989, for some discussion). Assuming that all L-selection is represented in terms of lexical tree structures and that all such structures are projected into the syntax via the rule in (4), the specifier–head relation must be defined without reference to form government or subcategorization. In recent theoretical approaches, the link between a head and its specifier has occasionally been represented as one of co-indexing between these positions through Specifier–Head Agreement. Chomsky (1986a: 24) adopts such a relation sporadically (in C^2 (the category of the clause) and in I^2 (the category of the sentence)) in order to account for certain government relations into specifier positions by external heads. This move has the flavour of expediency rather than theoretical commitment, but may be adopted as a general constraint on all well-formed representations, as in (16).

(16)   If α is the specifier of β, then α and β must be co-indexed.

The effect of the adoption of (16) into the theory, of course, depends on the precise import given to the co-indexing relation. If d-structure is a pure categorial representation of lexical dependencies, we might expect the use of co-indexing in d-structure to involve a close connection between the morphosyntactic properties of co-indexed elements. Indeed, we may require that categories which are co-indexed at d-structure are categorially compatible, where this property is interpreted in terms of category unification (Gazdar *et al.*, 1985: 27). Since lexical dependencies may be obscured at s-structure by the application of Move-α, c-compatibility seems inappropriate for co-indexing at this level, so that the rule in (17) must be seen as a general constraint on d-structure representations only. This restriction to d-structure could be captured by adopting (17) as part of X-bar theory and restricting the domain of this module to this level. As the mediator between the lexicon and the syntax, X-bar theory has no role to play at s-structure, while the Projection Principle restricts the creation of extra structure at this level.

(17)   If α and β are co-indexed at d-structure, then α and β must be c-compatible.

Because c-compatibility is identified with the unifiability of syntactic categories, certain categories may be marked as incompatible with each other because they belong to different categorial systems; for example, determiners, demonstratives, agreement and nouns form part of the nominal system, while tense, aspect and verbs form part of the verbal system. The adoption of (17) as a condition of d-structure representations (which could follow from some appropriate formalization in terms of feature-value sharing), imposes a rigorous constraint on permissible d-structure specifiers (namely, those that do not appear in specifier positions as the result of movement operations), preventing verbal specifiers of nominal heads and vice versa.[5] Indeed, this interpretation of a specifier captures something of the notion, occasionally proposed in the literature, that specifiers somehow complete or change the categorial nature of the structure in which they appear. To formalize this, we adopt the hypothesis that the category of a maximal projection in a tree at d-structure is determined, not just by the lexical category of the projection, but by that of any specifier as well. The category of a structure headed by X^0 containing a specifier Y^2 is thus the unification of X and Y, symbolized as $X \sqcup Y$ (Gazdar *et al.*, 1985: 27). While the fundamental relation between X^0 and its complement is one of lexical selection and indexical disjointness, that between X^0 and its specifier is one of categorial projection and indexical identity. The basic X-bar structure, then, is not just a tree generated according to the schemata in

(2), but a tree that also conforms to the co-indexing requirements in (11) and (16) with concomitant conditions on categorial compatibility imposed by (17), as shown in (18).

(18)   (Category of tree is $Y \sqcup X$)

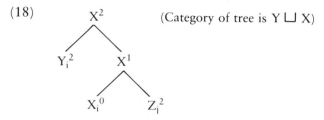

One of the implications of the link between co-indexing and compatibility is the possibility of a close morphological link between the specifier and its head. Given that head and specifier must unify, a variation in some morphosyntactic property of the head may affect the same morphosyntactic property in its specifier, if both expressions share that property. The adoption of (16) and (17) thus leads one to expect co-variation in form to exist between heads and specifiers and hence predicts the possibility that specifiers and heads may be in a concord relation. It is not being suggested that all concord relations reduce to specifier–head agreement, a position that is clearly untenable particularly for gender agreement, nor that all specifiers are necessarily in an agreement relation with their heads. All that is being suggested is that the dependence of d-structure specifiers on categorial compatibility with their heads lends itself to the possibility of co-variation.

Such a relation of concord is found between a subclass of the Det+N relation in English. The demonstratives *this/that* do not form-govern their nouns like the articles, according to the definition of this property in (1), because there is a recognizable formal relationship between the singular and plural demonstrative forms: co-varying the form of the noun requires a variation in the form of the demonstrative (and vice versa). L-selection is thus not the relation between Dem and N. The co-variation in number between them, however, indicates the close categorial link suggested by the generalized specifier–head relation defined in (16) and (17). However, because Dem+N and Det+N have the same distribution in English, they must ultimately be analysed as expressions of the same category. Under the assumption that verbs select Det, rather than N, as its complement, the determiner projection must be present in any tree analysing the Dem+N construction in order to satisfy the lexical-selection properties of the governing head. Hence, Dem+N must be realized as a (sub)tree rooted in Det² which has an empty head at d-structure. There are, therefore, two specifier positions that could accommodate a demonstrative phrase: [Spec, Det²] and [Spec, N²]. Because demonstratives co-vary with the number of the noun and do not co-occur with prototypical determiners like *the* (for example, *these the books*, *the these books*), the hypothesis is adopted that they are generated in d-structure as specifiers of N, not Det. The d-structure representation of the phrase *these books* is thus given by the tree in (19).

(19)

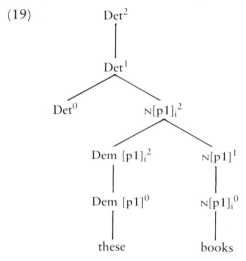

Because the determiner position is empty in (19), something must move into it at s-structure to satisfy the PFLP. Assuming that X^0 governs any sister and a specifier co-indexed with the head of that sister (Chomsky, 1986a: 25), then *these* may move into the governing Det⁰ position, according to (14).[6] Movement of Dem to Det is a substitution operation and thus, like d-structure co-indexing, the two categories must be c-compatible. The resultant category of the matrix head at s-structure is further determined as the unification of the categories of the associated positions. In this example, therefore, the movement of the demonstrative *these* into the determiner position gives rise to a unified demonstrative/determiner head and hence to the surface interpretation of *these* as a determiner. This is advantageous because, as noted in table 4.1, the demonstrative is a morphosyntactic locus with respect to Dem+N in that it is a locus of definiteness (*all these books* versus *all some books*). The difference between the fact that lexical determiners are form governors but that demonstratives are concord-controlled by the noun is captured by its analysis as a specifier of N at d-structure rather than its governor. Thus, we exploit the different representations for lexical dependencies, d-structure and their surface manifestations.

The lack of co-occurrence between determiners and demonstratives in English is not, of course, directly predicted by this analysis, because they are not expressions of the same lexical category (and thus in complementary distribution). Ungrammatical expressions like *these the penguins*, however, are accounted for by the fact that such a phrase would require the demonstrative to be in the specifier position of the determiner phrase at s-structure. According to (16), the demonstrative must be co-indexed with *the*. For this to be the case, the demonstrative, the determiner and the noun must all share the same index. However, the constraint in (11) requires the determiner to have an index disjoint from N. If such were the case, however, the demonstrative would also need to be disjoint, because of its d-structure position as the specifier of N, but this leads again to a violation of (16). An insoluble contradiction thus results and neither of the indexing patterns shown in (20) leads to grammaticality.[7]

(20)

    a. $^*[_{Det}2$ these$_i$ $[_{Det_i^0}$ the] $[_{N_i^2}$ t$_i$ $[_{N_i^0}$ penguins]]]

    b. $^*[_{Det}2$ these$_i$ $[_{Det_i^0}$ the] $[_{N_i^2}$ t$_i$ $[_{N_j^2}$ penguins]]]

The impossibility of demonstratives appearing with a preceding determiner, as in *the these penguins*, may be accounted for in a number of different ways, none as immediately satisfying as the preceding account of the ungrammaticality of *these the penguins*. The reason for this restriction may, however, be sought in a constraint that disallows the recursion of functional categories. It is well known that functional categories do not stack (for example, *the the penguin*, *the happy the penguin*, *this that penguin*). Such a constraint, however, only operates within particular boundaries and the repetition of categories is permitted in expressions like *the book of the student* or *this penguin in that hole*. The relevant bounding conditions seem to be determined by government and θ-marking. If a lexically filled node α^0 governs a node β^2, then β must be categorially distinct from α, unless α^0 θ-marks β^2. Furthermore, the category of any node, γ^2, governed in turn by β^0 must also be distinct from α, unless again β^0 θ-marks γ^2. In other words, any lexically filled chain of nodes related by government occurring between two θ-marked nodes in some tree contains only one instance of a category. It is also that every node in such a chain must be c-compatible and so form what Jane Grimshaw in unpublished work has dubbed an Extended Projection. The definition of this notion is given in (21) where the symbol $\sqcap$ indicates category intersection and $CAT(\xi)$ indicates the category of the node, ξ.

(21)   In a tree, $[_{\alpha}2 \ldots \alpha^0 [_{\beta}2 \ldots \beta^0 [_{\gamma}2 \ldots] \ldots] \ldots]$, if α^0 is lexically filled and neither β^2 nor γ^2 is θ-marked, then $CAT(\alpha) \sqcap CAT(\beta) = CAT(\alpha) \sqcap CAT(\gamma) = \emptyset$ and $CAT(\alpha)$ is c-compatible with $CAT(\beta)$, which is c-compatible with $CAT(\gamma)$.

This constraint prevents the acceptance of expressions like *the this penguin*, under the assumption that demonstratives in English are marked as definite. Since definiteness is also a property of Det (possibly its sole defining property), the government of a common noun phrase containing a demonstrative in its specifier position by a lexically realized determiner is disallowed, as shown in (22).

(22) $*[_{\text{Det}}2 [_{\text{Det}[+\text{Def}]}^0 \text{the}][_{N}2 [_{\text{Dem}[+\text{Def}]_i}^2 \text{this}] [_{N_i}^0 \text{penguin}]]]$

The analysis of demonstratives given above not only entails a close categorial connection between a specifier and its head, but also the closeness of the former to a higher governing head. In (21), there is movement from a specifier position into a higher governing position licensed by co-indexing and c-compatibility. There is also a negative selection relation between a higher governing position (Det^0) and the specifier of its complement (Dem). If specifiers are susceptible to external selection, then one might expect to find that the appearance of certain specifiers is required to satisfy the L-selection properties of a higher governor. Such seems to be the case in the auxiliary system in English. The central part of this system shows a relation between the auxiliary verbs *have* and *be* and verb forms containing the affixes: perfective -*ed*, progressive -*ing* and passive -*en*. According to the PFLP, the recognition of the affixes as independent elements entails that the construction should not be analysed in binary fashion as Aux+VP but as Aux+Af+VP. There then arises the problem of where to attach the projections of these three categories.

The relation between the affixes and the following verbal phrase must be one of L-selection, since each exponent requires different properties of its complement. Thus, the perfective affix requires a non-perfective complement, the progressive requires a non-perfective, non-progressive complement and the passive requires a non-perfective, non-progressive and non-passive complement (these negative selectional properties being derivable from (21)). Hence, VP may be analysed as the complement of Af projected from the lexicon. There is also a selectional relation between the auxiliary verbs *be* and *have* and the affixes, but this is stricter than that between the affixes and their complements: *have* must appear with the perfective *-ed* and *be* must appear with non-perfective *-ing* and *-en*. The strict perfective/ non-perfective contrast in the appearance of the auxiliaries indicates, not lexical selection, but categorial compatibility, even though no co-variation is present. Analysing *have* as the perfective auxiliary verb (V[+Aux, +Pf]) and *be* as the non-perfective auxiliary verb (V[+Aux, −Pf]), this strict relation between the affix and its associated auxiliary may be most perspicuously analysed as one of specifier–head co-indexing and consequent c-compatibility. The analysis of the auxiliaries as specifiers rather than governing heads receives some support from the fact that each of the participial categories, perfective, progressive and passive, may appear without accompanying auxiliaries, as illustrated by the examples in (23). This is explained if the auxiliaries are optional specifier elements, but not if they are the matrix heads of their respective constructions.

(23) a. These clothes need washing (*dial.* washed)
      b. Leaving the corpse unburied, Rambo charged back into the undergrowth
      c. Inhabited as it is by penguins, Antarctica is not the world's most inviting continent

The obligatoriness of the auxiliary in the Aux+VP construction, on the other hand, is attributable to the selection of a verbal element by the higher verb. Affixes select for a following verbal expression in order to satisfy the fact that they require a verb to attach to at s-structure (in order to avoid the Stray Affix Filter of Baker (1988)). If d-structure is constructed by the adjunction of trees projected from the lexicon, as mentioned in section 4.2, the relation between the categories of adjoining structures and the nodes to which they are adjoined needs to be defined. If this relation is not just one of unifiability, but categorial extension (in the sense of Gazdar *et al.*, 1985: 27), then the complement of an affix must not only contain categorial information compatible with the L-selection properties of the former, but it must have that information specified as part of its categorial structure: if an affix selects for a verb then a phrase containing a verb must appear in the complement. The affixes themselves are not, however, categorially specified as verbal (since they are not actually verbs) and therefore need to appear with some verbal element to license the attachment of their structure to a higher affix. The theory of X-bar structure adopted above allows a verb to provide this missing property if it appears in specifier position, thus unifying its category with that of the head, to yield the categorial definition of the whole structure (18). Since the only verbal specifiers allowed with the affixes are *have* and *be* (because of co-indexing and c-compatibility), embedding an affix under a governor that requires a verbal complement requires the projection of an auxiliary at d-structure.

As an example, the d-structure of *have been singing* is given in (24). The higher perfective affix selects a non-perfective verbal complement which is satisfied by a structure headed by *-ing* as long as it is associated with a co-indexed auxiliary verb in specifier position. The latter ensures that the category of the complete embedded structure is $v[+Aux, -Pf, +Pr, -Pas]$ an extension of the category $v[-Pf]$ which is L-selected by the higher affix *-ed*. The s-structure of *have been singing* is then straightforwardly derived from (24) by head movement of *be* to adjoin to *-ed* and of *sing* to adjoin to *-ing*.

(24)

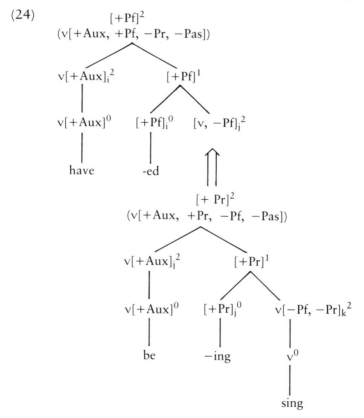

We see from this analysis that certain head-like properties which are similar on the surface may derive from very different structures. A verb embedded under an affix surfaces as adjoined to that affix and appears after an auxiliary. It thus appears that the auxiliary form-governs the verb and so the construction seems like an instance of straightforward verb plus complement constructions, like V+NP. For example, it appears from sentences like those in (25) that Aux is a proper governor although the actual proper governor is the higher node in which the auxiliary appears at s-structure.

(25)   a. I thought she might have bought silk stockings, and bought silk stockings she has.
        b. I thought she might be buying silk stockings, and buying silk stockings she was.

However, the fact that the auxiliary appears in [Spec, V^2] rather than as a complement means that the properties of the constructions differ. In particular, the V^2 (including the affix) appears as a distributional equivalent and a morphosyntactic locus of the phrase. It is to a consideration of the distributional properties of specifier structures that we will now turn.

4.4 Specifiers and distributional properties

Let us first consider the property of being the obligatory constituent in a phrase. We have seen that specifiers may be required to be present to satisfy the selectional requirements of a higher governor, as in the analysis of the auxiliary construction sketched in section 4.3. Because of the constraint that specifiers and their heads must be co-indexed, however, the head need not be overtly realized. The lexical head of a structure containing a specifier (or indeed a complement) is obligatory because without the lexical category there could be no X-bar projection and no co-indexing of the specifier with a head required by (16). However, according to the PFLP in (10), a node can be empty provided that it is associated through co-indexing with a node that contains phonetically realized material. Since a specifier, like Aux in (24), must be co-indexed with its affix head it can PF-license the latter position, which can therefore remain empty provided the specifier is phonetically realized. With respect to the Aux+VP construction, this means that the VP (with its affix) is not obligatory. That this is the case in English is illustrated in (26), which contrasts with the generally obligatory nature of verbal complements like noun phrases in such constructions.

(26)   a.   I thought Rambo might have shot the cat and he had
        b.   *I thought Rambo might have shot the cat and he had shot

Assuming that the VP complement of a null affix is required for the purpose of interpretation, the auxiliary phrase in the conjunct of (26) has the d-structure shown in (27).

(27)

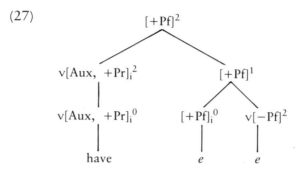

Here, the auxiliary node not only co-indexes the affix head, as normal, but also the VP complement of the past-participle affix. No co-indexing between the head and its complement VP occurs at d-structure, because of the restriction that co-indexed nodes at this level be c-compatible (main verbs are [−Aux], by assumption). However, because there is no lexical head, the complement V^2 is not L-selected; nothing blocks the co-indexing of the empty V^2 with the head at s-structure. Where this occurs, the V^2 is PF-licensed by the auxiliary via the co-indexed empty head and so the structure is permitted.

The contrasting pattern in obligatoriness observed between Aux+VP and V+NP is mirrored in an interesting fashion with the two exponents of the noun phrase that we are concerned with, that is, Det+N and Dem+N. In the former construction, if pronouns are excluded from consideration, the noun is obligatory, while in the latter it is optional. The reasons for this difference again lie in the fact that N is a complement with respect to Det but a head with respect to Dem. Thus, since a determiner like *a* L-selects its complement through form government of number, this complement cannot be co-indexed with its governing head and so cannot be PF-licensed by it, as shown in the structure in (12b), above. In the Dem+N structure, on the other hand, an overt demonstrative in specifier position licenses an empty nominal (and an empty Det position by head movement, as seen in section 4.3). The structure underlying the pronominal use of a demonstrative is shown in (28) where the licensing of the head N is clearly indicated by the index shared with the demonstrative in the matrix determiner position. From these two structures, we get the contrast in grammaticality between *Rambo shot a* and *Rambo shot this.*

(28)

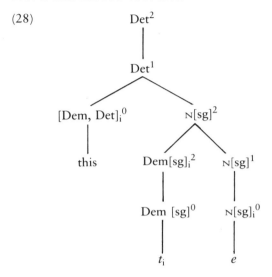

Like determiners in general, demonstratives are optional. But this results from the fact that the latter are specifiers and thus not projected from the lexicon. Furthermore, they are not required to satisfy the selectional properties of an external governor, like auxiliaries, and so are not specifically selected by any governing item. Furthermore, the demonstrative also falls out as being a distributional equivalent because of its ability to license the empty nominal head, as shown in (28), and by the fact that at s-structure an expression of this category must appear in the matrix determiner position to satisfy the PFLP, as discussed above. The noun in this construction is also a distributional equivalent, as it is in Det+N, a result that follows from the optionality of demonstratives (being specifiers and not selected by Det) and the existence of a class of nominal expressions that can move into an empty determiner position, that is, proper names.

Distributional equivalence between these expressions depends on a number of factors, some of which are independent of the properties of the structures assigned by the grammar. The definition of this head-like property given in (1.3b) above entails that X is a distributional equivalent in a construction X+Y if there are expressions in X that can appear on their own in the same (or similar) environments as other expressions in X combined with expressions in Y. One of the prerequisites for this to occur in a constituent-structure analysis is that the category of X is approximately equal (or similar enough) to that of X+Y to allow substitution of X for X+Y. So, for example, both Aux and VP are the distributional equivalents of Aux+VP (although not of Af + VP). This is predicted by the current analysis, because the categorial specification of both types of expression satisfies the same L-selected environments. Thus, a non-auxiliary verb phrase satisfies the selectional requirement of tense and any of the affixes, because the latter select only for the non-specification of properties like Pf and Pr, while main verbs are by default non-perfective and non-progressive. The auxiliaries also satisfy the requirements of the same environments because of their strong compatibility with the affixes. It would be possible, therefore, to analyse expressions where the verb phrase and the affix are omitted from the construction (for example, *Rambo might have*) as just containing an instance of the auxiliary without the affix or the VP. Whether this is feasible depends on the necessity or otherwise of the appearance of a phonologically empty VP for interpretation purposes. On either analysis, however, the current approach predicts the distributional equivalence of Aux and VP with the Aux+VP construction.

4.5 Conclusion

The theory presented in the last three sections takes L-selection (subcategorization and form control) and local concord control as the primary determinants of headedness. The distributional properties shown by structural heads and their satellites, on the other hand, are primarily determined by the interaction of co-indexing, c-compatibility, head movement and the PFLP. As discussed in sections 4.2, 4.3 and 4.4, the optionality or obligatoriness of an expression in a construction depends on several factors. In the first place, a lexical head is obligatory if (and only if) it has no associated specifier and no c-compatible complement. If one or other of these conditions fails to hold, then a head is realized optionally. For non-heads, however, obligatoriness follows from external selection (if a specifier) or L-selection by all expressions in the category of the head (for example, VP being selected by all the verbal affixes). Otherwise non-heads are optional. This is summarized in (29).

(29)   In a construction, X+Y:
        a. X is optional iff Y is a c-compatible complement or if Y is an associated specifier. It is obligatory otherwise.

    b. Y is obligatory iff it is L-selected for by all expressions in X or if there is an external governor selecting for X ⊔ Y. Y is optional otherwise.

Apart from non-affixal categories that satisfy the generalization that there is always an instance of category X^0 that fails to take complements (13), distributional equivalence follows from considerations of categorial compatibility. As we have seen, X is distributionally equivalent to X+Y if its categorial specification is sufficiently similar to that of X+Y to satisfy the selectional properties of external governors. This may happen if X is a specifier containing major feature specifications (such as Aux) or if X is the structural head that L-selects for Y. In the latter case, Y cannot satisfy the selectional requirements of a higher governor because it is necessarily distinct from X according to the constraint in (11). However, if Y is c-compatible with X (that is, part of an extended projection with X) then substitution head movement may take place for certain expressions in Y. In this case, Y is itself a distributional equivalent of X+Y. These results are summarized in (30).

(30)   In a construction, X+Y, X is distributionally equivalent to X+Y iff
    a. there are expressions in X that L-select for no category or property and Y is not a specifier; or
    b. the category X is approximately equal to the category of X+Y; or
    c. X is the specifier of Y; or
    d. X is the complement of Y and c-compatible with it.

In sections 4.2 and 4.3, it was shown how four of the patterns shown by the head-like properties in table 4.2 can be accounted for. Where X subcategorizes for Y, in X+Y, the head-like properties all converge on X. From subcategorization, it follows that X has the ability to form-govern Y but not to control the concord in Y, because X L-selects Y and thus, by the constraint in (11), they must have disjoint indices. No variation in the properties of X therefore directly induces a concomitant variation in the properties of Y. Furthermore, the head is obligatory with respect to its complement if it θ-marks it and is a distributional equivalent if the statement in (13) is universally valid.

Where X does not θ-mark its complement, however, it is likely to be affixal or at least a non-major category. It is thus not necessarily obligatory where there is a c-compatible specifier (for example, the verbal affixes), nor is it necessarily a distributional equivalent, if its specifier is externally selected. In both these constructions, the other constituent Y has none of the head-like properties, because of disjoint indexing. Where X does not subcategorize for Y, however, it is either a form controller or a concord controller. In both cases, neither X nor Y is obligatory but they are distributional equivalents.

The fifth pattern in table 4.2, type 4, exemplified by the A+N construction in English, has not yet been discussed. This pattern has neither of the constituents subcategorizing for, or controlling the form of, the other. However, the distributional properties all converge on one of the elements. This too follows from the interaction of X-bar theory, co-indexing and the PFLP if we make the assumption that, in English, adjuncts are not co-indexed with their governing heads.[8] This could be achieved by adopting a (parameterized) constraint against co-indexing elements at s-structure, except through movement. Because d-structure co-indexing requires categorial compatibility, adjectives cannot be co-indexed with nominal heads in English (they disagree in value for the feature V) and so cannot license an empty head or be distributionally equivalent to A+N. Hence, these properties can only be exhibited on the N, uniquely identifying this as the head of the construction.[9]

The variant of X-bar theory presented above thus provides an account of the variation in the distribution of the head-like properties across different constructions depending on the strength of the selection between elements. This variation in the patterns of head-like properties observed within a single language has implications for patterns of headedness cross-linguistically. It is possible that a construction that is only weakly headed in one language may be strongly headed in another and thus that parametric variation in syntactic properties will be observed across superficially similar constructions in different languages. Such a study is, however, the topic of another discussion, but it has been shown that the framework laid out here provides the basis for an account of the patterns of headedness observed across different constructions and in different languages.

NOTES

1. I am grateful to the participants of the Talking Heads Round Table for their comments on an earlier draft of this chapter and to Mary E. Tait for the long hours of talking about the content. All errors are, naturally, my own.

2. Where symbols like NP and VP are used in the exposition below, reference is being made to the traditional linguistic notion of noun phrase and verb phrase. Where superscripts are used to indicate bar levels, as in N^2 and V^2, reference is being made to theoretically defined projections of particular categories.

3. There is a very weak interpretation of the property (apparently assumed in Zwicky, 1985, and Nichols, 1986), that is defined where all members of X are able to appear in construction with some expression of Y (that is, the partition of X may trivially consist only of X itself). This latter interpretation is satisfied if the expressions of a certain category can appear with a co-constituent of some other category, while the former actually divides categories into distinct subcategories. Only the stronger interpretation of subcategorization is significant for headedness, however, since only this property is selective. For example, in the V+NP construction in English, the NP properly partitions V into two partially disjoint non-null subsets, while V partitions NP into NP and $\emptyset$, since every NP can appear after some verb (modulo sense restrictions and case forms). If weak categorization were significant, NP would be identified as the head of V+NP as well as V.

4. The semantics of this structure is straightforward and head movement of this sort may be seen as akin to the type raising of a property (the property of being Rambo) to an individual (a proper principal filter on the set of properties) in the sense of Keenan and Faltz (1985).

5. It may be that the constraint in (17) may not hold if the head θ-marks its specifier, allowing noun phrases to be generated as specifiers of verbs at d-structure. This weakening would permit indirect objects to appear in this position, as suggested in Tait (1991).

6. The head noun *books* cannot move across the demonstrative to give **books these* because of a minimality constraint preventing the movement of a matrix head over that of a lexically filled specifier (Cann and Tait, 1989). This is only a reflex of relativized minimality (Rizzi, 1990) if adjacency is incorporated into the definition of closest possible governor.

7. Precisely analogous arguments provide an account of the **[that t] filter in English. The argument is somewhat involved, but the grammaticality pattern shown in (i) to (iv) follows from the fact that lexical Comp L-selects its complement I^2 through form government (finiteness). In the object dependency in (i), the trace in [Spec, C^2] can be co-indexed with the complementizer, because it is not required to share the index of Infl governed by Comp. In (ii) and (iii), however, the subject extraction is blocked because either indexing pattern with respect to the trace and Comp leads to a violation of (16) (as in (ii)) or (11) (as in (iii)). Where no lexical Comp appears, no L-selection occurs between Comp and Infl and so (11) is not relevant, and the trace, Comp and I^2 can all be co-indexed, leading to a grammatical sentence.

(i) What$_i$ did Conan$_j$ I$_j^0$ believe t_i that$_i$ Rambo$_k$ I$_k^0$ had shot t_i?

(ii) *What$_i$ did Conan$_j$ I$_j^0$ believe t_i that$_k$ t_i I$_i^0$ had shot Rambo$_k$?

(iii) *What$_i$ did$_j$ -C$_i$ Conan$_j$ I$_j^0$ believe t_i that$_i$ t_i I$_i^0$ had shot Rambo$_k$?

(iv) What$_i$ did Conan$_j$ I$_j^0$ believe t_i C$_i^0$ t_i I$_i^0$ had shot Rambo$_k$?

8. This is not, however, true for languages that show concord between adjectives and nouns, with concomitant changes in the distribution of the head-like properties predicted.

9. Expressions like *the poor* are ignored here, because of the necessity of the definite determiner which must be the element that licenses the omission of the N (if, indeed, this should be analysed as a construction with an empty nominal head).

5 Head-hunting: on the trail of the nominal Janus

ANDREW RADFORD

5.1 Introduction

This chapter poses the question: 'What is the head of modified nominal structures such as *good students, these students* or *many students*?' The answer I shall give here is one inspired by classical mythology: namely, that like the ancient Roman god **Janus**, such structures are **double-headed**. The theoretical framework used here will be that of **Government–Binding theory**; the specific descriptive claim being made is that modified nominals incorporate multiple phrasal projections (with each modifier heading a separate projection), and that each phrasal 'layer' of the structure comprises both an **immediate head** (the modifier) and an **ultimate head** (the modified N): thus, for example, the immediate head of the expression 'good students' is the Adjective *good*, but its ultimate head is the Noun *students*. The analysis will proceed in a bottom–up fashion: accordingly, I start by looking at the innermost NP 'core' of nominals.

5.2 The internal structure of Noun Phrases

Consider the internal structure of nominals such as the following:

(1) a. *ministry of defence* INSTRUCTIONS **to all employees**
     b. *government* CRITICISM **of the press**
     c. *Labour Party* POLICY **on defence**
     d. *military police* INVOLVEMENT **in torture of prisoners**
     e. *university management* ALLEGATIONS **of a concerted student campaign of disruption**
     f. *European Community* DEMANDS **for monetary union**
     g. *student* ASSESSMENT **of lectures**
     h. *Department of the Environment* PLANS **for a new motorway**

The overall string in such examples is traditionally considered to have the categorial status of a Noun Phrase: its head in each case is clearly the capitalized Noun, since the number properties of the capitalized Noun determine the number properties of the overall nominal, so that, for example, a nominal such as *Ministry of Defence instructions to all employees* is a plural nominal precisely because it is a projection of the head plural Noun *instructions*.

However, what is rather less obvious is the internal constituent structure of nominals such as those in (1). Superficially, such strings would appear to have the thematic and syntactic properties of a typical [*specifier*+HEAD+**complement**] structure. Thus, a string such as *Ministry of Defence instructions to all employees* would appear to have the simplified superficial syntactic/thematic structure (2) below:

(2)

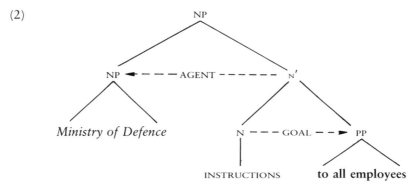

A structure such as (2) conforms to the canonical pattern of θ-role assignment in English (with the AGENT argument being externalized and the GOAL argument internalized), and likewise conforms to canonical configurational properties, so that, for example, the **head/ complement parameter** is properly set in that the head Noun *instructions* precedes its PP complement *to all employees*.

However, given that English has 'passive' constructions in which the θ-role assigned to an internal argument in active structures is externalized, we might also expect to find nominals which show this 'reversed' pattern of θ-role assignment. In this context, it is interesting to consider θ-role assignment in pairs such as the following:

(3)   a. *student* evaluation **of lectures**
      b. *lecture* evaluation **by students**

In (3a), the AGENT argument *student* is externalized (that is, projected into the italicized specifier position within the containing NP) and the PATIENT argument *lectures* is introduced by the Preposition *of*, which is typically used to introduce the internal argument of a nominal or adjectival head. By contrast, in (3b) it is the PATIENT argument *lecture*, which is externalized, and the AGENT argument *students* is introduced by the Preposition *by* which is typically used to introduce an unexternalized AGENT argument.

We can find further evidence in favour of analysing the italicized expression in nominals such as (1) as the specifier (and external AGENT argument) of its containing nominal, namely that (like other specifiers) it can serve as the controller of PRO; for example, in structures such as the following:

(4)   a. *Ministry of Defence* reluctance PRO to admit mistakes
      b. *opposition* attempts PRO to secure themselves a place on the committee
      c. *government* unwillingness PRO to compromise with the opposition
      d. *Department of the Environment* plans PRO to commission a new railroad linking London to Dover

Thus, the assumption that nominals such as (1) are Noun Phrases with an internal constituent structure along the lines of (2) above would seem to have a certain amount of initial plausibility.

An interesting variant of the pattern found in (1) above is that found in nominals like those in (5):

(5)   a. *enemy* **heavy artillery** losses
      b. *government* **income tax** reforms
      c. *opposition* **corruption** allegations
      d. *European Community* **sheep meat** subsidies
      e. *Ministry of Defence* **satellite intelligence** procurement

It seems plausible to suppose that the italicized nominal serves the thematic role of AGENT, whereas the bold-printed nominal serves that of PATIENT. Since canonical AGENTS are specifiers and canonical PATIENTS are complements, we might therefore suggest that an NP such as (5a) has the structure (6) below:

(6)

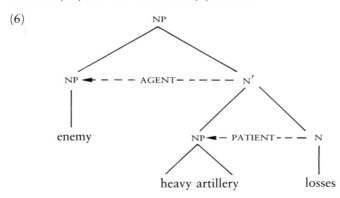

What makes it all the more plausible to consider the first nominal to be an AGENT specifier and the second to be a PATIENT complement is the fact that the former is often paraphrasable by a *by*-phrase, and the latter by an *of*-phrase:

(7)   a. losses *of heavy artillery* **by the enemy**
        b. reforms *of income tax* **by the government**
        c. allegations *of corruption* **by the opposition**
        d. subsidies *of sheep meat* **by the European Community**
        e. procurement *of satellite intelligence* **by the Ministry of Defence**

A further piece of evidence which suggests that it is plausible to treat nominals such as those in (2) as structures of the form [specifier+complement+head] relates to the fact that the putative specifier and complement cannot be substituted for each other (that is, cannot have their relative ordering changed), as we see from the ungrammaticality of examples such as the following:

(8)   a. ***heavy artillery** *enemy* losses
        b. ***income tax** *government* reforms
        c. ***corruption** *opposition* allegations
        d. ***sheep meat** *European Community* subsidies
        e. ***satellite intelligence** *Ministry of Defence* procurement

This suggests that the two occupy different structural positions (precisely as is claimed in (6) above).

There are a number of interesting properties which seem to differentiate post-head arguments in structures like (2) and (6) from pre-head arguments, as we can see in relation to paradigms such as the following:

(9)   a. these recent attacks [on *the students*]
        b. these recent attacks [by *the students*]
        c. these recent *student* attacks
        d. *these recent *the student(s)* attacks

(Note that (9c) is ambiguous, and can have the interpretation of (9a) or (9b).) For one thing, post-head arguments (like *the students* in (9a) and (9b)) are potentially determinate nominals (that is, nominals which can be premodified by a Determiner of their own), and thus would appear to have the status of Determiner Phrases (DPs). By contrast, pre-head nominals are intrinsically indeterminate (that is, cannot be premodified by a Determiner of their own – as we see from the grammaticality of (9c) and the ungrammaticality of (9d)), and thus appear to have the status of simple Noun Phrases (NPs).

A second (arguably related) property of the pre-head arguments in structures like (2) and (6) is that they would appear to be occupying caseless positions, and thus to be licensed by some set of principles (perhaps thematic in nature) other than those of Case theory. The fact that pre-head nominals seem to be in caseless positions might be related to their status as NP rather than DP constituents if we take the view that case is a property of DP rather than NP constituents. To see why we might want to suggest that case (in English) is a property of DP rather than NP, consider a sentence such as:

(10)   [*We students of linguistics*] berate you professors, and you professors berate [*us students of linguistics*]

Following Abney (1987), we might suppose that the bracketed nominals in (10) have the simplified structure (11):

(11)   [$_{DP}$ [$_D$ we/us] [$_{NP}$ [$_N$ students] of linguistics]]

Interestingly, the case properties of the overall DP are overtly realized only on the head D of DP, not on the head of N of NP. What this might lead us to suggest is that case in English is a property of DP, but not of NP. In the light of this, consider possible differences between structures such as (12a) and (12b) below (on the interpretation in which (*the*) *students* is a PATIENT complement of the N *attacks*).

(12)   a. [$_{NP}$ [$_{N'}$ [$_{NP}$ student] [$_N$ attacks]]]
        b. [$_{NP}$ [$_{N'}$ [$_N$ attacks] [$_{PP}$ [$_{P'}$ [$_P$ on] [$_{DP}$ the students]]]]]

We might suppose that an N or N-bar can only directly θ-mark an argument to its left, so that the NP *student* in (12a) gets a θ-role directly from the N *attacks* when functioning as an internal PATIENT argument (though it would get its θ-role from N-bar when functioning as an externalized AGENT). Since Nouns are not (direct) case assigners, the NP *student* here will be caseless. By contrast, in (12b), the argument is a DP *the students*, and thus requires both case and a θ-role. The DP *the students* cannot get case from the head Noun *attacks* (since Nouns are not direct case assigners), nor can it get a θ-role from the Noun *attacks* (since N and N-bar assign direct θ-roles leftwards). In consequence, the Preposition *on* has to be used, firstly in order to transmit the PATIENT θ-role from the Noun *attacks* to its internal argument *the students*, and secondly in order to assign case to the DP *the students*.

A third property which differentiates pre-head from post-head arguments is that post-head arguments carry number properties (as we can see from the plural +*s* suffix in 'attacks on the *students*'), whereas pre-head arguments generally appear to show no number contrast (so that *student* is uninflected in '*student attacks*'). Moreover, the same pattern shows up with AGENT nominals, as we can see from contrasts such as the following:

(13)   a. allegations by *the university authorities*
        b. *university authority* allegations

If we assume that number properties are AGR properties, and that AGR is a functional property carried by Nouns which are constituents of functional DP constituents in English, then we might suggest that only DP arguments will contain (NP complements headed by) Nouns with number properties, not NP arguments. Given all these assumptions, it follows that DP arguments differ from NP arguments in respect of their D-properties (determinacy properties), θ-properties (thematic properties) K-properties (case properties) and AGR-properties (agreement or, more specifically, number properties).

It is interesting to note that these differences between pre-head NP arguments and post-head DP arguments are also found in other structures, as we can see by comparing the bracketed passive participle structures in (14a) and (14b):

(14)   a. rumours [inspired by *the university authorities*]
        b. [*university authority* inspired] rumours

In (14a) the italicized AGENT nominal is determinate (cf. *the*), carries AGR properties (cf. the plural +*s* suffix) and is indirectly θ-marked and case-marked by the Preposition *by*. In (14b), on the other hand, the italicized AGENT is intrinsically indeterminate (cf. the absence of *the*), lacks AGR properties (cf. the impossibility of plural +*s*), occupies a caseless position and is directly θ-marked by the participle *inspired*. The conclusion which structures like (13) and (14) seem to lead us to is that post-head nominal arguments are DPs, whereas pre-head nominal arguments are NPs.

5.3 Pre-nominal and post-nominal Adjectives

Thus far, our discussion has been concerned essentially with nominal expressions used as arguments of nominal heads; but given that nominals can be modified by adjectival expressions, an obvious question to ask is how we handle the syntax of adnominal Adjectives. What, for example, is the structural position occupied by Adjectives used to premodify nominals? What I shall suggest here is that we can differentiate between two different types of prenominal Adjectives:

namely (1) those occupying an argument position internal to NP; and (2) those occupying a modifier position external to NP. The claim that NP-internal Adjectives can function as arguments would seem to be borne out by alternations like the following, where the italicized adjectival seems to have the same complement interpretation as the bold-printed nominal:

(15)   a. enemy **troop** losses/enemy *military* losses
       b. government **money** policy/government *monetary* policy
       c. government **tax** reforms/government *fiscal* reforms

Conversely, in structures such as the following, the (italicized) Adjective appears to function as an external argument (namely subject), and hence precedes the (bold-printed) internal argument:

(16)   a. *Spanish* **troop** movements/***troop** *Spanish* movements
       b. *ministerial* **defence** cuts/***defence** *ministerial* cuts
       c. *editorial* **policy** decisions/***policy** *editorial* decisions

Similarly, in structures such as (17), the italicized Adjective acts like an external argument in being able to serve as a controller for PRO:

(17)   a. the *Spanish* decision PRO to revalue their currency
       b. the *American* reluctance PRO to agree to a ceasefire
       c. the *allied* desire PRO to portray themselves as defenders of democracy

If it is indeed the case that Adjectives (of an appropriate type) can function as arguments of NPs, then an NP such as *Spanish fiscal reforms* would have a structure such as (18):

(18)   [NP [AP Spanish] [N′ [AP fiscal] [N reforms]]]

where *fiscal* is the AP complement of the N *reforms*, and *Spanish* is the AP specifier of the N-bar *fiscal reforms*. Although being used in the typical nominal function of arguments, the italicized Adjectives in (17) lack functional AGR properties (as we see from the fact that they cannot take the Noun plural +s suffix). Perhaps because of this, they also lack functional case properties, and so are not subject to case-licensing conditions on their distribution. The position they occupy is arguably determined by the direction of direct θ-role assignment, in that (as we suggested earlier) N directly θ-marks its internal argument leftwards, and likewise N-bar directly θ-marks its external argument leftwards. There is an interesting parallel here with the participle construction illustrated in (14) above, as we can see from examples such as (19) below:

(19)   a. [*Libyan government* sponsored] terrorism
        b. [*Libyan* sponsored] terrorism

In (19a), the italicized AGENT expression would seem to be an NP; but in (19b) the italicized AGENT seems to be simply an AP, so lending further support to our suggestion that Adjectives (of an appropriate type) can be used as pre-head arguments. What pre-head nominal and adjectival arguments have in common (in English) is that both are purely **lexical** expressions which carry thematic properties but lack **functional** properties (hence are indeterminate, caseless and agreementless).

Having given a brief characterization of adjectival arguments, let us now turn to consider **adjectival modifiers**. It seems clear that adjectival modifiers are positioned externally to NP, as we see from word-order facts in sentences such as the following (where the modifying Adjective is italicized):

(20)   a. *recent* [government tax reforms]
        b. *[government *recent* tax reforms]
        c. *[government tax *recent* reforms]

It therefore follows that NP-external adjectival modifiers (that is, attributive Adjectives) must precede NP-internal adjectival arguments – a claim borne out by contrasts such as the following:

(21)   a. There was **considerable** [*Spanish* reluctance PRO to devalue their currency]
        b. *There was [*Spanish* **considerable** reluctance PRO to devalue their currency]

Moreover, the claim that Adjectives can be either arguments or modifiers provides a straightforward way of accounting for the ambiguity of nominals such as (22):

(22)   a *Jewish* leader

Under the analysis proposed here, the ambiguity would be *structural* in nature, and would reside in the position occupied by the Adjective *Jewish*. On one interpretation, *Jewish* would be an Adjective which functions as an NP-internal argument so that (22) would mean 'a leader of the Jews'. (Note that *Jewish* could not be analysed as an NP here, since it can never be used as a nominal – cf. the ungrammaticality of *a Jewish/*the Jewish(es).) On another interpretation, *Jewish* would be an NP-external modifier, and (22) would mean 'a leader who is Jewish'. Of course, there are other correlates of this structural ambiguity: for example, *Jewish* can be premodified by *really* in its modifier use, but not in its argument use. Similarly, *Jewish* can be positioned post-nominally in its modifier use (cf. 'I have never met [a leader *so Jewish*]'), but not in its argument use.

Mention of the fact that in its non-argument use, *Jewish* can be used post-nominally as well as pre-nominally raises the question of whether or not pre-nominal modifying Adjectives might be analysed in essentially the same way as post-nominal Adjectives. In earlier work (Radford, 1981, 1988), I suggested that both pre-nominal attributive Adjectives and post-nominal Adjectives serve as *adjuncts* to the sister nominals which they are immediately adjacent to, and thus occupy the same hierarchial position (differing only in their linear position). Given our arguments here that non-argument adnominal Adjectives are external to the Noun Phrases they modify, a natural extension of this analysis would be to posit that such Adjectives head APs which function as adjuncts to the NPs they modify. In more concrete terms, what this would mean would be that the bracketed nominals in sentences such as (23):

(23) a. [*Available funds*] are limited
      b. [*Funds available*] are limited

would have the simplified adjunction structures indicated in (24):

(24) a. [$_{NP}$ [$_{AP}$ available] [$_{NP}$ [$_{N}$ funds]]]
      b. [$_{NP}$ [$_{NP}$ [$_{N}$ funds]] [$_{AP}$ available]]

Treating all adnominal (non-argument) adjectival expressions as APs which serve as adjuncts to NPs in this way offers the obvious advantage of providing a unitary account of the syntax of pre-nominal and post-nominal Adjectives. Moreover, the *adjunct* analysis correctly predicts that post-nominal APs (being adjuncts external to NP) will follow post-nominal arguments (which are internal to NP), as we can illustrate in terms of examples such as the following:

(25) a. [students *of linguistics*] **good at phonetics**
      b. *[students **good at phonetics** *of linguistics*]

If (as we are suggesting here) *of linguistics* is a complement of *students*, and **good at phonetics** is an adjunct to the NP *students of linguistics*, then the word-order facts in (25) fall out in precisely the way we should expect them to.

Furthermore, if we assume that adjectival adjuncts are generated by a rule of the form (26) below (or by the more general rule schema which subsumes (26)):

(26)   NP = AP*, NP

(where AP* indicates 'one or more Adjectival Phrases', and ','
indicates bidirectional concatenation, that is the Adjectival Phrases
can precede or follow the expressions they modify), then we correctly
predict that both pre-nominal and post-nominal (non-argument)
Adjectives can be recursively stacked, so resulting in structures such
as:

(27)   a. Are there [actors *available* **suitable for the part**]?
        b. Are there [**suitable** *available* actors]?

Thus, the adjunct analysis seems at first sight to have some merit.

A further apparent advantage of (26) is that it provides us with an
interesting way of handling the **scope ambiguity** of a phrase such as
my first disastrous marriage (from Radford, 1988: 222), as illustrated
by pairs such as the following:

(28)   a. *My first disastrous marriage* caused me even more hassle than
           my second (= my second disastrous marriage)
        b. *My first, disastrous, marriage* was only forgotten after my
           second, very happy, marriage

The two italicized strings differ both in their intonation contours
(marked by the presence or absence of a comma) and in the semantic
function of the Adjective *disastrous*: in (28a), it is a *restrictive*
modifier, whereas in (28b) it is an *appositive* modifier. Equivalently,
we might say that the two structures differ in respect of the *scope* of
the Adjectives: in (28a), *disastrous* has scope over *marriage*, and *first*
has scope over *disastrous marriage*; in (28b), both *first* and *disastrous*
have scope over *marriage*. In accordance with (26), we can account
for the scope ambiguity here by positing that modifying Adjectives
can be either linearly stacked (that is, iterated), or hierarchially
stacked. Assuming for the moment that the two italicized nominals in
(28) are DPs, this would mean that they have the respective structures
indicated in (29) below (where the two APs are stacked hierarchially
in (29a) and linearly in (29b)):

(29)   a. [$_{DP}$ [$_D$ my] [$_{NP}$ [$_{AP}$ first] [$_{NP}$ [$_{AP}$ disastrous] [$_{NP}$ marriage]]]]
        b. $_{DP}$ [$_D$ my] [$_{NP}$ [$_{AP}$ first] [$_{AP}$ disastrous] [$_{NP}$ marriage]]]

If we posit that an adnominal AP has scope over any nominal which it
c-commands, then it follows that *disastrous* will have scope over the
NP *marriage* in both structures, and that *first* will have scope over the
NP *disastrous marriage* in (29b), but only over the NP *marriage* in
(29b). The fact that it enables us to provide a natural account of the

scope of adnominal Adjectives clearly lends added plausibility to the NP-adjunct analysis.

However, a closer look at examples like (27) should alert us to a potential problem: namely, that *suitable* licenses a PP complement *for the part* when used post-nominally, but not when used pre-nominally. Moreover, this is not in any sense a lexical idiosyncrasy of the Adjective *suitable*, since the same is true of other Adjectives (for example, *available* and *proud*) as we see from paradigms such as the following:

(30) a. resources *available to us*/*available to us resources
      b. people *suitable for the job*/**suitable for the job* people
      c. mothers *proud of their children*/**proud of their children* mothers

Abney (1987: 326) argues that it is a systematic fact about English that 'pre-nominal Adjectives may not have complements'. The obvious question to ask is how we are to account for this under the adjunct analysis.

One possible answer would be to invoke Williams' (1982) **head-final filter**, and posit that premodifying expressions must be head-final, and so cannot contain post-modifiers. This would then enable us to account for alterations such as the following:

(31) a. an environment *free* **of pollution**
      b. a **pollution** *free* environment
      c. *a *free* **of pollution** environment

The data would then be exactly as expected: when the italicized Adjective is post-nominal, it can have a following (bold-printed) complement; when the Adjective is pre-nominal, it can have a preceding complement, but not a following complement. Likewise, the *head-final filter* would correctly predict contrasts such as the following in German (from Lyons, 1991: 36):

(32) a eine **auf sich** *stolze* Frau
         an   **of herself** *proud* woman

      b. *eine stolze **auf sich** Frau
         a   proud **of herself** woman

Thus, the adjunct analysis would seem to account for the relevant data, provided we assume some version of Williams' filter.

However, there are both theoretical and descriptive reasons for calling into question our reliance on the *head-final filter* in the adjunct analysis of adnominal Adjectives given above. From a theoretical perspective, the general problem posed by any such filter is that it is non-explanatory, since it amounts to mere *stipulation* of an unexplained fact: that is, it simply says that premodifying phrases cannot contain post-head constituents, without saying *why* they cannot. From a descriptive perspective, the problem posed by the filter is that it would seem to be falsified by premodifying phrases such as those bracketed below:

(33)   [*after* **dinner**] speeches; [*under* **the counter**] transactions; [*up* **to the minute**] news reports; [*off* **piste**] skiing; an [*in* **depth**] survey; a [*with* **profits**] policy; the [*on* **board**] computer; an [*out* **of date**] design; the [*end* **of term**] celebrations; a [*far* **from perfect**] performance; your [*next* **to last**] chance; the [*ban* **the bomb**] campaign; a [*better* **than average**] student

In each of these structures, the italicized constituent would appear to be the head of the bracketed premodifying phrase, and yet is not final within its containing phrase, so calling into question the observational adequacy of the *head-final filter* (which wrongly predicts that such structures are ungrammatical).

Interestingly, although pre-nominal comparative Adjectives can be postmodified by a *than*-phrase, they cannot be post-modified by an expression which serves as a thematic complement of the Adjective: cf. the following contrasts (where we assume that **at phonetics** is θ-marked by the Adjective *good/better*, but *than average* is not):

(34)   a. There are few *better* **than average** students in my class
        b. *There are few *better* **at phonetics** students in my class

Why should it be that post-nominal Adjectives permit a following thematic complement, whereas pre-nominal Adjectives do not? Abney (1987: 326–38) suggests that the reason why pre-nominal Adjectives do not permit thematic complements is that the Noun Phrase premodified by the Adjective is itself the complement of the Adjective. What this means is that pre-nominal Adjectives are the heads of their containing phrases, and that the Noun Phrases which they modify are the complements of the head Adjectives. If we continue to suppose that post-nominal adjectivals are adjuncts, then this would mean that nominal pairs such as *available resources* and *resources available to us* would have the respective simplified structures indicated in (35) below:

(35)   a. [$_A$ [$_A$ available] [$_{NP}$ [$_N$ resources]]]
        b. [$_{NP}$ [$_{NP}$ [$_N$ resources]] [$_{AP}$ [$_A$ available] [$_{PP}$ to us]]]

Pre-nominal Adjectives would thus be the heads of their containing phrases, whereas post-nominal Adjectives would be adjuncts to the nominals they follow. A structure such as (35a) would involve *complementation* (since a modified nominal is analysed as the complement of the Adjective which modifies it), whereas a structure such as (35b) would involve *adjunction* (with the adjoined AP having an essentially predicative interpretation, and thus being interpreted in much the same way as a restrictive relative clause like *that are available to us*).

Analysing pre-nominal and post-nominal Adjectives as the heads of their immediately containing expressions would provide us with a straightforward account of the properties of an Adjective like *fond*, as illustrated in (36):

(36)   a. She is fond *of chocolate*/*She is fond
        b. a woman so fond of *chocolate*/*a woman so fond
        c. a fond *embrace*/*a fond

Given the analyses in (35), we could say that the essential property of *fond* is that it requires a following complement: in its predicative use as a post-nominal adjunct, its complement is a KP like *of chocolate* (that is, a phrase headed by the K constituent or 'genitive case particle' *of*), while in its attributive use it requires an NP complement like *embrace*.

What adds plausibility to the head analysis of pre-nominal Adjectives is the fact that we find (in a number of languages) structures in which pre-nominal Adjectives take KP complements introduced by the same 'genitive case particle' (*of* or its counterpart) which is used to introduce the complement of many predicative Adjectives: for example, Abney (1987: 324) notes that in non-standard forms of English we find structures such as the following:

(37)   a. too big *of a house*
        b. as nice *of a man*
        c. how long *of a board*

where the pre-nominal Adjectives *big/nice/long* have the same *of*-phrase complement as predicative Adjectives in structures such as 'fond *of* chocolate'. In French, we find seemingly similar structures:

(38)   a. un drôle *de* garçon
         a   weird (*of*) boy
        b. une drôle *de* fille
         a   weird (*of*) girl

    c. des   drôles *de* garçons
       some weird (*of*) boys
    d. des   drôles *de* filles
       some weird (*of*) girls

where the Adjective likewise has a KP complement introduced by the same genitive particle *de* 'of' which is used to introduce the complement of many predicative Adjectives (cf. 'fier *de* son fils', 'proud *of* his son'). And in Sardinian, we find what appears to be a similar construction (see Jones, forthcoming: 30, 52):

(39)   a. unu bette *de* pittsinnu
         a   big (*of*) boy
     b. sa ruja *de* mákkina
         the red (*of*) car

Thus, the analysis of pre-nominal Adjectives as heads taking NP or KP complements seems far from implausible.

    There are a number of interesting phenomena which lead us to the conclusion that attributive (premodifying) Adjectives exhibit different syntactic behaviour from predicative Adjectives, and that postmodifying Adjectives are used in an essentially predicative way. For example (as noted in Jackendoff, 1972), Adjectives like *mere* and *utter* can be used pre-nominally, but not post-nominally or predicatively:

(40)   a. *mere* excuses/*utter* chaos
     b. *excuses *so mere*/*chaos *so utter*
     c. *His excuses were *mere*/*The chaos was *utter*

Conversely, there are Adjectives which can be used post-nominally or predicatively, but not pre-nominally:

(41)   a. people *afraid of the dark*
     b. They were *afraid*
     c. *afraid* people

Some Adjectives favour one meaning when used pre-nominally, but another when used post-nominally or predicatively:

(42)   a. *present* students (antonym = *past*)
     b. students *present* (antonym = *absent*)
     c. Most of them are *present* (antonym = *absent*)

The same is true of *grand* in French:

(43)   a. un *grand* écrivain (a *great* writer)
     b. un écrivain *grand* (a *tall* writer)
     c. Cet écrivain est *grand* (This writer is *tall*)

What is particularly interesting about such data is that they suggest that post-nominal Adjectives are essentially predicative in nature, and distinct in a number of ways from pre-nominal Adjectives. Similar semantic differences between pre-nominal and post-nominal Adjectives in Sardinian are reported by Jones (forthcoming). Clearly, it would be difficult to provide any systematic description of the semantic differences between pre-nominal and post-nominal Adjectives if we were to posit that the two have the same function of adnominal adjuncts.

Further support for the claim that pre-nominal Adjectives are the heads of their containing nominals comes from the fact that pre-nominal Adjectives often combine with following NP complements to form a unit with an idiosyncratic (metaphorical) meaning which is not present when the Adjective is used post-nominally or predicatively. It is a feature of head+complement structures that they often have a metaphorical interpretation, as we see from expressions such as *break the ice, blow the whistle, smell a rat, kick the bucket, spill the beans, toe the line, bite the bullet, bite the dust, hit the roof*, etc. Significantly, many Adjective+Noun collocations also have an idiosyncratic metaphorical meaning: for example, *white elephant, red herring, blue stocking, grey matter, black sheep, cold turkey, hot rod, humble pie, blank cheque, sacred cow, damp squib, flying saucer, wet blanket*, etc. However, the idiomatic interpretation is often lost (or becomes 'forced') if the Adjective is used post-nominally or predicatively, so that a sentence such as *She is a blue stocking* can have the idiomatic interpretation 'She is a career woman', but not a sentence such as *She is a stocking (that is) blue as any I've ever come across*. Given that many head+complement structures are idiomatic collocations, treating pre-nominal Adjectives as the head of their containing nominals would provide us with a straightforward account of the fact that such pre-nominal Adjective collocations have an idiosyncratic metaphorical interpretation. Much the same point can also be made in relation to the fact that many pre-nominal Adjectives take on an idiosyncratic metaphorical meaning when combined with a specific (non-metaphorical) nominal complement – cf. expressions such as '*white* lie', '*black* market' '*purple* prose', '*spitting* image', etc.

Moreover, we might argue that treating pre-nominal Adjectives as heads and post-nominal Adjectives as adjuncts would provide a way of accounting for the semantic differences between pre-nominal/post-nominal Adjective pairs such as the following (where $\neq$ marks non-synonymy, and ! denotes an incoherent utterance):

(44)   a. She has friends different from me ≠ She has different friends from me
       b. He has a car bigger than his garage ≠!He has a bigger car than his garage
       c. He has a Volvo similar to my Renault ≠!He has a similar Volvo to my Renault

If pre-nominal and post-nominal Adjectives are both treated as adjuncts to NP (with pre-nominal Adjectives licensing extraposition of the *from/than/to* phrase), then we should expect the first member of such related sentence pairs to be synonymous with the second: the fact that this is not so is consistent with the view that pre-nominal and post-nominal Adjectives occupy different structural positions within their containing nominals.

A further way in which pre-nominal and post-nominal Adjectives may differ is in respect of their morphosyntactic properties: for example, in French (where Adjectives carry overt AGR properties), we find that pre-nominal Adjectives may exhibit different agreement patterns from post-nominal or predicative Adjectives. In this respect, consider the following contrast:

(45)   a. de *vieilles* gens
          some old (F PL) people
       b. des gens qui sont plus *vieux* que moi
          some people who are more *old* (M PL) than me
       c. des gens plus *vieux* que moi
          some people more *old* (M PL) than me

The Noun *gens* 'people' is feminine in French, but has the semantic property of denoting mixed-sex groups. Since masculine is the unmarked gender in French, expressions predicated of such nominals generally take masculine plural agreement – hence the use of the masculine form *vieux* in (45b) and (45c): this pattern of agreement is loosely termed *semantic* in traditional grammar. However, pre-nominal Adjectives require strict *syntactic* agreement (that is, agreement with the number/gender properties of the head Noun of their NP complement), so that the feminine form *vieilles* is required in (45a). It would seem that it is not unusual to find that *modification* requires strict syntactic agreement between a modifying and a modified head; by contrast, predication often seems to require a relation of 'semantic compatibility'. The two different agreement patterns can be illustrated in terms of a common (in both senses of the word) pattern of agreement found in sentences such as '*A northern team* are playing a southern team in the final'. In this type of structure, we have strict syntactic agreement between the modifier *a* and the Noun *team* which it modifies, but a relation of 'semantic compatibility' between the singular subject *a northern team* and the plural head Auxiliary *are* of the predicate phrase. We shall return to consider how to handle the strict syntactic agreement between head Nouns and their pre-nominal modifiers in section 5.5 below.

The dual pattern of agreement in French nominals such as (45) might be argued to be paralleled by the dual pattern of agreement found in Spanish nominals such as the following (brought to my attention by Iggy Roca):

(46) a. *simpaticas* mujeres y hombres
         nice [F PL] women and men
      b. hombres y mujeres (que son) *simpaticos*
         men and women (who are) nice [M PL]

The interpretation relevant to our discussion here is the one on which the Adjective *simpaticos/simpaticas* is construed with both conjuncts, so that the intended meaning is 'nice women and nice men'. Here we have a variant of the problem discussed in (45), namely that of agreement between an Adjective and a mixed-gender nominal. As before, we find that the *unmarked* agreement form (masculine) is required for predicative and post-nominal Adjectives; but this is not so with pre-nominal Adjectives, since these must be made to agree with the first conjunct. If pre-nominal Adjectives are heads, we might take the phenomenon to involve **exceptional agreement marking**, and to be analogous to **exceptional case marking**: in other words, we might suggest a parallelism between structures like (47a) and (47b):

(47) a. [$_{VP}$ [$_V$ **consider**] [$_{IP}$ *them* [$_{I'}$ to be wrong]]]
      b. [$_{AP}$ [$_A$ **simpaticas**] [$_{CP}$ *mujeres* [$_{C'}$ y hombres]]]

In (47a), a relationship of licensing through case holds (under government and strict adjacency) between the head V of the matrix VP and the specifier of its complement IP; and we might suppose that in (47b), a parallel relationship of licensing through agreement holds (under government and strict adjacency) between the head of the matrix AP and the specifier of the complement CP (CP = Co-ordinate Phrase). Given the canonical *rightward* directionality of government in head-first languages like Spanish, it would follow that the pattern of agreement found in (47) could not occur with post-nominal Adjectives in such languages.

A final piece of morphosyntactic evidence which would seem to suggest that pre-nominal Adjectives are the heads of the overall structures containing them comes from Rumanian. In Rumanian, Adjectives may either precede or follow nominals which they modify:

(48)   a. o *interesantă* **carte**
           an *interesting* **book**
        b. o **carte** *interesantă*
           a **book** *interesting*

As we see from these examples, Determiners and Quantifiers (like *o* 'a(n)') generally precede the expressions they modify. However, Rumanian has an enclitic definite article, so that, for example, the definite form of the Noun *oraş* 'town' is *oraşul*, 'town+the'. Within the DP framework, we might suppose that the enclitic Determiner originates as the head of a containing DP, and that the head N of its complement NP is then raised by **head-to-head movement** to be prefixed to the head Determiner in the matrix DP, as represented schematically in (49):

(49) $_{DP}[_D + _{UL}] [_{NP} [_N oraş]]]$

In the light of this observation, consider which constituent is raised to be prefixed to the italicized article in structures such as (50):

(50)   a. *oraşul*   vechi
           town+the old
           'the old town'

        b. *vechiul*   oraş
           old+the town
           'the old town'

Given our claim that the Noun is the head of Noun+Adjective structures, it is significant that the article is suffixed to the head Noun in (50a); but equally, given the assumption that the Adjective is the head of Adjective+Noun structures, we should precisely expect that the article ends up suffixed to the Adjective in (50b). The nature of the head-movement operation involved in the two structures is represented in simplified form in (51):

(51)   a. $[_{DP}[_D + ul][_{NP}[_{NP}[_N oraş]][_{AP}[_A vechi]]]]]$

        b. $[_{DP}[_D + ul][_{AP}[_A vechi][_{NP}[_N oraş]]]]$

Given the analysis proposed here, in both cases head-to-head movement results in a complement head being raised to be adjoined to the left of a head matrix Determiner. In (51a), the head of the complement of the matrix D is the Noun *oraş* 'town', so the enclitic article +*ul* ends up suffixed to this Noun; but in (51b), the head of the complement of the matrix D is the Adjective *vechi* 'old', so the enclitic article ends up attached to this Adjective.

To summarize: there is some evidence in support of the analysis in (35), under which pre-nominal restrictive Adjectives are modifying heads which select NP complements, but post-nominal Adjectives are predicative adjuncts to NPs.

5.4 Determiners and Quantifiers

The obvious question that remains to be asked at this point is what structural position(s) Determiners and Quantifiers occupy within nominals: we shall begin by looking at Determiners, returning to consider Quantifiers briefly at the end of this section. Since Determiners are positioned in front of adjectival modifiers, we might suppose that they head a separate phrasal projection from D to DP (as suggested, for example, in Fukui, 1986; Hellan, 1986; Abney, 1987; Ritter, 1988; Grosu, 1988; and Fassi Fehri, 1990). Given this (and earlier) assumptions, a string such as *the recent government tax reforms* would have the structure (52):

(52) $[_{DP}[_{D}the][_{AP}[_{A} recent][_{NP}[_{NP} government][_{N'}[_{NP}tax][_{N} reforms]]]]]$

The resultant nominal would be a multilayered structure in which not just the head Noun *reforms*, but also the premodifying Adjective *recent* and the Determiner *the* project into separate phrasal constituents (the N *reforms* into the NP *government tax reforms*, the A *recent* into the AP *recent government tax reforms* and the D *the* into the DP *the recent government tax reforms*).

Of course, if Determiners can be projected into Determiner Phrases, then we should expect to find evidence that Determiners license specifiers of their own. This expectation might seem to be borne out by examples such as the following:

(53)   a. [*What* a fool] I was!
        b. I have never before witnessed [*so tragic* an accident]
        c. Tu   veux [*encore* une pomme]? (French)
            You want [*again* an apple]?
            'Do you want another apple?'

    d. N-a   venit [*nici* **o** persoană] (Rumanian)
       Not-has come [*not* **a** person]
       'Not a single person came'

It seems plausible to suppose that the bracketed strings in (53) are DPs headed by the bold-printed Determiner, and that the italicized pre-determiner expressions function as the specifiers of the Determiners.

    The observation (made in relation to examples such as (53)) that Determiners license specifiers of their own suggests an interesting analysis of structures involving so-called 'genitive *'s*'. Consider, for example, how we might deal with a possessive *'s* structure such as that in (54):

(54)   the government's recent tax reforms

Following a suggestion attributed by Abney (1987: 79) to Richard Larson, we might suggest that possessive *'s* (in this kind of use) be analysed as a head Determiner which licenses an NP or AP complement and a DP specifier. Given these (and earlier) assumptions, (54) would have the skeletal structure indicated in (55):

(55)   [$_{DP}$[$_{DP}$*the government*][$_{D'}$[$_D$'s] [$_{AP}$recent [$_{NP}$tax reforms]]]]

There are a number of interesting points of comparison between the determinate structure (55) and its indeterminate counterpart (56):

(56)   [$_{AP}$[$_A$recent] [$_{NP}$[$_{NP}$*government*] [$_{N'}$ tax reforms]]]

In (56), the italicized nominal *government* is an NP which functions as the specifier of a containing NP, and follows the adjectival modifier *recent*; by contrast, in (55) the italicized nominal *the government* is a DP which functions as the specifier of a containing DP, and precedes the adjectival modifier *recent*. If we posit that Nouns are not case assigners and that genitive *'s* is a functional category which (like INFL) assigns case to its specifier, and if we further posit that DPs are case-dependent but NPs are case-resistant, then it follows that the NP *government* (being case-resistant) can occur in a caseless position as the specifier of NP but not in a case-marked position as the specifier of DP, and that conversely the DP *the government* (being case-dependent) can occur as the specifier of DP, but not as the specifier of NP.

    There are a number of empirical arguments in support of analysing possessive *'s* as a head Determiner in English: for example, like demonstrative Determiners in English, possessive *'s* can be used both *pre-nominally* and *pro-nominally*:

(57) a. *These houses* are bigger than **those**
      b. *Mary's house* is bigger than **John's**

Moreover, there are strong distributional parallels between 's and the definite Determiner *the*: they are the only two Determiner constituents which can precede the post-determiner Quantifier *every*:

(58) a. Congressmen pander to **the** *every whim of the president*
      b. Congressmen pander to *the president's every whim*

In addition, both *the* and possessive nominals can be preceded by the same range of pre-determiner Quantifiers, as we can illustrate in terms of (59):

(59) a. *all/both* **the** problems
      b. *all/both* **John's** problems

And significantly, possessive 's and other Determiners are mutually exclusive, as we see from examples such as the following:

(60) *__the president's__ *this/that/a/the* friend

(Nominals like (60) do not seem to be semantically ill-formed in any way, since they have coherent paraphrases – cf. 'a/the friend of the president', 'this/that friend of the president's'.) Given that Determiners do not license DP complements, what this suggests is that possessive 's belongs to the same category as items like *this/that/a/the* – that is, to the category of third-person Determiners. Thus, it seems reasonable to posit that possessive 's is a Determiner which carries much the same morphosyntactic and semantic properties as *the*, but differs from *the* in that it licenses (indeed, *requires*) a possessor DP as its specifier (perhaps because 's is a suffix, or perhaps because it must obligatorily discharge case onto an overt specifier, in much the same way as a finite INFL constituent like *will* in English obligatorily requires an overt specifier to discharge nominative case onto), and in that it can be used *pronominally* as well as *pre-nominally*. Interestingly, 's generally requires a nominal rather than pronominal specifier (so we have '*which party's* policy?', but not *'which's* policy?').

Thus far, our discussion of possessives has focused on *nominal* possessives (that is, expressions in which the possessor is a nominal); however, an obvious question to ask is how we deal with *pronominal* possessives (expressions in which the possessor is a pronoun) like *our/ours, your/yours, her/hers, their/theirs, my/mine*, etc. The traditional way of dealing with pronominal possessives (suggested, for example by Bloomfield, 1933) is to analyse them as Determiners. Within the DP framework, this would mean that a nominal such as *your car* would have the simplified structure (61):

(61) $[_{DP}[_D your] [_{NP}[_N car]]]$

However, if pronominal possessives are head Determiners, then we might expect that (like possessive *'s* and other Determiners) they license specifiers of their own. In this connection, it is interesting to note the occurrence of structures such as the following in Dutch (from Stuurman, 1991):

(62)   *Jan* **z'n** vrienden
        Jan his friends
        'Jan's friends'

It seems reasonable to suppose that the possessive pronoun *z'n* here is the head of the overall DP, and that *Jan* is its specifier, so that a string like (62) has the structure (63):

(63) $[_{DP}[_{DP}Jan][_{D'}z'n][_{NP}vrienden]]]$

(I shall assume here that *Jan*, being a definite nominal, is premodified by a null definite Determiner, and thus has the status of a DP: in many languages, proper names are premodified by the definite article.) We might then see the relationship between the head and specifier of a possessive DP in (63) as very much akin to the relationship between INFL and its specifier: thus, the head agrees with the specifier (*Jan* is third person singular, so the head pronoun *z'n* is also third person singular), while the specifier is case-marked by the head: similarly, INFL agrees with (and assigns case to) its specifier.

  Given this assumption, we might suppose that pronominal possessives carry a set of AGR properties, marking agreement with their specifier: this specifier is overt (= *Jan*) in (63), but can also be covert. Thus, a pronominal possessive in Dutch licenses either an overt or a covert specifier. By contrast, pronominal possessives in English license only a null specifier, not an overt specifier, as we can see from contrasts such as the following:

(64)   a. **his** friends
        b. **John* **his** friends

(where **his** is the head, and *John* is the specifier). The only possessive morpheme which licenses an overt specifier in English is *'s*, which (perhaps because of its lack of any overtly marked AGR properties, and/or because it is a suffix which needs to be attached to an appropriate host, and/or because it must obligatorily discharge case features onto an overt DP specifier) requires an overt specifier. If this is so, then we have the following range of licensed and unlicensed possessive DP structures in English:

(65) a. [$_{DP}$[$_{DP}$the boy][$_{D'}$[$_D$'s/***his**][$_{NP}$father]]]
      b. [$_{DP}$[$_{DP}$e][$_{D'}$[$_D$*his*/*'s][$_{NP}$father]]]

Where the head D of a possessive DP is *'s*, an overt specifier is required; where the head D is a pronoun, the specifier must be null in (though it can be overt in Dutch).

The parallel drawn here between the D system and the I system raises an interesting question, in the light of the observation made by Chomsky (1989) that INFL in languages with rich inflection systems carries both subject agreement (= AGR-S) and object agreement (= AGR-O) properties. If we re-interpret AGR-S to mean 'specifier-agreement' (that is, agreement between a head and its specifier), then we might say that pronouns such as *his* in English and *z'n* in Dutch agree with their specifiers (whether overt or covert), and so carry AGR-S properties. This would lead us, however, to expect to find languages in which possessive Determiners exhibit AGR-O properties as well as AGR-S properties – that is, languages in which possessive pronouns agree with their complements as well as their specifiers.

In fact, French is just such a language. As we see from table 5.1, possessive pronouns inflect for agreement both with their 'under-stood' specifier (more specifically, with the *person/number* properties of the specifier), and with their complement (more specifically, with the *number/gender* properties of their complement). The initial

Table 5.1 Pre-nominal possessive pronouns in French

AGR-S properties (*possessor*)	AGR-O properties (*possessee*)		
	M SG	F SG	PL
1SG 'my'	mon	ma	mes
2SG 'your'	ton	ta	tes
3SG 'his/her/its'	son	sa	ses
1PL 'our'	notre		nos
2PL 'your'	votre		vos
3PL 'their'	leur		leurs

Note: 1/2/3 = first/second/third person; M = Masculine; F = Feminine; SG = Singular; PL = Plural consonant of the pronoun ($m+/t+/s+/n+/v+/l+$) generally seems to carry the AGR-S features (identifying the person and number of the possessor), while the remainder of the pronoun carries AGR-O features (identifying the number and gender of the complement). Thus, in a form such as *sa*, *s+* carries the AGR-S properties and identifies the possessor as third person singular (his/her/its), whereas *+a* carries the AGR-O properties and identifies the possessee as feminine singular. In contrast to French, possessive pronouns in English mark only AGR-S properties, and hence do not carry complement-agreement properties.

An obvious question which arises from our discussion here is how we handle the contrast between pairs of nominals such as *we politicians* and *our politicians*. If both *we* and *our* are pre-nominal Determiners taking NP complements, what is the difference between them? The answer suggested here is that *our* carries AGR-S properties (but no overt AGR-O properties, and no overt case properties), and so is interpreted as having a null first person plural specifier/possessor: cf. our discussion of (65) above. By contrast, *we* does not license a specifier, but carries AGR-O properties (it takes a plural complement) and overt case properties (it is overtly marked as nominative).

One type of pre-nominal modifier remains to be discussed, namely **Quantifiers**. Quantifiers seem to fall into two different distributional classes, as we can illustrate by contrasting the plural Quantifiers *tous* 'all' and *plusieurs* 'several' in French. The (masculine plural) Quantifier *tous* 'all' in French can generally premodify only a **determinate** (masculine plural) nominal (that is, a masculine plural nominal premodified by a Determiner), so that we can have '*tous* **les garçons**' ('all the boys'), '*tous* **ces beaux arbres**' ('all these beautiful trees') and '*tous* **nos ancêtres**' ('all our ancestors'), but not ***'*tous* **(beaux) arbres**' ('all (beautiful) trees'). By contrast, the (masculine/feminine plural) Quantifier *plusieurs* 'several' can modify only an **indeterminate** plural nominal (that is, a plural nominal not premodified by a Determiner), so that we can have '*plusieurs* **questions**' ('several questions') and '*plusieurs* **faux pas**' ('several false steps'), but not ***'*plusieurs* **ces arbres**' ('several these trees'). How can we account for the fact that *tous* quantifies a *determinate* nominal, whereas *plusieurs* quantifies an *indeterminate* nominal? Within the framework adopted here, it seems natural to suppose that quantification of a determinate nominal involves quantification of a DP, whereas quantification of an indeterminate nominal involves quantification of an NP. But what is the structural relation between the Quantifier and the quantified expression?

Given our general assumption that pre-nominal modifiers are the heads of their containing nominals, a natural answer would be to suppose that quantified nominals have the status of Quantifier Phrases headed by their Quantifiers. On this assumption, nominals such as *tous ces arbres* 'all these trees' and *plusieurs arbres* 'several trees' would have the respective structures (66a) and (66b) below:

(66)   a. $[_{QP}[_{Q}tous][_{DP}[_{D}ces][_{NP}[_{N}arbres]]]]$
         b. $[_{QP}[_{Q}plusieurs][_{N}[_{PN}arbres]]]$

We could then say that both quantified nominal structures would be Quantifier Phrases, and would differ only in that the complement of the Quantifier *tous* 'all' is a DP, whereas the complement of the Quantifier *plusieurs* 'several' is an NP. Pre-determiner Quantifiers would then differ from pre-nominal Quantifiers in respect of their complement-selection (that is, subcategorization) properties, for example in respect of whether they license an NP or DP complement.

5.5 Percolation and co-headedness

Under the analysis outlined in the previous sections, *students of linguistics* is a Noun Phrase, *good students of linguistics* is an Adjectival Phrase, *many students of linguistics* is a Quantifier Phrase and *these students of linguistics* is a Determiner Phrase. However, there is an obvious problem posed by such an analysis: namely, that we no longer have any unitary characterization of a *nominal* expression, since each different type of nominal has a different categorial status (as NP, AP, QP or DP). Yet, in spite of putative differences in their categorial status, these various types of nominal can all serve as arguments, and can all be antecedents of an anaphor such as *themselves*, as we see from examples such as the following:

(67)   a. *Students* sometimes underestimate **themselves**
         b. *Good students* sometimes underestimate **themselves**
         c. *Many students* sometimes underestimate **themselves**
         d. *These students* sometimes underestimate **themselves**

Clearly, we want to avoid saying that the antecedent of an anaphor like *themselves* can be like an NP like *students*, or an AP like *good students*, or a QP like *many students*, or a DP like *these students*. What we want to be able to say is that all these various different kinds of constituent (NP, AP, QP, DP) have in common the fact that they are *nominal* constituents. One way in which we might seek to do this is by positing that the nominal properties of the complement NP *students* in an AP such as *good students*, a QP such as *many students* or a DP such as *these students* somehow percolate up to the containing AP, QP, or DP constituent. We could then say that what all the various italicized nominals in (67) have in common is the fact that they all have a Noun as their **ultimate head**. Of course, for such an account to be workable, we need to be able to formalize the notion of **percolation**: but how can we do this? Abney (1987) attempts to handle percolation in terms of an **inheritance** principle: however, for reasons outlined in Radford (1989), the principle is unworkable. How, then, are we to deal with percolation?

Before attempting to develop an alternative account, let us ask ourselves just what intuition is being captured by saying that in an AP such as *good students*, a QP such as *many students* or a DP such as *these students*, the nominal properties of the head Noun *students* percolate up to the overall AP, QP or DP constituent. What we are trying to say is that *good students* is an Adjective-modified Noun Phrase, that *many students* is a Quantified Noun Phrase and that *these students* is a Determinate Noun Phrase. The implicit assumption behind this analysis is that modified expressions are co-headed, in the sense that the head of the modifying Phrase is the **immediate head** and the head of the modified Phrase is the **ultimate head**. In these terms, the immediate head of a string such as *good students* would be the Adjective *good*, but its ultimate head would be the plural Noun *students*: the immediate head of a string such as *many students* would be the Quantifier *many*, though its ultimate head would be the Noun *students*; and likewise, the immediate head of a string such as *these students* would be the Determiner *these*, but its ultimate head would be the Noun *students*. More concretely, we might suggest that *good students* is an ANP constituent, *many students* is a QNP, and *these students* is a DNP. To say, for example, that *many students* is a QNP is to say that it is a Quantified Noun Phrase, that is, a Phrase whose immediate head is the Quantifier *many*, and whose ultimate head is the Noun *students*. In contrast, an unmodified nominal such as *students (of linguistics)* would be an NP, that is, a constituent whose immediate and ultimate head is the same Noun, *students*.

An obvious question to ask is how we could extend the **co-headedness** account to deal with multiply modified phrases such as *all these small cars*. One possibility would be as follows. We might suppose that *cars* is an NP, that is, a constituent whose immediate and ultimate head is the same Noun *cars*. We might also suppose that *small cars* is an ANP (an Adjective-modified Noun Phrase), in that its immediate head is the Adjective *small* and its ultimate head is the

Noun *cars*. We might further suppose that *these small cars* is a DNP (Determinate Noun Phrase), that is, a Phrase whose immediate head is the Determiner *these* and whose ultimate head is the Noun *cars*. Finally, we might suppose that the overall expression *all these small cars* is a QNP (Quantified Noun Phrase), that is, a Phrase whose immediate head is the Quantifier *all* and whose ultimate head is the Noun *cars*. Given these assumptions, the string *all these small cars* would have the simplified structure (68):

(68) $[_{QNP}[_Q all][_{DNP}[_D these][_{ANP}[_A small][_{NP}[_N cars]]]]]$

We could then attain a unitary characterization of the notion of a *nominal constituent* as a 'constituent whose ultimate head is a Noun'. Thus, the NP *cars*, the ANP *small cars*, the DNP *these small cars* and the QNP *all these small cars* would all be 'nominal constituents' in (68) – and so, indeed, would all of the italicized expressions in (67). The essential intuition behind this analysis is that the categorial properties of the ultimate head of a constituent percolate up to each successively larger phrasal projection of the ultimate head.

While it seems intuitively plausible to posit co-headed constituents such as QNP (= Quantified Noun Phrase) and DNP (= Determinate Noun Phrase), it might seem rather less plausible to posit a category of ANP constituents (Adjective-modified Noun Phrases). However, there is some empirical evidence that ANP forms a 'natural syntactic class', in the sense that it is precisely this kind of constituent which appears to occur as the complement of the plural partitive Quantifier *d(e)* 'some' in non-negative sentences in French:

(69)   a. On a choisi *des/*de* **vins**
             'We chose some wines'
         b. On a choisi *des/*de* **vins excellents**
             'We chose some excellent wines'
         c. On a choisi **d'excellents vins**/*des **excellents vins**
             'We chose some excellent wines'

Such data suggest that *de* (in non-negative sentences) is only used to quantify an ANP like *excellent vins*, not a simple NP such as *vins*, nor a complex NP such as *vins excellents* (the latter comprising an NP *vins* to which the AP *excellents* has been adjoined to form the larger NP *vins excellents*, as we argued in section 5.3). Thus, we might say that the partitive Quantifier *d(e)* in French (in non-negative sentences) selects an ANP complement, and hence that ANP is a 'natural' phrasal constituent.

The **co-headedness** account sketched above provides an interesting account of a number of aspects of the syntax of modified nominals which previously proved problematic. For example, under the analysis in section 5.3, both nominal expressions such as *fond memories* and adjectival expressions such as *fond of chocolate* would be assigned the same categorial status of AP, in spite of obvious distributional differences between the two. Under the revised account here, *fond memories* would be an ANP (a Phrase whose immediate head is the Adjective *fond* and whose ultimate head is the Noun *memories*), whereas *fond of chocolate* (in which *fond* is a predicate, not a modifier) is an AP (a Phrase whose immediate and ultimate head is the Adjective *fond*). Similarly, the co-headedness framework would allow us to account for the fact that pre-nominal Adjectives can be recursively stacked, but not pre-nominal Determiners. Let us suppose that both restrictive adjectival modifiers and Determiners select an (A)NP complement. It follows that a restrictive Adjective like *small* can combine with an NP complement like *cars* to form the ANP *small cars*. The resultant ANP can in turn serve as the complement of another restrictive Adjective like *Japanese*, so forming the larger ANP constituent *Japanese small cars*. Since Determiners can take an ANP complement, the resulting ANP can combine with a Determiner like *these* to form the DNP *these Japanese small cars*. But the resulting DNP cannot serve as the complement of another Adjective or Determiner, since premodifying Determiners and Adjectives take an (A)NP complement, not a DNP complement (hence the fact that structures like **the many students* and **these the students* are ungrammatical in English, even though they do not appear to be semantically incoherent, in that they have well-formed counterparts in Italian and Arabic respectively). Clearly, a mass of descriptive details need to be accommodated, but the general outlines of a co-headedness approach should be clear. As noted earlier, the core assumption underlying the analysis is that the categorial properties of the ultimate head of a nominal percolate up through all its phrasal projections.

The co-headedness framework also provides us with a principled account of the strictly morphosyntactic agreement which holds between modifiers and heads, as illustrated by the Italian counterpart of (68) above, viz. (70):

(70) $[_{QNP}[_Q tutte][_{DNP}[_D queste][_{ANP}[_A piccole][_{NP}[_N macchine]]]]]$

As we see from (70), all three premodifiers (*tutte* 'all', *queste* 'these' and *piccole* 'small') agree in number and gender with (and carry the same feminine plural +*e* ending as) the Noun *macchine* 'cars'. Within the co-headedness framework, we can say that agreement holds between the immediate and ultimate heads of a phrase, so that the immediate A head *piccole* of ANP, the immediate D head *queste* of DNP and the immediate Q head *tutte* of QNP all agree with their ultimate N head *macchine*. In a morphologically rich language like Latin in which Nouns carry morphologically realized case properties as well as number and gender properties, the co-heads of Nouns will agree with their ultimate head Nouns in *case* as well as number and gender. In a morphologically impoverished language like English, the relevant agreement patterns are less immediately obvious, but are latent in that, for example, Quantifiers like *both*, Determiners like *these* and Adjectives like *various* are inherently plural, and so can serve as the immediate heads only of a nominal whose ultimate head is plural. In more general terms, we can say that the co-headedness framework provides us with a natural characterization of the strict morphosyntactic agreement relation between modifying and modified heads: 'agreement' in our terms is a morphosyntactic relation between co-heads, such that the immediate head of a nominal assumes the morphological properties of its ultimate head N.

This characterization of agreement as a relation between co-heads enables us to provide an interesting account of the agreement pattern found in structures such as (71) below, where a modifying Adjective has a genitive NP complement (in our terms, a KNP complement headed by the genitive K (case particle) *de* 'of'):

(71)   a. une drôle   *de* fille (French)
         one strange *of* girl
         'a STRANGE girl'

      b. sa manna *de* ampulla (Sardinian, from Jones, forthcoming)
         the BIG   (*of*) bottle
      c. cudda *de* mákkina (Sardinian, from Jones, forthcoming)
         THAT (of) car

We might suppose that in (71a), *fille* is an NP, *de fille* is a KNP, *drôle de fille* is an ANP and *une drôle de fille* is a QNP, so that (71a) has the structure (72) below:

(72)   [$_{QNP}$[$_Q$une][$_{ANP}$[$_A$drôle][$_{KNP}$[$_K$de][$_{NP}$[$_M$fille]]]]]

Given that the assumption that the immediate head of a nominal (where it carries agreement morphology) agrees with its ultimate N head, it would then follow that the immediate A head *drôle* of ANP and the immediate Q head *une* of QNP would agree with the ultimate head N *fille*. (The immediate K head *de* of KNP would not agree with its ultimate N head *fille* – or would agree vacuously – since K carries no overt agreement morphology.) Similarly, we might posit that (71b) has the structure (73):

(73) $[_{DNP}[_D sa][_{ANP}[_A manna][_{KNP}[_K de][_{NP}[_N ampulla]]]]]$

It would then follow that the immediate head A *manna* of ANP and the immediate head D *sa* of DNP would agree with their ultimate head N *ampulla*. In much the same way, we might posit that (71c) has the structure (74):

(74) $[_{DNP}[_D cudda][_{KNP}[_K de][_{NP}[_N mákkina]]]]$

The immediate head D *cudda* of DNP would then agree with its ultimate head N *mákkina*. Thus, the co-headedness framework would allow us to provide a unitary account of agreement not only in structures where Adjectives and Determiners take an NP complement, but also in structures where they take a 'genitive' KNP complement.

5.6 Pronouns

Thus far, we have argued that the co-headedness framework provides us with an interesting account of a number of aspects of the morphosyntax of *nominal* constituents, and allows us to attain a unitary definition of a *nominal* constituent as 'a constituent whose ultimate head is a Noun'. We shall now go on to argue that the framework also provides an interesting account of the morphosyntax of Pronouns, and allows us to attain a unitary definition of a **pronominal** constituent as 'a constituent whose ultimate head is a Pronoun (that is, pronominal N)'. The simplest type of Pronoun we find in English is the pronominal count Noun *one(s)*, in the type of use illustrated in (75) (see Radford, 1990, for arguments that *one* is pro-N, not pro-N-bar or pro-NP):

(75)   a. Do you like the red *ones*, or would you prefer a blue *one*?
        b. The picture I like best is the *one* of you in a monokini

In this particular use, *one* lacks the specific sense properties of count Nouns like *sweater* or *picture*, and yet seems to have the morphological characteristics of a typical count Noun, in that – like a typical count Noun – it has a plural form in +s. Within the co-headedness framework, the pronoun *one* (in this use) would be analysed as a simple pronoun whose sole head is a pronominal count N. This head pronominal N can in turn serve as the ultimate head of a more complex nominal such as *a blue one* in (75a). Such an expression would be analysed as having the structure (76):

(76) $[_{DNP}[_{D}a][_{ANP}[_{A}blue][_{NP}[_{N}one]]]]$

Under this analysis, the NP *one*, ANP *blue one* and DNP *a blue one* all have the countable Pronoun (that is, pronominal count N) *one* as their ultimate head.

Just as we find nominal constituents which are co-headed, so too we find pronominal constituents which are co-headed. Obvious potential examples of co-headed Pronouns are Quantified Pronouns like *someone, anyone, no-one* and *everyone* in English. We might analyse these as co-headed expressions comprising an ultimate pronominal N head *one* premodified by a Quantifier such as *some, any, no* or *every*. One way of executing this idea would be to suppose that such Quantified Pronouns are QNP constituents whose immediate head is a Q constituent with an NP complement whose immediate and ultimate head is the pronominal N *one*. We might then suppose (following Abney, 1987: 286–7) that the head Q and N constituents are subsequently 'fused' together into a single compound word by a syntactic operation of head-to-head movement. Within the co-headedness framework outlined here, this would mean that *everyone* is derived in the manner represented schematically in (77):

(77) $[_{QNP}[_{Q}every][_{NP}[_{N}one]]]$

Such an analysis would amount to claiming that the relevant Pronouns are **syntactic compounds** (that is, the Q and N components within them originate as heads of separate Phrases, but are fused together by operation of head-to-head movement in the syntax). We need to posit that the two morphemes ultimately form a single compound word in order to account for differences in stress pattern and vowel reduction in pairs such as *every body* (in the sense of 'every corpse', where the orthographic *o* vowel of *body* is stressed and cannot be reduced to schwa) and *everybody* (in the sense of 'everyone', where the *o* vowel of *body* is unstressed and can be reduced to schwa).

Plausible though such a syntactic-compounding analysis might seem, on closer inspection it turns out to be fraught with phonological, morphological, syntactic and semantic problems. From a phonological perspective, one problem is that a syntactic-compounding analysis would provide no explanation for why *no* is pronounced /nou/ in the words *no*/*nobody*/*no-one*, but /nʌ/ in the compound *nothing*, and /n/ in the word *none* (if this is a compound of *no+one*, and /ʌ/ is the initial segment of *one*). From a morphological viewpoint, a further problem is that we have no principled explanation of why the relevant compounds have no plural in +*s* when used as Pronouns, even though their ultimate heads are countable N constituents like *thing*/*body*/*one* which (in their nominal uses) do indeed have +*s* forms: indeed, if *none* is analysed as a compound of *no+one*, it is even more puzzling why the form *one* without plural +*s* is inherently singular in other uses, and yet *none* can be either singular or plural in modern colloquial English ('None **is/are** suitable'). From a syntactic point of view, a further problem is that the type of head-to-head movement (that is, syntactic compounding) operation in (77) would have to be heavily lexically restricted in order to account for the fact that we have a Pronoun *everything* but no Pronoun **eachthing*, and a Pronoun *somehow* but no Pronoun **nohow* (in British English): moreover, we have to find some explanation for why *head movement* adjoins the complement head to the *left* of the matrix head in cases such as (48), but to its *right* in cases such as (77). From a semantic point of view, the compounding analysis would fail to provide any principled account of the fact that *one* has a potentially unrestricted interpretation (for example, it may have an animate or inanimate antecedent) in an expression like *a good **one*** (and indeed in the Pronoun *none*), but has a restricted (human) interpretation in *someone*. Equally problematic from a semantic point of view is the fact that *body* has the sense of 'corpse' in its nominal use in an expression such as *a blood-stained **body***, but has the sense of 'person' in its pronominal use in expressions such as *anybody*. In short, analysing Pronouns like *everyone* as syntactic compounds poses numerous potential problems.

Since many of the phonological, morphological, syntactic and semantic properties of such Quantified Pronouns appear to be lexically idiosyncratic, an alternative approach would be to analyse them as **lexical compounds**. We might then say, for example, that *everyone* is a lexical compound of the Quantifier *every* and the pronominal N stem *one* (having the sense of 'person' in this pronominal use). More concretely, we might suppose that the overall compound has the status of a QN – that is, a Quantified pronominal N – as in (78):

(78)   [$_{QN}$[$_Q$every][$_N$one]]

We might interpret (78) as claiming *everyone* is a compound which comprises the pronominal N stem *one* (the ultimate head of the compound), and the premodifying Quantifier *every*. It would seem that the pronominal N in such compound Quantified Pronouns sometimes has a more restricted range of interpretation than in other uses. For example, the pronominal count Noun *one(s)* can freely have an animate or inanimate antecedent in expressions such as *a nice one*, but is intrinsically human in interpretation in Quantified Pronouns such as *someone/anyone/no-one/everyone*; likewise, the French pronominal N *uns* 'ones' can be animate or inanimate in expressions such as 'les *uns*' ('the *ones*', often contrasted with *les autres* 'the others') and in the plural Pronoun *quelques-uns* 'some (ones)', but is intrinsically human in the singular form *quelqu'un* 'someone'. In the light of the observation that the N head in a Quantified Pronoun has a restricted (for example, human) interpretation, it is interesting to consider the interpretation of the pronouns *somebody/anybody/ nobody/everybody*. It seems implausible to posit that these items incorporate the Noun *body*, since although *body* has the sense of 'corpse' in a nominal expression such as 'a blood-stained *body*', it does not have the same sense in a Pronoun such as *somebody*. On the contrary, *body* in expressions such as *somebody/anybody/nobody/ everybody* seems to have precisely the same restricted (human) interpretation as the pronoun *one* in *someone/anyone/no-one/ everyone*. It therefore seems reasonable to suppose that the *body* morpheme in a Quantified Pronoun like *everybody* is in fact a pronominal N, just like the *one* morpheme in a Quantified Pronoun such as *everyone*. By extension of the same reasoning, we might similarly suppose that the *thing* morpheme in compound Quantified Pronouns such as *something/anything/nothing/everything* is also a restricted pronominal N: more specifically, it is a singular pronominal count N restricted to an inanimate interpretation. The pronoun *thing* (and its counterpart in other languages) in compound Pronouns is morphologically distinct from its Noun counterpart: for example, in English, the Pronoun *thing* is inherently singular, so that we have '*nothing* interesting', but not *'*nothings* interesting'; in French/ Italian, the pronoun *chose/cosa* 'thing' which appears in compound pronouns like *quelque chose* 'something'/*qualcosa* 'something'/*che cosa?* 'what (thing)?' is masculine in gender, whereas its Noun counterpart *chose/cosa* is feminine. Thus, there is a certain amount of evidence in support of claiming that the head N element in this type of Quantified Pronoun is always pronominal, even though it resembles an item which otherwise functions as a Noun.

The more general implication of the lexical compound analysis in (78) is that not just (compound) phrases, but also (compound) words may be co-headed. Just as a compound Phrase can be built up out of separate phrasal projections of a modified (ultimate) head and a modifying head (so that N projects into an NP which combines with Q to form QNP), so too a compound word can be formed out of a modified (ultimate) head and a modifying head (so that Q combines with N to form QN). We could then say that a QNP (Quantified Nominal Phrase) can either be a projection of a single compound head Quantified (pro)nominal (QN), or a projection of two separate simplex Q and N heads (with a head nominal or pronominal N projecting into the NP complement of a head Q which in turn projects into a QNP). We might suppose, for example, that the Pronoun *somebody* and its non-pronominal counterpart *some body* (meaning 'some corpse') are QNPs with the respective structures indicated in (79) below (where we use *b'dy* to designate the vowel-reducible Pronoun *body* meaning 'person', and *body* to designate the vowel-irreducible Noun *body* meaning 'corpse'):

(79)   a. $[_{QNP}[_{QN}[_Q\text{some}][_N\text{b'dy}]]]$ (= 'someone')
        b. $[_{QNP}[_Q\text{some}][_{NP}[_N\text{body}]]]$ (= 'some corpse')

This would mean that the Pronoun *someb'dy* is in effect a quantified pronominal N, whereas the nominal *some body/corpse* is a Quantified Noun Phrase. Thus, a phrasal category like QNP can be the maximal projection either of a compound QN (Quantified Pronoun) head, or of two independent simple Q and N heads (a head nominal or pronominal N projecting into the NP complement of a head Q which in turn projects into a QNP).

A natural question to ask is whether the co-headedness account could be extended to pronominal Quantifiers which do not incorporate an overt pronominal N morpheme. There are a number of such pronouns which have similar semantic properties to items such as *someone*, in two respects: firstly, they are 'free' pronouns, in the sense that (like *free* relative pronouns) they have no antecedent; and secondly, they have a restricted interpretation (such as inanimate or human). For example, English *what?* (and indeed its Rumanian counterpart *ce?*) (as a pre-nominal Q can quantify both inanimate and human expressions (cf. '*What* **ideas** have you had?' '*What* **politician** would ever dream of telling the truth?'), though its pronominal counterpart ('*What* did you see?') is intrinsically inanimate. We might accordingly suggest that *what* in its pronominal use is a *wh-*

Quantifier which quantifies a null inanimate pronominal N (whereas, conversely, the Pronoun *who* is a *wh*-Quantifier which quantifies a null pronominal human N). If we treat such pronouns as lexical compounds like *someone/something*, then *what?* in its pre-nominal and pronominal uses (in sentences such as '*What* (film) did you see?') would have the categorial status of a simple Q head taking an NP complement in its pre-nominal use, but of a compound QN head in its pronominal use:

(80) a. $[_{QNP}[_Q\text{what}][_{NP}[_N\text{film}]]]$
       b. $[_{QNP}[_{QN}[_Q\text{what}][_Ne]]]$

where *e* denotes an empty N with a restricted (inanimate) interpretation. The Italian counterparts of the English interrogative pronoun *what?* are interesting in the context of our discussion here. One such counterpart is *che cosa?* 'what thing?', which comprises the pre-nominal Quantifier *che* and the pronoun *cosa* (different from the Noun *cosa* 'thing' in that the Pronoun is masculine in gender whereas the Noun is feminine): a second counterpart is *che?* 'what?', which (in our terms) involves the Quantifier *che* quantifying a null inanimate pronominal head with a restricted, inanimate interpretation (that is, a null counterpart of *cosa*); a third counterpart is *cosa?*, which might be analysed as involving an overt inanimate pronominal N *cosa* quantified by a null *wh*-Quantifier. The fact that either the Q or the N can be null in Italian interrogative *wh*-Pronouns might lead us to ask whether we find quantified Pronouns in which both Q and N are null: in this connection, it is interesting to note the claim by Obenauer (1976) that the French interrogative Pronoun *quoi?* 'what?' has a null variant, and that young children sometimes produce *wh*-questions containing a null *wh*-Pronoun, for example, 'Daddy doing?' corresponding to the adult question '*What's* Daddy doing?'. If pronominal Quantifiers with a restricted interpretation are treated as lexical compounds, their idiosyncratic phonological, morphosyntactic and semantic properties can be directly specified in their lexical entries (for example, whether the ultimate pronominal N head is overt or covert, masculine or feminine, singular or plural, restricted or unrestricted in interpretation, etc.).

However, many (indeed most) pronominal Quantifiers are rather different from *what?* or *who?* in two respects: firstly, they are 'bound' Pronouns in that they require an antecedent in order to be interpretable; and secondly, they have a potentially unrestricted (for example, animate or inanimate) interpretation. We can illustrate these two properties in relation to pronominal Quantifiers such as those italicized in (81):

(81)   We saw *many/few/some/several/three/both/none/neither*

Such sentences are uninterpretable unless the Pronouns are assigned an antecedent; but the antecedent is potentially unrestricted, in the sense that it is not required to be intrinsically human or inanimate. Interestingly, many such pronominal Quantifiers are often paraphrasable (when they denote countable entities) by structures of the form Quantifier+*one(s)*:

(82)   a. *Which one(s)*/**Which** do you like best?
         b. I don't think *any one*/**any** of them is adequate
         c. *Each one*/**Each** has his faults
         d. You can have *either one*/**either**
         e. *Neither one*/**Neither** will pass the exam

We might accordingly suggest that the difference between *which one(s)?* and pronominal *which?* is simply that *which* quantifies an overt pronominal N head *one(s)* in the first example, but a null pronominal N head in the second, as in (83) (where *e* designates an empty N head):

(83)   a. [$_{QNP}$[$_Q$which][$_{NP}$[$_N$one(s)]]]
         b. [$_{QNP}$[$_Q$which][$_{NP}$[$_N$*e*]]]

The more general implication would be that all unrestricted pronominal Quantifiers involve quantification of a pronominal N head, and that this N head is overt in expressions such as *which one(s)?*, but covert in unrestricted Pronouns such as *which?* We might then suppose that the empty pronominal head *e* in (83b) is interpreted in much the same way as the overt pronominal head *one(s)* in (83a). It should be self-evident that an analysis such as (83b) would be entirely consistent with a co-headedness analysis of Pronouns, since a Pronoun like *which?* is treated as a co-projection of an overt Q head and a null N head.

Clearly, although our discussion here relates to Quantified Pronouns, it can be generalized to Determinate Pronouns (that is, pronominal Determiners) in a straightforward fashion. For example, we might suppose that strings such as *these cars*, *these* and *this* are DNP (Determinate Noun Phrase) constituents with the respective simplified structures indicated in (84a–c):

(84)   a. [$_{DNP}$[$_D$these][$_{NP}$[$_N$cars]]]
         b. [$_{DNP}$[$_D$these][$_{NP}$[$_N$*e*]]]
         c. [$_{DNP}$[$_{DN}$[$_D$this][$_N$*e*]]]

Thus, a DNP could be headed either by two simplex heads (with N projecting into an NP complement of a D which projects into DNP), or by a compound DN head, incorporating a null (restricted) pronominal N as its ultimate head and an overt premodifying Determiner. The empty head pronominal N has an unrestricted interpretation in Pronouns like *these\those*, but may have a restricted (inanimate) interpretation in Pronouns like *this/that* (since such Pronouns can only be interpreted as inanimate in expressions such as *I don't like this/that.*

We might extend this analysis to 'personal Pronouns' like *we/you/ they*, and suppose that they are Determinate Pronouns, that is, Determiners which determine a null pronominal N head. What lends plausibility to such an analysis is the fact that items like *we* and *you* can serve as Determiners for an overt nominal (in sentences such as '*We* **linguists** respect *you* **psychologists**'). Moreover, in some varieties of English *we\you* can serve as Determiners for the pronominal N *ones* (hence we find the compound Pronouns *we'uns* and *you'uns* in Ozark English – as noted in Jacobs and Rosenbaum, 1968: 98). Even third-person pronouns such as *they* and *them* can be used as prenominal Determiners in some varieties of English, as we can see from examples such as the following:

(85) a. Tell Cooper to shift *they* stones there (Devonshire, from Harris, 1991: 23)
   b. It was like this in *them* days, years ago, you see (Somerset, from Ihalainen, 1991: 156)

Hence, it is far from implausible to say that in their pronominal use personal Pronouns like *they/them* comprise a Determiner which determines a null pronominal N. In many languages third-person Pronouns can also be used pre-nominally (so that, for example, French *les* corresponds both to the English Determiner *the* and to the English Pronoun *them*, and likewise *le* corresponds to both 'the' and 'him', and *la* to both 'the' and 'her'), so analysing personal Pronouns as comprising a null pronominal N constituent premodified by a Determiner is by no means implausible. Indeed, we might even speculate that the null Pronoun 'little *pro*' involves a null D determining a null pronominal N: given that Pronouns typically carry case, this would provide a natural way of accounting for Rizzi's (1986) observation that 'little *pro*' is subject to case constraints on its distribution.

One interesting consequence of the analysis proposed here is that Pronouns like *what?* or *someb'dy* are analysed as both semantically and syntactically distinct from Pronouns like *which?* The two types of

Pronoun differ in their semantic properties in that *what?* and *someb'dy* are analysed as **free, restricted** pronouns (that is, as antecedentless Pronouns which are restricted to having an inanimate or animate interpretation), whereas *which?* is analysed as a **bound, unrestricted** Pronoun (that is, a Pronoun which requires an antecedent, but which permits a potentially unrestricted choice of antecedent). The two also differ in their syntactic structure, in that *what?* and *someb'dy* quantify a restricted pronominal N (which is null in the case of *what?* but has the form *b'dy* in the case of *someb'dy*), whereas *which?* quantifies a null unrestricted pronominal NP. The syntactic differences between the two types of Pronoun can be represented as in (86) and (87):

(86)   a. $[_{QN}[_Q what][_N e]]$
       b. $[_{QN}[_Q some][_N b'dy]]$ (= 'someone')
(87) $[_{QNP}[_Q which][_{NP}[_N e]]]$

There are two pieces of empirical evidence which support assigning different structural representations to restricted Pronouns like those in (86), and unrestricted Pronouns like that in (87). The first comes from the distribution of the item *else* in English. Within the framework developed here, we can characterize the use of this item by positing that *else* occurs only after **quantified restricted Pronouns** (that is, Pronouns in which a Quantifier quantifies a pronominal N which is restricted to being interpreted as, for example, human or inanimate). This accounts for the fact that we can have *everyone else, anybody else, nothing else, somewhere else, who else?, what else?*, and *all else* (cf. *If all else fails. . .* , where *all* means 'everything' and so involves quantification of a restricted inanimate Pronoun), since all of the relevant Pronouns involve quantification of a restricted pronominal N. By the same token, the proposed analysis also accounts for the impossibility of **which else?*, **whose else?*, *several else, *both else , *many else, *most else, since all of these involve quantification of an unrestricted null bound NP. (It would be implausible to argue that these expressions are semantically incoherent, since they have coherent paraphrases with *other(s)*: compare, for example, *which other ones?* and *which others?*.) Likewise, if *else* can only follow *quantified* restricted Pronouns, we can account for the ungrammaticality of *this else, *that else (in the sense of 'this/that other thing'), since although these have a restricted (inanimate) pronominal N as their ultimate head, they are not *quantified* pronouns, but rather *determinate* pronouns (that is, they are pronominal Determiners, not pronominal Quantifiers).

A second piece of empirical evidence in support of assigning different structures to restricted and unrestricted Pronouns comes from **postpositional** structures such as those italicized in the following dialogues:

(88)   a. 'She was stabbed' – '*What with?*'
       b. 'She was really rude' – '*Who to?*'
       c. 'She's just come back' – '*Where from?*'
       d. 'She's given us an assignment to do' – '*When for?*'

There are many interesting features of the italicized construction in (88). The one that most concerns us here is that it is not possible with *unrestricted wh*-Pronouns like *which?* or *whose?*:

(89)   a. 'She was stabbed with one of these knives' – *'*Which with?*'
       b. 'She went to someone's flat' – *'*Whose to?*'

Clearly, the Pronouns in (88) have a restricted interpretation, in that *what?* means (roughly) 'which things?', *who?* means 'which person?', *where?* means 'which place?', and *when?* means 'which time?'; equally clearly, the pronouns *which?* and *whose?* are unrestricted in interpretation, and require a discourse antecedent. The obvious question to ask is why it should be that restricted *wh*-Pronouns can occur in this type of postpositional structure, whereas unrestricted *wh*-Pronouns cannot. One point to note in this connection is that although *wh*-heads can occur in this type of postpositional structure, *wh*-phrases cannot – contrast the grammaticality of the italicized structure in (88a) above with the ungrammaticality of that in (90):

(90)   a. 'She was stabbed' – *'*What kind of instrument with?*'
       b. 'She's been talking' – *'*How many people to?*'

What this might suggest is that postpositional structures like *what with?* are compound heads of some kind in which a *wh*-head is adjoined to a postpositional head. Such a compounding analysis would provide a natural account of contrasts such as that between (88a) and (90a), since in (88a) a *wh*-head (a compound QN head) has been adjoined to a Postposition, whereas in (90a) a *wh*-phrase (a QNP) has been adjoined to a Postposition (in violation of structural principles of Universal Grammar (UG) which determine that only heads – not phrases – can be adjoined to other heads). Given the *compound* analysis, the ungrammaticality of structures such as (89) can be accounted for straightforwardly by positing that *which?* and *whose?* are phrasal QNP constituents (as in (87) above), and hence cannot in principle be adjoined to a postpositional head.

Thus far, we have suggested that the head of an NP can be a pronominal N, the head of a QNP can be a pronominal Quantifier and the head of a DNP can be a pronominal Determiner. The obvious question to ask at this point is thus whether an ANP can be headed by a pronominal Adjective. There are numerous structures in a variety of languages in which an Adjective without an overt nominal complement can be used in a nominal position – compare, for instance, the use of the French Adjective *autres* 'other' in a sentence such as (91):

(91)   [D'*autres*]   sont affectés plus profondément (French)
        [(Some) others] are   affected more deeply

Given that the bracketed adjectival structure in (91) occurs in a nominal argument position, we might suppose that *autres* is a co-projection of a head Adjective *autres* and a null plural pronominal N constituent which is unrestricted in interpretation (and so can be human, or inanimate). Note that it would be implausible to analyse *autres* here as a simple Noun, since (as we saw earlier in relation to examples such as (69) above) only ANPs are quantified by the partitive Quantifier *d(e)* 'some' in non-negative sentences in French, not simple NPs. Not surprisingly (in the context of our earlier discussion), the null pronominal N head of a pronominal Adjective may have a restricted interpretation; consider, for example, sentences such as the following:

(92)   a. Lo *importante*   es que diga   la verdad (Spanish)
           The important (**thing**) is that (he) tell the truth
        b. Many *Welsh* despise the *English* (= Welsh/English **people**)

Here, the Adjective *importante* in (92a) is interpreted as qualifying an inanimate N (cf. the translation 'the important **thing**'); by contrast, the Adjectives *Welsh/English* in (92b) qualify an empty N which is morphologically plural and intrinsically human in interpretation (cf. the paraphrases *Welsh* **people** and *English* **people**).

If we are right, then each of the four types of constituent which co-head nominals (N, D, Q and A) has a pronominal counterpart, so that we find pronominal N constituents like *one*, pronominal Quantifiers like *each*, pronominal Determiners like *we* and pronominal Adjectives like *English*. It may well be that restricted pronominal Q, D and A constituents are lexical compounds of an (overt or covert) pronominal N ultimate head and a Q, D or A premodifier, and thus have the status of QN, DN and AN constituents.

NOTE

This is a revised version of a paper presented at the Talking Heads Round Table. I am grateful to Bob Borsley, Dick Hudson, the editors and an anonymous reviewer for helpful hints on an even more primitive (pre-neoclassical) version of this chapter.

6 The headedness of noun phrases: slaying the nominal hydra

JOHN PAYNE

6.1 Introduction

How many heads does a noun phrase have?[1] In the traditional generative conception, the answer is simple: the noun phrase has a single head which is a noun. We shall call this the single-head hypothesis. In the single-head hypothesis, other typical noun-phrase constituents (articles, demonstratives, quantifiers, numerals, adjective phrases, adpositional phrases, relative clauses, etc.) are all treated as modifiers of the head noun.

An alternative to the single-head hypothesis which has recently gained in popularity is the idea that the noun phrase contains at least one head, and possibly a multiplicity of heads, in addition to the noun. Each such head, typically but not necessarily a functional category such as a determiner, numeral or quantifier, has its own phrasal projection and takes another noun-phrase constituent as its complement. We shall call this the multi-head hypothesis.

Section 6.2 of this chapter provides a preliminary discussion of the single-head hypothesis (6.2.1) and the multi-head hypothesis (6.2.2). In section 6.3, which is the heart of the chapter, five specific arguments are then presented which lend support to the single-head hypothesis: incorporation (6.3.1), subcategorization (6.3.2), the position of possessor phrases (6.3.3), apposition (6.3.4) and agreement and government (6.3.5). In conclusion, section 6.4 lists the consequential syntactic and morphological properties which focus on the noun as the central constituent of the noun phrase.

6.2 Two hypotheses of noun-phrase structure

In this section, we present an initial comparison of the single-head and multi-head hypotheses.

6.2.1 The single-head hypothesis

In the single-head hypothesis, the noun phrase has a single head which is a noun. With the noun as the unique head, other typical noun-phrase constituents (articles, demonstratives, quantifiers, numerals, adjective phrases, adpositional phrases, relative clauses, etc.) are treated as stacked modifiers, each modifying progressively larger nominal constituents containing the head. Schematically, this conception of the noun phrase can be represented as follows:

(1)

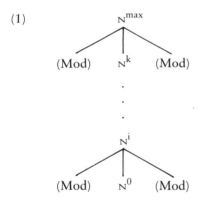

Here N^0 (or N) is the head noun, N^{max} (or NP) is the maximal nominal node representing the whole noun phrase and N^{i-k} are any intermediate nominal nodes. The N^{i-k} may or may not be distinct from N^{max}, N^0 and each other, but $i \geq 0$, $k \geq i$ and $max \geq k$. Modifiers occur either to the left or right, typically in binary trees.

A classic instantiation of this scheme is Jackendoff's three-level analysis of noun phrases within the X-bar framework (Jackendoff, 1977a). PP complements of the head noun (like *of Leslie* in (2)) are daughters of N^1 and sisters of N^0. Restrictive modifiers such as adjective phrases and relative clauses are daughters of a recursive N^2, determiners (such as the definite article) are daughters of N^3 and sisters of N^2, while non-restrictive modifiers are daughters and sisters of N^3:

(2)

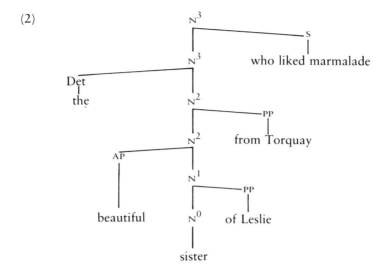

The beautiful sister of Leslie from Torquay, who liked marmalade

Other authors reduce the level of N^{max}, for example to N^2 as in (3) from Gazdar *et al.* (1985: 126):

(3)

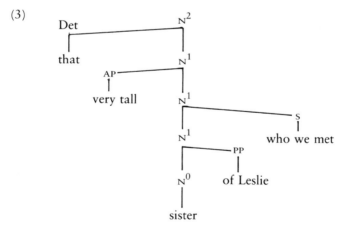

That very tall sister of Leslie who we met

Yet other authors increase it, for example to N^5 as in the Russian example (4) from Babby (1985: 6; 14, footnote 6):

(4)   te   poslednie pjat´ bol'šix butylok vina
        those last   five   big   bottles of-wine

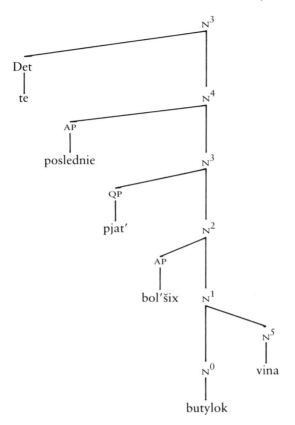

The apparent successes of this type of analysis are largely syntactic: for example, higher-level modifiers are more remote from the head than lower-level modifiers on the same side, and ordering restrictions automatically follow. We have *the very tall sister* rather than **very tall the sister*, and *the sister of Leslie from Torquay* rather than **the sister from Torquay of Leslie* (though in this second case the violation seems to be a lesser one). In the Russian example (4), *poslednij* 'last' is one of a small group of adjectives which can precede numerals and occurs as a modifier at the N^4 level, unlike *bol'šoj* 'big', which is an N^2 modifier.

However, much of the syntax accounted for by the multiplication of levels can be made to follow from semantic principles: for example, in the Montagovian semantics provided for noun phrases by Gazdar *et al.* (1985), an N^0 like *woman* denotes a set of individuals (for example, the set of women). APs like *very tall*, PPs like *from Torquay* and relative clauses like *who we met* ultimately denote functions from sets of individuals to sets of individuals, and can therefore apply to N^0 nodes yielding N^1 nodes. These also denote sets of individuals (for example, the set of very tall women, the set of women from Torquay, the set of women who we met). However, determiners denote functions from sets of individuals to sets of sets of individuals, the general type of N^2. Since adjectives do not take sets of sets of individuals as their arguments, it therefore follows simply from semantic principles that adjectives apply to nouns before determiners do.

Similarly, not all modifiers are interpreted as functions: for example, a relational N^0 like *sister*, just like a nominalized N^0 such as *dislike* or *gift*, is treated by Gazdar *et al.* (1985) as denoting a function which takes the denotation of its complement as argument, yielding an N^1 denotation. For example, the function denoted by *sister* takes the denotation of *of Leslie* as its argument and yields as value the set of sisters of Leslie. This N^1 can then be further modified by prepositional-phrase postmodifiers such as *from Torquay*, giving the order *sister of Leslie from Torquay* rather than *sister from Torquay of Leslie*. In this case, the ordering constraint again follows from the correct application of function to argument: *sister* denotes a function which must combine with an argument before any further modification is possible.

The multiplication of levels permitted by schema (1) therefore seems in some respects like a chimera: much of the work can be done by function–argument structures. More fundamentally, the issue arises as to what correspondence (or lack of it) should exist between the semantic types and the syntactic levels. Different syntactic levels seem in some cases to represent semantic objects of different types (for example, N^2 and N^1 in Gazdar *et al.*, 1985), and in other cases different syntactic levels denote semantic objects of the same type (for example, N^1 and N^0 when N^0 is non-relational). Equally, the same syntactic category can correspond to different semantic types (such as relational and non-relational N^0).

The issue that must be faced by the single-head hypothesis is therefore: what use can be made of the notion that the noun is the head of the noun phrase? Is there any independent justification for the idea that there is a chain of N nodes linking the head and the maximal category, despite the evident partial non-correspondence between these nodes and the semantic types they represent?

6.2.2 *The multi-head hypothesis*

An alternative to the single-head hypothesis is the idea that the noun phrase contains at least one head, and possibly a multiplicity of heads, in addition to the noun. We shall call this the multi-head hypothesis, represented schematically in (5):

(5)

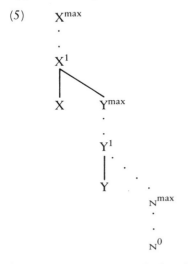

Note that the term *multi-head* as we use it here implies that each head has its own projection.

Typically, the node X^{max} representing the whole noun phrase is taken to be a DP (determiner phrase), giving a version of the multi-head hypothesis known as the DP-hypothesis (Hellan, 1986; Abney, 1987; Szabolcsi, 1987; Löbel, 1989; Olsen, 1989; and so on). In some versions, D(et) is the only head in addition to N, and additional modifiers like quantifier phrases and adjective phrases are attached within NP (for example, Olsen, cited by Löbel, 1989: 142):

(6)

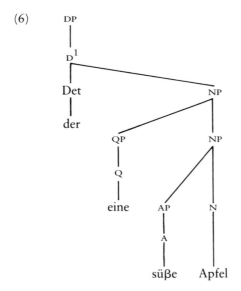

der eine süße   Apfel
the one sweet apple

In other versions, quantifiers and adjectives head their own phrases
(Abney, 1987: 338–9):

(7)

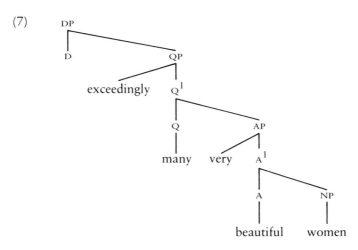

exceedingly many very beautiful women

A claimed analogy with clausal structures leads to the creation of a nominal-agreement node, representing the agreement of a possessed noun with a possessor. DP can then be equated with IP in clauses (Abney, 1987; Horrocks and Stavrou, 1987 (for English)), or treated as parallel with CP (Horrocks and Stavrou, 1987 (for Greek); Szabolcsi, 1987). Szabolcsi's representation of a Hungarian NP with a possessor has DP replaced by CN″, and the nominal equivalent of IP as IN″:

(8)

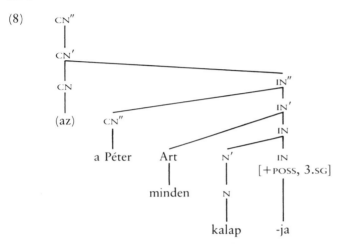

(8)   a   Péter minden kalapja
       the Peter every   hat-his
       'Peter's every hat'

The multi-headed analyses illustrated above are as able to cope with ordering constraints as the single-headed analyses discussed in section 6.2.1. In (7), for example, determiners select QPs as their complements, Qs select APs and As select NPs. The ordering Det–Q–A–N follows straightforwardly. To the extent that complement selection is not involved in the predication of order, multiple levels within a given category can be invoked. In (10), for example, *minden* precedes *kalap* within IN″ because it is attached at a higher level. Evidently, a multi-headed analysis in which every single noun-phrase modifier has its own head and phrasal projection (a 'hydra' like (7)) will rely on complement selection alone for its basic order predictions.

Where the multi-headed analyses seem at first sight to win in principle is in the possibility of providing an isomorphic semantics.

Since DP is a different kind of node from N, there is no reason why the two should represent identical semantic types. Szabolcsi (1987), indeed, provides a fully compositional semantics for the tree in (8), with each node assigned a properly typed interpretation. It should be noted, however, that not every multi-headed analysis has this property. In particular, the assignment of the node AP to the phrase *very beautiful women* in (7) would imply, for isomorphism to hold, a different semantic type for *very beautiful women* and just *women*. Abney, in fact, has to propose a rather unintuitive 'inheritance principle', whereby the AP 'inherits' NP status from its complement.

The semantic status of nodes like QP is also problematic: if Q is taken to include numerals, expressions like *few, many* and *several*, and possibly the indefinite articles *a, some* and zero, then Q has a natural interpretation as a cardinality attribute, that is, a special kind of first-order predicate, rather than as a quantifier in the sense of generalized quantifier theory (Loebner, 1987). Given a semantic theory of plurality such as that of Link (1987), a common noun such as *woman* denotes a set of individuals, a plural proper noun like *women* denotes the set containing all the possible i-sums (individual sums) of the individuals denoted by *woman*, and *seven women* picks out all the i-sums which have seven individuals in them. *Seven women* therefore denotes an object of the same type as the simple plural noun *women*, and the same problem arises with QP in the 'hydra' analyses as with AP. Even classic Ds like definite determiners are perhaps not totally immune to this line of criticism: they simply pick out contextually defined i-sums (Link, 1987: 153).

It is not, therefore, evident that a multi-headed analysis of noun phrases has any fundamental advantage over a single-headed one. Both are capable of handling basic ordering facts, and the apparent semantic advantage of the multi-headed analysis dissolves under closer examination.

6.3 Arguments in favour of the single-head hypothesis

In this section, we turn to five specific arguments which seem to favour the single-head hypothesis.

6.3.1 Incorporation

The analysis of incorporation typically concentrates on the incorporation of nouns into verbs in so-called 'incorporating' languages like Onondaga, Southern Tiwa, Mohawk, Nahuatl, Niuean and many others (for a full survey see Mithun, 1984). Baker (1988) treats noun incorporation formally as a case of head-to-head movement: a head noun moves into a verb which subcategorizes the noun phrase containing the head noun. When the head noun is modified, the modifiers are left behind in their original structural positions.

Compare the unincorporated (9a) and its incorporated counterpart (9b) from Southern Tiwa (Baker, 1988: 94):

(9) a. Wisi seuan-in bi-mū -ban
        two man -PL 1.SG-see -PAST
        'I saw two men'

     b. Wisi bi-seuan -mū -ban
        two 1.SG-man-see -PAST
        'I saw two men'

According to Baker, these have the structures (10a) and (10b) respectively (using English morphs):

(10) a.

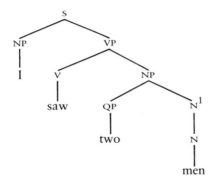

b.

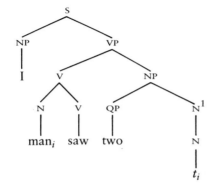

The head noun *seuan* is raised from N and adjoins to V, leaving behind a trace which is antecedent-governed. The antecedent-government condition in this analysis is an important one: it prevents, for example, an incorporation in which the head noun of a subject is lowered into a verb. Structures like (11) are predicted to be universally ill-formed:

(11)

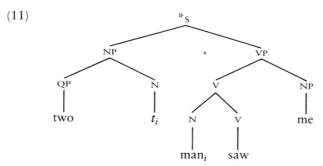

two men saw me

One consequence of Baker's original adoption of the antecedent-government condition is that it will only hold in (10b) as long as the noun is the head of the object noun phrase. In a structure in which the Q element heads its own projection, there will be an intervening QP node which blocks government:

(12)

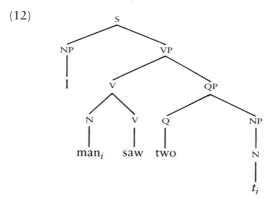

The same consideration would, of course, apply to noun phrases in which DP rather than QP was the highest node, and a determiner rather than a quantifier was stranded.

In a resolution of this inconsistency between the DP hypothesis and the analysis of incorporation, Baker and Hale (1990) propose an extension to Rizzi's (1990) relativized minimality principle, and a division between lexical and functional heads. Determiners, and presumably also quantifiers, are taken to be functional rather than lexical heads. As such, they do not count as potential antecedent governors for a lexical trace such as the trace of N in (12), the incorporated noun can antecedent-govern its trace, and the 'long-distance' incorporation of nouns into verbs is permitted. The functional categories within the noun phrase are in effect rendered invisible as far as incorporation of the lexical head noun is concerned.

Unfortunately, while this distinction between lexical and functional heads within the noun phrase might succeed in making the analysis of noun incorporation into verbs compatible with the DP hypothesis and the antecedent-government condition, it fails to take into account a very restricted set of languages in which incorporation of nominal modifiers into nouns is also permitted. The languages in question are the Paleo-Siberian languages Chukchi and Koryak.

A typical example of adjective incorporation in Chukchi is (13):

(13) a. nə- tur-qine- te   kupre- te
          new   -INST net   -INST
          'with a new net'

      b. tur-kupre- te
          new-net   -INST
          'with a new net'

In the unincorporated (13a), the adjective and the noun are independently case-marked and the adjective root is in addition marked by the circumfix *nə- ... -qine* as a free lexical item. In the incorporated (13b), which is the preferred version with oblique cases (Comrie, 1981: 251), the adjective is incorporated into the noun, losing the circumfix, and the resulting complex is marked by a single case.

Not only adjectives, but other nominal modifiers can be incorporated, including determiners, possessors and quantifiers (including numerals). Examples of determiner and possessive pronoun incorporation from the Palana dialect of Koryak (Žukova, 1980: 77–8) are presented in (14):

(14) a. Yoten- ra   -k
          this   -house- LOC
          'in this house'

      b. Yəmək -ra   -k
          my   -house -LOC
          'in my house'

The pattern of incorporation is essentially the same: the incorporated items in (14) lack independent case endings (although the demonstrative may take such endings in isolation: compare *gutinek* 'in this'). Words are subject to vowel-harmony rules, so in (14a) the 'recessive' high vowels *u* and *i* of the determiner *guttin* change to their 'dominant' low counterparts *o* and *e* under the influence of the dominant *a* of the noun *ra* 'house' (the loss of consonant doubling is also phonological).

An example of numeral incorporation is presented in (15) from Chukchi (Skorik, 1968: 259):

(15)   Ɣa   -ŋəron   -kopra -ma
        COMIT -three   -net   -COMIT
        'with three nets'

The comitative, which is a circumfix, surrounds the noun and the incorporated numeral. The direction of incorporation is particularly clear in this case, since numerals themselves have no case declension. The noun *kupre* 'net', which in isolation has 'recessive' vowels *u* and *e*, changes to *kopra* with 'dominant' vowels *o* and *a* under the influence of the dominant *a* vowels of the comitative circumfix.

Especially fascinating examples of numeral incorporation in Chukchi are provided by those in which the final element of a complex numeral is incorporated into a noun, leaving the rest of the numeral behind (Skorik, 1968: 260):

(16)   a. məngətken ŋireq parol
           ten   two   plus
           'twelve'

        b. məngətken ŋireq parol -kopra-ta
           ten   two   plus -net   -INST
           'with twelve nets'

The element *parol* 'plus' is added to all complex numerals ending in a digit, but is omitted in complex numerals where the final element is a ten or hundred. Vowel harmony shows that *parol-kopra-ta* forms a single word. Such examples of stranding are strikingly similar to those like (9b), in which the head noun is incorporated into the verb, stranding the nominal modifier, and suggest strongly that a unified analysis is necessary for incorporation into verbs and incorporation into nouns.

Now, if a multi-headed analysis is selected for noun phrases in Chukchi, a serious problem arises with the antecedent-government condition. The representation of (14a), for instance, would essentially have to be as in (17):

(17)

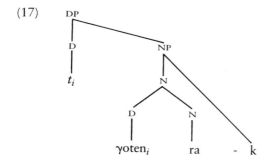

However, the determiner in such an analysis would have to be *lowered* into the noun (and similarly for numeral quantifiers, possessors and adjectives). In this case, the trace is not in a position where it can be governed by its antecedent. Indeed, the trace is in a position where it itself governs its antecedent, surely an inadmissible situation.

Similar considerations apply to possessors, adjectives and quantifiers. On the assumption that the final element in a Chukchi numeral is its head, the representation of (16b) under the multi-head analysis would be essentially as in (18):

(18)

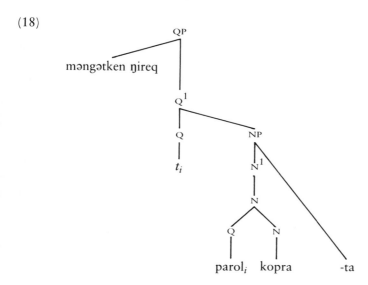

Again, the quantifier head would have to be *lowered* into the noun, into a position where it is governed by its own trace.

The alternative single-head analyses of (14a) and (16b) could be as in (19) and (20):

(19)

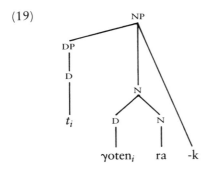

(20)

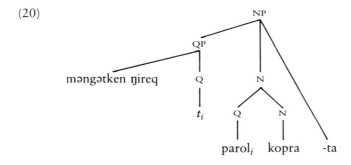

Here, at least, under some version of maximal command, it would be possible to have *parol* governing its trace. In fact, there is evidence that some kind of relaxation of this kind is required in any case for incorporation into verbs in Chukchi, since adjuncts and adverbials are freely incorporable as well as objects.[2] Skorik (1977) comes to the conclusion that verbal modifiers of any kind can be incorporated into verbs, and this is clearly parallel to the general incorporation of modifiers into nouns.

However, it is not even necessary to accept the formal analysis of incorporation in order to appreciate the force of the evidence from Chukchi and Koryak. In these languages, we have incorporation into nouns as well as incorporation into verbs. These two processes seem to be exactly parallel: for example, stranding of non-head constituents is possible in both cases. The obvious generalization is that incorporation is a process which takes (heads of) modifiers and inserts them into heads. A generalization of this kind depends, however, on the idea that the noun is the head of the noun phrase just as the verb is the head of the verb phrase. Determiners, quantifiers, possessors and adjectives must all be modifiers.

6.3.2 Subcategorization

The subcategorization argument against the multi-headed analysis is based on the comparison between the verbal subcategorization of clauses and the verbal subcategorization of noun phrases.

Baltin (1989: 3–5) argues that verbs subcategorize for clauses according to different complementizer types, and this is all the information that is necessary for the lexical entry. For example, a verb like *wonder* subcategorizes for a [+WH] complementizer like *whether* or *if*. Once *whether* has been chosen, both finite and non-finite clauses are possible, but *if* permits only a finite clause:

(21)   a.
        I wonder $\left\{ \begin{array}{c} \text{whether} \\ \\ \text{if} \end{array} \right\}$ hydras ever die

        b.
        I wonder $\left\{ \begin{array}{c} \text{whether} \\ \\ \text{*if} \end{array} \right\}$ to slay a hydra

The crucial point is that the finite versus non-finite distinction depends on the complementizer and not on the verb. There are no verbs in English which require a *whether* complementizer and at the same time block either the finite or non-finite option. It would therefore be reasonable to assume that the complementizer was acting as a head.

Probably, Baltin's argument is too strong. In discussion, Arnold Zwicky pointed out that the English complementizer *that* permits indicative and subjunctive complements, and the choice of indicative versus subjunctive is dependent on the matrix verb rather than the complementizer. For example, *insist* takes *that* followed by a subjunctive verb form, while *know* takes *that* followed by the indicative:

(22)   a. I insist that Hugo play for England
        b. I know that Hugo plays for England

The general case seems to be that verbs certainly subcategorize their complement clauses according to the choice of complementizer, but some aspects of the choice of verb form in the complement clauses may also be dependent on the matrix verb. These facts fit nicely with an analysis in which both complementizer and verb have head status in complement clauses.

By contrast, however, verbs in English do not seem to subcategorize for different determiners or quantifiers. If a verb permits a noun-phrase complement, it permits any noun-phrase complement regardless of its determiner or quantifier. We do not have a set of verbs x which only permit objects beginning with, for example, the quantifier *every*, and another set y which only permit objects beginning with *each*. In this respect, determiners and quantifiers behave no differently from adjectives, which likewise have no effect on verbal subcategorization, and, to extend the comparison to clausal complements, no differently from general verbal modifiers such as adjuncts. The role of determiners and quantifiers within noun phrases seems markedly different from the role of complementizers within complement clauses.

The argument can be extended to include a rather more restricted notion of subcategorization. English verbs subcategorize for different types of clause according to gross category: in a standard GB analysis, for example, verbs subcategorize for CP, IP or 'small clause' complements. In a more surface approach, the choice might be CP or VP. An analogy for noun phrases would be a division of the set of English verbs into those which select DPs, those which select QPs and those which select NPs. This, however, is difficult to imagine: there are no two different verbs x and y such that, for example, x only occurs with noun phrases which contain determiners and y only occurs with noun phrases which contain quantifiers. The simple solution is that verbs subcategorize for NP, PP, CP, VP and so on, but not DP, QP or similar nodes.

6.3.3 The position of possessor phrases

One of the interesting properties of the multi-headed analysis is the prediction that it makes about the possible position of possessor phrases. To take a simple English example, possessors can occur either as complements of N ('*of*-genitives'), or in a higher position in which they appear to be in complementary distribution with determiners ('*s* genitives'). One of the early developments in the multi-headed analysis was, however, the realization that a more appropriate position for the '*s* type of genitive would be the specifier position of DP rather than the D position itself. Abney (1987), for example, first suggests an analysis in which D contains the '*s* of the '*s* genitive (23a), but then suggests that D, by analogy with I, is an empty case assigner assigning '*s* to the noun phrase in specifier position (23b):

(23)   a.

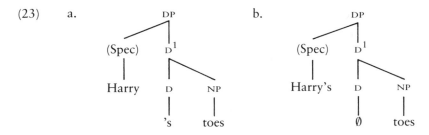

The notion that the possessor might be in the specifier position of DP received immediate support from languages like Greek (Horrocks and Stavrou, 1987) and Hungarian (Szabolcsi, 1987), in which possessors and overt determiners are not in complementary distribution. From this, it is a small step to the suggestion that the two possessor positions might be related by movement. Horrocks and Stavrou (1987), for example, suggest that the possessor in complement position after the noun in Greek can move to specifier of DP by a rule analogous to *wh*-movement:

(24)

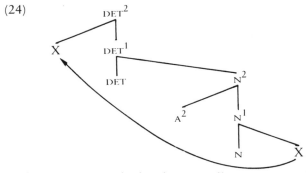

In diagram (24), which schematically represents this movement, the two possessor positions are marked by X, and the direction of movement by an arrow.

Unfortunately, however, although the initial position in the noun phrase and the immediate complement position of the noun are very common positions for possessors, this distribution is by no means universal. A striking alternative is provided by Farsi, which attaches possessors in a fixed position after any adjective phrases and before any prepositional phrases or relative clauses:[3]

(25)   yek doxtar -e   zibā   -ye   jān   az   Abādān
        one daughter -EZAFE beautiful -EZAFE   John from Abadan
        'one beautiful daughter of John from Abadan'

The possessor cannot be treated as the complement of *doxtar*, since it is separated from *doxtar* by a classic adjectival adjunct. Nor can it be treated as a specifier of *yek*, since it is enclosed on the right by a classic PP adjunct. A movement analysis seems implausible, since *doxtar* appears to lack an immediate complement position as such, and no obvious landing site is available. Even if a 'hydra' were assumed with the specifier position of AP as a landing site, it would be difficult to find a mechanism to block the possessor ending up ungrammatically between two adjectival modifiers.

If, on the other hand, possessors are treated as general modifiers of N within the single-head analysis, a range of positions for possessors beyond the two assumed by the multiple-headed analysis becomes available. The analysis of (25) would be essentially as follows (Hoodfar, 1983: 23–41):

(26)

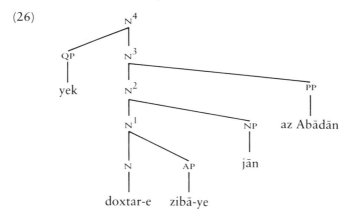

As Hoodfar shows, each of the intermediate nodes N^1, N^2 and N^3 can be justified by different processes of deletion and substitution.

6.3.4 *Apposition*

Lehmann (1982) argues that agreement relations between noun-phrase-internal constituents are triggered by the noun phrase. To the extent that noun-phrase-internal constituents share agreement features such as case, number and gender, they are marked as jointly participating in reference to the same overall referent. In this sense, agreement imparts autonomy to the agreeing constituents, and it is not surprising that in languages which permit constituents to be either marked or unmarked, the marked constituents are the ones which have greater autonomy.

A clear example of this is the case marking of noun-phrase constituents in Walbiri (Hale, 1976, cited by Lehmann, 1982: 263). The unmarked position of modifiers is post-nominal, and a case suffix is attached to the noun phrase as a whole:

(27) **maliki waṛi -ŋki ∅ -tji**   yaḻku-ṇu ŋatju
      dog   big -ERG ASP -OBJ.1.SG bite -PRT me(ABS)
      'The big dog bit me'

Should, however, the elements be permuted around the sentence, a case suffix is attached both to the noun and the adjective:

(28) waṛi -ŋki ∅ -tji   yaḻku-ṇu **maliki -ḻi**
      big -ERG ASP -OBJ.1.SG bite -PRT dog   -ERG
      'The big dog bit me'

The language we shall concentrate on in this section, Dama or Nama (Hottentot),[4] exhibits a similar phenomenon, but the permutation of elements is restricted to within the overall noun phrase. It therefore represents an intermediate stage between the rather free word order of noun-phrase constituents permitted by Walbiri and the rather fixed order of noun-phrase constituents found in languages like English, which have little noun-phrase-internal agreement marking. The permutation of noun-phrase constituents pivots around the noun, which may therefore be said to have a special status within the noun phrase.

All noun phrases in Dama end with a person, number and gender marker. Nominal modifiers which precede the noun occur in a fixed order, and a single person, number and gender marker is postposed to the whole noun phrase:

(29) [horaga ne !nona ≠ kini]-di
      all   this three book -3.FEM.PL
      'all these three books'

Example (30) shows the possessor construction. The possessor noun phrase *!Gombate* has its own independent marker *-s* (third person feminine singular) and is followed by the possessive postposition *di*. Otherwise, the principles which underlie the noun phrase in (30) are the same as in (29). The order of constituents within the noun phrase is fixed, and there is a single person, number and gender marker postposed to the whole noun phrase:

(3) [[!Gombate]-s   di !nona ≠ kini]-di
     !Gombate -3.FEM.SG of three   book-3.FEM.PL
     '!Gombate's three books'

Any of the individual constituents in (29) and (30) can act as a noun phrase in its own right if suffixed by the appropriate marker:

(31)   a. [[!Gombate]-s   di]-di
           !Gombate   -3.FEM.SG of -3.FEM.PL
           'ones of !Gombate'

        b. [!nona]-di
           three   -3.FEM.PL
           'three'

        c. [≠ kini]-di
           book   -3.FEM.PL
           'books'

The most important point, however, is that a noun phrase can also be constructed out of a sequence of such constituents each bearing its own person, number and gender marker. In this type of noun-phrase construction, the first constituent consists of the noun and any fixed-order, unmarked premodifiers, and is postposed by the appropriate person, number and gender marker. The subsequent constituents each have their own independent person, number and gender markers, and their relative order is free:

(32)   a. [ne !nona ≠ kini]-di   [!Gombate-s   di]-di
           this three book   -3.FEM.PL !Gombate -3.FEM.SG of -3.FEM.PL
           'these three books, the ones of !Gombate'

        b. [≠ kini]-di   [ne !nona]-di   [!Gombate-s   di]-di
           book   -3.FEM.PL this three -3.FEM.PL !Gombate -3.FEM.SG of -3.FEM.PL
           'the books, these three, the ones of !Gombate'

The separate individual constituents in (32a) and (32b) look like independent noun phrases in apposition. However, case markers are obligatorily suffixed only to the end of the whole global noun phrase, rather than to each individual subconstituent. This shows that the entire construction is a single noun phrase.

The conclusion to be drawn from this set of examples is that Universal Grammar must permit the existence of noun phrases constructed on an appositional pattern as well as the strict hierarchial pattern of English or the free scrambling pattern permitted in languages like Walbiri. In the appositional construction of noun phrases illustrated above, the noun is clearly the pivotal element. If we take the noun to be the head of the construction, we can say that modifiers which precede the head are fixed in order and do not have the person, number and gender marking of the whole noun phrase. All post-head constituents must be appositional, are permutable amongst themselves and each carries its own person, number and gender marker. No such generalizations are statable if the determiner *ne* or the quantifier *!nona* is taken to be the head.

6.3.5 *Agreement and government*

In the most simple case, noun-phrase-internal agreement involves the marking of shared features such as gender, number, case and definiteness on noun-phrase constituents. Virtually any feature can be marked on any constituent or combination of constituents (see Lehmann, 1982, for a survey), so it is not obvious how the head of the noun phrase might be identified on a 'morphosyntactic locus' basis (see Zwicky, 1985; and Hudson, 1987, for a discussion of this criterion for headedness across a number of constructions). However, cases of non-agreement such as that presented by Corbett (this volume) do raise some very important issues.

The problem arises from elements like numerals in Russian which in certain cases cause expected agreement features (those that would otherwise percolate from the maximal noun-phrase node) to be overridden. A relatively simple case is provided by numerals ending in 5–9, 10–20, 30, 40 etc. Such numerals cause an expected nominative or accusative case to be overridden by the genitive on the noun and lower adjectival or participial modifiers, while plural number is maintained:

(33)   a. te   poslednie bol′šie   butylki
          that (NOM.PL) last (NOM.PL) big (NOM.PL) bottle (NOM.PL)
          'those last big bottles'

       b. te   poslednie pjat′   bol′šix   butylok
          that (NOM.PL) last (NOM.PL) five (NOM) big (GEN.PL) bottle (GEN.PL)
          'those last five big bottles'

Equally, numerals 21, 31, 41 etc. cause plural number to be replaced by singular, and numbers ending in 2, 3 and 4 create a complicated situation in which the noun appears in a form which in most cases is identical to the genitive singular, but sometimes genitive plural (adjectival nouns like *rabočij* 'worker') and very rarely in an old dual form which occurs nowhere else (nouns like *šag* 'step'), while the adjective and participle are nominative or genitive plural (with some determining factors).

Such complications after numerals are by no means unusual: they occur throughout Slavonic and Uralic, for example. Equally, not only numerals are responsible for shifts in expected agreement patterns. Determiners in German cause similar problems, giving rise to the so-called strong and weak declensions. For example, the determiner *der* in *der süße Apfel* 'the sweet apple' causes the adjective *süß* to assume a case form which it would not otherwise take, the weak inflection *-e* rather than the strong nominative inflection *-er* as in *ein süßer Apfel* 'one sweet apple'.

These relations seem at first sight to follow quite naturally from a multi-headed analysis in which the numeral or determiner is a head, governing the form of its complement. However, the relationship is not always completely one-sided: inherent features of the noun like gender can reciprocally determine the form of the numeral or the determiner. For example, the Russian numeral 'two' has two gender forms, *dva* (masculine and neuter) and *dve* (feminine):

(34)   a. dva   magazina
             two (NOM.MASC) shop (GEN.SG.MASC)
             'two shops'

          b. dve   knigi
             two (NOM.FEM) book (GEN.SG.FEM)
             'two books'

As far as gender is concerned, the relationship here looks like a typical case of the 'agreement' of a noun-phrase-internal modifier with its head noun.

Equally, the typical relation between numeral and noun seems very different from the government relation imposed by classic governors such as verbs and nouns. Nouns which govern the case or form of their complements do not suddenly fail to do so when put into a different, usually oblique case, yet this is a typical behaviour for a numeral.[5] To take Russian as an example, if the noun phrases in (33) are put into an oblique case such as the instrumental, genitive, dative or prepositional, we obtain the following pattern:

(35)   a. temi   poslednimi bol'šimi   butylkami
             that (INST.PL) last (INST.PL) big (INST.PL) bottle (INST.PL)
             'with those last big bottles'

          b. temi   poslednimi pjat'ju   bol'šimi   butylkami
             that (INST.PL) last (INST.PL) five (INST) big (INST.PL) bottle (INST.PL)
             'with those last five big bottles'

In (35b), the numeral 'five' ceases to 'govern' the genitive case, and the noun and adjective take the instrumental case of the whole noun phrase. When the numeral 'five' itself is genitive, the noun and adjective are genitive plural.

Cann (this volume: 44–5) attempts a formal definition of the difference between form government and agreement (concord):

(36)   a. *Form governor*: X is a governor in X+Y if there is some group of inflectional variants, $x_1, ..., x_n$ in X that all induce the same proper binary partition on the expression-forms of Y according to their morphological form.

        b. *Concord controller*: X is a concord controller in X+Y if there is some group of inflectional variants, $x_1, ..., x_n$ in X which induce different binary partitions on expression-forms of Y according to their morphological form.

Cann's definition of form governor clearly captures the classic case in which a noun X, no matter what its own inflectional form is, governs the same case of its complement Y. Equally, the definition of concord controller captures the classic case in which a noun X controls the various agreement forms of a modifying adjective Y.

What, then, is the relationship between a Russian numeral and its noun? It is interesting to note that under Cann's definition this relationship is not one of form government, since the inflectional variants of the numeral do not all induce the *same* binary partition on expression-forms of the following noun: the noun is typically genitive if the numeral is nominative, accusative or genitive, and instrumental if the numeral is instrumental. Might the relationship instead be one of concord? In terms of gender, the answer is clearly positive. In terms of case, although it might at first sight seem strange, Cann's definition of concord controller seems closer to the facts than his definition of form governor: nothing in the definition of concord controller requires that the binary partition induced by the controlling noun be the 'obvious' one. An instrumental noun as in (35b) co-occurs with an instrumental numeral, whereas a genitive noun as in (33b) co-occurs with a nominative numeral. Of course, a genitive noun can also co-occur with an accusative or genitive numeral, but the partition induced is still a binary one: genitive nouns do not co-occur with instrumental, dative or prepositional numerals, and they do co-occur with nominative, accusative and genitive numerals.

The result of this discussion is that the typical relationship between a numeral (or determiner) and its noun is not obviously one of government, and may instead be more akin to a relationship of agreement. The idea of a relationship of agreement fits well with the single-head analysis of noun phrases in which the noun, as head, is the controller of agreement.

By contrast, the multi-head analysis provides a structure which is more compatible with form government. Indeed, if a noun phrase consisted of many heads, each of these heads might be expected in principle to be form governor. For example, we could hypothesize a language similar to Russian, but in which the determiner changed the expected case of the numeral, the numeral changed the expected case of the adjective, and the adjective changed the expected case of the noun. This is not what happens: at most one constituent seems to be able to act in this way in any given noun phrase. The more 'hydra-like' the structure, the more unexpected this observation becomes.

We could, of course, allow for this single constituent to be selected as the one extra head in addition to the noun when it triggered 'form government'; but this would lead to essentially identical syntactic structures in the same language being assigned one or two heads – hardly a happy conclusion. Perhaps the hydra should rather be slain.

6.4 Conclusion

In section 6.2 of this chapter, we attempted to demonstrate that with respect to some basic properties (basic word-order predictions, semantic plausibility), the multi-head hypothesis of noun-phrase structure has no significant advantages over the single-head hypothesis. However, in section 6.3, a number of specific syntactic and morphological arguments were presented which seem to point towards the superiority of the single-head hypothesis. The consequence is a model of the noun phrase in which the noun is the unique head, and determiners, numerals, adjectives and possessor phrases are all modifiers of that head.

Particular properties of the head noun which emerge are:

1 The noun is the category into which incorporation is possible (like the verb in verb phrases).

2 The noun is the category whose maximal projection determines verbal subcategorization (as opposed to the determiner, which does not).

3 The noun is the category which acts as the structural pivot in appositional noun phrases.

4 The noun is the category which acts as controller of agreement (concord) in noun phrases.

Of course, within the limited scope of this chapter, we have not been able to address all of the issues concerned with a comparison of the single-head and multi-head hypotheses. The intention has simply been to demonstrate that, despite the current popularity of multi-head analyses, the single-head analysis has many positive attributes.

NOTES

1. I keep *noun phrase* as a neutral term which does not prejudge the issue of headedness. Symbols like NP, on the other hand, have theoretical status. I am grateful to the participants in the Talking Heads Round Table, and also to members of the Linguistics Program, University of Florida, Gainesville, for their reactions to earlier versions of this chapter. The views expressed are, of course, solely my own.
2. The problems for Baker's analysis of incorporation raised by the incorporation of adjuncts and adverbials in Chukchi were first raised by Andy Spencer in a lecture to the Linguistics Association of Great Britain, UMIST, September 1989. We see no reason, however, for accepting Spencer's conclusion that incorporation in Chukchi must be lexical compounding.
3. Ezafe in example (25) is an obligatory construction marker which precedes all adjective and noun modifiers in Persian noun phrases.
4. The Dama examples in this section are based on work with an informant. For a published account of the very closely related Nama see Hagman (1974).
5. A notable exception seems to be provided by the prescriptive rules of standard Arabic, which require numerals 3–10 to be followed invariably by the genitive plural, 11–99 to be followed invariably by the accusative singular and hundreds and thousands to be followed by the genitive singular. However, since these rules deviate from those in the dialects, they are frequently not applied correctly (see Fischer and Jastrow, 1977: 385).

7 Head- versus dependent-marking: the case of the clause

NIGEL VINCENT

7.1 Introduction

In this chapter[1] I wish to consider the implications of juxtaposing three strands of recent syntactic research that have tended to remain independent of each other. Although there are undeniably differences of emphasis and occasionally of principle, it is part of the contention of this chapter (a) that there is much to be gained from an attempt to bring them together, and (b) that there is less of real substance keeping them apart than is perhaps sometimes thought. The approaches in question are:

1 The line of typological research inaugurated by Nichols (1986), in particular her fundamental distinction between head-marking and dependent-marking languages.

2 The focus in the recent generative literature on the properties of functional categories and their projections (Chomsky, 1986a; Abney, 1987; Speas, 1990 and a whole host of other references).

3 The study of the processes of grammaticalization as a mechanism of syntactic change (Heine, Claudi and Hünnemeyer, 1991; Heine and Traugott, 1991; Hopper and Traugott, forthcoming).

I will begin with a brief characterization of each.

7.2 Head-marking versus dependent-marking

This typology assumes a theory-independent and cross-linguistic agreement as to which is the head and which the dependent in any given syntactic construction, and then classifies languages according to whether the head–dependent relation is marked on the head or the dependent. Thus, compare the following:

(1)   Maltese bin   Alla
              son of God
(2)   Latin   filius Dei
              son of God

The Maltese[2] noun *iben* 'son' has a special form *bin*, the so-called construct state, which is required when it has a nominal dependent. The dependent nominal *Alla* 'God' occurs in the same form as it would if it were an independent element. The marking of the possessive construction appears on the possessum, here regarded universally as the head, and the construction is therefore head-marked (HM). Conversely, in Latin it is the dependent *Dei* which signals its function by its changed form, being in the genitive case, and thus Latin is here dependent-marking (DM). Nichols (1986) demonstrates how, when languages are approached in the light of this distinction, they exhibit a clear tendency to fall consistently into one or other type across a wide range of constructions. A language which has a head-marked possessive construction, for example, can also be expected to show head-marking of other adnominal elements, in adpositional phrases and in clausal relations. She then goes on to explore some structural and diachronic implications of her typology, a number of which we shall return to below.

Beside the examples in (1) and (2) we may compare the Italian or English constructions in (3):

(3)   Italian   figlio di Dio
              son   of God

In such instances there is a separate element, the preposition *di* or *of*, whose function seems to be to mark the dependency. Nichols explicitly leaves such situations out of account, commenting: 'Languages of the isolating type will be left out of the discussion tirely – although their "grammatical words", "function words", "empty words", etc. presumably also exhibit head-marking and dependent-marking tendencies' (1986: 59).[3] By contrast, the grammar of functional categories has become central to recent debates within Government–Binding (GB) theory. Such developments can be expected to yield dividends when we come to consider the extension of Nichols' typology into the grammar of 'isolating' languages.

7.3 Functional categories

One of the principal motivations for the development of X-bar theory was to permit the expression of generalizations about the types of configurational structure that can be projected from a given category. In particular, there is an X′ level which comprises the category X plus its complements and an X″ level which comprises the X′ and a specifier. Chomsky (1986a), in a famously brief passage (compare Lightfoot, 1990), proposes the extension of this system to include not only lexical (N, V, A, P) but also functional (COMP, INFL) categories. Since then there has been a veritable explosion of such functional projections. (Abney, 1987 for DP; Rivero, 1988 for ASPP; Chomsky, 1989 for FP; Laughren, 1989 for KP; Pollock, 1989 for TP, AGRP, NEGP; etc.[4]) What these all have in common is that function words such as complementizers, auxiliaries and determiners now head their own projections and take maximal projections of lexical categories as complements, instead of, as before, being the fillers of ancillary slots within lexical projections.

7.3.1 Functional categories and the HM/DM distinction

This new view of the syntax of functional categories greatly complicates – though we will argue below that it at the same time adds considerable interest to – the task of seeking to relate Nichols' dichotomy to the generative tradition of phrase-structure building. On the old view, where NP = [DET N], and assuming that possessors are a kind of DET, it was a straightforward matter to express the head/dependent-marking distinction exemplified in (1) and (2) in tree form, if so desired. This sort of automatic transfer from one theory to another is clearly what underlies Nichols' (1986: 57) remark that 'Linguists of divergent theoretical persuasions are in almost complete agreement as to what is the head and what is the non-head in a given construction.' Compare now one possible structure imposed within the DP hypothesis for a genitive construction in English (see Stowell, 1989, for good discussion and Radford (this volume) for an analysis that adopts the structure in (4)):

(4)

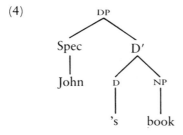

Here what Nichols would consider the dependent-marking *'s* is the head of its own projection. There is a consequent need to re-assess the applicability of the HM/DM distinction to elaborated syntactic structure of the kind in (4). Note in passing that an alternative version of DP might be (5a), with a null D and *'s* inserted as a case assigned by D, just as I assigns (nominative) Case to the subject in (5b).

(5) a.   b.

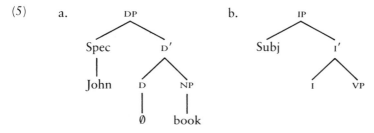

Both (4) and (5a) change the status of an English possessor construction from the point of view of the HM/DM distinction. In (4), the element *'s* is the head. Moreover, on the version of this analysis argued for by Radford (this volume), the specifier agrees with the head, just as with subject–verb agreement. This latter phenomenon is explicitly recognized by Nichols as a kind of HM. Example (5a), by contrast, involves DM, though the possessor is now Spec of DP rather than Spec of NP. Under both (4) and (5a), a construct state would come out as a kind of dependent marking, since the possessum, which is now treated as an argument of the possessor, bears the phonological reflex of the syntactic construction (for a DP-inspired analysis of the Hebrew construct state, see Ritter, 1988).

 We will not proceed further with this line of argument for the present, but three lessons can already be drawn.

1 The extension of X-bar theory has considerably widened the gap between current phrase-structure theory and the traditional assumptions of dependency that had been built into early theories of category projection. At the same time, the extra layers of syntactic structure have increased the range of analyses in principle possible for any given set of data. Any attempt at comparing and reconciling Nichols' work and the generative tradition is thereby made both more complicated and, we shall argue, more feasible.

2 The comfortable assumptions about head versus dependency which underpin Nichols' generalizations are rudely disturbed. We

cannot establish heads and dependents by simple inspection but need to resort to more detailed, complex, often language-internal and sometimes theory-internal, argumentation.[5]

3 We need to be clear about the criteria involved in deciding cases of headhood, since it is evident that Nichols' typology could, so to speak, be stood on its head if we were to adopt a different set of decisions as to what constitutes the head of any given construction. Conversely, of course, Nichols' impressive results may be taken as a strong argument in favour of the traditional values and may help us to decide in cases – such as the relation between complementizer and the accompanying clause – where traditional grammar is not clear. One suggestive possibility is to decompose the traditional and intuitive notion of head into a number of further, more primitive notions. This is the approach argued for by Zwicky in this volume, who distinguishes three separate concepts: Head (versus Dependent), Functor (versus Functee), Base (versus Specifier). In the clear cases, such as the verb in a verb–object dyad, the traditional 'head' is also functor and base. Zwicky argues that the controversial cases are so precisely because these logically distinct properties do not converge and different analysts have chosen to give priority to one rather than the other. Nichols' generalizations will still stand, therefore, but not necessarily for the subproperty that Zwicky names Head. In fact, as far as I can see, Nichols' (1986: 57) intuitive concept of head corresponds most closely to Zwicky's Base. However, the proper working out of these issues will have to wait for another occasion.

The 'grammatical words' which have figured so prominently in recent generative work have also been the subject of intensive and original investigation, albeit from a very different direction and usually with very different methodological and metaphysical predilections, by scholars interested in the process of syntactic change known as 'grammaticalization', which we will now briefly consider.

7.4 Grammaticalization

The classic definition of this phenomenon is due to Meillet (1912: 131): 'L'attribution d'un caractère grammatical à un mot jadis autonome.' Examples are legion: the evolution of the Latin noun *casa* 'house' into the French preposition *chez*; the shift of the English *do* from full verb to causative to carrier of tense and negation; the etymological source of the Gulf Arabic conjunction *yoom* 'when' in a noun meaning 'day'; and so on. One of the concerns of recent work has been to show how there are recurrent cross-linguistic patterns whereby grammatical markers of a certain type are frequently found to have semantically similar sources. Thus, future auxiliaries often derive from verbs of motion: compare English *be going to*, French *aller*, Lango *bino* 'come' and 'future'; Lotuko (Eastern Nilotic) uses both *tuna* 'come' and *leten* 'go' as future auxiliaries. Similar studies have been carried out on the origin of conditional markers, complementizers, a variety of tense and aspect markers, articles and so on. (Heine and Traugott, 1991, provide a number of further studies over a range of families, and Hopper and Traugott, forthcoming, give a valuable synthesis.) There thus appear to be natural paths of syntactico-semantic development akin to the recurring dimensions of phonetic change first classified by historical linguists in the last century.

These paths of grammaticalization are often convergent. That is to say, one type of grammatical marker can be shown to come from a number of different sources. Thus, future markers – in addition to deriving from motion verbs – are also commonly descended from verbs of volition (English *will*, Rumanian *voi* < Latin *velle* 'to wish', Greek *tha* < *thelo hina* 'I want so as to...', Swahili *-ta* < *taka* 'want') and from expressions of obligation (French *-ai* < Latin *habere* 'have (to)', Sardinian *devere* 'future' < Latin *debere* 'must') (Fleischman, 1983; Bybee and Pagliuca, 1985).

In addition to raising the question of the semantic routes by which 'grammatical' or 'function' words arise, work on grammaticalization has made us aware of one significant fact, though it is not one that is generally stated explicitly, namely:

(6)   Function words are always etymologically derived from lexical words.

An appropriate name for (6) might be Gabelentz's Law, since a virtually identical assertion is to be found in the writings of the nineteenth-century German scholar: 'Alle Afformativen waren ursprünglich selbständige Wörten' (1891: 250–1, cited in Heine and Reh, 1984: 68). At first sight (6) might seem to state the obvious: what else, after all, could function words derive from? The point is that function words do not continue as such over long stretches of time. Rather, they represent intermediate stages in a historical evolution from independent lexical items to morphologically bound affixes and ultimately inclusion as part of the opaque make-up of an arbitrary linguistic sign.[6]

Let us now consider the generalization in (6) in relation to the two approaches we have so far discussed.

7.4.1 HM/DM and grammaticalization

As far as the HM/DM distinction is concerned, the problem is to determine the way in which changes of category may impinge upon the typological classification of the language or construction in question. Consider the case of complementizers which derive from verbs of saying (Lord, 1976). At the ungrammaticalized stage we will have:

(7)   [VERB + SENTENCE]$_{VP}$

The whole will be a VP, of which – by common consent – the V is the head. If the verb becomes a complementizer, and if one believes in CPs, then it is reasonable to suppose that the VP becomes a CP. Grammaticalization has taken place and has changed the category of the construction but has not altered its head–dependent structure. If, on the other hand, a CP is thought of as being a kind of sentence (as the old S-bar notation implied), then grammaticalization would involve loss of head status, and might have different consequences for the typological classification of the language. Similar considerations arise when a lexical preposition such as Latin *de* 'down from, concerning' develops into a grammatical, case-assigning preposition such as French *de*, Italian *di*, etc.

7.4.2 Functional categories and grammaticalization

From the GB perspective the problem is to decide on the proper characterization of languages without overt functional categories: for example, Japanese and Russian with no articles, Latin with no articles, few auxiliaries and very limited use of complementizers. As long as X-bar theory was based solely on the properties [±N, ±V] there was not really a problem of general applicability, since it is reasonable to take the noun/verb split to be universal (Schachter, 1985). One solution, of course, is to maintain the universalist position by postulating empty Cs and Ds, but to many this will seem unduly procrustean. Alternatively, the applicability of the concept head will have to be relativized to language type: some languages will have a functional head system and some will not, and even for those which do have functional heads, the details of the system may vary from language to language (on this point compare Iatridou, 1990). This latter conclusion is defended in Fukui and Speas (1986), for example, where it is argued that Japanese does not have functional projections. Vincent (1989) made a similar suggestion for Latin, thus seeing the historical evolution of COMP, DET and INFL items in Romance as a linked set of changes due to the emergence of a functional head system. The PF-Licensing Principle (PFLP) discussed by Cann (this volume) represents a step towards a version of GB in which there is an explicit criterion which predicts when functional categories may be recognized by a grammar. Changes of the kind documented under the rubric of grammaticalization may then be thought of as proceeding down to a point when the distribution of the relevant item is such as to permit recognition by the PFLP. Functional projections will then be induced with attendant re-organization of the structural possibilities of the language.

7.4.3 *The status of morphological elements*

Another issue of importance which emerges via the study of grammaticalization is the status of morphological elements. A common subsequent stage in grammatical evolution is from independent function word to bound morpheme: for example, the French future markers *-ai*, *-as*, *-a*, which derive from Latin *habeo, habes, habet* (compare French *j'ai, tu as, il a*). A normal intervening stage here would involve cliticization. If headhood can be retained even after grammaticalization, as we hinted in the case of VP > CP, can it be retained even after morphologization? Put another way, can a morpheme be the head of a construction? On this issue constituency and dependency grammarians seem for the most part to be diametrically opposed. Hudson is quite explicit, within his Word Grammar, about denying syntactic statements access to the internal structure of the word. Within the generative tradition, by contrast, morphemes are standardly taken to be the heads of words (Scalise, 1988, gives a review of this point), though views vary as to the accessibility of these items to grammatical process (see Speas, 1990: 240–7, for some discussion – henceforth we will follow Speas in referring to the view that morphemes are not accessible to syntax as the Lexical Integrity Hypothesis (LIH)). Indeed, in most current variants of GB, affixes may even project like full categories (see Cann, this volume). For Nichols, morphemes are largely treated as markers of the head–dependent relation rather than as members of it, so the question does not directly arise. Commonly noted (though still putative) equivalences such as that between adpositions and case markers (or less commonly between case markers and complementizers – compare Simpson, 1988) suggest that these issues may be more complex than a simple yes or no, and that the historical perspective may add an important, though largely overlooked, dimension to the question.

So far in this chapter I have sought to set out positions and identify issues. In what follows I will focus on one particular question, namely that of clausal marking, and try to show how the three approaches I have identified can be, if not totally reconciled, at least brought together to contribute to a broader understanding of the problem. The data will be mostly from Latin, a DM language with very little in the way of (overt) functional categories; Italian, a DM language with a well-developed system of functional projections, and Maltese, a language tending towards HM and with some functional structure. I will also cast the occasional sideways glance at a number of Australian languages, drawing on data discussed by the contributors to Austin (1988) and on the treatment of the HM Amerindian language Lakhota outlined in Van Valin (1985).

7.5 Complementizers and the DM/HM dichotomy

Generative grammar and the HM/DM distinction offer a useful complementarity of perspectives from which to examine the structure of the clause, and in particular the nature and role of the complementizer within the clause. In dependency terms, a verb and its sentential argument constitute a head–modifier dyad just as a verb and a nominal argument do. And indeed in some languages, the marking is identical in that the verb of the sentential argument may bear a case suffix directly (see Dench and Evans, 1988; Evans, 1988; Simpson, 1988). We will return to the complementizing function of nominal case in section 7.7 below. More commonly, though, the sentential argument is preceded or followed by an item whose principal function is to mark the clause as embedded, a so-called complementizer. It is easy to show by standard tests (Bresnan, 1974) that the complementizer forms a constituent with its clause. From this it follows that an example such as (8) exhibits dependent-marking (H = head, D = dependent, M = marking):

(8)   Fred [^{H}believes ^{D}[^{M}that [the earth is flat]]]

Indeed, as Nichols notes, 'canonical subordination is a consequence of the choice of dependent-marking strategies' (1986: 64).

Whereas the HM/DM approach naturally asks about the role of the complementizer *vis-à-vis* the verb (or adjective, noun or preposition) which is its governor, the generative tradition has been more concerned about its status within the clause to which it is attached, and has recently espoused the view that it is the head of its own dependency dyad,[7] viz (where IP = the old S: see below):

(9)   [C IP] $_{CP}$

Synthesizing the two approaches is not difficult: C is the head of its own dyad but at the same time is the marker of the dependency of that dyad on an external head. In other words, Nichols' approach requires three primitives – Head, Dependent and Marking – and the same item or morpheme may fulfil more than one of these roles.[8] However, this situation does not arise in Nichols' original paper, as we have noted, for two accidental reasons: she assumed a version of what we called above the Lexical Integrity Hypothesis; and second, she more or less arbitrarily excluded function words from her initial consideration. Yet, neither of these restrictions is crucial. The LIH has various forms, one of which – argued by Speas (1990) – is that it holds for derivation but not for inflection. Nichols' position is perfectly consistent with such a variant. The extension of the HM/DM typology to function words is an empirical matter, and one which the present chapter attempts to begin to address.

7.6 Predictions of CP within a HM/DM approach

It is one thing to show that the HM/DM approach and that of generative grammar can be reconciled. The more interesting question is whether there is anything to be gained by such a move. I will argue that there are indeed positive consequences here and that the gain is reciprocal. Let us consider things from the HM/DM perspective first. Once Nichols has established the existence of the HM/DM opposition she goes on to extract a number of generalizations. One is that HM languages seem to preponderate among the languages of the world,[9] and that this is – or ought to be – unwelcome news to the GB model, which in its insistence on notions such as government and Case (with a capital C!) appears to perpetuate traditional assumptions about the naturalness of DM. This criticism will be to some degree defused if we can show that some aspects of GB provide a framework within which Nichols' generalizations can find more detailed articulation.

A second point is that, within this general preference for HM, there are types of construction which are preferentially HM or DM. In particular, she notes (1986: 75–6), on the one hand, that the grammar of the clause inherently favours head-marking and, on the other, that embedded sentences tend to be dependent-marked. Sentential complementation is of interest not least because it falls at the point of convergence of these two claims. If, as seems natural, we treat a sentential complement as an argument, then we might expect it to be marked preferentially on the governing verb. However, the mere fact of its being sentential would lead us to anticipate dependent-marking. I have not yet done extensive cross-linguistic testing, but my impression from reading grammatical descriptions is that the sentential property wins out (unless the complement involves a nominalized verb form – see section 7.7). This is most obviously revealed in the widespread occurrence of complementizers in languages which are otherwise strongly HM (compare, for example, the discussion of Lakhota in Van Valin 1985).[10]

If the grammar of the clause is inherently likely to be HM, then the view that C is head of CP makes a number of further properties fall neatly into place. What Nichols means by clause is the combination of a verb and its arguments. Since the CP is a larger unit of a generally clausal type, we might also expect it to show HM effects, as indeed it does. The following is a preliminary list of some complementizer-related phenomena which can be argued to fall under the rubric of HM.

7.6.1 The finiteness of the complement clause

The distinction between finite and non-finite clauses is a type of DM effect: the form of the clause signals its dependency on a controlling verb. The location of the marker of finiteness may, on the other hand, be taken as a diagnostic of the head. Classically, of course, finiteness is identified on the verb form, but it is also indexed on the complementizer in a number of instances. Thus, English *that* is always accompanied by a finite verb. The finiteness of the clause is signalled both on the verb and in the choice of complementizer, a type of double marking. In some languages the choice is not between an element and zero; rather, finite and non-finite verbs have their own distinct complementizers, as in the Romance languages. These all have a descendant of Latin *quid/quod/quia* as the basic complementizer for finite clauses and a prepositional item – for example, Italian *a* or *di* – with non-finite clauses. Thus:

(10)   Italian
    a. dice   che non hai   capito
       he says COMP NEG you-have understood
       'He says you have not understood'

    b. dice   di   non aver   capito
       he says COMP NEG have-INF understood
       'He says that he has not understood'

Contrast this with the behaviour of the Swedish element *att*, which introduces both finite and non-finite clauses so that the marking rests entirely on the V (or I) position (Börjars, 1987). Conversely, in Maltese the verb form never changes but whether we have the equivalent of finite or non-finite in other languages depends on the presence of the complementizer. Thus:

(11)   Maltese
    a. ix-xhud   qal li   kienet ix-xita
       the-witness said COMP was   the-rain
       'The witness said it was raining'

    b. beda   jimxi
       he-began he-walks
       'He began to walk'

Example (11a) would be ungrammatical without the complementizer *li*, and (11b) would be ungrammatical with it. The verb form *jimxi* 'he walks' is the same as would be used in an independent main clause.

    All the foregoing examples attest to the fact that finiteness may be marked at the C position, on the main verb (or in I position), or by some combination of the two.

7.6.2 Mood

Closely related to finiteness is mood, and again when it shows up in the form of a separate set of verb inflections as in the subjunctives of many Indo-European languages, it appears to be a clear DM phenomenon (Nichols 1986: 64). There are, however, instances where the complementizer may also vary according to the mood. Calabrese (1992; forthcoming) discusses one such case in the dialects of the Salentino area of southern Italy. These dialects – probably under Greek influence – have lost many of the uses of the Latin infinitive that survive, and indeed are extended, elsewhere in the Romance area. Instead, they have a distinction between two complementizers:

ku < Latin *quod* and *ka* < Latin *quia*. Calabrese sums up the distribution as follows:

ka behaves like the complementizers *che* of Italian or *that* of English...*ku* is used to introduce the clausal complement of a verb that requires this clausal complement to be infinitival in a language like Italian if its subject is understood to be identical to an argument of the main clause, and ...*ku* introduces the clauses which, in a language like Italian, typically require the subjunctive mood if their subject is not identical to an argument of the matrix.

What in other dialects involves an alternation at V or I here involves a choice at C, as would be expected if C is itself both a head and a marker of dependency.

7.6.3 Polarity

Another property that is commonly marked on the complementizer is negation. Two possibilities exist: (a) a special negative complementizer; or (b) a negative element incorporated into the complementizer position. A residue of the latter is to be found in the etymology of English *than* from *that+not*. Interestingly, for the same function of marking a comparative clause other varieties of English use *nor*. Contrast this with the situation in a number of Romance languages where comparatives have the same complementizer as in other types of embedding, but where there is sentence-internal pleonastic negation:

(12)   French
        Jean est plus riche que nous n'avions pensé
        'John is richer than we thought'

Other languages with such elements are Welsh (Borsley, 1986) and possibly Maltese. The unmarked complementizer in Maltese is *li*, which is found not only in relatives and with verbal complements, but is also used after prepositions when the latter take sentential arguments. Thus:

(13)   Maltese
        wara li   telqu
        after COMP they-left
        'after they left'

One may compare in this respect French *après que*, *sans que*, etc. Some prepositions, however, instead of *li*, take *ma* (see Sutcliffe,

1936: 207): *qabel* 'before', *bla* 'without', *minnghajr* 'without', *bhal-ma* 'as'. Thus, beside (13) we find:

(14)   qabel ma telqu
         before COMP they-left

With the exception of *bhalma* 'as', for which a different explanation is possible,[11] it is striking that the corresponding prepositions in French take the same pleonastic negation as in the comparatives:

(15)   French
         avant que Pierre ne vienne
         before COMP Peter NEG come-SUBJ
         'before Peter comes'

Furthermore, just as the French negative in these contexts is not completed with the particle *pas*, so in Maltese the verbal negation which usually involves a prefixed *ma* and a suffix *-x* (for example, *ma telqux* 'they did not leave') is here found without *-x*. Note too that etymologically the negative suffix *-x* in Maltese is a reduced form of the noun *xejn* 'thing' just as the French negative particles *pas*, etc. are reduced forms of Latin nouns with originally emphatic function. We might speculate, therefore, that the reinforcing function of these items was not appropriate in certain kinds of adjunct and hence their synchronic absence. Be that as it may, the parallelisms between these two cases are quite remarkable, and make the point that what in one language may be marked within the clause may in other languages be signalled on the complementizer. Moreover, the difference here parallels other differences between the two languages in that French is basically DM whereas Maltese shows a lot of HM properties.

Many other languages show attraction of negation to C position as, for example, in Finnish, where the negative auxiliary *ei* may be attached to the complementizer *etta* to form the compound C/I element *ettei* (Kenesei, 1991). This same effect is found with the negative conditional marker *ellei* 'if not' (compare English *unless*). Another context where negation is commonly marked at C is in purpose clauses, as in the distinction between Latin *ut* 'in order to' and *ne* 'in order that not' (once again compare English *lest*, with the same use of *less* as a negative complementizing element as in *unless*). For an interesting dissection of the historical processes at work in the genesis of a polarity distinction in the introducers of purpose clauses in the Oceanic language To'aba'ita, see Lichtenberk (1991: 66–75).

7.6.4 *Arguments of the complement clause*

In a number of varieties of Arabic, including the classical language, a marker co-referential to the subject of the complement is cliticized to the complementizer. Thus in the Gulf Arabic example (16):[12]

(16)   Gulf Arabic
        fakkart   inn-ak   bitiiji
        I-thought COMP-2.SG.OBJ 2.SG.SUBJ-come
        'I thought that you would come'

Note that in this example we have not simply got cliticization of the subject onto the complementizer. The suffix -*ak* is the same as that used to form a clitic object of a finite verb, so that we have genuine marking of one of the arguments of the clause on the complementizer. An alternative pattern attested in Levantine Arabic exhibits a third person singular pronoun attached to the complementizer, apparently as a kind of cataphoric reference to the succeeding clause. Thus:

(17)   Levantine Arabic
        fakkart   inn-uh   bitiiji
        I-thought COMP-3.SG.OBJ 2.SG.SUBJ-come
        'I thought that you would come'

Here the clausal argument in its entirety is marked on the head exactly as in the case of the more familiar instances of verbs being marked for their dependents.

7.6.5 *WH-movement*

It is tempting to see WH-movement as a special case of an element of the clause appearing in complementizer position, and thus as a kind of head-marking, particularly in view of the frequency with which complementizers are derived historically from WH-words. Such a conclusion would have followed quite naturally on the older view, according to which fronted WH-words occupy the complementizer position. However, under the CP hypothesis, the WH-word moves to Spec of C rather than to C (Lightfoot, 1990). A second difficulty is that in a number of languages WH-movement (whether at s-structure or Logical Form (LF)) is to the left even though the complementizer position is clause-final.

It is certainly not impossible that these difficulties can be removed with further analysis. Thus, Roberts and Vincent (1991) begin the task of classifying the elements that can occur in the C-system of a language, and attempt to state the relation between the pronominal properties of C and D. However, we must for the moment leave it an open question as to whether it might not be possible to motivate the existence of WH-movement phenomena in the attested cross-linguistic preference for HM in clause-level constructions.

7.6.6 *Head-to-head movement*

In discussing the marking of finiteness and mood in sections 7.6.1 and 7.6.2 above, we noted the relations between marking at the complementizer position and marking at the verb or auxiliary (INFL) position. Properties of this kind have been studied within GB under the rubric of head-to-head movement. A classic example is the analysis of the distribution of English auxiliaries as involving a rule of I-to-C movement (compare Pollock, 1989). Similar sorts of data have also been adduced in the treatment of verb-second effects in Germanic and earlier stages of the Romance languages – see the contributions to Battye and Roberts (forthcoming). The movement aspects of these analyses are probably not crucial, but the data analysed provide further support for the view that there are two related head positions in a clause, C and I. The unified analysis in GB can find a unified explanation in the HM/DM distinction.

7.6.7 *Summary*

The phenomena surveyed in sections 7.6.1–6 constitute areas in which recent generative work has made considerable progress. The list is not exhaustive by any means. See Sadock (1991: ch 5.5) for documentation of some further relevant cases and interesting discussion from an intriguingly different theoretical perspective. Indeed, many of the issues that arise bring with them complex and to some extent theory-bound argumentation, but it may be that we have gone as far as we can in theory-neutral terms. The Zwicky–Hudson debate in *Journal of Linguistics* (Zwicky, 1985: Hudson, 1987) was for the most part conducted theory-neutrally, and served very well to clear the ground for future discussions (also Zwicky, this volume). The next stage is to try and see to what extent the insights of one theory or approach can be reconciled with those of others.

7.7 Complementizing case

Given that complements are arguments of their governing verbs, it is not surprising to find that in many (most?) languages there is the possibility of a nominalized verb form in the complement, as in English *I like swimming*. If NPs in such a language also inflect for case, we should in turn expect the possibility of case-marked nominalizations serving as complements. Such a phenomenon is not unknown in Indo-European (compare the Latin supine – Vincent, 1992), but it is especially well developed in a number of Australian languages (as shown in the contributions to Austin, 1988, particularly Simpson, 1988, and also Dench and Evans, 1988). The following is a simple example from Simpson (1988: 212, her (18)):

(18)   Warlpiri
        yula-nja-ku jati-jarri-ja
        cry-NOM-PURP start-INCH-PAST
        'She burst into tears' (lit. started to cry)

It is notable that the Purposive marker *-ku* is identical to the Dative case suffix, something which is reminiscent of the general tendency for purpose clauses to be expressed by Datives or directional prepositions (as with English *to*, French *à*, to name two well-tried examples). Perhaps more striking are the instances where this same phenomenon is found but the verb form shows no other evidence of nominalization. In the following Kayardild example from Evans (1988: 229, his (22)), the finite verb *thaa-thuu-nth* 'will return' bears the 'oblique' suffix (labelled here COBL for 'complementizing oblique'). Moreover, the argument of that verb and the modifier of the argument agree and take the same suffix, which is therefore distributed over every word of the clause:

(19)   Kayardild
        ngada murnmurdawa-th [ngijin-inja thabuju-ntha
        I-NOM be glad-ACT   my-COBL   brother-COBL
        thaa-thuu-nth]_COBL
        return-FUT-COBL
        'I am glad that my brother is coming back'

The issue that concerns us here is the status of these case markers. Both Evans and Simpson are surely right in claiming that case suffixes and complementizing suffixes are the same morphological elements rather than homophonous ones, and case is, of course, the classic form of dependent-marking. The question is: are these cases (and by extension all nominal cases) also to be seen as heads of their phrases? If so, they would then parallel the standard treatment of the adpositions which exercise the same or similar functions in 'analytic' languages. This analysis would entail a relaxing of the strongest form of the Lexical Integrity Hypothesis, though it would be compatible with a weaker version such as that espoused by Speas (1990) to the effect that syntactic generalizations may refer to inflectional but not derivational morphology. There is not space here to explore all the implications of these constructions, but it is clear that the phenomenon of 'complementizing case' provides an important new angle on the question not only of what is the head of the CP but also of the NP/DP/KP.[13] (See section 7.9 below for some further discussion of this question.)

7.8 HM complement strategies

So far we have discussed patterns of complementation that can be classified as DM. It is natural to ask what kinds of strategy would count as HM. One obvious possibility is that the governing verb is marked with an affix or clitic to indicate the presence of a sentential complement (see, however, note 7). In such circumstances it is not uncommon to have a complementizer present as well, so that what we have is technically double marking rather than pure head-marking. A slightly more complex case is attested in Maltese and some other Semitic languages, where the subject of the complement clause is marked with a clitic on the head verb. Thus, compare (20a) and (20b) (Sutcliffe 1936: 166):

(20)   Maltese
        a. irrid-kom   taqraw
           1.SG.SUBJ-want-2.PL.OBJ 2.PL.SUBJ-read
           'I want you to read'

        b. irrid   li   taqraw
           1.SG.SUBJ-want COMP 2.PL.SUBJ-read
           'I want you to read'

In (20a) there are two finite verbs, the first of which bears a second person plural object suffix (contrast *quasamkom* 'He broke you (pl)') and no complementizer is possible. In (20b) the first finite verb, *irrid* 'I want', does not have the pronominal suffix and the complementizer is obligatory. While (20b) looks like a classic instance of a complement dependent-marked by the complementizer, (20a) is pure HM. That is to say there is no change of verb form nor any function word; the presence of the dependent is signalled solely by the affix on the head. There is an interesting parallelism here with the pattern of Lakhota complementation described in Van Valin (1985: 387–91), though the complementizer is optionally present in the Lakhota equivalent of the Maltese pattern (20a). Another parallel case from Old Russian has been brought to my attention by Johanna Nichols:

(21)   Old Russian
        my   že ix   že ne vemy kto   sut'
        we-NOM PTC them-ACC PTC NEG know who-NOM   are-3.PL
        'and we don't know who they are'

The type of Maltese pattern described above is in one respect akin to what is found with so-called 'Raising' verbs in English, namely the subject of the subordinate verb is apparently encoded as the object of the main verb. Of course, there is at the same time a major difference: the subordinate verb in the Maltese example (and also in the Lakhota examples Van Valin describes) is finite rather than non-finite. A corollary of this is that the second person plural is marked twice in example (20a), once as the object of *irrid* and once as the subject of *taqraw*. Classical raising is thus a double-marking strategy: the 'raised' object is an HM property and the infinitive verb is a DM property.[14] On this view, we can also derive an account of the unusual (that is, 'marked' in the other sense!) nature of 'Raising' in English, since such a pattern has two exceptional properties: (a) it is an HM strategy in an otherwise DM language; and (b) it is an HM strategy in a preferentially DM construction.

7.9   C in relation to other functional categories

Having established the utility of C as head of CP in the light of both generative approaches and the HM/DM distinction, it is natural to ask what other categories C relates to, and therefore whether our argumentation can be extended beyond the domain of the clause. A number of generalizations both synchronic and diachronic suggest a close link between complementizers and pronouns. Thus, English *that* in its complementizing function is historically derived from the demonstrative pronoun. Indeed, Noonan (1985) asserts that pronouns cross-linguistically provide the most common etymological source of complementizers.[15] In other languages, complementizers overlap with articles (Lakhota as reported by Van Valin, 1985). But of course, articles commonly overlap with pronouns too: English *the* is also historically from the same source as *that*, and in the majority of the Romance languages the articles and clitic pronouns are linked developments from the distal deictic *ille*. These morphological overlaps between pronouns and determiners are part of the argument behind what has come to be known as the DP-hypothesis (Abney, 1987; Stowell, 1989; and see Lyons, 1977: 392 and 452–66, for an adumbration of the same line of thought), which in turn is linked to the CP-hypothesis via the principles of X-bar as extended to functional categories (Fukui and Speas 1986; Speas, 1990). An intriguing question, though one that there is not space to follow up here, is the extent to which the role of D may be construed in HM/DM terms as we have suggested is appropriate in the case of C. There is certainly some evidence in favour of the view that D is the slot where categories of the DP may be signalled (case in Germanic and number and gender in, for example, Romance) when they are not marked on the noun.[16] It is also argued in Vincent (1989) that the co-emergence of the categories D and C in Romance is a linked development of a 'natural class' of changes.

Other historical sources of complementizers are verbs and preposition/conjunctions.[17] The case of verbs we have already touched on, noting that while there may be the kind of semantic 'bleaching' familiar from other instances of grammaticalization, there is preservation of headhood: V changes to C and therefore VP changes to CP. With prepositions we also get semantic bleaching as in the development of the Romance non-finite complementizers exemplified in French *à* and *de* from Latin *ad* 'to' and *de* 'concerning, down from' (Vincent, 1990). Borsley (1986) discusses a different sort of prepositional complementizer in Welsh. There is a clear intuitive connection between the roles of prepositions and cases, and it is worthy of note that prepositions seem more commonly to be linked to subordinating conjunctions than to complementizers of argument clauses (and indeed, as in our Maltese and French examples above, often co-occur with them). This provides an interesting parallel to the observation in Simpson (1988: 212) that 'most clauses with complementizer suffixes do not represent clausal arguments. They normally represent adjuncts. In this they resemble LOCATIVE case-suffixes.' As we noted in section 7.7, there is much that remains to be worked out in the relation between CP and DP and between CP and PP (and KP).[18] It seems clear, however, that the triple focus of generative grammar, the HM/DM distinction and grammaticalization will offer a fuller account than could be achieved by any one of these alone.

7.10 Conclusion

Much of this chapter has been preliminary and tentative, suggesting links and parallels rather than new analyses and extensive theoretical

argumentation, and raising at least as many questions as are answered. While it is not possible to agree with Nichols' optimistic
assertion that 'Linguists of divergent theoretical persuasions are in
almost complete agreement as to what is the head and what is the
non-head in a given construction' (1986: 57), it is possible to see the
phenomenon of heads as an important area of convergence in
syntactic theorizing, and one where the juxtaposition of different
approaches offers the opportunity of new and fruitful syntheses.

NOTES

1. Some of the ideas in this chapter were first worked out and given a
   public airing during a short stay in the Department of Linguistics, La
   Trobe University. I am grateful to Barry Blake for arranging this visit
   and to the British Council for contributing towards the costs. At that
   time I received useful comments, questions and advice from Peter
   Austin, Edith Bavin, Barry Blake and Kate Burridge. I have benefited
   from discussing questions of headedness, functional categories and
   constituent marking with Kersti Börjars and Linda Roberts. I am also
   grateful to Bob Borsley, Oscar Collinge, Grev Corbett, Dick Hudson,
   Jim Miller, John Payne, Katherine Perera and Johanna Nichols for their
   comments and suggestions.
2. For help with the Maltese data, which recur at various points in this
   chapter, I am indebted to Albert Borg and Manwel Mifsud of the
   Institute of Linguistics in the University of Malta. It is interesting to note
   that whereas the two Semitic languages in Nichols' list, Arabic and
   Hebrew, come out as almost perfectly balanced between the two polar
   extremes of HM and DM – and are classified by Nichols as 'double
   marking' – Maltese has a much larger number of head-marking properties. The consequence of this directionality of change – particularly in
   the light of prolonged contact with two dependent-marking languages,
   Italian and English – deserves further study.
3. Johanna Nichols informs me that in compiling her statistics she sometimes included 'grammatical' words that had a clear marking function.
   However, it remains true that there is no systematic exploration within
   Nichols (1986) of the role of such items.
4. It might be instructive to attempt a comprehensive survey of all the new
   projections that have been proposed in an attempt to see (a) what, if
   any, internal contradictions are generated, and (b) how much of the
   syntactic structure thereby generated is actually required. There is an
   undefended assumption in all this work that, once a new item or
   category is required by the syntax of a particular language, the
   appropriate way to encode it is via the constituency representations that

X-bar imposes. In most instances I do not share this assumption, though I think it is most defensible for DET, COMP and INFL, the categories whose role and structure I explore in this chapter. These other questions I will put on one side. See also Cann (this volume) for discussion of this issue.

5. One might compare in this respect Greenberg-style generalizations about word order. In their original formulation they were (perhaps necessarily) couched in terms of crude, superficial grammatical categories. Subsequent work has taken these up and sought to reconcile them with the demands of more explicitly formulated theories; see, amongst others, Hawkins (1982, 1983); Travis (1984, 1989); Giorgi and Longobardi (1991). It does not, of course, follow that Greenberg and his colleagues would necessarily agree with the way their work has been interpreted within the generative tradition; see, for example, Croft (1990) (although, curiously, this work also omits any reference to Nichols' typology). See also Dryer (forthcoming) for an update on research into word-order universals. The important point, rather, is that results and generalizations obtained within one approach can inform work in another. It is this same spirit of cross-paradigm reconciliation that underlies the present chapter.

6. There are some notorious exceptions to this principle, as both Johanna Nichols and Oscar Collinge have reminded me: for example, the Indo-European pronominal bases have been resistant to change over not just centuries but millennia; likewise, the core prepositions of a language are often of considerable antiquity (Meillet and Vendryes, 1948: ch. 8). More work is clearly required to sort out the most resistant subclasses of grammatical elements, but the mere fact that the counter-examples fall into classes (pronouns and (some) prepositions as opposed to, say, articles and auxiliaries) suggests that there are principled explanations to be offered here rather than a random series of exceptions that might invalidate our generalization under (6) altogether.

7. The view that the complementizer (or conjunction, in older terminology) is head of the clause to which it attaches is not unique to generative work. Indeed, it seems to be essential to adopt this view in any strict dependency approach (compare Hudson, 1987).

8. Bob Borsley suggests another instance of such overlap of roles. In Welsh a noun phrase (or perhaps DP) like *darlun o'r dynion* 'a picture of the men' contains the preposition *o* which functions as a marker of the dependency. In *darlun ohonynt hwy* 'a picture of them', we find the inflected form of the preposition, giving us head-marking on the marker.

9. Johanna Nichols informs me that on the larger sample of languages she has studied to date the balance between DM and HM in nearer to a 50–50 per cent split.

10. Another possibility might be that, even in a language which head-marks arguments of the clause, this marking would not be triggered by the

presence of a clausal argument. The latter point is difficult to investigate, however, since the expected marking in such circumstances
would be that appropriate to a third person singular object, and this is
commonly zero (cf. Lakhota, Abkhaz). In certain circumstances Navajo
has overt marking for third person singular objects, and in those
instances, as far as I have been able to determine, the presence of a
sentential argument is morphologically signalled. We discuss the question of HM patterns of complementation in a little more detail below
(section 7.8).

11. In its complementizing function, *ma* has a wider distribution than
    indicated here; see Sutcliffe (1936: 183). There seems to be a conver-
    gence of two different elements, one a negative and one a relative
    pronoun, but more thorough historical investigation than I have been
    able to undertake may show some connection.

12. I owe this example to Clive Holes, to whom I am grateful for discussion
    of this phenomenon more generally.

13. One possible solution would be to follow Szabolcsi (forthcoming) in
    suggesting that D in the nominal corresponds to C in the sentence, while
    case corresponds to INFL. This, however, would imply that the case
    phrase (KP) is an argument of D, which conflicts with the idea of case and
    adpositions being in some sense equivalent, an idea which requires DP to
    be an argument of P. (See also note 16.)

14. It should be noted that this account requires us to accept an analysis
    whereby *her* in *I believe her to be a genius* is indeed the object of *believe*,
    as would be the case on the original raising analyses of Rosenbaum
    (1967) and Postal (1974) or on the LFG account of Bresnan (1982b). I
    believe that there are independent grounds for preferring such an
    analysis over the one involving Exceptional Case Marking which is
    standard within GB, but it would take us too far from the point to go
    into this matter (see Vincent, forthcoming). It is also important to keep
    English 'Raising' distinct from the accusative and infinitive construc-
    tions of the classical languages (for Latin see Vincent, 1990, and for
    Greek, Philippaki-Warburton and Catismali, 1990).

15. Sometimes the pronoun in question is a WH-word, as in the case of the
    Romance complementizers *que*, *che*, etc. and as in English *who*, *which*
    (see also section 7.6.3). We will leave for another occasion the full
    exploration of the implications of these morphological overlaps.

16. There is some debate within the GB literature as to whether the
    sentential analogue of DP is IP or CP (Szabolcsi, 1989). The historical
    arguments seem to favour CP, as we have argued in the text, though
    instances of D evolving into I might be found in the way etymological
    pronouns have taken on copular functions in Semitic or in the develop-
    ment of pronominal clusters into 'auxiliaries' in some Australian
    languages (see Bowe, 1990: 62–5, for discussion). The matter, however,
    deserves more detailed discussion than we are able to give it here.

17. We accept the arguments of Jackendoff (1973) and Emonds (1976) that prepositions and conjunctions are part of a single grammatical category. For explicit argumentation linking these to complementizers, see Vincent (1980), Edmonds (1985: ch. 7).

18. A start is made in this direction in Roberts and Vincent (1991), where it is argued that there is a natural relation between c and d as functional categories but not between c and any of the major categories. The argument there is conducted largely on synchronic grounds, and leads to the conclusion that the connections between c and n or v (as evidenced in the latter case by v2 effects, for example) are indirect rather than direct. c is argued instead to have direct links with other functional categories such as c and i. At this point diachronic questions are clearly of significance since the fillers of i are usually verbal in etymological origin. Likewise p covers items that behave as functional markers (for example, Case assigners) and as full lexical predicates, and again commonly the former derive from the latter.

8 *Heads in discourse: structural versus functional centricity*

JOHANNA NICHOLS

8.1 Introduction

Ellipsis, deletability and the question of what fragment of a constituent can stand alone are problems which figure in many discussions of what constitutes the head of a constituent; see Zwicky's definition of *base* (this volume). The very persistence of this issue in the literature would lead one to expect that there would be distinct cross-linguistic consistency in the deletability and retainability of parts of constituents. In addition, and more generally, it would lead one to expect that the notion of head would lead to useful cross-linguistic generalizations about deletability and obligatoriness of parts of constituents. This chapter offers a first step towards a cross-linguistic investigation of whether and how heads figure in constraining constituent-reducing operations of the type that arise in connected discourse. A comparison of just two of the languages discussed – Russian and Chechen-Ingush – suffices to show that languages can differ substantially in whether heads can be deleted, or dependents left to stand alone, by these discourse operations.[1] In part for this reason, and in part because the relevant tendencies are only statistical, constituent-reducing operations will probably not prove to be a useful cross-linguistic indicator of head and non-head status. On the other hand, they do appear to shed light on some of the larger questions of how constituents are defined, grammaticalized and used in individual languages.

In what follows I will simply assume that the verb is the head of the clause. Since the argument is that there is neither cross-linguistic consistency in what can be deleted in ellipsis nor correlation between deletability and morphological type, the conclusions would be equally valid for any decision as to what is head. What is absolutely essential for the comparative typological approach taken here is that there be a cross-linguistically consistent, strictly syntactic definition of head and non-head; without this, there would be no basis of comparison, and any answer to the hypothesis of correlation between morphological marking type and deletability of heads raised below would be circular. This chapter is offered not only as a cross-linguistic study of heads in discourse but also as a demonstration of the indispensability of a universal syntactic definition of *head* to cross-linguistic work.

In terms first proposed by Bloomfield (1933) an **endocentric** constituent is one whose distributional privileges as a constituent are the same as those of its head alone; an **exocentric** constituent is one whose distribution is different from that of its head. For example, the English PP is exocentric, because the distribution of a PP is different from that of a preposition; the English NP is endocentric, because an NP and a noun have the same privileges of occurrence. Nichols (1986) claims that the distinction of exocentric versus endocentric arises only in languages with a good deal of dependent-marking morphology; in predominantly head-marking languages, all constituents appear to be endocentric. For instance, in strictly head-marking languages like Abkhaz, Lakhota or Tzutujil, a verb and a clause have the same external distribution, and an adposition and a PP have the same external distribution. The visible surface reflex of this situation is that in a consistently head-marking language an adposition can always stand alone without an independent object to form a PP, and a verb can stand alone to constitute a sentence. In a dependent-marking language like Russian, in contrast, a preposition cannot be used without an object and a verb can generally not stand alone.[2]

This familiar kind of centricity has to do with abstract grammatical properties and distributional privileges of constituents and their heads, and I will call it **structural centricity**. Once we look at how constituents and their heads are actually employed in connected texts, another aspect of centricity emerges, one I will call **functional centricity**. Rules which delete or otherwise remove parts of constituents can affect either heads or non-heads of those constituents, and functional centricity has to do with this opposition. When a constituent-reducing operation applies, one can ask either what has been removed or what remains. This chapter concentrates on what remains of the reduced constituent, although a taxonomy could equally well be based on what is removed. I will use the following terms for two types of constituent-reducing operations.

Isolation of dependent, implemented by head removal: deletion or other excision of the head of the constituent, leaving a lone dependent or dependents, as in gapping in English (here and below, relevant portions of examples are in boldface):

(1)   Mary left at 2:30 and **John at 3:00.**

or as in replies to NP-focused WH-questions:

(2)   What did you give him? – **A book.**

Gapping can remove more than just the head, but it consistently leaves a dependent or dependents isolated.

Isolation of head, *or dependent removal*: deletion, etc. of one or more non-heads in a constituent. The result may be a bare head, or it may be a head with partial valence. A bare head is illustrated by answers to yes–no questions in Russian:

(3)   Ty   s   nami pojdeš'?   –**Pojdu.**
         You with us   go-2.SG   go-1.SG
         Will you go with us?   – Yes (lit. 'I'll go')

A head with partial valence is illustrated by answers to WH-questions focused on the verb or VP in English:

(4)   What did you do?   –   **Called the police.**
                                Gave him the papers.
                                Postponed my vacation.

By isolation is meant a variety of kinds of syntactic autonomy, ranging from the complete autonomy of independent utterances in (2) or (4) to the semi-autonomy of the reduced co-ordinate as in (1), or a stranded element as in examples to follow below.

The reduced structures surveyed here include some of those usually put forth in distributionally based arguments for headedness and for endocentric versus exocentric status. Therefore I have chosen to present constituent-reducing processes as an issue in centricity; a constituent reducible to a lone dependent is **functionally exocentric,** and one reducible to a head is **functionally endocentric.** Functional centricity has little bearing on the structural centricity of constituents, since functional centricity is established by considering reduced constituents and such reduced constituents, though they have been used in arguments for headedness, do not provide the strongest arguments (for an overview of the arguments see the introduction to this volume).

The rest of this chapter examines head removal and dependent removal in four languages and draws some more general conclusions about their probable cross-linguistic distribution.

8.2 Hypothesis and survey design

Since head-marking languages are structurally endocentric, with heads able to stand alone or representing an entire constituent, one might expect them to be functionally endocentric as well. That is, one would expect them to make frequent use of lone heads in discourse. Correspondingly, since the constituents of dependent-marking languages are structurally exocentric, one might expect them to be functionally exocentric as well; lone heads should not occur in discourse, and isolated dependents should occur. Such patterns would use the morphological structure of the language to maximal communicative efficacy: in a head-marking language, the head bears the morphological information about the syntax of the constituent, and the head is left intact by constituent-reducing processes; while in a dependent-marking language, the dependents bear the morphological information, and they are left intact.

This chapter is a pilot study testing these hypotheses. It surveys four languages with a substantial dependent-marking component but otherwise different morphosyntax, to see whether they are indeed all prone to use isolated dependents but not isolated heads. The four languages prove to differ substantially in their use of constituent-reducing operations. The languages are the following: Russian, a language with a good deal of morphology, almost all of it dependent-marking; Chechen-Ingush, also with a good deal of morphology and radically dependent-marking, but differing from Russian in being ergative; English, with little morphology, most of it dependent-marking; and Nunggubuyu, a radically non-configurational language with a good deal of head-marking morphology in addition to some dependent-marking morphology.

Most of the material used below is elicited, although obviously a full-blown cross-linguistic comparison would need to be based primarily on text surveys. This chapter is offered as hypothesis-generating, and I hope it will encourage text work by specialists in languages of critical types.

The only zero-producing processes not considered here are controlled ones such as those that produce non-finite verb forms (notably infinitives).

8.3 Russian

Like all Indo-European languages preserving the inherited morphology, Russian is strongly dependent-marking. Consistent with what one might expect on structural grounds (see section 8.2 above), Russian makes extensive use of head-removing operations and only limited use of dependent-removing operations. The only clear example of an adjunct-removing operation I have found is the tendency to reply to yes–no questions by using a bare verb, as in (3) above. The bare verb is the most natural answer to a simple yes–no question, and consultants report it to be more natural than *Da* 'yes' in all contexts.[3] *Da* and/or other words can also be added to the verb, as in the third answer in (5). (Here and below, # indicates a stylistically marked or less natural form.)

(5) Ty emu peredala moe pis′mo?   — **Peredala.**
     you him gave   my letter   gave
                                          — **#Da**
                                          yes
                                          — **Da, peredala emu**
                                          yes gave   him
         'Did you give him my letter?'   'Yes'

Colloquial Russian has numerous examples with anaphoric zeros (anaphors are in boldface):

(6) Dva dnja Ivan ne naxodil sebe mesta. **Ø** proboval napit′sja, no ešče xuže stalo – protivno. **Ø** brosil. Na tretij den′ **Ø** sel pisat′ rasskaz v rajonnuju gazetu. On časten′ko čital v gazetax rasskazy ljudej, kotoryx obideli ni za čto. **Emu** tože xotelos′ sprosit′ vsex: kak že tak možno?!
                                                 (Šukšin, 1975: 84)
     'For two days Ivan was beside himself. **He** (Ø) tried to drink, but it just made things worse – he didn't feel like it. **He** (Ø) gave it up. The next day **he** (Ø) sat down to write a story to the regional newspaper. **He** had often read in newspaper stories of people who had been hurt for no reason. **He** also wanted to ask everyone: how can people do such things?'

It can be argued (see Nichols, 1985b) that in colloquial Russian zero is the natural anaphor for the theme of the paragraph, and the form shifts to overt only when there is a shift in temporal reference, in the syntactic function of the subject, or in other factors (the last two sentences in (6) illustrate changes in temporal reference and syntactic function). These anaphoric zeros appear to be zero word forms of personal pronouns which become overt under certain conditions. That is, rather than actual syntactic removal we have here to do with morphologically and phonologically zero realizations of syntactically present inflectional forms.

Dependent-isolating processes are numerous in Russian. The following five constructions are the clearest examples.

Replies to WH-questions

(7)   Čto on dal svoemu synu? – **Knigu.**
      what he gave his   son   book-ACC
      'What did he give his son?' – 'A book.'

Gapping

(8)   Miša čital 'Vojnu i   mir', a   **ja – 'Annu Kareninu'**
      M.   read War   and Peace and/but I   A.K.
      'Misha was reading "War and Peace", and I [was reading] "Anna
      Karenina".'

In Russian, unlike English, gapping is extremely frequent and its output is not stylistically marked.

Verbless sentences (see Mel'čuk, 1979a). In these constructions the verb is missing, but its arguments bear the cases it governs. The combination of cases and context makes it possible to recover the meaning and sometimes even identify a specific lexeme for the zero verb. Verbless sentences differ from gapping in that gapping involves deletion under identity, while the zero verb is not related by identity or any other resemblance relation to any previous verb in the context; verbless sentences are usually single main clauses, while examples of gapping, like (8), involve overt co-ordination. Example (10) below is interesting and unusual in that its second clause might in principle be viewed as the result of gapping; but the crucial first clause clearly is not. English glosses for zero verbs are bracketed in the following examples.

(9)   On mne ni slova
      he me not word-GEN
      'He didn't [say] a word to me.'

(10)   Tat'jana v les,   medved´ za nej.
      T.   into forest, bear   after her
      'Tat'jana [ran] into the forest and the bear [came running] after her.'
                                              (Pushkin)

Formulas

(11)   S   novym godom!
      with new   year
      'Happy new year!'

(12) Ščastlivogo puti!
      happy   journey-GEN
      'Happy journey!'

The case frame and the conventions of usage enable one to identify the verb in such formulas. Example (11), for instance, can be restored to the correct but unidiomatic (13), with *pozdravljat'* 'congratulate', which governs the preposition *s* 'with':

(13) (Ja) pozdravljaju tebja s   novym godom
       I   congratulate you with new   year

The verb of (12) would be *želaju* '(I) wish', which takes a genitive object.

Conventionalized hesitation phenomena. Corresponding to English *um, uh, whatchamacallit*, etc., a Russian may insert *èto* 'this' or *èto samoe* 'this very', appropriately case-inflected or provided with a preposition. In (14), *daleko* is a predicate governing a prepositional phrase *do* 'to' + genitive, and the verb *popast'* 'get in, be admitted', literally 'fall', of (15) governs a prepositional phrase of direction or a directional adverb.

(14) Kak daleko **do ètogo**... do cerkvi?
      How far   to this   to church
      'How far is it to the...uh...church?'   (conversation)

(15) Znaeš   kuda on popal? On popal **v èto**...v
      know-2.SG where he got.in   he got.into this to
      pedinstitut
      pedagogical.institute
      'You know where he got accepted? He got accepted to
      a...whatchamacallit...pedagogical institute.'   (conversation)

That is, the conventional hesitation filler in Russian is a dependent. It is followed by a pause, then a syntactically and intonationally isolated dependent.

In summary, in Russian usage, in a variety of contexts the dependents of a constituent may stand alone and represent the entire constituent. Replies, gapping, verbless sentences and formulas involve elliptical 'clauses' where the head is absent and the dependents alone constitute the clause. The conventional hesitation filler guarantees that in the event that a speaker has difficulty in recalling a word the head will not be stranded, even temporarily, without a dependent. On the other hand, lone heads in Russian seem limited to answers to certain kinds of questions and stylistically extreme (colloquial) examples with anaphoric zeros, and the anaphoric zeros may belong to morphology rather than syntax. Thus the majority of constituent-reducing processes would appear to be head-removing and to leave isolated dependents. The incidence of bare verbs as answers to yes–no questions and of anaphoric zeros is higher in speech as represented in literature, but probably not in real speech. Table 8.1 gives frequencies for head-isolating and dependent-isolating processes in a survey of ten pages of a published transcription of live spoken Russian. These figures show that most constituents (70 per cent) are unreduced. But of those that are reduced, isolated dependents are almost three times as common as isolated heads. Of the 13 examples with isolated heads (verbs), 6 had anaphoric zero subjects and 2 were imperatives which normally lack overt subjects. If we disregard the imperatives, the number of isolated verbs reduces to 11 (6 per cent); if we also disregard the verbs with anaphoric zero subjects, it is further reduced to 3 (2 per cent). Thus the total number of secure examples of truly isolated heads (verbs) would be only a tiny fraction of the number of isolated dependents.

Table 8.1 Constituent fragments in spoken Russian

Constituent					
NP (from s)	24	(14%)			
PP (from s)	11	(6%)	Total dependent-isolating	38	(22%)
Verbless s	3	(2%)			
v (from s)	13	(8%)	Total head-isolating:	13	(8%)
Full s	120	(70%)	Total unreduced:	120	(70%)
Total clauses	171	(100%)		171	(100%)

Source: Zemskaja and Kapanadze (1978: 42–52)

8.4 Chechen-Ingush

Chechen and Ingush are closely related languages spoken in the north central Caucasus and belonging to the Nakh family of Northeast Caucasian. They will be treated as a single language here because they form a single speech community and because they are identical in the respects investigated here. Chechen-Ingush is strictly dependent-marking, and the structural centricity of its various constituents is the same as that of its Russian or English counterparts. However, rules for deletion and reduction in Chechen-Ingush use dependent removal but almost never remove heads, even in constructions where head removal is cross-linguistically common.

Replies to yes–no questions illustrate dependent removal. There is no equivalent to 'yes' or 'no' in Ingush; the main verb is repeated instead, and a directional or locational pre-verb is removed along with the dependents:

(16)   Ingush
        A:ra- vealar- ij yz?   – Vealar
        out   went   Q he   went
        'Did he go out?'   'Yes'

Chechen-Ingush texts have many anaphoric zero dependents as a result of co-referential deletion, all of them due to controlled deletion in chained clauses. Like many languages of northern Eurasia, Chechen-Ingush almost entirely lacks clause and sentence co-ordination, using chaining instead. These zero dependents at first glance appear to be additional examples of dependent removal, but since they are controlled and involve non-infinitive verbs they are not counted here.

Head removal is extremely rare. It is unusual even in answers to WH-questions, where bare NPs are cross-linguistically common:

(17)   Ingush
        Fy   dennad cuo   voʕaa?   – a. Sowɣat dennad
        what gave   he-ERG son-DAT   gift   gave
                                        b. #Sowɣat.
        'What did he give his son?'   – 'A present'.

The (b) answer, which is the only possibility in English and the unmarked possibility in Russian, is marked in Ingush, where it requires special intonation.

Further examples where heads are conspicuous in their non-removal are found in formulaic utterances. While English and Russian use verbless formulas like *Happy New Year*, *good night* or (11)–(12), Chechen and Ingush regularly include a verb:

(18)   Ingush
        De dika xojla ħuona
        Day good may be you-DAT
        'Good day', literally 'May/let the day be (a) good (one) to you'

(19)   Chechen
        Neq'dika xülda ħaⁿ
        road good may be you-GEN
        'Have a good trip!', literally 'May the road be a good one for you'

English and Russian use bare adjectives or adverbs in expressions like 'Good!', 'OK', Russian *xorošo* 'good', etc., but Chechen and Ingush include verbs here too:

(20)   Chechen
        Dika du
        good is
        'Good.'

The ubiquitous conventional hesitation filler in Chechen-Ingush is *die ħuona*, a phrase whose first element is apparently a verb and the second is the dative second-person pronoun. That is, it seems to have a head, and certainly it is not an isolated dependent. Unlike the common hesitation phrase of Russian, this one does not fill an argument position in the clause, but is rather an appendage of some kind to a clause member or to a whole clause.

The use of dependent removal and avoidance of head removal interact to decrease the number of bare NPs and increase the number of clauses in Chechen-Ingush texts. Another source of additional heads in Chechen-Ingush texts is embedding of mentioned forms as arguments in relative clauses on relatively empty antecedent nouns. For instance, where both English and Russian insert various proper names and mentioned forms into a text as NPs, Chechen-Ingush typically treats them as clauses. Example (21) shows a citation following a quote in an academic text in Chechen. The reference is to a source in Russian.

(21)   Chechen
        'Sbornik svedenij o kavkazskix gorcax' c'ie   jolu
        [journal title: in Russian]   name being
        kniːga,   vypusk 1, Tiflis 1868.)
        book-NOM vol.
        '(*Sbornik svedenij o kavkazskix gorcax* 1, Tbilisi 1868.)'
        literally '(Book/journal whose title is *Sbornik...*)'

The Chechen text embeds the journal title as predicate nominal in a relative clause on *kniːga* 'book'. In English or Russian, the title would ordinarily be used alone as an NP, as in the translation above. Example (21) is an NP in Chechen just as its translation is; what is distinctive about Chechen here is that it cannot use a mentioned NP as a syntactic NP, but must embed it under an ordinary NP. An analogue in colloquial Chechen is (22), where the mentioned word is embedded as direct object in a relative clause:

(22)   Chechen; partially constructed example
       Muːxa xir du örsiːⁿ   mattaħ   'naž' boːxu doš?
       how will.be Russian language-LOC oak saying word
       'What is Russian for "oak"?', 'What is "oak" in Russian?', literally
       '...the word meaning "oak"...'

To summarize: in Chechen-Ingush a constituent is normally
reduced to its head in discourse contexts where this is impossible in
English and possible but not necessary in Russian. On the other hand,
almost never do dependents stand alone in Chechen-Ingush.[4] Though
Chechen-Ingush is dependent-marking, like Russian, its tendencies in
reducing constituents are diametrically opposed to those shown for
Russian. Comparison of Russian and Chechen-Ingush suffices to
falsify the hypothesis (section 8.2) of correlation between morphosyntactic type and discourse centricity. It should also be noted that
the dependent-removing processes of Chechen-Ingush are few and
apparently not frequent in texts, so that Chechen-Ingush might best
be described as a language that generally removes neither heads nor
dependents.

If head/dependent marking does not predict the differing
constituent-reducing processes of Russian and Chechen-Ingush, what
does? There are three differences between Chechen-Ingush and
Russian that seem relevant in this connection. One is the strength and
clarity with which Chechen-Ingush grammaticalizes its constituents
and constituent boundaries. A constituent much like a VP (it is
probably some kind of $\bar{V}$, and its most frequent manifestation is a
verb and its nominative argument; for details see Nichols, forthcoming a; b) serves as the domain for a distinctive and striking intonation
contour consisting of alternating high and low pitches with a
pronounced internal downstep. The same constituent is the domain
for second-positioning of certain clitics and interrogatives and rigid
word-order rules that cannot be disrupted by the pragmatically based
word-order changes that apply outside this constituent. In lieu of
sentence co-ordination Chechen-Ingush uses clause chaining historically identifiable as co-ordination of these VP-like constituents. The
NP has the same downstepped intonation contour and rigid word
order. In Russian, in contrast, the immediate and salient properties
such as word order and intonation seem to be describable in terms of
dependency relations like verb–argument rather than constituents.
Evidence for a Russian VP can be uncovered by argumentation, but
this is very different from that of Chechen-Ingush, where the grammatical evidence for the VP-like constituent is of the kind that must be

stated in any elementary descriptive grammar. Chechen-Ingush, in short, is a highly configurational language, while Russian is not.[5]

The second potentially relevant difference between Chechen-Ingush and Russian is that Chechen-Ingush sentence structure is built on subordination, chaining and control, while Russian makes primary use of co-ordination and non-controlled anaphora. Co-ordination in general imposes requirements of identity or equivalence of the co-ordinated structures, and this facilitates head removal, since it is often the heads that function as the identical or equivalent elements. Three of the five constituent-reducing processes of Russian enumerated above – answers to WH-questions, gapping and conventionalized hesitation phenomena – involve co-ordination or some other form of syntactic repetition, with deletion under identity. Thus it may be that a co-ordination-based grammar is associated with a propensity to remove heads, or at least with tolerance of head removal, while a control-based or subordination-based grammar inhibits head removal.

The third potentially relevant difference between Russian and Chechen-Ingush is that Russian is an accusative language while Chechen-Ingush is profoundly ergative. The morphology is consistently ergative, and – what is probably most important for constituent reduction – the lexicon is consistently ergative: every verb governs a nominative (S or O in the terms of Dixon, 1979), no case-changing rule applies to those nominatives, and no valence-changing operation affects those nominatives. Both case-changing and valence-changing operations do affect non-nominative arguments, notably subjects of transitives (the A of Dixon, 1979) and indirect objects. The obligatory nature and immutability of the nominative in the lexicon is paralleled by obvious impressionistic closeness of verb and S/O in the syntax, and the fact that verb and S/O behave as a closely bound unit would appear to be consistent with the non-removability of the verb and/or non-isolability of at least its closest dependent.

8.5 English

English has very little morphology, but what it does have is dependent-marking. The functional centricity of English is split in type, with both head-isolating and dependent-isolating processes well established.[6] Head-isolating processes include those that strand prepositions:

(23)   What book did you look that up **in**?

Isolation of dependents is visible in answers to WH-questions:

(24)   What did you give him? – **A book.**

as well as gapping, which can remove a verb, as in (25), or the head noun of a NP, as in (26):

(25)   Susan is from Michigan and **Ann from North Dakota.**

(26)   They brought one six-pack of beer and **two of Coke.**

A construction that involves both head removal and dependent removal is right node raising:

(27)   Susan is fond of, while Mary looks askance at, profanity.

(28)   equal to or greater than five

The segments *Susan is fond of, while Mary looks askance at* and *equal to or greater than* show dependent removal and partial valence in each conjunct; the segments *profanity* and *five* are isolated dependents.

Constructions like (27)–(28) and (29) create co-ordinated object-less prepositions with the object factored out by right node raising. Example (30) does not co-ordinate prepositions but involves an anaphoric process that leaves the second preposition objectless.

(29)   Would you like your tea **with** or without sugar?

(30)   Would you like your tea with sugar or **without**?

In Russian, analogues to (27)–(29) are generally impossible where the co-ordinated words govern different cases; see (31), showing that *s* 'with' governs the instrumental and *bez* 'without' governs the genitive, and (32b), showing that co-ordination of these two prepositions is impossible. Similarly, in (33), *ravno* 'equal (to)' takes dative and *bol'še* 'more (than)' takes genitive, and co-ordination, as in (33b), is unacceptable. An anaphoric zero and consequently an objectless preposition or other relator is possible, though felt by some to be colloquial or stylistically marked: (32a) and (33a).[7] Co-ordination with no reduction, as in (31), is always acceptable.

(31)   Kak ty p'eš' čaj, s   saxarom ili bez   saxara?
        how you drink tea with sugar-INSTR or without sugar-GEN
        'How do you drink your tea, with sugar or without it?'

(32)   a. Kak ty p'eš' čaj, s   saxarom   ili **bez**?
          how you drink tea with sugar-INSTR or without
          'How do you drink your tea, with sugar or without?' (colloquial)

       b. *Kak ty p'eš' čaj, s   ili bez   saxara?
           how you drink tea with or without sugar
           'How do you drink your tea, with or without sugar?'

(33)   a. ravno dvum   ili **bol'še**
          equal two-DAT or more
          'equal to or greater than two'

       b. **ravno** ili bol'še dvux[8]
          equal or more   two-GEN
          'equal to or greater than two'

Co-ordination is fully acceptable where both co-ordinates take the
same case: see (34b) and (35b). Here too some speakers find that the
variant with anaphoric zero is slightly less natural, though also fully
acceptable: (34a) and (35a).

(34)   a. Kogda ty prideš', do   uroka   ili **posle**?
          when you come before class-GEN or after
          'When are you coming, before class or after?'
       b. Kogda ty prideš', **do**   ili posle uroka?
          when you come before or after class-GEN
          'When are you coming, before or after class?'

(35)   a. bol'še dvux   ili **men'še**
          more two-GEN or less
          'more or less than two'
       b. **bol'še** ili men'še dvux
          more or less   two-GEN
          'more or less than two'

These examples show that bare prepositions or other case-governing
heads are tolerated in Russian only under two conditions: there may
be co-ordination of the heads, so that in a sense the factored-out
dependent is shared by the two heads (which is possible only when
the two heads govern the same case); or a dependent can be removed
by an anaphoric process.

8.6 Nunggubuyu

As an example of a more exotic language let us consider Nunggubuyu, a well-described language of Australia that is radically non-
configurational and has a good deal of head marking at the clause
level.

Heath (1984: 612–15) shows that many dependents, and perhaps also some heads, occur intonationally isolated in texts. Such examples appear to involve detachment, not ellipsis. True ellipsis is evidently involved in gapping, of which I have observed one example (here and below, underlining marks English intrusions):

(36)   wu-gu-ru "net" wirima+maya-na waː-dhurabada,
         they   they call it   white people
         nu-raː-'yun   wara-wuru-wuruj "nanʸja"
         as for us   Aboriginals   net
                                        (Heath, 1984: 501, ex. (15.xiv))
         'They call it "net", the white people, but we aboriginals [call it] "nanʸja".'

and in the few instances of what appear to be verbless sentences that occur in the texts; for example:

(37)   "him go cemetery", wara-white men,
                                  noun class marker
         nu-raː-'yunᵍ   gudugudu,   nu-raː-'yunᵍ
         as for us (EXP1) sacred burial ground as for us
         wara-wuru-wuruj wara-oldme-old-men
         Aboriginals   old men (redupl.)
         ' "He goes to the cemetery" , [say] the white people; as for us, we call it "gudugudu", us old Aboriginals.'   (Heath, 1980: 259, 50.5)

Ellipsis also appears to be involved in the construction Heath (1984: 612–15) describes as an **echo**, where some part of a constituent is repeated after the full constituent. Since Heath's term pertains to text analysis while I am analysing syntax, and since I also analyse preposed partial repetitions as involving the same syntactic process, I will simply refer to all of them by the discourse-neutral term **repeat**. Repeats are moderately frequent in the texts of Heath (1980). They can involve either head removal or dependent removal. (In the examples below I give Heath's smooth translation followed by my own clause-by-clause analysis, displayed line by line, with bold face indicating the elliptical repeats.) An example with head removal is:

(38)   nᵍi=ya-nᵍgi anji,   ba-gu nᵍi+wudhi aba ragij, a-wurugu-ruj
         she went   Jabiru there she perched then first at a billabong
         a-nᵍagara-wugag, **a-ngᵍara-wugag wurugu,**
         huge   huge   billabong
         a-nᵍagara-wugag wurugu, ba-gu xxx nᵍi+buri nᵍara-nᵍari-gay
         huge   billabong then   she sat   her nest
         adaba ba-gu, **ba-gu nᵍara-nᵍari-gay**
         then   there   there her nest

'Jabiru (crane) went along. She was perched there first (i.e. before the others arrived), at a huge billabong (pond). She sat there, (at) her nest.'   (Heath, 1980: 67; 10.1)'

Jabiru went along.
She perched first at a huge billabong.
Huge billabong.   [repeat with verb and adverbs removed]
Huge billabong.   [same]
Then she sat on her nest there.
Her nest there.   [repeat with verb and one adverb removed]

Examples with dependent removal are:

(39)   aba ni-ga na-ni-wiya-yun^g adaba ni=ya-n^{g}gi, oː-'ba-ni
        then he   son   then   he went   that
        anaː-gugu naː-'+galima-n^y, **naː-'+ga̲li̲ma-n^y**
        water   he got water for him
        ni-yan^{g}ga=ya-n^{g}giː::
        he went
        'As for the son, he went along. He collected water for him. He got it for him (the father) and went along back.'   (Heath, 1980: 69; 10.5)

        As for the son, he went along.
        He fetched water for him.
        (He) fetched for him.   [repeat with direct object deleted]
        He went along back.

(40)   am! n^{g}iwu=n^{g}a-n^g a̲daba **ya̲ː-ji   wu=buri,** ya̲ː-ji
        eat she ate it   then here   it   sat   here
        wu-nuga-n^{g}u=buri ana-nuga, ama-gulmun-duj
        stone   sat stone   in the belly
        'She swallowed it so that it, the stone, was sitting in her belly.'
                                        (Heath, 1980: 53; 7.9)

        She ate it,
        then **it sat here,** [independent and incorporated subjects both removed]
        the stone sat here in the belly.

For consistency with the other three languages surveyed above, this analysis of Nunggubuyu has been phrased in terminology suggesting a constituent analysis: repeats are elliptical forms of pristine clauses and they contain identifiable absences of identifiable constituents. In reality Nunggubuyu, a highly non-configurational language, does not obviously have either a pristine category S or identifiable constituents thereof (Heath, 1986). This is a language for which it is more appropriate to classify 'elliptical' strings by what is present than by what has been deleted. But the findings would be the same on that analysis. Nunggubuyu repeats can be either verbless nouns or nounless verbs. I will continue to speak of elliptical clauses and head or dependent removal for convenience, but without implying commitment to a configurational analysis of Nunggubuyu.

While Nunggubuyu can remove either heads or dependents, a count done on one text shows that dependent removal is much more common than head removal. The results are given in table 8.2. Clear cases of removal are infrequent (7 clauses out of 194), but most of them involve dependent removal (6 out of 7). There are another 16 instances of verbless constituents which might be viewed as repeats with head removal but are probably better analysed as nominal sentences with predicate adjectives (12 examples) or intonationally isolated nouns co-ordinate to noun arguments (4 examples) (see Heath, 1986: 387–8, 391 for the better analyses). Nunggubuyu is a pro-drop language in which a bare verb can be a complete sentence. Thirty-eight of the 153 non-repeat clauses are bare verbs; there are 35 bare verbs which repeat such bare verbs, and these repeats might well be included among the examples of repeats with dependent removal. There would then be a total of 35+6 = 41 examples of dependent removal as against 17 examples of head removal, both totals including unclear as well as clear cases. The 6 clear cases of dependent removal create bare verbs. Therefore a total of 38 + 35 + 6 = 79 clauses, repeats and non-repeats, consist of bare verbs, but at most only 17 constituents are analysable as bare nouns, and a more conservative figure is 1. Thus, regardless of whether one counts clear cases alone or clear and unclear cases, and regardless of whether one counts removals or remaining fragments, Nunggubuyu removes dependents (or isolates heads) much more often than it removes heads (or isolates dependents). Nunggubuyu must then be functionally endocentric.

Table 8.2   Constituent fragments in Nunggubuyu text

Noun(s) or pronoun(s) as repeat of S	1	(clear case of head removal)
Adjectival predicate	12	(formally much like head removal)
Bare noun in co-ordination	4	(formally somewhat like head removal)
Verb with partial valence (repeats of S)	6	(clear cases of dependent removal)
Bare verb as repeat of bare verb	35	(vacuous dependent removal)
Full S (including unrepeated bare verb)	153	

Text: Heath, 1980: 108–17, text 16; see also Heath, 1984: 589ff.

8.7 Suggestive analogues in word formation

Derivational processes in morphology show the same cross-linguistic opposition between removal of heads and removal of dependents. The Indo-European languages offer numerous instances of lexicalization of a construction with head removal. The stranded dependent comes to function as an autonomous word while carrying what was originally the marker of its syntactic relation in a particular construction. An example is English *seldom*, where the *-m* is a fossilized case suffix. Russian examples are *domoj* 'home(wards)', a fossilized dative of 'home, house', in which neither this form of the ending nor this function of the dative case is currently used; and *peškom* 'by foot', an instrumental (productive in this form and this function) of a noun lost from the language. Lexicalizations like these are to be expected in languages that can isolate inflected dependents, that is, languages with functionally exocentric constituents. Examples like these illustrate a diachronic mechanism that is of interest in the identification of functional centricity.

Further examples come from lexicalization of what were originally dependents in NPs. In Russian, last names like *Ivanov* and *Kuzmin* go back etymologically to possessive adjectives but are now autonomous words. In Chechen-Ingush, adjectives end in *-Vn*, identical to the genitive case ending, and this suggests that the category of adjectives arose in lexicalized possessive nouns. An example is *noxčii^n* 'Chechen, of the Chechen'.

Functionally endocentric languages can then be expected to exhibit lexicalized stranded heads, and there is some evidence that they do. Tzutujil, a Mayan language, uses possessive prefixes on abstract nouns, as in the following, derived from *chee7* 'tree, wood' (Dayley, 1985: 150; note that 7 is used for the glottal stop in Mayan practical orthographies).

(41)   r-   chee7 aal
        3.sg tree -ness
        'quality or fact of being (like) tree or wood; treeness, woodness'

Ordinarily, nouns with possessive affixes like *r-* 'third person singular' are used as heads of NPs with dependent possessors. But abstract nouns like this one have possessive inflection as part of their lexical form, and they can therefore be described as stranded by lexicalized dependent removal. Another example of lexicalized dependent removal comes from Mangarayi, a language of Australia (Merlan, 1982: 74); N = gender marker, Abs = case marker):

(42)   Ø- miyar- awu
         NAbs forehead its
         'cloud', literally '(It)s forehead'

The identity of the historical possessor is lost, but evidently this word represents the stranded head of an earlier locution characterizing clouds as someone's or something's forehead.

The examples presented in this section show lexicalized head removal in dependent-marked constituents (adverbs in Indo-European languages; the former possessor of NPs in Russian and Chechen-Ingush), and lexicalized dependent removal in head-marked constituents (former heads of possessive NPs in Tzutujil and Mangarayi). Of course, such lexicalization is visible only when it freezes morphology, and therefore the only visible examples will be dependent-marked (former) dependents (as in Russian and Chechen-Ingush) and head-marked (former) heads (as in Tzutujil and Mangarayi). A frozen stranded head noun in Russian or dependent noun in Tzutujil would be indistinguishable from an ordinary noun, since Russian has no head-marking and Tzutujil no dependent-marking on nouns in NPs. That is, these examples rather mechanically reflect morphology and only secondarily point to functional centricity types.

8.8 Conclusions

This survey has shown that isolation of heads and dependents in contexts of ellipsis or other discourse-based processes is not cross-linguistically uniform. Languages can prefer to isolate heads (Nunggubuyu), dependents (Russian), both (English), or neither (Chechen-Ingush). They can prefer to remove heads (Russian), dependents (Nunggubuyu), both (English) or neither (Chechen-Ingush).

Nor is preference for one or the other type of constituent reduction fully predictable from head/dependent marking. Only two of these four languages support the hypothesis of consistency in functional and structural centricity: Russian, which is dependent-marking and more prone to remove heads than dependents, and Nunggubuyu, which has a good deal of head-marking morphology and is more prone to remove dependents than heads. Chechen-Ingush, which is radically dependent-marking yet never removes heads, is a strong counter-example to the hypothesis of consistency. English, which is dependent-marking yet removes both heads and dependents with equal ease, is a weaker counter-example. Still, if head/dependent-marking does not predict constituent reduction, it is clear that morphology in general constrains the syntax of ellipsis. The clearest example is the comparison of Russian and English co-ordinate reduction (section 8.5), where a same-case constraint on co-ordination restricts possibilities of deletion.

Three of the languages – all but Chechen-Ingush – have both head-removing and dependent-removing processes among their syntactic rules. What differentiates the languages is not the absolute presence or absence of certain types of removal in their grammars but the relative frequencies of the two kinds of removal in actual usage.

In order to raise hypotheses conducive to further cross-linguistic research, several factors have been identified here as possibly inclining a dependent-marking language to use one or the other type of constituent reduction: configurationality, profound ergativity, co-ordination-based versus chaining-based grammar, amount of morphology, presence of head-marking morphology in addition to dependent-marking morphology.

The processes surveyed here will obviously not be useful tests for what is and what is not head in a given constituent: there is cross-linguistic variation, and the tendencies are statistical rather than categorical. In any event, the examples given above have concentrated on the treatment of verbs and their arguments, an area of grammar where there appears to be a majority stance, namely that the verb is the head. On the other hand, preferences in constituent reduction do appear to have something to do with the role played by constituents and/or the salience given to heads in the overall grammar of a language. That is, they may prove to bear on the kind of functional analysis to which a refined understanding of head and non-head status will be applicable. It is for this reason that this chapter has attempted to present generalizations and hypotheses in a form appropriate for construction of a cross-linguistic comparative framework.

A variety of different constituent-reducing processes have been surveyed here, not all of them found in all four of the languages. Reference to heads and dependents appears not to be part of the strict description of any of these processes. This means that functional centricity is not part of the grammar of any of the languages. Rather, it has the status of an observation on the grammar: a number of different processes in Russian remove heads and leave dependents standing alone; no process does this in Chechen-Ingush; etc. That is, functional centricity is a convergence in the effects or outputs of rules none of which necessarily refer to heads or non-heads. It is the kind of construct that is appropriate to cross-linguistic work, but one which probably has no place in the formal description of individual languages.

NOTES

1. Fieldwork on Chechen-Ingush was conducted in Tbilisi, Georgia, and Groznyj, Chechen-Ingush ASSR, as a participant in the ACLS-Academy Exchange of Senior Scholars (1984, 1989) and the Exchange of Senior Scholars with the Soviet Ministry of Higher Education (1979, 1981), supported by the International Research and Exchanges Board. I am grateful to the Oriental Institute of the Georgian Academy of Sciences, the Soviet Academy of Sciences and Groznyj State University for hospitality and research facilities. My deepest gratitude to the speakers of Chechen and Ingush who have worked with me on these occasions. Renewed thanks to my Russian-speaking colleagues for their patient consideration of yet another round of linguistic curiosities.

Travel funding that made it possible to attend the Talking Heads Round Table was provided by the Center for Slavic and East European Studies, University of California, Berkeley.
2. A Russian verb can stand alone only when its arguments can all be interpreted as anaphoric zeros, including when it is an answer to a yes–no question. Even here there are restrictions, as will be discussed below.
3. This firm conviction of all my consultants is belied by text examples, where the bare verb is rare in answers to yes–no questions. This may be because most of my yes–no examples come from narrative literature with direct speech representing colloquial Russian, and this representation of speech is quite different from actual colloquial Russian speech; for example:

– Mark Ivanovič, – načal Pirogov,... – Al'bert Gribov kogda-to rabotal u vas v aèroklube?
– Da, zamečatel'nyj byl texnik.
'Mark Ivanovich', Pirogov began,... 'Did an Albert Gribov ever work in your flying club?'
'Yes, he was a wonderful technician'   (Šeludjakov, 1972: 9–10)

A real spoken dialogue would probably have the interrogator first asking if Mark Ivanovich had known an Albert Gribov, then asking whether Gribov had worked for the club. That question (that is, *Rabotal li on u vas v aèroklube?* 'Did he work in your flying club?' could more easily be answered with the bare *Rabotal* 'worked'. The text example compresses two points of new information – Gribov's name and the question about his employment – into a single sentence, where actual spoken Russian would probably establish only one new point per sentence. Even then, to judge from examples in Zemskaja and Kapanadze (1978) and others I have overheard, a speaker would be more likely to answer *Da, rabotal* 'Yes, (he) worked' than simply *Rabotal* '(He) worked' (though, to judge from my elicitation, the same speaker, if asked to rank acceptability, would maintain that *Rabotal* was the better answer).

4. It is interesting that in Chechen-Ingush the same abstract tendency is visible in other parts of the grammar. Negation is a verbal affix or clitic; while English and Russian can negate nouns, adjectives, adverbs, pronouns, etc. (*not potatoes, not bad, not there, not me*), Chechen-Ingush can negate only verbs: *dika daːc* 'not good', literally '(it) isn't good'. That is, just as dependents cannot be isolated, neither can they be negated.

5. I take configurationality to be a scalar rather than dichotomous property. I follow such sources as Hale (1983) and Heath (1986) in understanding configurationality as the tendency to grammaticalize constituents in general (and not just as having versus lacking a vp constituent).

6. Terms for syntactic rules are defined in McCawley (1988).

7. The syntactic difference between the (a) variants (with co-ordination) and (b) variants (with anaphoric zero) in (32)–(35) is reflected in the intonation contours: in the (a) variants the entire co-ordinated phrase, including the shared dependent, constitutes a single intonation domain with a single sentence accent on the second conjunct; while in the (b) variants there are two sentence accents, one on each head.

8. Sentences like (33b) are accepted only by speakers familiar with contemporary mathematical usage, in which words like *ravno* 'equal' and *bol'še* 'more' are gradually ceasing to govern cases and turning into particles, so that one can even hear, for example, *ravno dva* 'equal to two' (*dva* is nominative). In the final stage of the process, (*) *ravno ili bol'še dva* '≥ 2' will involve co-ordination of dependents, not heads.

9 Heads in Head-driven Phrase Structure Grammar

ROBERT D. BORSLEY

9.1 Introduction

Head-driven Phrase Structure Grammar (HPSG) is the only current approach to syntax with 'head' in its title.[1] Obviously, then, heads play an important role in the framework. As its founders, Pollard and Sag, stress, HPSG is also a unification-based approach (see Pollard and Sag, 1987). This means that whether or not an expression is well formed depends on a variety of factors, none of which takes precedence over any other. I will argue that there is a conflict between these two features of the framework. More precisely, I claim that a fully general characterization of the head–mother relation requires a default principle which is incompatible with a purely unification-based approach (as in Pollard and Sag, 1987: 8). It seems to me that this is true within the standard version of HPSG, but it is particularly true if HPSG is revised in ways that I have argued for elsewhere (Borsley, 1987, forthcoming). A unification-based approach is not something that should be given up lightly, since it offers a simple picture of how grammars function and is attractive from a computational point of view.[2] However, if it precludes the capturing of a linguistically significant generalization, it should be abandoned, and it seems to me that this is the case.

In a sense, this chapter is rather narrowly focused, since it is concerned with the correct formulation of one principle in one not very widely assumed framework. However, the argument that I develop is potentially relevant to any framework in which heads have mothers, any constituency-based framework, in other words. Heads are likely to have much the same properties in any constituency-based framework, and unification is likely to play a central role in any fully formalized framework. Thus, it seems likely that the argument I develop here is not just relevant to HPSG.

The chapter is organized as follows. In section 9.2, I outline the standard version of HPSG presented in Pollard and Sag (1987). Next I look more closely at the relation between head and mother in standard HPSG and argue for a default version of HPSG's Head Feature Principle (section 9.3). Then, in section 9.4, I summarize the case for a revised version of HPSG that I present in Borsley (1987, forthcoming). Section 9.5 makes the case that the proposed revisions provide further motivation for a default Head Feature Principle. Then, in section 9.6, I discuss the broader relevance of the chapter's argument, and finally I give a summary (section 9.7).

9.2 Standard HPSG

The essential details of the standard version of HPSG can be illustrated fairly briefly. As we will see, heads play a major role, constraining both the sisters and the mothers with which they co-occur.

Central to standard HPSG is a feature SUBCAT, whose value is a list of signs, which are combinations of syntactic, semantic and phonological information.[3] For simplicity, however, I will assume that the list consists of categories. The list indicates both what complements an item takes and what kind of subject it requires. The complements are listed in the order most oblique to least oblique and are followed by the subject.[4] Thus, for a ditransitive verb like *spares*, we will have the following category:

(1)   v[LEX+;SUBCAT<NP, NP, NP[3SG]>]

The feature specification [LEX+] distinguishes lexical categories from phrasal categories. For a simple transitive verb like *likes*, we will have the following category:

(2)   v[LEX+;SUBCAT<NP, NP[3SG]>]

Finally, for a simple intransitive verb like *sleeps*, we will have the following:

(3)   v[LEX+;SUBCAT<NP[3SG]>]

SUBCAT can also have the empty list, represented as '<>', as its value. This situation occurs with both Ss and NPs, which are analysed as v[LEX−;SUBCAT<>] and N[LEX−;SUBCAT<>], respectively. (Thus, 'NP' in (1)–(3) is an informal notation.)

The most obvious feature of HPSG is that it has very few rules. In particular, it has very few immediate dominance (ID) rules. In HPSG, such rules state that certain signs can have certain other signs as immediate constituents. It will not misrepresent the framework too much, however, if we assume that they state that certain categories can immediately dominate certain other categories. The two rules that we need to consider here are the following:

(4)   a. [SUBCAT$<[]>$] $\rightarrow$ H[LEX+], C*
          b. [SUBCAT$<>$] $\rightarrow$ H[LEX−], C

I will call (4a) the head–complement rule and (4b) the subject–predicate rule. '[]' stands for an arbitrary category, 'H' for a head, and 'C' for a non-head. We can paraphrase these rules as follows:

(5)   a. A category with a single member SUBCAT list can immediately dominate a lexical head and any number of non-heads.
          b. A category with an empty SUBCAT list can immediately dominate a phrasal head and a single non-head.

Nothing in these rules ensures that we have the right kind of non-heads or that we have the right kind of mother, that a nominal head has a nominal mother, a verbal head a verbal mother and so on. The former is ensured by the Subcategorization Principle and the latter by the Head Feature Principle (HFP). We can formulate the Subcategorization Principle as follows:

(6)   The value of SUBCAT in a head is the value of SUBCAT in its mother together with the sisters of the head.

The HFP can be formulated as follows:

(7)   The value of HEAD in a mother is identical to the value of HEAD in its head.

HEAD is a feature which groups together all other features except SUBCAT, the so-called BINDING features, for example, the feature SLASH involved in the analysis of unbounded dependencies, and the feature LEX. Given the Head Feature Principle and the Subcategorization Principle, the rules in (4) allow trees like the following:

(8)

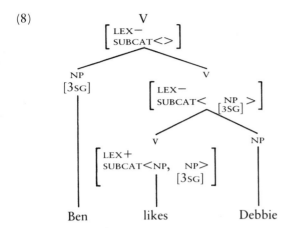

Example (8) illustrates clearly the way in which HPSG is a unification-based framework. Both of the subtrees that it consists of conform to a rule, to the two principles and to certain linear precedence rules (which we need not discuss), and none of these takes precedence over any of the others.

A further point that we should note is that specifiers are equated with subjects within the standard version of HPSG. Like subjects, they are analysed as realizations of the final item on a SUBCAT list. Thus, a simple common noun like *book* has the following category:

(9)   N[LEX+;SUBCAT<Det>]

Given this category, we will have trees like the following:[5]

(10)

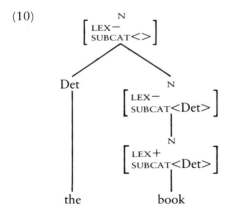

Examples (8) and (10) illustrate the way that heads constrain both their sisters and their mother in HPSG. In both areas, HPSG differs in important ways from the related Generalized Phrase Structure Grammar (GPSG) framework. Heads constrain their sisters in GPSG but only indirectly as a result of their association with various different ID rules (Gazdar *et al.*, 1985: 31–5). HPSG seems a clear advance on GPSG here. Heads constrain their mothers directly in GPSG through the Head Feature Convention (HFC) (Gazdar *et al.*, 1985: 94–9). This differs from the HFP of HPSG in a number of ways. Most important in the present context is that whereas the HFP is an absolute principle, the HFC is a default principle. It stipulates that head and mother have the same value for HEAD features unless some rule requires otherwise.[6] It is cited in Gazdar (1987) as an important illustration of the role that default inheritance can play in linguistic analysis. It is not so clear that HSPG represents an advance over GPSG here. The fact that rules take precedence over the HFC means, however, that GPSG, unlike HPSG, is not a purely unification-based framework. This is an important difference between the two frameworks.

9.3 Heads and mothers in standard HPSG

We can now look more closely at the relation between heads and mothers in standard HPSG. I will begin by introducing an important methodological assumption. Then I will look at some further structures which, given this assumption, provide some motivation for a default HFP.

What should we expect of an analysis of the head–mother relation? It seems to me that it is reasonable to impose the following requirement:

(11)   All similarities between a head and its mother should be attributed to the same principle unless there is evidence that some other principle is responsible.

I am assuming here that there can be similarities which should be attributed to a different principle from the main principle that is responsible for head–mother similarities. A case in point is provided by unbounded dependency constructions.

In HPSG, unbounded dependency constructions are analysed in terms of a feature SLASH whose value is a set of signs. For simplicity, however, I will assume that its value is a set of categories. We can look first at the bracketed subordinate clause in the following:

(12)   I wonder [what John did]

This will have something like the following structure:

(13)

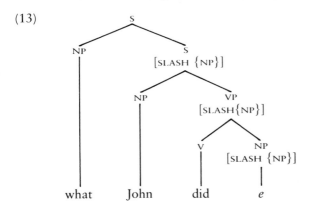

The important point about this example in the present context is that the lower S and the VP which is its head on HPSG assumptions have the same value for the feature SLASH. One might suppose that this should be attributed to the principle that is responsible for other head–mother similarities and this is essentially the position of GPSG, where unbounded dependencies are analysed in terms of a SLASH feature, whose value is a category (Gazdar *et al.*, 1985: 137–68). However, as Pollard and Sag (forthcoming) note, there is evidence against this position. Consider the following:

(14)   What did John do?

This will have something like the following structure:

(15)

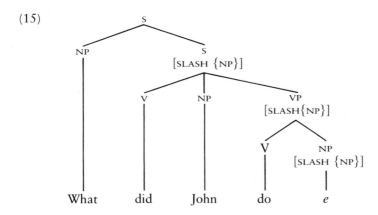

Here, the lower S and the complement daughter have the same value for SLASH. It is clear that the SLASH specification of the lower S must appear on the complement daughter. If we allowed local trees like (16), we would allow examples like (17).

(16)

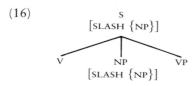

(17)   *Who did a picture of annoy John?

It is fairly clear, then, that we need a principle referring to both heads and complements to ensure the correct distribution of the SLASH feature, and this is essentially what Pollard and Sag (forthcoming) propose. Thus, in (13), we have a similarity between head and mother which should not be attributed to the HFP.

We can turn now to some further types of structure in which we have similarities between head and mother which, given the principle in (11), should be attributed to the HFP, but which can only be attributed to the HFP if it is a default principle. Firstly, we can look at head–adjunct structures, exemplified by the bracketed strings in the following:

(18)   a. Ben [slept in the bath]
         b. the [man with a bike]

It is widely assumed that adjuncts appear in structures of the following form and this assumption is shared by HPSG:[7]

(19)

Such structures have figured prominently in GPSG arguments for a default formulation of the HFC (see, for example, Pullum, 1985: 346–8). The important point about them for GPSG is that head and mother are identical in all respects including bar level, and thus provide evidence against the idea characteristic of much work in X-bar theory that head and mother are identical in all respects except bar level. In HPSG, they are also identical in all respects including the value of SUBCAT. Hence, we must ask how we can ensure that they have identical values for SUBCAT.

The same question arises with filler–gap structures, exemplified by topicalization sentences and WH-questions such as the following:

(20)   a. Beans I like.
        b. What do you like?

The essential structure of such examples is as follows:

(21)
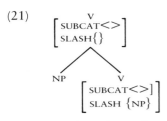

Here, head and mother are not identical because the head is [SLASH{NP}] while the mother is [SLASH{}]. However, they do have the same value, <>, for SUBCAT. Again, then, we must ask how we can ensure that we have identical values for SUBCAT.

One way in which we might ensure that head and mother have the same value for SUBCAT in these two types of structure is with a revised Subcategorization Principle. It is clear, in fact, that it must be revised anyway. As we have formulated it, there should be no sisters where head and mother have the same value for SUBCAT. If we use the term complement in an extended way to refer both to complements in the narrow sense and to specifiers and subjects, but not to either adjuncts or fillers, we might reformulate the Subcategorization Principle as follows:

(22)   The value of SUBCAT in a head is the value of SUBCAT in its mother together with the complement sisters of the head.

So formulated, the principle will ensure that the appropriate complement sisters appear when head and mother have different values for SUBCAT and also that head and mother have the same value for SUBCAT when there is no complement sister. Here, then, we have a way of ensuring that head and mother have the same value for SUBCAT in the two types of structure that we are concerned with. It appears, however, that this approach is incompatible with the principle in (11). As far as I can see, there is no reason to attribute these similarities between head and mother to a different principle from other similarities in the way that there is with the similarity that we were concerned with in (13). It seems to me, then, that this is not a satisfactory approach.

One might also ensure that head and mother have the same value for SUBCAT in these two types of structure by stipulating this in the relevant rules. This too, however, is incompatible with (11). It seems that this too is not a satisfactory approach.

If there is no good reason for attributing these similarities between head and mother to a different principle from other similarities, then they should be attributed to the HFP. It is not too difficult to do this. Firstly, we need to add SUBCAT to the features which constitute the value of HEAD and to reformulate the HFP as follows:

(23)   The value of HEAD in a mother is identical to the value of HEAD in its head unless some rules says otherwise.

Then, we can reformulate the two rules as follows:

(24)   a. [SUBCAT<[]>] → H[LEX+;SUBCAT<...>], c*
        b. [SUBCAT<>] → H[LEX−;SUBCAT<[]>], c

I use '<...>' here to stand for any list. The important point about these rules is that they stipulate that head and mother have different values for SUBCAT. They will ensure that head and mother have different values for SUBCAT in head–complement and subject–predicate structures but the HFP will ensure that they have the same value for SUBCAT in head–adjunct and filler–gap structures. Finally, we can reformulate the Subcategorization Principle so that it is only operative where head and mother have different values. We can propose the following:

(25)   When head and mother have different values for SUBCAT, the value of SUBCAT in the head is the value of SUBCAT in its mother together with the sisters of the head.

I have argued, then, that head–adjunct structures and filler–gap structures provide reasons for reformulating the HFP as a default principle. In both types of structure, head and mother have the same value for SUBCAT. It is possible to ensure this without invoking a default HFP, but there is no real reason to think that some other principle is responsible. Thus, a default HFP seems the right approach. But as we noted earlier, if we have a default HFP, HPSG will no longer be a purely unification-based framework.

9.4 Revised HPSG

We can turn now to the revised version of HPSG that is proposed in Borsley (1987, forthcoming). The central feature of this version of the framework is that the SUBCAT feature is replaced by three separate valency features: a restricted SUBCAT feature, which just indicates what complements an item takes; a SUBJ feature, which indicates what sort of subject an item requires; and a SPEC feature, which indicates what sort of specifier an item requires.

A number of arguments are advanced in Borsley (1987, forthcoming) for the proposal that subjects should be analysed as the realization of a separate SUBJ feature. We can note just two here. One argument is that it allows a more restrictive notion of possible non-head category. Within the standard framework, non-heads are either [SUBCAT<>] categories, [SUBCAT<[]>] categories (subjectless infinitives, predicative APs, etc.) or minor categories like Det or Deg. In the revised framework, they are either [SUBCAT<>] categories or minor categories. Another argument is that the proposal allows one to recognize heads that require a complement but not a subject. Within the standard framework, an item requires a subject if it requires anything at all. Within the revised framework, however, an item can be analysed as [SUBJ<>;SUBCAT<[]>]. Such an analysis seems appropriate *inter alia* for prepositions in complement and adverbial PPs.

Given a separate SUBJ feature, we will have the following categories instead of (1)–(3).

(26)   V[LEX+;SUBJ<NP[3SG]>;SUBCAT< NP, NP>]

(27)   V[LEX+;SUBJ<NP[3SG]>;SUBCAT<NP>]

(28)   V[LEX+;SUBJ<NP[3SG]>;SUBCAT<>]

Similarly, instead of (8), we will have trees like the following:

(29)

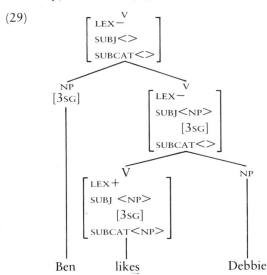

We will consider how the rules and principles should be reformulated in the next section.

The main argument for a SPEC feature distinct from SUBJ is that there are items that have both a specifier and a subject. Consider, for example, the following:

(30)   With Debbie a candidate, anything could happen.

(31)   With Ben too drunk to stand up, the party came to an end.

In (30), the noun *candidate* takes both a specifier *a* and a subject *Debbie*. Similarly, in (31), the adjective *drunk* takes both a specifier *too* and a subject *Ben*.

Given a separate SPEC feature, we will have the following categories for a simple common noun like *book*.

(32)   N[LEX+;SUBJ<>;SPEC<Det>;SUBCAT<>]

(33)   N[LEX+;SUBJ<NP>;SPEC<Det>;SUBCAT<>]

Example (32) is the category that we need for such a noun when it heads an argument NP, while (33) is the category that we need for such a noun when it heads a predicative NP. Given (32), we will have trees like the following:

(34)
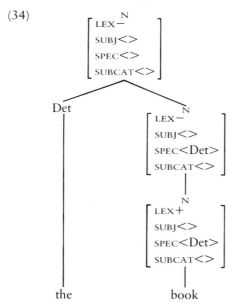

Example (33) will give us a similar tree with [SUBJ<NP>] instead of [SUBJ<>].

Andrew Radford has pointed out to me that examples like (30) and (31) would not necessitate a SPEC feature if determiners like *a* and degree words like *too* were analysed as heads, as proposed in Abney (1987) and elsewhere, for example Radford (this volume). I am sceptical, however, about the viability of such an analysis. I sketch an argument against the assumption that determiners are heads in Borsley (forthcoming) and other arguments are advanced in Payne (this volume). It is worth adding, however, that the argument that I develop in the following section would not be affected in any major way if a SPEC feature proved to be unnecessary.

9.5 Heads and mothers in revised HPSG

We can now look more closely at the relation between head and mother in the revised version of HPSG. I will argue that there is further motivation here for a default version of the HFP.

The relation between head and mother is obviously more complex given a number of separate valency features than it is if we have just a single SUBCAT feature. There are three different types of structure to consider: head–complement structures, specifier–head structures and subject–predicate structures. The position of the three valency features in the three types of structure can be summarized as follows:

(35) a. *Head–complement structures*
       The value of SUBCAT is any list in the head and the empty list in the mother.
       The value of SPEC is the same in the head and the mother.
       The value of SUBJ is the same in the head and the mother.
    b. *Specifier–head structures*
       The value of SUBCAT is the empty list in the head and the mother.
       The value of SPEC is a non-empty list in the head and the empty list in the mother.
       The value of SUBJ is the same in the head and the mother.
    c. *Subject–predicate structures*
       The value of SUBCAT is the empty list in the head and the mother.
       The value of SPEC is the empty list in the head and the mother.
       The value of SUBJ is a non-empty list in the head and the empty list in the mother.

In each type of structure, head and mother have different values for one of the valency features but the same value for the other two. The question to ask, of course, is: how can we ensure the identical values?

One might try to attribute the identical values to a revised version of the Subcategorization Principle. It is not at all clear to me, however, how exactly this approach could be implemented, and, of course, it would face the objection that it treats certain similarities between head and mother as different from others without any good reason.

One might also stipulate the identities in the rules. Specifically, one might propose the following rules for the three types of structure:

(36)   [SUBJ $\boxed{1}$;SPEC $\boxed{2}$;SUBCAT<>] → H[LEX+;SUBJ $\boxed{1}$;SPEC $\boxed{2}$], C*

(37)   [SUBJ $\boxed{1}$;SPEC<>;SUBCAT<>] → H[LEX−;SUBJ $\boxed{1}$;SUBCAT<>], C

(38)   [SUBJ<>;SPEC<>;SUBCAT<>] → H[LEX−;SPEC<>;SUBCAT<>], C

Following standard HPSG practice, I use numerical tags here to indicate that two features have the same value. Thus, the head–complement rule in (36) stipulates that head and mother have the same value for SPEC and SUBCAT; the specifier–head rule in (37) stipulates that head and mother have the same value for SUBJ and SUBCAT (the empty list in the latter case); and the subject–predicate rule in (38) stipulates that head and mother have the same value for SPEC and SUBCAT (the empty list in both cases). These rules would capture the position of the three valency features in the three types of structure. Again, however, we are treating certain similarities between head and mother as different from others without any good reason for doing so; so this is not a very satisfactory approach.

It is worth noting that the situation here is somewhat different from that in standard HPSG. In standard HPSG, head and mother sometimes have the same value for SUBCAT and sometimes have different values. In the revised framework, we can say that it is normal for head and mother to have the same value for these features. It is only when the value of a valency feature on a head is realized by sisters of the head that head and mother have different values for this feature and this is only the case in one type of structure. It seems to me, then, that we have rather stronger motivation here for a default version of the HFP than we have in standard HPSG.

If we have a default version of the HFP, we can formulate the three rules as follows:

(39)   [SUBCAT<>] → H[LEX+;SUBCAT<...>], C*

(40)   [SPEC<>] → H[LEX−;SPEC<[]>;SUBCAT<>], C

(41)   [SUBJ<>] → H[LEX−;SUBJ<[]>;SPEC<>;SUBCAT<>], C

Each rule will ensure that head and mother have different values for one of the valency features (the mother having the value <> in each case). The HFP will ensure that they have the same value for the other valency features. More precisely, it will ensure that head and mother have the same value for SPEC and SUBJ in structures licensed by the head–complement rule, that head and mother have the same value for SUBJ and SUBCAT in structures licensed by the specifier–head rule (in the latter case the empty list), and that head and mother have the same value for SPEC and SUBCAT in structures licensed by the subject–predicate rule (in both cases the empty list).

One other thing that we need to do in the revised framework is to reformulate the Subcategorization Principle so that it governs all three valency features. It is not difficult to do this. We can propose the following:

(42)   For any valency feature F, when head and mother have different values for F, the value of F in the head is the value of F in its mother together with the sisters of the head.

This will ensure that heads have the appropriate complement, specifier and subject sisters. It will also ensure that heads have the right filler sisters if we identify SLASH as a valency feature (though not as a HEAD feature). Given this, we might provide for filler–gap structures with the following rule:

(43)   [SLASH{...}] → H[MAJ V;SUBJ<>;SPEC<>;SUBCAT<>;SLASH{...[]...}], C

Notice that there is no need here to specify that the mother is [SUBJ<>], [SPEC<>] and [SUBCAT<>] since the HFP will ensure that.

It appears that the case for a default version of the HFP is strengthened quite considerably if the SUBCAT feature of standard HPSG is replaced by three separate valency features. This lends further support to the view that HPSG cannot be a purely unification-based framework.

9.6 The broader relevance of the argument

In this final section, I want to suggest that the foregoing discussion is not just relevant in the context of HPSG. Rather, it is potentially relevant for any framework in which heads have mothers, any constituency-based framework in other words. I will develop this point with reference to the Government–Binding (GB) theory.

Like HPSG, GB assumes a small number of ID rules (although they are not normally called ID rules). We can formulate the main rules as follows:

(44)   a. $X'' \rightarrow Y'', X'$
       b. $X' \rightarrow X, Y''*$

Example (44a) provides for specifier–head structures and (44b) provides for head–complement structures. They suggest that head and mother are identical except for bar level in both types of structure. If this were the case, it would be unsatisfactory to state it in the rules. Rather, it would call for a principle, something like the following:

(45)   A mother and its head are identical except for bar level.

This is a relative of the HFP, of course. But it is easy to show that (45) is too simple. This becomes clear if we consider the valency properties of heads.

   In GB, it is assumed that the valency properties of heads are largely predictable from the θ-roles with which they are associated. A distinction is drawn between internal and external θ-roles, and the following assumption is made about internal θ-roles:

(46)   The internal θ-roles of a head are assigned to its complements.

The situation with external θ-roles is rather more complex. It depends in part on how the bracketed strings in the following, which for GB are small clauses, are analysed:

(47)   Debbie considers [Ben a fool]

(48)   Debbie considers [Ben foolish]

(49)   Debbie wanted [Ben out of the room]

(50)   Debbie made [Ben do it]

One proposal, advanced in Stowell (1981), is that they involve structures of the following form, where X is N, A, P or V.

(51)

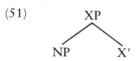

The situation with external θ-roles also depends on how the subjects of ordinary clauses are analysed. A widely accepted proposal, advanced, for example, in Sportiche (1988), is that they originate as VP-specifiers and are moved to the IP-specifier position. On this analysis, (52) has the derivation in (53).

(52)   Ben may annoy Debbie.

(53)

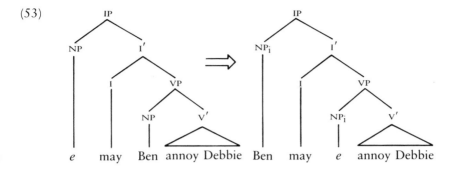

If we accept both of these proposals, we might make the following assumption.

(54)   The external θ-role of a head is assigned to its specifier.

A further plausible assumption is the following:

(55)   A category can only assign a θ-role to a sister.

Given this assumption, an X′ must inherit the external θ-role specification of its head. A final assumption that it seems natural to make is the following:

(56)   A category does not inherit a θ-role specification from its head if the θ-role is assigned to a sister of the head.

Given this assumption, an X′ will not inherit the internal θ-role specification of its head, and an X″ will not inherit the external θ-role specification of its head.

We can return now to the head–mother relation. Given the assumptions that we have just made about θ-roles, it seems natural to propose the following principle:

(57)   A mother and its head are identical unless some rule or principle allows them to differ.

The rules in (44) will allow a mother and its head to differ in bar level and the principle in (56) will allow a mother and its head to differ in θ-role specifications. In the present context, of course, the important point is that (57) is a default principle. Given such a principle, a fully formalized version of GB cannot be purely unification-based.

There are obviously alternative assumptions that one might make about θ-roles, and it is possible that some will eliminate the need for a default HFP. Moreover, GB is not the only constituency-based framework. It seems quite likely, however, that a fully general characterization of the head–mother relation will require a default principle in any constituency-based framework and hence be incompatible with a purely unification-based approach to syntax. Thus the argument developed is not just relevant to HPSG.

9.7 Conclusions

We have looked at the head–mother relation both in the standard version of HPSG presented in Pollard and Sag (1987) and in the revised version proposed in Borsley (1987, forthcoming). I have argued that there is motivation within both versions of the framework for a default version of the HFP.[8] The argument would be of limited interest if it was relevant only to HSPG. I have shown, however, through a consideration of GB that it is probably relevant to any constituency-based framework. And so, while this chapter is about heads in HPSG, it is not just about heads in HPSG.

NOTES

1. I am grateful to Carl Pollard, Nigel Vincent and Andrew Radford for a number of helpful comments on an earlier version of this chapter. All remaining imperfections are my responsibility.
2. In Borsley (1990), I outline an HSPG-based computational grammar of English, which incorporates a number of the ideas of Borsley (1987, forthcoming). It does not, however, incorporate a default version of the HFP.
3. Pollard and Sag (forthcoming) propose that SUBCAT takes a list not of signs but of SYNSEM objects, combinations of syntactic and semantic information. The idea here is that heads restrict the syntactic and semantic properties of their sisters but not their phonological properties.
4. In Pollard and Sag (forthcoming), the order of the list is reversed. However, this change is of no significance.
5. One might question whether it is desirable to have a non-branching phrasal node in examples like this, and also whether it is desirable to have such a node in sentences with a simple intransitive verb such as *Ben slept*. In fact, in Borsley (1987, forthcoming), I assume that it is undesirable. If one takes this view, one must, of course, allow specifiers and subjects to combine with a lexical category.
6. This is something of a simplification because it ignores co-ordinate structures, which are analysed within GPSG as multiply headed. Where a mother has a number of heads, the HFC requires it to have the HEAD feature specifications which are common to all the heads.

7. Pollard and Sag (1987) assume that heads select the adjuncts with which they combine through an ADJUNCTS feature. Pollard and Sag (forthcoming) propose that adjuncts select the heads with which they combine through a MOD feature. In the present context, however, it is not important which of these positions is adopted. Pollard and Sag's (1987) analysis allows structures in which a number of adjuncts are sisters and structures in which adjuncts are sisters of complements as well as structures like (32).

8. Essentially, my argument is that the standard, absolute HFP is too weak because it cannot account for situations in which head and mother have the same value for features that encode the valency properties of heads. It may be that the standard HFP is also too strong. Pullum (1991) argues on the basis of English nominal gerund phrases that a head and mother may differ in their basic categorial status. For example, a verbal head may have a nominal mother. This is ruled out by the standard HFP, but is quite compatible with a default HFP. Thus, while valency features provide particularly strong motivation for a default HFP, they are probably not the only features that are relevant.

10 *Heads and lexical semantics*

SCOTT McGLASHAN

10.1 Introduction

This chapter discusses the syntactic and semantic relations between the 'head of a phrase' and the phrase itself.[1] In particular, the phrase is a 'kind of' the head since the latter provides both the semantic and syntactic type of the phrase (Hudson, 1987: 115–16). For example, the noun can be treated as head in noun phrases and its systematic priority over other categories in the phrase, such as adjectives and determiners, is manifest in the syntactic and semantic type of the phrase.[2]

There are three reasons for discussing these syntactic and semantic relations. The first is to introduce a unification framework which characterizes them in terms of a dependency approach to combination: categories in a binary phrase are combined as 'head' and 'modifier' (or 'dependent') (Hays, 1964; Anderson, 1977: 92–100; Hudson, 1984: 75–9; Miller, 1985: 25–31). The second reason is to show that this framework provides a better account of these relations than frameworks where categories are combined as functor and argument (Ajdukiewicz, 1935; Vennemann and Harlow, 1977; Flynn, 1983; Calder *et al.*, 1987; Zeevat, 1988). The third – and most important – reason is to introduce evidence which demonstrates that the semantic relations between heads and phrases are not necessarily transparent: the phrase can exhibit semantic properties which conflict with those of the head. This evidence leads to a revision of the framework where semantic conflicts are resolved on the basis of the head–modifier distinction.

10.2 The Head–Modifier Principle

The framework adopted is a unification grammar in which categories combine as head and modifier to yield a result category for the phrase. Before describing the framework in detail, we outline three aspects of dependency grammar which motivate it: specification, category constancy and obligatoriness.

The first aspect is that the modifier category syntactically and semantically specifies the head category. As Jespersen (1924:96) says, 'the chief word [head] is defined (qualified, modified) by another word, which may be defined (qualified, modified) by a third word'. With *large elephants*, for example, the noun *elephants* is semantically specified by the adjective *large*: the size of the elephant is specified as large. The modifier may also specify syntactic properties of the head; in *two elephants* the quantifier *two* confirms the plural number on the head *elephants*. These examples illustrate two effects of specification on the head: the addition of new properties; and confirmation of existing properties.[3]

The second aspect is category constancy: the syntactic and semantic type of the result category is provided by the head rather than the modifier category (Hjelmslev, 1939). With *pink elephants*, for example, the result category is syntactically a 'kind of' noun, not an adjective, and semantically a 'kind of' entity rather than a property of an entity.

The third aspect is obligatoriness: the head category is obligatory to the phrase (Hjelmslev, 1939; Miller, 1985: 27; Anderson, 1986: 55). The notion of obligatoriness, however, must be approached with caution, since the absence of a category can indicate either optional or elliptical status (Zwicky, 1985: 13). Head categories are obligatory since they provide the syntactic and semantic types of the result category; without these, the result category would not be defined. Consequently, when the head category is absent, it must be elliptical rather than optional: it is implicit in the discourse and when reconstructed from context provides the syntactic and semantic types of the phrase (Matthews, 1981: 38–45). For example, in the context of talking about two films, the head noun (*film*) can be elided as in *I didn't see either* (Nichols, this volume). Modifier categories, on the other hand, are not obligatory in this sense. In phrases where they are obligatory, it is the head category which provides the types; for example, the result category in the auxiliary–verb phrase (*the elephant*) *may like hay* is semantically a 'liking' event not a property such as possibility.[4] Modifier categories are obligatory in such constructions in order to provide properties necessary for the result category, properties which are not provided by the head itself. For example, the result of combining a verb with an auxiliary verb must be specified for tense and if this is not inherent in the verb (*like*), then it must be provided by the auxiliary-verb modifier (*may*).

These three aspects underpin combination: phrases are characterized as the category which results from the extension of a head category through specification by a modifier category. The head category provides the syntactic and semantic type of the result category so long as the modifier category does not change properties of the head which define its syntactic or semantic type.[5] The head category is also obligatory since it is necessary for specification by the modifier category and for the existence of the result category.[6]

In this framework, each category is defined for the attribute-value pairs given in (1) (Andry *et al.*, forthcoming):[7]

(1)   category = phonology $\wedge$ syntax $\wedge$ order $\wedge$ semantics $\wedge$ constraints
            phonology = member-of (orthographic form)
            syntax = head $\wedge$ modifier
                  head = type
                        type = noun $\vee$ verb $\vee$ adjective $\vee$ auxiliary
                        $\vee$ determiner $\vee$ adverb
                        modifier = set-of (category)
                  order = directionality $\wedge$ adjacency $\wedge$ optionality
                  directionality = pre $\vee$ post
                  adjacency = next $\vee$ nonext
                  optionality = optional $\vee$ obligatory
            semantics = type $\wedge$ set of-(property)
                        type = member-of(type hierarchy)
            constraints = set-of (constraint)
                        constraint = name $\wedge$ type condition arg*
                              name = member-of(constraint-name)
                              type = necessary $\vee$ default
                              condition = path $\vee$ constraint
                              arg = path $\vee$ constraint

Combination is characterized in terms of the unification of part of the head category with the whole of the modifier category, as well as constraints which relate this part to other parts of the head category (Shieber, 1986: 14–24; Pollard and Sag, 1987: 28–50). Unifying categories composed of attribute-value pairs impose two restrictions on specification: compatibility and subsumption. With compatibility, only categories with compatible attribute-value pairs can unify. With subsumption, all attribute-value pairs in each unifying category must be contained in their unification: information cannot be lost or changed, only confirmed or added. In this way, unification supports the two effects of specification described above.

The syntax attribute of categories is broadly analogous with that in Categorial Grammar (see section 10.3). In particular, the head–modifier distinction has been 'pushed' inside the syntax attribute so that each category is defined for a head attribute, here describing its syntactic type, and a modifier attribute whose value is a set of categories with which it can combine. Combinational information in dependency rules is specified in the categories themselves, thereby reducing both the number and complexity of rules. For example, the rule for intransitive verbs, $V(N^*)$ (Robinson, 1970: 262), is characterized using a general combinational rule – the Head-Modifier Principle (HMP) – together with the category structure in (2), where the value of <syntax head type> is verb and the value of <syntax modifier first syntax head type> is noun.[8]

$$(2) \quad \left[\text{syntax :} \left[\begin{array}{l} \text{head : [type : verb]} \\[1em] \text{modifier :} \left\langle \left[\begin{array}{l} \text{syntax : [head: [type : noun]]} \\[1em] \text{order:} \left[\begin{array}{l} \text{directionality : pre} \\ \text{optionality : obligatory} \end{array} \right] \end{array} \right] \right\rangle \end{array} \right] \right]$$

Note that the relative ordering and optionality of these categories is specified in the value of the modifier's **order** attribute: the noun is obligatory (**obligatory**) and precedes the verb (**pre**), although they are not necessarily adjacent since no value is specified for the attribute **adjacency**.

A concept is described in terms of the semantic attribute of a category through its type attribute and a set of properties. The type identifies the location of the concept in an inheritance hierarchy. Types are ordered in terms of subsumption such that more general types subsume more specific types and, conversely, types which are subsumed by more general types inherit properties from them. Apart from the root of the hierarchy, which defines *mode* properties, each type is defined for either atomic or complex *core* properties: atomic properties are characterized with a value attribute; and complex properties are characterized with one or more role attributes, where each role expresses a relation between the concept itself and another concept in the hierarchy.[9] In this hierarchy shown in figure 10.1, the root type TOP is defined for mode properties, such as **polarity** and **definite**, whose values are themselves of the type PRE-PROPERTY. The TOP type subsumes four general types of concept which in turn inherit

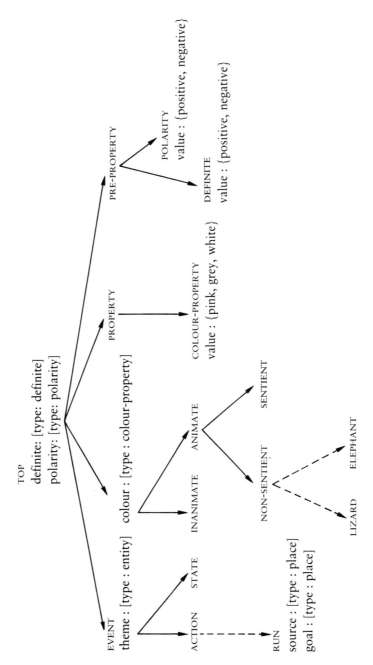

Figure 10.1 A portion of a concept hierarchy

the mode properties: EVENT, ENTITY, PROPERTY and PRE-PROPERTY.[10] The type EVENT, for example, is defined for a core property, **theme**, which relates it to concepts of the type ENTITY. This property is inherited by the type RUN, which is also defined for the roles **source** and **goal**. Likewise, ENTITY is defined for the role **colour**, which relates it to concepts of the type COLOUR-PROPERTY, itself subsumed by the type PROPERTY, and this property is inherited by subsumed types such as ELEPHANT.

Finally, each category is defined for a set of constraints which explicitly relate substructures within the category. The name of the constraint specifies the relation between the arguments in the constraint. For example, an equality constraint specifies a re-entrancy relationship between path arguments. The type of a constraint indicates whether the relation is necessary or a default; while default relations may hold, necessary relations must hold for the category to be well formed. Conditions indicate that the relation is conditional; necessary constraints must hold if the condition is satisfied; default relations may hold if the condition is satisfied.

One purpose of constraints is to define the relation between the modifier attribute of a category and its head attribute.[11] The effect of this is to pass information from a modifier category, which unifies with an **active** modifier in the modifier set, up to the head attribute of the head category, which then becomes the result category for the phrase. For example, a constraint may define a re-entrancy relation between the semantics of a modifier category and a role in semantics of the head category. In (3), the semantics of the 'subject' of *run* is equated with the value of the **theme** role by means of an equality constraint which unifies the value of <syntax modifier first semantics> with that of <semantics theme>:

(3)

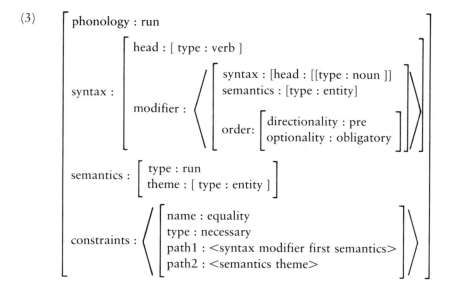

$$
\left[
\begin{array}{l}
\text{phonology : run} \\[4pt]
\text{syntax :}
\left[
\begin{array}{l}
\text{head : [type : verb]} \\[4pt]
\text{modifier :}
\left\langle
\left[
\begin{array}{l}
\text{syntax : [head : [[type : noun]]} \\
\text{semantics : [type : entity]} \\[4pt]
\text{order:}
\left[
\begin{array}{l}
\text{directionality : pre} \\
\text{optionality : obligatory}
\end{array}
\right]
\end{array}
\right]
\right\rangle
\end{array}
\right] \\[30pt]
\text{semantics :}
\left[
\begin{array}{l}
\text{type : run} \\
\text{theme : [type : entity]}
\end{array}
\right] \\[20pt]
\text{constraints :}
\left\langle
\left[
\begin{array}{l}
\text{name : equality} \\
\text{type : necessary} \\
\text{path1 : <syntax modifier first semantics>} \\
\text{path2 : <semantics theme>}
\end{array}
\right]
\right\rangle
\end{array}
\right]
$$

Accordingly, when *run* combines with a noun in the subject position, such as *elephants* in *elephants run*, the subject's semantic type and properties are equated with those of the **theme**: the semantic type of **theme** in (3), for example, subsumes the semantic type of *elephants* in (6) below.

While the semantic constraint in (3) is appropriate for complement modifiers, it is inappropriate for attribute modifiers since these modifiers can be iterated and on each iteration a different attribute modified. Attribute modifiers can be divided into two types: mode modifiers, such as determiners, auxiliaries and intensive adverbs, which modify mode properties of the head and are subsumed by the general semantic type PRE-PROPERTY; and core modifiers, such as adjectives and adverbs, which modify its core properties and are subsumed by the type PROPERTY. Consider the categories for *the, pink* and *elephants* given in (4), (5) and (6) respectively:

(4)

$$
\left[
\begin{array}{l}
\text{phonology : the} \\
\text{syntax : [head : [type : determiner]]} \\[4pt]
\text{semantics :}
\left[
\begin{array}{l}
\text{type : definite} \\
\text{value : positive}
\end{array}
\right]
\end{array}
\right]
$$

(5)

$$
\begin{bmatrix}
\text{phonology : pink} \\
\text{syntax : [head : [type : adjective]]} \\[4pt]
\text{semantics :}
\begin{bmatrix}
\text{type : colour} \\
\text{value : pink}
\end{bmatrix}
\end{bmatrix}
$$

(6)

$$
\begin{bmatrix}
\text{phonology : elephants} \\[6pt]
\text{syntax :}
\begin{bmatrix}
\text{head : [type : noun]} \\[4pt]
\text{modifier :}
\left\langle
\begin{array}{l}
\begin{bmatrix}
\text{syntax : [head : [type : determiner]]} \\
\text{semantics : [type : pre-property]}
\end{bmatrix} \\[6pt]
\begin{bmatrix}
\text{syntax : [head : [type : adjective]]} \\
\text{semantics : [type : property]}
\end{bmatrix}
\end{array}
\right\rangle
\end{bmatrix} \\[10pt]
\text{semantics :}
\begin{bmatrix}
\text{type : elephant} \\
\text{definite : [type : definite]} \\
\text{polarity : [type : polarity]} \\
\text{colour : [type : colour]}
\end{bmatrix} \\[8pt]
\text{constraints :}
\left\langle
\begin{bmatrix}
\text{name : equality} \\
\text{type : necessary} \\
\text{path1 : <syntax modifier NUMBER semantics>} \\
\text{path2 : <semantics ROLE>}
\end{bmatrix}
\right\rangle
\end{bmatrix}
$$

The category for *elephants* given in (6), specifies an equality relation where the paths included typed variables: NUMBER in **path1** varies over the set of modifiers; and ROLE in **path2** varies over the roles in its semantics. When the mode modifier *the* in (4) combines with this category, it unifies with the first active modifier (DEFINITE is subsumed by PRE-PROPERTY) and application of the constraint then equates its semantics with the **definite** role contained in the head category's **semantics** attribute. Likewise, the core modifier *pink* in (5) unifies with the second active modifier (COLOUR PROPERTY is subsumed by PROPERTY) and the constraint equates its semantics with the **colour** property in the head's **semantics**. The semantics of the result category is shown in (7):

(7)

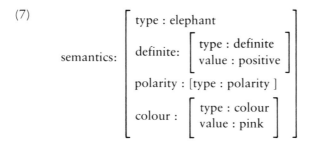

$$\text{semantics:} \begin{bmatrix} \text{type : elephant} \\[4pt] \text{definite:} \begin{bmatrix} \text{type : definite} \\ \text{value : positive} \end{bmatrix} \\[8pt] \text{polarity : [type : polarity]} \\[6pt] \text{colour :} \begin{bmatrix} \text{type : colour} \\ \text{value : pink} \end{bmatrix} \end{bmatrix}$$

Since this constraint does not specify which role the modifier's semantics is to be equated with, different occurrences of attribute modifiers can be equated with different roles in the head. The only restriction is that the structures must be compatible; this rules out phrases like *black pink elephants*, where incompatible colour properties are specified. Furthermore, the only difference between the constraints for complement and attribute modifiers is that in the former case both the ROLE and NUMBER are specified.

The head–modifier assignments in this framework are based upon traditional assignments (Chomsky, 1970: 210; Jackendoff, 1977b; Gazdar and Pullum, 1981). Table 10.1 gives the head of simple phrases together with their syntactic and (general) semantic type. What underlies these assignments is the general semantic type of the combining categories. Within the dependency tradition, the priority of heads has been motivated on the basis of ranking; for example, in dependency case grammar categories are ranked on the basis of a syntactic type constructed out of semantic properties, such as N – potentially referential – and P – potentially predicative (Anderson, 1989b). An alternative to Anderson's approach is to rank categories on the basis of their general semantic type, as shown in (8) (> signifies outranking):

Table 10.1   Assignments with the Head–Modifier Principle

Phrase	Head	Modifier	Example
noun–verb	verb, EVENT	noun, ENTITY	elephants run
verb–noun	verb, EVENT	noun, ENTITY	saw elephants
adjective–noun	noun, ENTITY	adjective, PROPERTY	grey elephants
verb–adverb	verb, EVENT	adverb, PROPERTY	run slowly
determiner–noun	noun, ENTITY	determiner, PRE-PROPERTY	the elephant
auxiliary–verb	verb, EVENT	auxiliary, PRE-PROPERTY	may run
adverb–adjective	adjective, PROPERTY	adverb, PRE-PROPERTY	very grey

(8)   EVENT > ENTITY > PROPERTY > PRE-PROPERTY

Since > is a transitive relation, this ranking underpins the priority of heads over modifiers and is systematically reflected in the assignments in table 10.1.

In sum, this framework offers a combinational approach to heads, informed by both the dependency and unification traditions. This approach is summarized in the Head–Modifier Principle in (9):

(9)   *Head-Modifier Principle* (HMP)
   a. Categories in a binary construction combine as head C^H and modifier C^M to yield a result category C^R.
   b. $C^R = C^H$ after specification of C^H by C^M and application of a category constraint within C^H.
   c. Specification: C^H is specified by C^M iff there exists a C such that $C \in C^H$:<syntax modifier> and $C \sqcup C^M$.
   d. Category constraint: C^H: <syntax modifier NUMBER semantics> $\sqcup$ C^H: <semantics ROLE> where NUMBER ranges over the set of modifiers and ROLE over semantic role attributes defined for C^H:<semantics type>.
   e. The distinction between head and modifier categories is based upon the ordering of general semantic types in (8).

10.3 Comparison with the Functor–Argument Principle

In this section, we briefly compare the Head–Modifier Principle with another combinational principle, the Functor–Argument Principle.

10.3.1 *The Functor–Argument Principle*

The Functor–Argument Principle (FAP) is based upon a distinction between functor and argument categories: the functor category specifies the argument of a function (the 'take' category) as well as the result of the function (the 'make' category). Accordingly, the prioritized category in a phrase is identified as the functor category, as opposed to the head category. Identifying which category in a phrase is the functor and which is the argument, however, is not a straightforward task. As Zwicky (1985: 4) observed, either category can, in principle, be assigned the status of functor with sufficient ingenuity. For this reason, we pay particular attention to Keenan's observations on the correlation between surface form and logical form.

Keenan claims that the directionality of agreement relations between expressions is systematically based upon the directionality of semantic variation. This is captured in the following principle:

(10)   *Meaning–Form Dependency Principle* (MFDP)
        Given *A* and *B* distinct constituents of a syntactic structure *E*, *A* may agree with *B* iff the semantic interpretation of expressions of *A* varies with the semantic interpretation of expressions of *B* in the interpretation of *E*.   (Keenan, 1979: 168)

Pursuing the question of whether 'there [is] any correlation between what varies in meaning with what and the logical structures assigned to agreement pairs' (Keenan, 1989: 170), Keenan develops a second principle:

(11)   *The Functional Dependency Principle* (FDP)
        Given *A* and *B* distinct constituents of a SF [surface form] *E*, *A* may agree with *B* iff in the LF [logical form] of expressions of *E*, the LFs of expressions of *A* are interpreted as *functions* taking the interpretations of expressions of *B* as arguments.   (Keenan, 1979: 172)

Taking these principles together, one interpretation of Keenan's position is that semantic variation is a characteristic of functor categories but not argument categories: that is, the semantic interpretation of functor categories varies with that of argument categories, but not vice versa. For example, Keenan argues that the interpretation of a transitive verb varies with the interpretation of its direct object as he shows for *cut*:

(12)   a. cut finger ('to make an incision on the surface of')
        b. cut cake ('to cut all the way through'; 'to divide into portions for the purpose of serving')
        c. cut lawn ('trim')
        d. cut heroin ('diminish the potency of by adding a physically comparable substance')

Likewise, in noun phrases the interpretation of adjectives, such as *flat*, varies with the interpretation of nouns as shown in (13).

(13)   a. flat beer ('lacking normal taste')
        b. flat road ('without bumps or depressions')
        c. flat voice ('too low in pitch')

On the basis of semantic variation, then, verbs can be treated as functors with nouns as their arguments and adjectives as functors with noun arguments.

This approach can be captured in the Functor–Argument Principle:

(14)   *Functor–Argument Principle* (FAP)
      a. Categories in a binary construction combine as functor C^F and argument C^A to yield a result category C^R.
      b. $C^R = C^F$ after a unification U and application of a function F.
      c. U: C^F:C^{take} ⊔ C^A.
      d. F: C^F specifies a function F which maps between C^F:C^{take} and C^F:C^{make}.
      e. The distinction between functor and argument categories is based upon semantic variation as described in the MFDP and the FDP above.

The assignments arising from the FAP, broadly in accord with Keenan (1979), are given in table 10.2.[12] Comparison with the assignments in table 10.1 demonstrates that the FAP and HMP assign priority to different expressions in some of these phrase types. In particular, functor categories differ from head categories in adjective–noun, verb–adverb, determiner–noun, auxiliary–verb and adverb–adjective phrases. Even if the correlation between the functor–argument distinction and the head–modifier distinction were inverted so that argument categories were correlated with head categories, the problem would still persist: arguments do not correspond to heads in noun–verb and verb–noun phrases. However, a relation can be established between these assignments through an additional principle – the Endotypic Principle (Vennemann and Harlow, 1977; Bouma, 1988).

Table 10.2   Assignments with FAP

Phrase	*Functor*	*Argument*
noun–verb	verb|noun	noun
verb–noun	verb|noun	noun
adjective–noun	noun|noun	noun
verb–adverb	(verb|noun)(verb|noun)	verb|noun
determiner–noun	noun|noun	noun
auxiliary–verb	(verb|noun)(verb|noun)	verb|noun
adverb–adjective	(noun|noun)(noun|noun)	noun|noun

The Endotypic Principle is based upon the distinction between endotypic and exotypic functors. An endotypic functor is a functor of the form X/X: that is, its take and make categories are identical. As a corollary, exotypic functors are functors of the form X/Y.

(15)   *The Endotypic Principle* (EP)
In a construction consisting of a functor *F* and an argument *A*, *F* is
the head, *unless* it is endotypic in which case *A* is the head.
A functor which is not a head is a specifier (attribute).
An argument which is not a head is a specifier (complement).

Of the functors given in table 10.2, only verbs in verb–noun and
noun–verb phrases are exotypic: as functors, they correspond to
heads with their arguments as (complement) specifiers. The remaining functors are endotypic. For example, in adjective–noun phrases
the adjective is a functor which, syntactically, takes a category of the
type noun and makes a category of the type noun (noun/noun) and
semnatically it specifies a function mapping from the set of entities
into the set of entities ($<e>|<e>$). And similarly in verb–adverb
phrases, the adverb is a functor which takes a syntactic category of
the type verb/noun (that is, a verb category which itself takes a noun
category) and makes a category of the same type.

With the Endotypic Principle, then, the head–modifier distinction
can be derived from the functor–argument distinction. The problem
for the FAP, however, is that generalizations in serialization and
category constancy are couched in terms of the head–modifier
distinction not the more 'basic' functor–argument distinction. In
addition, the allegedly distinctive semantic characteristic of
functors – semantic variation – is not supported.

10.3.2 Serialization

Greenberg's implicational serialization universals captured cross-
language statistical regularities in the linear order of categories within
phrases (Greenberg, 1966). For example, if in a language, such as
Japanese, the direct object precedes the verb, then, typically, the
adjective will precede the noun and the noun the adposition. Such
apparent regularities can be accounted for in a systematic manner
with the following principle based upon the head–modifier distinction (Anderson, 1979: 7):

(16)   *Head–Modifier Serialization Principle*
Serialization in a phrase tends to follow systematically from the
relation between heads and modifiers: either modifiers precede
heads or heads precede modifiers.

Hawkins (1984) provides further support for the HMP in relation to
language-type frequency.[13] He formulates a principle which predicts
the relative number of language types on the basis of serialization of

heads and modifiers within phrases (Hawkins, 1984: 130–1):

(17) *Cross-Category Harmony Principle*
      The more similar the cross-category positioning of head, the more
      languages; the less similar, the fewer languages.

In both cases, then, the HMP in conjunction with serialization
principles appear to provide a straightforward account of word-order
generalizations. However, as Dryer (1988) has shown, there are other
factors at play in determining serialization. These include dominance
and harmony principles, areal influence, as well as the direction of
branching in branching as opposed to non-branching constructions.
One effect of this is that serialization principles based upon the
head–modifier distinction cannot be seen in isolation from other
principles: serialization is determined by the interaction of a number
of ordering principles and cannot be reduced to a single universal
principle. Principles such as those above, then, do not provide a
complete account of serialization: they simply provide a category-
based restriction on serialization.

Accounts based upon the FAP, however, require an additional
principle to provide restrictions on serialization. Keenan (1979)
employs a principle similar to, but more constrained than, the
Endotypic Principle:

(18) *The Dissimulation Principle* (DP)
      Functional expressions taking DNPs [determined noun phrases] as
      arguments and functional expressions taking CNPs [common noun
      phrases] as arguments tend to serialize on the opposite side of their
      argument expressions.   (Keenan, 1979: 188)

As Hawkins (1984) points out, while the DP may account for
serialization concerning noun phrases, it needs to be extended to
account for additional serialization facts such as the correlation
between adverb–adjective and adjective–noun serialization (Hawkins, 1984: 113–14). Vennemann, on the other hand, appeals to the
Endotypic Principle and is able to provide a general account of
serialization in terms of functors and arguments (Vennemann, 1976;
Vennemann and Harlow, 1977; Vennemann, 1984). Such an
account, however, relies upon a derived distinction – that between
heads and specifiers – and it is the latter distinction which captures
category restrictions on serialization. On the grounds of descriptive
economy, the HMP provides a better account since it is the
head–modifier (or specifier) distinction which underlies these restrictions.

10.3.3 Semantic category constancy

The FAP also requires the Endotypic Principle to account for the 'kind of' relationship. For neither the functor nor the modifier consistently provides the semantic type of the result category. In phrases with exotypic functors, the functor provides the semantic type. For example, in *elephants run*, the functor *run* is, semantically, a function from entities to truth values, a function which can be assigned the type EVENT. The argument restricts the domain of this function to entities of the type ELEPHANT. The resulting type is a more specific event: that is, the event of elephants running. In phrases with endotypic functors, it is the argument which provides the type of the result category. For example, in adjective–noun phrases like *pink elephants*, the functor describes a mapping from the set of entities onto the set of entities with the property PINK ($<e>|<e>$), but the argument provides the type of the set, that is, ELEPHANT. While the functor provides a restriction on the type of the set of entities, that is, entities with the property PINK, it is the argument which provides the type itself – entities of the type ELEPHANT with the colour property PINK. Consequently, the Endotypic Principle is required for a systematic account: heads, *qua* exotypic functors or arguments of endotypic functors, consistently provide the semantic type of the result category.

10.3.4 Semantic variation

According to the FAP, one of the distinctive characteristics of functors is that their semantic interpretation varies with their arguments, but not vice versa. This systematic asymmetry, however, is unsupported: variation in semantic interpretation is not simply unidirectional, for just as the argument can affect the interpretation of the functor, so the functor can affect the interpretation of the argument.

Consider, for example, the interpretation of verbs and adjectives. As functors, their interpretation can vary with the interpretation of their noun arguments, as illustrated in (12) and (13). Psycholinguistic evidence suppoprts not only variation in this direction, but also in the opposite direction. Murphy (1988) found that the interpretation of adjectives can systematically vary with the interpretation of nouns (see also Cruse, 1986: 152). For example, *long* has the interpretation 'great length', or a simple elaboration of this, in combination with *word* and *life*, but substantially different interpretations in combinations with nouns like *hand* ('expressed in complete sentences and without abbreviations'), *eye* ('towards the future') and *year* ('seeming to pass slowly'). Moreover, he also found that the interpretation of nouns varied with that of adjectives (see also Lakoff, 1987: 83–4). In some cases, the interpretation highlighted different senses of noun; *hand*, for example, took on interpretations which varied from 'side' as in *right hand* to 'anatomical hand' in *bleeding hand*. In others, variation highlighted different aspects of the same sense.

Anderson and Ortony (1975) report similar bidirectional variation in the interpretation of nouns and verbs. For example, the nouns *steak* and *soup* lead to different interpretations of *eat*: the act of eating is associated with different utensils as well as actions of the lips, teeth and tongue. Conversely, the interpretation of *piano* can vary in different verb contexts:

(19)   Pianos can be pleasing to listen to.

(20)   Pianos can be difficult to move.

In (19) the sound, but not the weight, of the piano is relevant, whereas in (20) the opposite is true. As Anderson and Ortony put it, 'in one context piano is a member of the same category as, say, harmonica, while in another it is certainly not. In the latter case, perhaps sofa would be a cohyponym' (1975: 169).

In sum, not only does the FAP require the Endotypic Principle to yield analyses which accord with serialization and semantic constancy requirements, but this evidence suggests semantic variation cannot distinguish functors from arguments. The HMP, on the other hand, provides a distinction which can directly account for these requirements and, since combination is based upon unification, an inherently bidirectional process, it can, in principle, account for this type of semantic variation. However, as section 10.4 demonstrates, there is a clear limit on the range of semantic variation which can be characterized through a simple unification approach.

10.4 Defeasibility

Defeasibility is a linguistic phenomenon which challenges simple unification-based approaches to category combination. The phenomenon is manifest in phrases where there is a conflict, usually a semantic conflict, between properties of the combining categories. The conflict is systematically resolved through the 'defeat' of one category by the other: the result category no longer has the property of the 'defeating' category since the property is replaced by one appropriate to the 'defeated' category. Defeasibility undermines two requirements central to the unification framework described in section 10.2: only compatible categories can combine; and their unification is subsumed by each category – there is no loss or change of information. While the framework needs to be extended to accommodate these challenges, the resolution of conflict seems to support its combinational principle.

Four types of semantic defeasibility will be briefly described: typicality defeat, intrinsic defeat, sortal defeat and general defeat. In these types, defeat can vary along a number of dimensions. One of these is dependence upon lexical semantics: that is, whether or not the occurrence of defeat is dependent upon specific semantic properties of the defeated category. Another is the nature of the defeated property. Possible properties of a concept can be classified as necessary properties or default properties (Murphy, 1988). Necessary properties are those which are essential for the concept to be categorized as it is; for example, **colour** is a necessary property of ENTITY. Default properties are 'typical' properties of the concept: that is, unless specified to the contrary, concepts will have these properties. For example, **four-legged** is a default property of ELEPHANT, unless, of course, they are disabled in the appropriate way. While necessary properties tend to play the major role in determining the application of concepts, default properties, especially perceptual properties like **shape**, play the major role in identifying instances of a concept. Finally, properties can be related to each other and these relationships can in turn affect defeat. For example, given a correlation between the **sweetness** of food and its **calorific value** – the sweeter food is, the more calories it typically contains – defeat of the **sweetness** property will also affect **calorific value** such that we can no longer infer that it is a high value (Franks, Myers and McGlashan, 1988).

10.4.1 *Typicality defeat*

The first type of defeat, typicality defeat, affects default properties and is lexically dependent. In an adjective–noun phrase like *grey elephants*, the value of the **colour** property specified by the modifier category is compatible with the default value **grey** of elephants. With *pink elephants*, however, the properties are incompatible and the default value specified by the head is defeated by the necessary value specified in the modifier category: while *elephants* are **grey**, *pink elephants* are **pink**. Psycholinguistic experiments also suggest that conflicts over default properties are systematically resolved in favour of the modifier category. When the properties of concepts such as *games* and *sports* are related for typicality, the (indirect) modifier *games* consistently plays a greater role in determining the typicality rating of properties in *sports that are also games* than the head *sports* (Hampton, 1987).

10.4.2 Intrinsic defeat

With the second type, intrinsic defeat, the properties of the semantic type of the defeated category are overridden independently of its lexical semantics. In noun phrases with privative adjectives such as *fake*, *former* and *false*, the adjective modifier consistently defeats the existence of the semantic type of the noun (Kamp, 1975); for example, while the concept underlying *Renoirs* asserts the existence of paintings by Renoir, *fake Renoirs* denies their existence. Likewise, modifiers of verbs such as *never* and *not* undermine the existence of a state or event; in *John never crossed the road*, there is a denial that a 'crossing' event took place. With this type of defeat, then, there is a conflict between the value of a mode property of the categories which is resolved in favour of the modifier category; for example, with *fake elephants* the modifier's value **negative** for **polarity** defeats the head's value **positive**. This makes problematic the subsumption relation between head and result categories: while *pink elephants* are clearly a 'kind of' *elephants*, *false beards* are not obviously 'kinds of' *beards*. In particular, the result category no longer contains necessary semantic properties of the head category; *false beards*, for example, do not grow on chins. Many of their default properties, especially those which play a diagnostic role, are preserved in the result category; with *fake Renoir*, for example, a sufficient number of diagnostic properties must be preserved so as to maintain the contrast with *fake Picasso* – a *fake Renoir* must at least appear more like a real Renoir than a *fake Picasso*.

10.4.3 Sortal defeat

The third type of defeat, sortal defeat, is similar to intrinsic defeat in that the subsumption relationship between the head and result category is undermined through the loss of necessary semantic properties of the head category, a loss which stems from the defeat of the head by the modifier (Franks, Myers and McGlashan, 1988; Franks, 1989). It differs from intrinsic defeat in three ways.

Firstly, the semantics of the head category is defeated as a consequence of the defeat of a core property. For example, in *chocolate elephants* the value of the **material** property **chocolate** of the adjective modifier defeats the **flesh** of the noun head. Since this property is necessary for the concept, its defeat entails that the subsumption relationship is no longer transparent – *chocolate elephants* are not real elephants. It does, however, retain default properties such as 'elephant shape' which differentiate *chocolate elephants* from *chocolate mice*. Furthermore, one of the concepts is elaborated as a result of defeat: *chocolate elephants* contain the default values **sweet** and **brown** which are not part of either concept but emerge from the elaboration of the modifier concept. Gentner (1981) provides psycholinguistic evidence to demonstrate that a noun modifier can defeat a verb head in a similar manner. For example, when subjects paraphrased sentences such as *the lizards worshipped*, they tended to produce paraphrases such as 'the small grey reptile lay on the hot rock and stared unblinkingly at the sun' (Gentner, 1981: 165). Here there is a conflict between the value of the **agent** role in the semantics of the verb and the modifier's semantics: SENTIENT is incompatible with LIZARD. Rather than simply replace the type of **agent** with LIZARD, the head concept is 'elaborated' into the type ANIMATE.

A second difference is that sortal defeat is lexically dependent. For example, *stone* is a modifier capable of giving rise to sortal defeat. In *stone bridge*, however, there is no defeat since the material properties specified in each category are compatible.

The third difference is that the discourse situation may play a greater role in determining which category has priority rather than the head–modifier distinction.[14] For example, if *the sunflower kissed the wall* were said in the context of a fancy-dress party, the most likely interpretation would be a metaphorical one in which semantic properties of the noun modifier were defeated: it would describe a person dressed as a sunflower rather than a real flower.

10.4.4 General defeat

The fourth type of defeat, general defeat, offers the strongest violation of compatibility and subsumption. The result category has neither the general semantic nor syntactic type of the head category. With other sorts of defeat, only the semantic type is undermined, and undermined to a limited extent. For example, with sortal defeat in *chocolate elephants*, while the semantic type of the head is undermined through loss of necessary properties, the result category clearly preserves its general semantic type (ENTITY) as well as the syntactic type (noun) of the head *elephants*.

Denominal verbs illustrate general defeat (Clark, 1983). In (21) *porch* is a noun with the general semantic type ENTITY.

(21)   Newspaper boys put newspapers in the porch.

In (22), however, the result category is a verb with the general semantic type EVENT.

(22)   Newspaper boys porch the newspapers.

This change in syntactic and semantic type can be seen as a manifestation of general defeat. In (22), the categories for *porch*, *the newspaper boys* and *the papers* are unable to combine since none can act as a head category. They can combine, however, if *porch* is selected as the head category and its syntactic and semantic types are systematically changed in order to accommodate the requirements of the modifier categories.

10.4.5 *Significance of defeat*

These types of semantic defeasibility demonstrate that categories with incompatible properties can combine successfully, although not all properties of the 'defeated' category are preserved in the result category. With typicality defeat, a default value in the 'defeated' category is overridden by a necessary value specified in the 'defeating' category and the default value is not preserved in the result category. With intrinsic defeat, the necessary value of a mode property in the 'defeated' category is overridden by a necessary value in the 'defeating' category and, as a result, necessary core properties are lost. With sortal defeat, the value of a necessary core property in the 'defeated' category is overridden by a necessary value in the 'defeating' category. And with general defeat, the semantic and syntactic types are replaced with those required by the 'defeating' category. As a consequence, the subsumption relationship between the 'defeated' category and the result category cannot be maintained: successful combination may involve the loss of information.

Two aspects of defeasibility, however, reinforce the HMP (rather than the FAP). The first is that modifiers, in general, have systematic priority in defeat: where there is a conflict, the modifier category is the 'defeating' category and the head the 'defeated' category. For the utility of the semantic type ranking given in (8) is that manifestations of priority either systematically follow from the ranking or go against it. With defeasibility, priority systematically goes against ranking: categories with semantic types of a lower rank can override properties of those with higher types.[15] The second aspect is that when defeat occurs, the head category still provides the basis for the result category. As Gentner says of noun–verb combinations: 'The verb meanings were not simply ignored. Other evidence from this study indicates that the verb preserved as much of its meaning as possible ... given an incompatible noun, the verb was typically extended until it fit' (Gentner, 1981: 165–6). Since the HMP identifies the result category as the head category after combination with the modifier category, it is the nature of combination which is in need of revision.

10.5 The Head–Modifier Principle revisited

With the definition of the HMP in (9) in section 10.2, combination will fail in phrases which manifest defeasibility. In particular, the category constraint (9d) will fail in phrases such as *the lizards worshipped* on account of semantic type incompatibility. Furthermore, if the concept representations are augmented to specify values for mode properties and to specify necessary and default values for core and mode properties, then the category constraint will also fail with *pink elephants*, *fake elephants* and *chocolate elephants* due to incompatibility between semantic properties of the categories. Most aspects of this combination principle, however, can be maintained through a more sophisticated approach to semantic representation, an approach in which constraints dynamically assign necessary and default properties to a concept, and property assignment is regulated by an assignment principle.

These constraints are informed by a theory-based approach to concept structure (Fillmore, 1982: Murphy and Medin, 1985; Lakoff, 1987). Theories are seen as 'commonsense' or 'folk' descriptions of the world: 'Representations of concepts are best thought of as theoretical knowledge or, at least, as embedded in knowledge that embodies a theory about the world' (Murphy and Medin, 1985: 298). Their utility lies in determining both the internal and external structure of concepts. In particular, theories underlie the organization of the concepts, such as the hierarchy in figure 10.1, the assignment of necessary and default properties to individual concepts as well as relations, especially explanatory and casual relations, between concepts. For example, Cohen and Murphy (1984) argue that our interpretation of compound concepts such as *engine repair* require knowledge about the use of vehicles, their parts and functions, as well as what can go wrong with them. Accordingly, 'the interpretation of a compound concept may be thought of as a hypothesis generated by background theories' (Murphy and Medin, 1985: 306).

In the revised framework, semantic constraints embody theories: constraints describe the assignment of necessary and default properties to a concept together with relations between these properties. For example, in a theory ELEPHANT may be defined for the property-assignment constraints shown in (23):

(23)

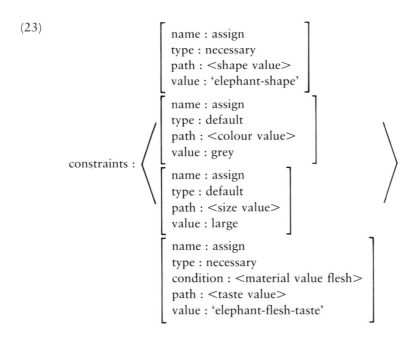

In (23), the first constraint necessarily assigns the **shape** property the value '**elephant-shape**'. Likewise, the second and third constraints assign default values for **size** and **taste**. The third constraint necessarily assigns a value for **taste** on the condition that <material value flesh> is defined for the concept. This property is defined by a constraint in the concept ANIMATE – it necessarily assigns the value **flesh** to the **material** property on the condition that <polarity value positive> is defined – and since ANIMATE subsumes ELEPHANT, the latter concept inherits the constraint. Furthermore, assignment of properties is based upon the following property-assignment principle:

(24)   *The Property-Assignment Principle* (PAP)
When concepts are assigned properties from two sources, one of these is a *prioritized* source (PS) and the other is a *non-prioritized* source (NPS).

Concepts in a subsumption relationship are prioritized: the concept with the more general type is the NPS and the concept with the more specific type is the PS.

Concepts in a head–modifier relationship are prioritized: the concept specified in the head category is the NPS and the concept in the modifier category is the PS.

A property P assigned a value by a constraint in PS has priority over P assigned by a constraint in NPS **unless** P is assigned a value by a default constraint in PS and P is assigned a value by necessary constraint in NPS.

This revised approach can, in principle, account for typicality, intrinsic and sortal defeat.[16] The value of the **colour** property *pink elephants* arises from an assignment 'conflict' between concepts in a head–modifier relationship: PINK has a necessary constraint which assigns the value **pink** and ELEPHANT has a default constraint which assigns **grey**. If both these constraints were to apply then the concept in the result category would be ill defined. With the PAP, however, this situation does not arise: since COLOUR (P) is assigned by a necessary constraint in the modifier (PS) and by a default constraint in the head (NPS), only the former constraint applies, thereby allowing the category constraint to succeed.

With the intrinsic defeat in *fake elephants*, the concept in the modifier category has a necessary constraint which assigns **polarity** the value **negative** and the concept in the head category has a necessary constraint which assigns the value **positive**. Application of PAP forestalls incompatibility by only applying the constraint in the modifier category: the concept in the result category has the value **negative**. Note also that most properties of ELEPHANT assigned by default are preserved: by default, *fake elephants* have the size, shape and colour of real elephants. What they lack is the value **flesh** for **material**: while the constraint is inherited from ANIMATE, it cannot apply since its condition – that **polarity** has the value **positive** – is not satisfied. Since this constraint does not apply, the condition (<material value flesh>) for the default constraint assigning **taste** the value 'elephant-taste' is not applied.

While dynamic assignment of properties and the PAP forestall failure of the category constraint, sortal defeat also requires elaboration of one of the combining concepts. In phrases such as *the lizards worshipped*, the result category has the type ANIMATE for the **agent** role, not the type assigned by the head or the modifier categories. This arises from elaboration of the head concept: with EVENT head concepts, the type for the role is replaced by one which subsumes the types assigned by the modifier (LIZARD) and head (SENTIENT) concepts. With the sortal defeat in *chocolate elephant*, it is the modifier concept which is elaborated. The concept associated with the adjective modifier *chocolate* has a necessary constraint which assigns **material** the value **chocolate**. The concept ELEPHANT inherits a necessary constraint from ANIMATE which assigns it the value **flesh**. According to the PAP, the modifier constraint has priority over the inherited head constraint and the concept of result category has **chocolate** as the value of **material**. As a result, the constraint on ELEPHANT which assigns a value for **taste** cannot apply. However, the other default constraints can: *chocolate elephants* are by default 'elephant-shaped', large and grey. Unfortunately, this is counterintuitive: *chocolate elephants* are typically sweet, brown and small. This problem does not arise if the modifier concept is elaborated: with ENTITY head concepts, the modifier concept is replaced by one which includes the property it assigns. The concept underlying *chocolate* can be elaborated into a concept of the type CHOCOLATE-ENTITY defined in (25):

(25)

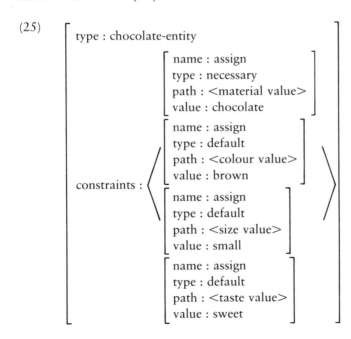

With this as the modifier concept, PAP ensures that properties of the result concept are assigned the appropriate values: **material, taste, size** and **colour** are assigned the values specified by CHOCOLATE-ENTITY constraints, but **shape** is assigned by the constraint in ELEPHANT since necessary constraints of heads (NPS) apply rather than default constraints of modifiers (PS).

The effect of defeasibility on the HMP is the replacement of the category constraint definition in (9d) with that given below:

(9)   d. Category constraint: C^H:<syntax modifier NUMBER semantics> matches C^H: <semantics ROLE> where NUMBER ranges over the set of modifiers and ROLE over semantic role attributes defined for C^H: <semantics type> if:

1 the constraints in C^H: <semantics> and C^H:<syntax modifier NUMBER semantics> are applied in accordance with the Property-Assignment Principle in (24);

2 application of the Property-Assignment Principle results in a necessary core property of C^H:<semantics> no longer holding, then elaborate C^H: <syntax modifier NUMBER semantics> if its type is PROPERTY or elaborate C^H: <semantics> if its type is EVENT;

3 C^H: <semantics> $\sqcup$ C^H: <syntax modifier NUMBER semantics>.

With this category constraint, the Head–Modifier Principle is able to account for these examples of defeasibility by restricting the application of constraints and, where necessary, elaborating concepts, prior to unification. Clearly, it will need to be generalized in order to account for other examples including those exhibiting general defeat.

10.6 Conclusion

In this chapter, we have described a unification-based framework whose combinatorial principle is based upon the head–modifier distinction in dependency grammar. The underlying motivation for the priority of the head in phrases was a semantic ranking in which the semantic type of a head systematically outranked that of the modifier. An alternative combinatorial principle, based upon the distinction between functor and argument, was shown to require an additional principle, the Endotypic Principle, for an adequate treatment of serialization and semantic category constancy. In addition, an alleged distinctive characteristic of functors, semantic variation in interpretation, was shown to be no less applicable to argument categories. Defeasibility evidence, however, presents a challenge to this framework, since in some phrases the categories have incompatible values for properties and the result category does not necessarily preserve those of the head category. This challenge was met through an approach to semantics in which properties of a concept are assigned by theory-based constraints and the application of these constraints was partly based upon the priority of modifiers over heads. The general consequence of defeasibility for linguistic theory is that subsumption cannot be maintained as a general effect of combination – modifiers can **change** heads.

NOTES

1. My thanks to participants at the Talking Heads Round Table for comments on an earlier draft of this chapter, especially my co-editors. The work was supported in part by the Commission of the European Communities under project P2218 (SUNDIAL).
2. See Radford (this volume) for an alternative treatment.
3. There is a third effect, namely changing properties of the head. This is discussed in section 10.4.
4. See Hudson (1987: 115) for an alternative treatment, where the auxiliary provides the semantic type; for example, *may like* describes a kind of possibility rather than a kind of liking.
5. This limit on specification is one way in which head categories have priority over modifier categories: category constancy, a combinatorial effect associated with head categories, has priority over specification, a combinatorial effect associated with modifier categories.
6. Since head categories are lexical categories and result categories are identical to head categories after extension, result categories are merely extended lexical categories. The head–modifier relation is treated as a basic relation between lexical categories, and constituency as a derived relation (Anderson and Durand, 1986: 2).
7. For expository convenience, the value of the phonology attribute is simply an orthographic form and the syntactic head property is only defined for syntactic type – morphosyntactic properties, such as person, number and case, can be defined by analogy with 'order' properties.
8. Paths, such as <syntax modifier first syntax head type>, identify substructures within the category. The set values have been given an arbitrary ordering to facilitate identification; *first* in a path identifies the first category in an ordered set.
9. The motivation for dividing mode and core properties of concepts derives from the process of 'anchoring' concepts in a discourse model

where core, but not mode, properties can form part of the model. Mode properties merely guide the anchoring process.

10. These types are, in part, derived from work in formal semantics, especially within Situation Semantics (Barwise and Perry, 1983; Fenstad *et al.*, 1987).

11. Constraints can, of course, be used to define relations within attributes of a category, such as semantic relations and syntactic relations like agreement.

12. With auxiliary–verb, verb–adverb and adverb–adjective phrases, no assignments are given in Keenan (1979). With the first and second phrases, we have assumed the analyses given in contemporary categorial grammars such as Unification Categorial Grammar (UCG) (Calder *et al.*, 1987: 18–35). With the third construction, the assignment is taken from Hawkins (1984: 113–14). In addition, the direction of combination is ignored: '|' covers both forward and backward combination.

13. But note that Hawkins has subsequently abandoned the head–modifier distinction (Hawkins, this volume).

14. This is also a characteristic of general defeat described in section 10.4.4.

15. In this way, the semantic type ranking bears comparison with the sonority hierarchy in phonology (Anderson and Durand, 1986: 16).

16. Space prohibits an account of general defeat in this chapter.

11 Heads, parsing and word-order universals

JOHN A. HAWKINS

11.1 Introduction

Two key issues in the discussion of heads are: how is 'head' to be defined, and are there clear linguistic generalizations that provide evidence for this notion? The debate between Hudson and Zwicky in the *Journal of Linguistics* (Hudson, 1987; Zwicky, 1985) illustrates the difficulties inherent in answering the first question. There is disagreement over which grammatical properties define, or correlate with, heads, and hence over the precise set of categories that are supposedly instances of this generalization. With regard to the second question, one grammatical area that has been cited as relevant is word order (see, for example, Zwicky, 1985: 10–11). It is often proposed that heads are consistently positioned either before or after non-heads within their respective phrasal categories. Vennemann (1974) formulates a Natural Serialization Principle for this regularity, and reformulates it in Vennemann (1984) in terms of the typological distinction between 'pre-specifying' (that is, modifier before head) and 'post-specifying' (head before modifier) languages.

This chapter will consider what word-order universals as currently formulated suggest about the notion 'head of phrase'.[1] I will argue, with Hudson, that there is a significant generalization here, but that it is not ultimately the kind of generalization he proposes. Indeed, the notion 'head' can probably be dispensed with altogether, as a property of Universal Grammar. Instead, I believe the underlying generalization involves a principle of parsing: the relevant categories provide unique 'Mother Node Construction'. They enable the language user to recognize the existence and nature of the syntactic grouping of words to which the word and category in question belong, and so inform the listener about abstract syntactic structure on-line. A noun signals the occurrence of a noun phrase, a complementizer the occurrence of a subordinate clause and so on. Unique mother node recognition is a crucial component of a theory of parsing that I have recently developed in Hawkins (1990, 1992ab, forthcoming), which makes many correct predictions for word-order universals in conjunction with an efficiency metric, Early Immediate Constituents.

The major proposal of this chapter will be that heads are a proper subset of mother node constructing categories, but not a linguistically significant subset. The significant generalization in this area will be shown to involve the uniqueness relation between a mother node and the daughter category or categories that can construct it and render it predictable. Seen from this perspective, many properties that have been ascribed to heads are really properties of the larger set of mother node constructing categories, and the justification for heads then becomes correspondingly moot.

The parsing theory to be proposed has a number of consequences for grammars, that is for the form and content of grammatical rules and principles: first, there are consequences for constituency and the categorial status of mothers and daughters; second, there are consequences for the linear ordering of daughters within their phrasal categories; third, this approach provides a simple and intuitive explanation for why a number of other grammatical properties are correlated with mother node constructing categories, and derivatively with heads. I will accordingly argue that parsing principles can explain many fundamental properties of syntax, including those aspects of the head of phrase generalization that appear to be theoretically well motivated and empirically correct.

The order of presentation is as follows. In section 11.2 I show that the most recently formulated word-order universals do not provide good evidence for a grammatical notion of 'head of phrase', as most people define this term, and I illustrate the parsing principles, Mother Node Construction and Early Immediate Constituents, that I believe do provide an explanation for a wide range of these universals. Section 11.3 considers Mother Node Construction in relation to constituency and category membership. Section 11.4 illustrates the predictions for linear order in greater detail. Section 11.5 examines the grammatical properties that have been argued to correlate with heads and proposes that those that appear to support a head of phrase generalization are more correctly definable as properties of mother node constructing categories. And section 11.6 summarizes the conclusions.

11.2 Word-order universals and parsing

This section enumerates some problems for the consistent head-ordering generalization and outlines an alternative theory of word-order universals.

11.2.1 *Problems with consistent head ordering*

The most recent empirical and theoretical work on word-order universals conducted by Matthew Dryer and myself does not provide good evidence for a grammatical 'head of phrase' generalization. When non-heads (variously referred to as 'dependents', 'modifiers', 'specifiers', etc.) are non-branching categories, such as single-word adjectives in relation to nouns, Dryer (1988, 1992) has shown that the proposed ordering correlations with other non-heads and heads cross-categorially simply do not hold. Both adjective orders, pre-nominal and post-nominal, are productively attested in both OV and VO language types, and the same is true for many other non-branching categories in relation to their purported heads. Even when non-heads are branching categories, however, there are numerous complications for the original intuition of consistent head ordering across categories. Dryer (1992) points out that there are correlations between, say, Aux and VP ordering (where Aux is some tense- or aspect-marked auxiliary verb) and other head–modifier pairs, but that this correlation supports consistent head ordering only on the assumption that the Aux is the head, which not all theories accept. More seriously, there are empirical problems involving a number of what I have called 'left–right asymmetries' (Hawkins, 1988, 1990). For example, in OV languages both pre-nominal and post-nominal relative clauses are productively attested, whereas VO languages co-occur almost exceptionlessly with the post-nominal type. The noun is generally regarded as the head in this head–modifier pair, and hence while VO languages provide evidence for a head-ordering correlation, OV languages do not. The same asymmetry is found in {Comp, s} ordering within s̄. OV languages are productively attested with s̄[s Comp] and with s̄[Comp s], VO languages only with s̄[Comp s]. Again, OV languages provide productive counter-examples to consistent head ordering, on the assumption that both Comp and v are heads.

Faced with facts such as these, the response I made in Hawkins (1983, 1984) was to try to incorporate the original insight of consistent head ordering, as illustrated in Vennemann's (1974, 1984) papers, within a set of interacting explanatory principles, the others being the Heaviness Serialization Principle (accounting for left–right asymmetries involving 'heavy' categories such as relative clauses) and the Mobility Principle (accounting for single-word adjectives). Supplementing the heads generalization in this way provided a means of preserving both the grammatical construct of head, and its predictions for those head–dependent pairs that were not skewed by mobility or heaviness considerations, namely the branching dependent categories for which Dryer (1988, 1992) has proposed his Branching Direction Theory. This theory is formulated as follows in Dryer (1988: 191).

(1)   *Dryer's Branching Direction Theory*
       Languages tend toward consistent left-branching or consistent right-branching. I.e. languages tend toward one of two ideals, one in which branching categories *precede* nonbranching categories, the other in which branching categories *follow* nonbranching categories.

I now believe that the interacting principles of Hawkins (1983, 1984) were insufficiently general and *ad hoc*, and that there is a much simpler explanatory theory of word-order universals, outlined in Hawkins (1990). This theory dispenses with all of the principles I proposed earlier, including consistent head ordering. Dryer's Branching Theory in (1) also dispenses with it. His theory will need to be modified in order to account for the above left–right asymmetries (which are unproblematic for him only in conjunction with methodological assumptions for measuring correlations, which I consider questionable in these cases), but, in general, branching direction provides an improved descriptive statement of the cross-categorial regularities compared with consistent head ordering.

11.2.2 An alternative theory of word-order universals

The basic intuition that underlies my current explanation for word-order universals is a simple one. I believe that words occur in the orders they do so that hearers can recognize syntactic groupings and their immediate constituents (ICs) as rapidly and efficiently as possible. Different orderings result in more or less rapid IC recognition. Consider the following pair of constituent orders in English, that are re-arranged by the rule of Heavy NP Shift:

(2)

a. I $_{VP}$[gave$_{NP}$[the valuable book that was extremely difficult to find]$_{PP}$[to Mary]]

      1   2   3   4   5 6 7   8   9 10   11

b. I $_{VP}$[gave $_{PP}$[to Mary] $_{NP}$[the valuable book that was extremely difficult to find]]

   1   2   3   4

Example (2b) provides a more rapid presentation of the three ICs of VP than (2a): just four of the twelve words dominated by VP are sufficient for the hearer to recognize that this VP consists of a V, a PP and an NP, whereas eleven words are needed in (2a) before the third IC, the PP, is recognized.

This example suggests that the ICs of a constituent can be recognized on the basis of a proper subset of the words dominated by this constituent, and that the size of this proper subset may vary, with some orderings shortening the number of words required for IC recognition, thereby making it faster. I believe that this simple fact is the major determinant of word order, both in the grammar and in performance.

In order to give some substance to this claim, I need to define some key concepts of the processing theory of Hawkins (1990, 1992b, forthcoming). The first is Mother Node Construction. The basic idea here is that some words and categories enable the hearer to 'construct' a higher and more abstract structural grouping on-line. The preposition *to* in (2) signals the existence of a prepositional phrase, the determiner *the* the existence of a noun phrase, and so on. More generally, some words and categories are vital for parsing since they reveal the nature of higher constituent structure. This principle is defined in (3):

(3)   *Mother Node Construction* (MNC)

        In the left-to-right parsing of a sentence, if any syntactic category C uniquely determines a phrasal mother node M, in accordance with the PS-rules of the grammar, then M is immediately constructed over C.

Examples of Mother Node Constructing Categories (MNCCs), together with the traditional labels for the categories they construct, are given in (4):

(4)   Comp   : s̄

          N   : NP

          Det   : NP

          V   : VP

          Adj   : AdjP

          P   : PP

          Aux   : S

Some additional principles that construct phrasal nodes are defined in Hawkins (forthcoming), for example, Sister Node Construction and

Grandmother Node Construction. MNC is the most general and universal in terms of the number of structures to which it applies, and it will be the main focus of this chapter. Additional principles will be considered in sections 11.3.7, 11.4.2, and 11.5.2 below.

MNC enables us to define the concept of a constituent recognition domain, as follows:

(5)   *Constituent recognition domain* (CRD)
       The constituent recognition domain for a phrasal mother node M is the ordered set of words in a parse string that must be parsed in order to recognize all ICs of M, proceeding from the word that constructs the first IC on the left, to the word that constructs the last IC on the right, and including all intervening words.

Thus, the CRDs of (2a) and (2b) are the eleven and four words respectively that need to be scanned in order to recognize the three ICs of VP. Within this VP the V is the MNCC, and the two other ICs are each in turn constructed on their left flank within their respective CRDs (for NP and PP). The CRD for VP is shortened in this case when shorter daughter ICs precede longer ones, as in (2b).

More generally, I argue in Hawkins (1990) that ordering within all CRDs is determined by the principle of Early Immediate Constituents, operating in conjunction with an efficiency metric defined in (7):

(6)   *Early Immediate Constituents* (EIC)
       The human parser prefers to maximize the left-to-right IC-to-word ratios of the phrasal nodes that it constructs.

(7)   *Left-to-right IC-to-word ratio*
       The left-to-right IC-to-word ratio for a constituent recognition domain is measured by first counting the ICs in the domain from left to right (starting from 1), and then counting the words in the domain from left to right (again starting from 1). For each word and its dominating IC, the IC total is divided by the word total at that point, and the result is expressed as a percentage (for example 2/3, or the second IC of the domain divided by the third word, that is 67 per cent). The higher the percentage, the more loaded and informative is the constituency information at that point. An aggregate IC-to-word ratio for the whole constituent recognition domain is then calculated by averaging the percentages for all the words in the domain. The higher the aggregate, the more optimal is that order of words for processing. The IC-to-word ratio for a whole sentence can be defined as the average of the aggregate IC-to-word ratios for all constituent recognition domains in the sentence, that is, for all phrasal categories that the sentence dominates.

The workings of this metric are illustrated in (2′):

(2′)

a.   I $_\text{VP}$[gave$_\text{NP}$[the   valuable book that was   extremely difficult to

VP CRD:	1/1	2/2	2/3	2/4	2/5	2/6	2/7	2/8	2/9
	100%	100%	67%	50%	40%	33%	29%	25%	22%

           find]$_\text{PP}$[to Mary]]

	2/10	3/11
	20%	27%

                                                    = 47% aggregate ratio

b.   I $_\text{VP}$[gave$_\text{PP}$[to   Mary] $_\text{NP}$[the valuable book that was extremely difficult to

VP CRD:	1/1	2/2	2/3	3/4
	100%	100%	67%	75%

                                                               find]]

                                                 = 86% aggregate ratio

The aggregate ratio for (2′a) is much lower than for (2′b), ultimately because the number of words required for recognition of the same number of ICs is much less.

EIC makes a number of predictions for grammaticalized word orders across languages. For example, it predicts that basic orders will, in general, be those that provide the most optimal left-to-right IC-to-word ratios, given the average word lengths of their respective ICs. And for any basic orders whose ratios are not optimal, then the lower the ratio, the fewer exemplifying languages there will be. This predicts, and provides an explanation for, the consistent cross-categorial left- or right-branching regularity of Dryer's Branching Direction Theory (compare (1)). Consider the structures of (8) and (9):

(8) $_\text{VP}$[walked $_\text{PP}$[to $_\text{NP}$[stores $_\bar{\text{S}}$[that $_\text{S}$[Bill likes]]]]]

(9)   [[[[[Bill likes]$_\text{S}$ that]$_\bar{\text{S}}$ stores]$_\text{NP}$ to]$_\text{PP}$ walked]$_\text{VP}$

Example (8) is a typical right-branching structure for languages such as English. The two daughter ICs of the VP are the verb *walked* and the PP (which is immediately recognized and constructed on its left periphery in a prepositional language). Two words suffice, *walked* and *to*, to recognize the two daughter ICs of the VP, making a perfect 100 per cent IC-to-word ratio. Similarly, the two daughter ICs of the PP CRD (the preposition and NP) are recognized within a two-word viewing window, *to stores* (the second can either be a noun or a determiner, both of which guarantee recognition of NP; compare (4) above), and so on down the tree (*stores* and *that* permit recognition of N and $\bar{\text{S}}$ within NP, etc.). When branching categories consistently follow non-branching categories, and each branching category is recognized on its left periphery, the result is optimal IC-to-word ratios.

The left-branching structure of languages such as Japanese and Korean illustrated in (9) can be equally optimal. A tensed auxiliary or verbal affix will construct S immediately prior to the complementizer constructing S̄. Two adjacent words will accordingly provide recognition of the two ICs of S̄, S and Comp, making a perfect IC-to-word ratio. Immediately thereafter *stores* constructs NP, and hence a two-word viewing window, *that stores*, suffices for recognition of the two ICs of NP, S̄ and N, providing a perfect IC-to-word ratio. The postposition *to* then immediately constructs PP, whose ICs are NP and Postposition, recognized within an optimal two-word sequence, *stores to*, and similarly for the VP. Branching categories consistently preceding non-branching categories, with recognition of the former on the right periphery, are as optimal as the reverse.

EIC also explains the existence across languages of re-arrangement rules such as Heavy NP Shift and Extraposition, and defines some quite specific (and correct) predictions for their formulation. It predicts that heavy categories with left-flank mother node construction, such as $_\bar{S}$[Comp S] or $_{NP}$[N S̄] in English, will be re-arranged to the right, while heavy categories with right-flank mother node construction in Japanese-type languages, such as $_\bar{S}$[S Comp] or $_{NP}$[S̄ N], will preferably move to the left. The purpose of these rules is to re-arrange constituent orders and re-instate the processing advantages of basic orders precisely for those instances of categories in performance that are unusually long or unusually short. For example, PPs in English are over twice as long as NPs on average in texts that I have examined (see Hawkins, 1992b, forthcoming) and this explains the relative ordering of [V NP PP] within the VP in the unmarked case. A re-arrangement such as Heavy NP Shift exists for structures like (2) in which the NP is, in the marked case, longer than the PP, and the repositioning re-introduces a preferred EIC ratio for this minority of cases. The rate of application for Heavy NP Shift in performance is even directly proportional to the degree of improvement in EIC ratios from basic to transformed orders. Conversely, EIC predicts that very light categories, such as single-word particles or pronouns, will always gravitate to the left within their CRDs.

The left–right asymmetries referred to above and summarized now in (10) and (11) are explained in terms of a second and independently motivated parsing principle, the Minimal Attachment Linear Order Principle, defined in (12) (see Hawkins, 1990: 252):

(10)   *Relative clauses*
       VO languages $_{NP}[N \bar{S}]$ only
       OV languages $_{NP}[N \bar{S}]$ or $_{NP}[\bar{S} N]$

(11)   *Comp positioning*
       VO languages $_{\bar{S}}[Comp S]$ only
       OV languages $_{\bar{S}}[Comp S]$ or $_{\bar{S}}[S Comp]$

(12)   *Minimal Attachment Linear Order Principle*
       The human parser prefers linear orderings that invite correct
       minimal attachments of words and ICs to mother nodes on-line.

The relevance of (12) to linear order was first proposed in Antinucci,
Duranti and Gebert (1979), who argued that pre-nominal clauses in
languages such as Japanese and Korean provide many more opportu-
nities for misanalysing constituent structure on-line and producing
garden paths than do their post-nominal counterparts (something
that has been empirically supported in Clancy, Lee and Zoh, 1986).
Such misanalyses have been shown in the work of Frazier (1978,
1985) to be associated with a measurable processing cost. The
asymmetries of (10) and (11) can therefore be explained in terms of
our two parsing principles, Early Immediate Constituents (6) and the
Minimal Attachment Linear Order Principle (12), as follows. The
orderings $_{NP}[N \bar{S}]$ and $_{\bar{S}}[Comp S]$ satisfy both principles in VO
languages, whereas the reverse $_{NP}[\bar{S} N]$ and $_{\bar{S}}[S Comp]$ would satisfy
neither. Hence only the former occur. But for languages with OV it is
not possible to satisfy both principles at once within basic orders at
least: $_{NP}[N \bar{S}]$ and $_{\bar{S}}[Comp S]$ satisfy the Minimal Attachment Linear
Order Principle, but not EIC; $_{NP}[\bar{S} N]$ and $_{\bar{S}}[S Comp]$ satisfy EIC but
not the Minimal Attachment principle. Hence, both orders are
productively attested in these languages (as are so-called 'head-
internal relatives'; see Keenan, 1985), and transformational re-
arrangements of the imperfect basic order either to the right (for
$_{\bar{S}}[Comp S]$ etc.) or to the left (for $_{S}[S Comp]$) then succeed in producing
orders in performance that are optimal for both principles.

   The basic point in all of this is that I no longer consider principles
of a purely grammatical nature to be capable of explaining why
languages arrange words in the orders they do. Grammatical principles alone give us no good reason to expect distinctions between
long and short ICs, or different directionalities for re-arrangement
rules in typologically different languages, or left–right asymmetries
such as (10) and (11). On the other hand, a performance approach
provides a very simple explanation. This explanation also subsumes

the very regularities that led to grammatical principles such as Vennemann's Natural Serialization, or Dryer's Branching Direction (1), or generative principles of head ordering and Directionality of Case and θ-role Assignment (see Haider, 1986; Travis, 1989). Where these principles are correct, there is a performance motivation; where they are incorrect, there is also a performance motivation. Some of these principles may be useful for purely descriptive purposes within certain grammars, but the explanatory primitives here reside within a theory of language processing, plausibly innately based, and this suggests that we expand our search further to see how much else in syntax follows from principles of processing rather than from (ultimately innate) principles of grammar. The syntactic notion 'head of phrase' provides another testing ground for this general approach, which I shall now pursue in greater detail.

11.3 Mother Node Construction, constituency and category membership

Let us return to the central parsing principle of this chapter, Mother Node Construction (MNC), defined in (3) above, which I repeat for convenience:

(3)   *Mother Node Construction* (MNC)
       In the left-to-right parsing of a sentence, if any syntactic category C uniquely determines a phrasal mother node M, in accordance with the PS-rules of the grammar, then M is immediately constructed over C.

We need to spell out the assumptions underlying MNC, and define its consequences and predictions for grammars. We can then compare it with the theory of heads.

11.3.1 Axiom of Existence

Principle (3) assumes that mother node constructing categories do indeed exist, and that they have the parsing function described, that is, they enable the hearer to recognize and construct phrasal mother nodes on-line. I shall refer to this as the Axiom of the Existence of MNCCs, defined in (13):

(13)   *Axiom of Existence*
       For each phrasal mother node M there exists at least one daughter category C that can construct M on each occasion of use, in accordance with the PS-rules of the grammar.

11.3.2 *Axiom of Uniqueness*

Mother Node Construction would not be possible unless the syntactic category that constructs a phrasal mother node is unique to that mother node. Otherwise, how could the hearer correctly recognize one mother node from another? This is defined as the Axiom of Uniqueness in (14):

(14)   *Axiom of Uniqueness*
        Each MNCC will consistently construct a unique M on each occasion of use.

11.3.3 *Daughter construction*

The Axiom of Existence refers explicitly to the construction of a phrasal node by a daughter category, rather than, say, by a sister, or by some more distant node in the phrase-structure tree. Such alternative possibilities are not ruled out, but the axiom claims that what is systematic in parsing is the recognition of a mother by a daughter, and this is not a trivial claim. A principle of Sister Node Construction is, in fact, proposed in Hawkins (forthcoming) for structures such as $_{\bar{s}}$[Comp S] in English, in which Comp constructs an S as right sister in addition to the mother $\bar{s}$. But (13) requires that no phrasal node can be constructed *only* on this basis.

Imagine that a given phrasal node co-occurring with a verb is assigned the category NP, that is $_{VP}$[V NP]. Imagine further that some other phrasal node that is quite non-distinct from this latter in terms of the daughter categories it can dominate but that occurs in conjunction with, say, an adjective is assigned the category PP, $_{AdjP}$[Adj PP], that is, solely on account of the difference in sister categories. Axiom (13) would rule out this possibility. More generally, it claims that the existence of distinct sisters is not a sufficient basis for distinguishing phrasal categories without some additional distinction in the daughter categories dominated, and hence that syntactic rules will not discriminate between categories solely on this basis. At least partially distinct daughters are always required, at least one of which will construct the mother node.

The ultimate functional motivation for this, I would argue, is that categories that are to be treated as distinct by the syntax, such as NP and PP, must be recognizably distinct in performance. By containing at least one daughter that is an MNCC unique to M, higher constituent structure can always be readily and rapidly inferred. By contrast, making the identity of M entirely dependent upon a sister would not be generally efficient, for several reasons. First, if the determining categories, V and Adj in the example above, were to follow the dependent NP/PP, a decision about the categorial status of this phrase would have to be delayed until V or Adj were encountered, that is *after* NP/PP had been completely scanned. Decisions about the *attachment site* for a phrase must sometimes be delayed in parsing, but the actual categorial identity of a phrase should always be rapidly recognizable, and on-line indeterminacy and delay in this regard can be avoided if mothers are systematically constructed by daughters. Second, making a category dependent upon its sisters for recognition imposes a strong adjacency requirement on these ICs, regardless of their ordering. Any kind of distance between them will lessen the construction potential of the determining sister. Such adjacency may not always be desirable, however. V and a direct-object NP are most frequently adjacent in English, but when the NP is longer than following VP-dominated constituents, there is independent motivation to postpose it by Heavy NP Shift, and hence to destroy the adjacency. Third, sister construction imposes a strong predictability requirement on adjacent ICs, again regardless of ordering. Such predictability is not very frequent, however. Even a PP in English, whose immediate daughter constituents are limited to P and NP (and adverbial speci-fiers), does not allow us to infer an accompanying NP after P, because of stacked PPs such as $_{PP}$[from $_{PP}$[under $_{NP}$[the table]]]. Fourth, all rules of grammar that referred to a sister-dependent category would need to be made context-sensitive. Any time reference was made to NP in the example above, the sister V would have to be included in the rule specification, and this would both add an extra symbol and reduce the generality of the rule, by making it inapplicable to any NPs in other environments.

For all of these reasons, mothers are systematically constructed by daughters, and Sister Node Construction is limited to a handful of structures in which sisters are regularly adjacent and predictable, such as $_{\bar{S}}$[Comp S]. Even here, the S must also be constructed by a daughter MNCC, on account of (13).

11.3.4 *Possible plurality of MNCCs*

Axiom (13) explicitly allows for the possibility of more than one MNCC per mother node. Thus, both a noun and a determiner are capable of constructing a noun phrase, and in a language such as German one could add inflected adjectives as well, since these occur exclusively within NPs (the relevant parsing principle being Agreement Projection, as in Hawkins, forthcoming). The NP will be constructed on-line by whichever of these daughters comes first. In $_{NP}$[einige grosse Männer] in German, 'several large men', the NP will be constructed by the determiner *einige*, in $_{NP}$[grosse Männer] by the inflected adjective *grosse*, and in $_{NP}$[Männer] by the noun alone. This plurality of MNCCs will be argued in section 11.4.2 to provide an explanation for the systematic variation in [Det N] and [N Det] orders across languages, since both categories are equally capable of constructing their mother node. It also makes sense of numerous other variation facts within and across grammars, whenever alternative constructing categories exist for one and the same M. For example, alternative MNCCs are generally omissible, as long as one remains with which to construct M. A German NP may be constructed by $_{NP}$[$_{Det}$[einige]] alone, by $_{NP}$[$_N$[Männer]] alone and even on occasion by $_{NP}$[$_{Adj}$[grosse]] alone, all of which function as NPs by NP-sensitive rules, such as Passive, Subject–Verb Agreement and so on. Such alternations between different MNCCs provide the main empirical difference between the heads theory and the theory presented here, a point developed in sections 11.3.7 and 11.4.2.

11.3.5 *Uniqueness*

While a mother node may be constructed by a plurality of MNCCs, the converse fails: an MNCC cannot construct more than one mother. In other words, any MNCC must have a unique phrasal mother node M; compare (14). There is a clear functional motivation for this requirement, and it has major consequences for the formulation of PS-rules and for the distinctiveness of MNCCs in language use.

If MNCCs were not unique to their Ms in this way, there would be a systematic ambiguity with respect to which mother node was intended on a particular occasion. Making the wrong selection would result in structural misanalyses, garden paths and so on, all of which are known to cause processing difficulty, and would defeat the whole purpose of having MNCCs at all, which I regard, following Fodor (1983), as a means of providing an immediate, obligatory and reflex-like recognition of higher constituent structure on-line. Hence it would be impossible for a verb to construct both a VP and, say, an AdjP. More generally, if a language has an AdjP at all (see Thompson, 1988), it must also have a separate form class of categories distinct from verbs and nouns, namely adjectives, which can uniquely construct this higher phrasal node.

The consequences of this for PS-rules are quite profound. Each phrasal node will be rewritten so as to contain at least one MNCC that is unique to it. This does not necessarily require, as I shall argue in section 11.3.7, that the MNCC must be of the same general category as the mother node, though it often will be. But it does impose a constraint on the relationship between left- and right-hand categories in PS-rewrite rules. A rule such as VP → NP + PP would be an impossible rule, since there is no MNCC for VP; VP → Adj + PP would be impossible alongside AdjP → Adj + PP, on account of the non-uniqueness of Adj as an MNCC, and VP → V + PP and AdjP → V + PP would be impossible for the same reason.

11.3.6 Types of MNCCs

The Axioms of Existence and Uniqueness incorporate a prediction with regard to the kinds of categories that can be MNCCs: any daughter may be an MNCC, as long as it guarantees unique recognition and construction of the mother. As a result, both lexical categories and the so-called 'functional' categories – closed-class items such as determiners and complementizers – can serve in this capacity. The lexical category of nouns is unique to NP, and so are determiners. For other phrasal categories, only a lexical or only a functional category may be appropriate, for independent reasons.

11.3.7 No requirement of category constancy

One of the major defining features of the head of phrase generalization is often referred to as 'category constancy' (see, for instance, Vennemann, 1974). The basic idea is that the phrasal mother node must be of the same general category type as its head, or a 'projection' of its head, to use the language of grammatical models such as X-bar syntax (as in Jackendoff, 1977b). The noun phrase is headed by a noun; if, following Abney (1987), the determiner is regarded as a head, then the whole phrase is labelled a determiner phrase; and so on.

The principle of MNC, by contrast, does not insist on category constancy. It requires only that the phrasal mother be uniquely recognizable on the basis of the relevant daughter. Both a determiner and a noun can construct NP on this account. An Aux can construct S, which is not a projection of Aux in our terms, and Comp can construct a subordinate S. When additional parsing principles such as Grandmother Node Construction (GNC) are considered (see Hawkins, forthcoming), the number of these alternative phrasal node constructing categories (PNCCs) for a given M increases. A finite verb, V_f, will construct VP by MNC, and S by GNC, since it may be just as unique to S as Aux is. A Nominative-marked pronoun in English will also construct S by GNC (and NP by MNC). Correspondingly, an NP with non-Nominative case marking may signal the onset of VP, by GNC, just as effectively as a verb in many languages. We do not wish to say in these cases that each constructing category projects its categorial status to the relevant mother, since the mother would then have to receive several different category labels at one and the same time. (We also need to allow for one and the same constructing category to be able to construct a categorially distinct mother and grandmother.) Category constancy would have undesirable empirical consequences if it were a necessary feature of MNC, therefore.

Recall the German NP examples discussed in section 11.3.4, where a determiner, inflected adjective or noun could each stand alone and construct NP: $_{NP}[_{Det}[einige]]$, $_{NP}[_{Adj}[grosse]]$ and $_{NP}[_{N}[Männer]]$. A literal enforcement of the category-constancy requirement would force us to say that only *Männer* was an NP, since it is a projection of the noun, whereas *einige* and *grosse* are determiners and adjectives respectively, which should project their categories onto the mother. But all of these items are clearly instances of the same phrasal category, most plausibly NP, and are treated identically by grammatical rules that refer to NP. So if we adhere to category constancy for MNCCs, we create phrasal categories that complicate the grammar. More generally, any language that permits a phrasal category to be constructed by a plurality of MNCCs, different members of which may construct M on different occasions, will result in complications for the grammar if category constancy is adhered to.

There is a second argument that points in the same direction, involving cross-linguistic variation. Imagine the case of two languages, L_1 and L_2, sharing exactly the same phrasal category conventionally labelled NP with the same set of daughters, except that L_1 has the order $_{NP}[N\ Det]$ while L_2 has $_{NP}[Det\ N]$. Now, by the definition of Mother Node Construction given in (3) above, the mother node NP will be immediately constructed by the first MNCC encountered in the left-to-right phrase, that is, by N in L_1 and by Det in L_2. If we insist that the category that actually constructs the mother also projects its categorial status to this phrasal node, we will be forced to say that L_1 has an NP, whereas L_2 has a DetP. But this is an undesirable result, because L_1 and L_2 have exactly the same phrasal constituent in terms of everything that matters for constituency, namely domination and the set of categories dominated, and it would be bizarre in a theory of Universal Grammar to have to say that there are two constituent types, that just happen to be identical in all respects that involve constituency, that none the less look as different in their categorial status and labelling as, say, NP and VP. By contrast, if we do not insist on category constancy, we can say that L_1 and L_2 share an identical phrasal category, NP, and differ only in a minor ordering that is quite irrelevant from the point of view of constituency and that involves a difference in performance rather than competence: the category that actually constructs this identical phrase on-line differs between L_1 and L_2.

Category constancy is not a necessary feature of MNC, therefore, because of MNCC–M pairings such as Det–NP, Aux–S and Comp–S̄. None the less, there are other pairs for which category constancy does hold, namely V–VP, N–NP and P–PP, and more generally I want to claim that an MNCC *may* project its categorial status, as in these cases. Why is it that some do, whereas others do not?

The reasons for this, it seems to me, are independent of phrasal node construction *per se*, and involve semantics and other performance properties of the categories in question. Consider the VP. Within our theory, this node will be constructed by V, or alternatively by some non-Nominative NP uniquely dominated by VP (on the basis of GNC). Semantically, both V and VP are predicates, whereas NPs are arguments, so if any of these constructing categories is going to project its syntactic status, considerations of a semantic nature suggest it should be V, since V shares a fundamental semantic property with VP. Also, V defines relations of subcategorization and selection on its accompanying NPs, while NPs do not define such relations on co-occurring Vs. V again has priority from this point of view, and the phrase that dominates V can be naturally regarded as an expansion of the daughter category that determines which other ICs can co-occur and form a larger unit. But the reason for this asymmetry is not because V is stipulated to be a head; it is because a verb can render its 'predicate frame' (see Hawkins, forthcoming) or valency structure predictable in performance, whereas NPs that are Accusative-marked or semantic Patients and so on, do not do this, since they are distributed among too many verbs to guarantee predictability. Give the native speaker a verb such as *hit*, and he/she will immediately provide NP co-occurrence frames for it; give him/her an NP such as *the farmer* and there will be no such uniformity in the co-occurring verbs that are provided. Hence, analysing VP as a type of V is motivated both semantically and in processing terms.

Similar arguments apply to the NP. There is a semantic unity to N and NP, which is lacking with Det. Nouns define classes of entities possessing conceptual properties associated with lexical items, and NPs define more complex and restricted classes of this type. The determiner functions primarily to restrict the reference of nouns, rather than to define a class of entities *per se*, and when (as in German *einige*) it stands alone, there is generally a semantic noun class that is understood. For this reason there is semantic support for analysing the mother of N as a type of N, that is, NP, even though Det can also construct it syntactically.

Finally, there are no comparable reasons, beyond MNC and uniqueness, for saying that the mother of a complementizer such as *that* is a syntactic projection of Comp, that is, CompP. *That* exists, as I see it, solely in order to provide a clear syntactic boundary for parsing purposes. Since MNC alone is not sufficient to motivate a CompP, Comp does not project its syntactic status.

11.3.8 Comparing MNCCs and heads

If one compares the MNCCs illustrated in (4) above with the corresponding set of head categories that is generally assumed in the literature (see section 11.5 for a summary of the defining properties of heads), one sees that the two notions are close, but not identical. Both MNCCs and heads are daughter categories of their mother nodes (section 11.3.3). Both are unique to their mother nodes (section 11.3.5). MNCCs can be both lexical and functional categories, and many theories of heads now allow for both possibilities as well (section 11.3.6). They differ in two related respects only. There can be a possible plurality of MNCCs for a given mother, whereas there can only literally be one head of phrase, on the assumption that the head projects its categorial status onto the mother (section 11.3.4): the mother cannot have several node labels at once. There is, correspondingly, no requirement of category constancy for MNCCs, whereas there is for heads (section 11.3.7).

We therefore have two competing approaches to account for a set of grammatical regularities, the one in terms of an ultimately performance-driven notion of Mother Node Construction, the other in terms of a grammatical primitive, head of phrase. How can we decide between these two approaches? I shall offer three types of arguments in favour of Mother Node Construction.

First, we can focus on the major defining differences between them, involving the plurality of MNCCs versus heads, and category constancy. Any argument that supports the need for several 'heads' for one and the same phrasal node and for abandoning category constancy is an argument against the head of phrase generalization. I gave one such in section 11.3.7 involving the alternation between competing MNCCs in the German noun phrase. Whenever different categories construct the mother, there will have to be some technical manipulation within the heads theory that guarantees category constancy, despite the simplest evidence on the surface. Further arguments will be given in section 11.4.2. Second, I argued in section 11.2.1 that one major grammatical regularity that has been proposed in support of heads does not actually support it, namely word order. Instead, performance principles that include MNC were argued in section 11.2.2 to provide a better explanation of cross-linguistic ordering regularities. This point will be pursued further in section 11.4.1. Third, I shall argue in section 11.5 that proposed grammatical correlates of heads are really properties of constructing categories instead. I shall also suggest, in section 11.6, that the parsing theory is more explanatory than the heads theory.

11.4 Mother Node Construction and linear order

I argued in section 11.2.1 that word-order universals do not support a consistent head-ordering regularity. Where the sisters of proposed heads are non-branching categories, there are no cross-categorial ordering correlations; where the sisters are branching, there are correlations, but often only under assumptions that not all theories accept, and there are also straightforward counter-examples. It was shown in section 11.2.2 that the principle of Mother Node Construction, operating in conjunction with Early Immediate Constituents, can provide a more general explanation for cross-linguistic ordering regularities. In this section I examine two further respects in which MNC and the heads theory contrast with regard to ordering facts, and we shall see that in both cases MNC is supported.

11.4.1 Left-peripheral and right-peripheral MNC languages

EIC incorporates a prediction for the positioning of MNCCs within their respective phrasal categories. I repeat the definition of EIC for convenience:

(6)   *Early Immediate Constituents*
The human parser prefers to maximize the left-to-right IC-to-word ratios of the phrasal nodes that it constructs.

The prediction will be referred to as 'peripherality'. We saw in the Heavy NP Shift example of English in (2'b) above (*I gave to Mary the valuable book that was extremely difficult to find*) that higher ratios result when shorter ICs precede longer ones within a CRD. But IC-to-word ratios will still not be optimal unless the category that constructs the postposed NP actually occurs on the left periphery of this NP. Imagine that only a head noun were capable of constructing NP. The CRD for VP would then proceed from the verb on the left to the head noun on the right, resulting in a lower aggregate ratio. Compare (2'b), which we repeat, with (2''), in which the NP is constructed by N:

(2')

b.   I $_{VP}$[gave $_{PP}$[to   Mary] $_{NP}$[the valuable book that was extremely difficult to
   VP CRD: 1/1   2/2   2/3   3/4   find]]
            100%   100% 67%   75%   = 86% aggregate ratio

(2'')

        I $_{VP}$[gave $_{PP}$[to   Mary] $_{NP}$[the valuable book that was extremely difficult to
   VP CRD: 1/1   2/2   2/3   3/4   3/5   3/6   find]]
            100%   100% 67%   75% 60%   50%   = 75% aggregate ratio

The concept of a constituent recognition domain (see (5) above) refers to the ordered set of words that are needed to recognize all the ICs of VP, proceeding from the word that constructs the first IC to the word that constructs the last. Since N constructs NP in (2''), the CRD proceeds on this occasion from *gave* on the left to *book* on the right, and the calculation of the IC-to-word ratio is made as shown, in accordance with the procedure defined in (7) above.

It is for this reason also that complementizers constructing subordinate clauses occur exclusively on the left periphery in English-type languages. If Comp were medial within $\bar{S}$, the recognition of this latter would occur later, and IC-to-word ratios would be lower. (There could also be Minimal Attachment misrecognition problems.) In Japanese, on the other hand, complementizers occur on the right periphery:

(15)   a. Mary said $_{\bar{S}}$ [that John got married yesterday]

        b. Japanese
           [Kinoo   John-ga kekkonsi-ta to]$_{\bar{S}}$ Mary-ga it-ta
           yesterday John   got-married that   Mary   said

The rightward positioning of the Japanese complementizer *to* has the same advantage as the leftward positioning of *that* in English. The calculation of the matrix CRD will only start once *to* has actually constructed its mother and has made it clear to the listener that the initial material is a subordinate $\bar{S}$ rather than a main clause.

More generally, EIC leads us to predict that MNCCs will be peripheral within all phrasal categories, and that they will be consistently peripheral within a given language. In the typical right-branching structure of (8) above, all MNCCs are left peripheral:

(8) $_{VP}$[walked $_{PP}$[to $_{NP}$[stores $_{\bar{S}}$[that $_{S}$[Bill likes]]]]]

If such a language were to have, say, postpositions rather than prepositions, the CRD for the VP would no longer have an optimal IC-to-word ratio, since this domain would now proceed from *walked* on the left, which constructs VP, to the postposition *to* on the right constructing PP, as shown in (8'):

(8') $_{VP}$[walked $_{PP[NP}$[stores that Bill likes] to]]
VP CRD: 1/1   2/2   2/3 2/4 2/5   2/6
        100%   100% 67% 50%40% 33%
                                        = 65% aggregate ratio

The aggregate ratio in (8') is now significantly less than the optimal score for VP in (8).

Conversely, left-branching languages will achieve optimal IC-to-word ratios only on condition that their MNCCs are right-peripheral, as in (9):

(9)   [[[[[Bill likes]$_S$ that]$_{\bar{S}}$ stores]$_{NP}$ to]$_{PP}$ walked]$_{VP}$

If such languages were prepositional rather than postpositional, the VP domain would again have a much lower IC-to-word ratio, as shown in (9'), since the CRD now proceeds from the preposition *to* to the verb *walked*:

(9') $_{VP[PP}$[to $_{NP}$[Bill likes that stores]] walked]
VP CRD: 1/1   1/2   1/3 1/4 1/5   2/6
        100%   50% 33% 25% 20%   33%
                                        = 44% aggregate ratio

The EIC therefore predicts consistent peripherality for MNCCs, and the basic reason why it does so is that the CRD for each phrasal category can consist of other phrasal categories, and if all of these are recognized and constructed on the same periphery, CRDs can be much shorter and IC-to-word ratios much higher. This prediction is defined in (16):

(16)   *Consistent peripherality*
        MNCCs are, in the unmarked case, consistently left- or consistently right-peripheral within their phrasal categories.

From the point of view of language typology, (16) has the following consequences. There are only two peripheries to a phrasal category, the left side or the right side, so if the ordering of MNCCs is going to be consistent, there can only be two language types, which I shall refer to as 'left-mother-node constructing languages' or left-MNC languages for short, and 'right-MNC' languages. English is an example of the former, and Japanese of the latter. This different positioning of MNCCs has major consequences for the on-line processing of syntactic structure. In English, processing proceeds in a top–down manner, that is, down the syntactic tree, as in (15a); in Japanese it proceeds bottom–up, as in (15b).

EIC therefore predicts the existence of just two word-order types. MNCCs could, in principle, occupy some medial position within their phrasal categories, leading to an MNC-medial language type. But such a type would be incompatible with EIC and with (16). Of course, within a syntactic theory that assumes exclusively binary branching for all categories, the peripherality of all daughters is guaranteed, and no MNCC could be medial, hence there could be no medial type. But many theories do not assume binary branching, and I know of no compelling reasons for why this should be a universal of constituent structure. Some languages have been argued to have flat structures, particularly at the sentence level, and to lack a VP (Hale, 1983). Even for languages like English that do have a clear VP, I am not aware of compelling arguments for the binary structure $_{VP}[[V\ NP]\ PP]$ for (2a) above, rather than $_{VP}[V\ NP\ PP]$. So the prediction made by EIC that there will not be MNC-medial language types, in the unmarked case, is not a trivial claim.

A second prediction made by EIC for language typology involves the relative distribution of these two word-order types. Since each can provide optimal IC-to-word ratios, as illustrated in (8) and (9), it is predicted that they should be more or less equally attested across languages.

This frequency prediction is quite strikingly confirmed. Hawkins and Cutler (1988) and Hawkins and Gilligan (1988) examine a number of different language samples currently available and show that the distribution of left- versus right-MNC languages is almost exactly 50–50 (at least for VO versus OV, and PrNP versus NPPo orders). Where there are left–right asymmetries involving $_{NP}[N\ \bar{S}]$ versus $[\bar{S}\ N]_{NP}$ or $_{\bar{S}}[Comp\ S]$ versus $[S\ Comp]_{\bar{S}}$, there is no 50–50 distribution, of course, but the frequency skewing is now predicted by the conjunction of EIC and the additional parsing principle defined in (12) (Hawkins, 1990).

Principle (16) also makes a further frequency prediction. It does not rule out, categorically, the existence of languages with mixed left- and right-peripheral MNCCs; but it does claim that these are marked. More generally, EIC predicts that the frequency of marked structures such as (8') and (9') across languages will be in direct proportion to their EIC ratios. Some consequences of this prediction are pursued in Hawkins (1990), and are found to be confirmed.

A typology in terms of left-MNC and right-MNC languages contrasts with the alternative characterization in terms of head-initial and head-final languages, both theoretically and empirically. The existence of left-MNC and right-MNC languages is now directly motivated, and the absence of MNC-medial languages explained. The head-initial versus head-final typology is simply stipulated, and there is no explanation for the absence of head-medial languages. Such languages are quite compatible with the cross-categorial rule simplification idea that underlies X-bar theory, since some identical sisters across categories could in principle be ordered to the left of the head and some to the right. And indeed my earlier theory of Cross-Category Harmony, which was based on this X-bar intuition (Hawkins, 1983), incorporated exactly this prediction, which Dryer (1991) has now found is not supported in his own language sample. So at a very general level, EIC and consistent peripherality provide a more constrained and explanatory theory of word-order types than the heads theory.

Empirically, this theory subsumes and also explains Dryer's branching regularity and predicts the equal frequency of the two language types illustrated in (8) and (9), since they both achieve optimal scores. The heads theory simply has nothing to say about frequencies, and is again less explanatory from this point of view.

11.4.2 Predictions for alternative MNCCs

What about phrasal categories that can be constructed by a plurality of MNCCs? EIC makes a prediction for these cases, which contrasts with the heads theory. Consider left-MNC languages. It does not matter from our point of view which MNCC is leftmost, as long as one of them is, since each is capable of performing the same parsing job. For the NP we accordingly predict variation. The leftmost daughter may be a head noun (as in Yoruba), or it may be a determiner (as in English), but one of them must be leftmost, and this seems to be an exceptionless universal in VO and prepositional languages (Hawkins, 1983: 117–20).[2]

Such a prediction cannot be made in a theory in which NP is constructed by just one category, namely the head noun. The variation would have to be accounted for by saying, for example, that Det-initial languages such as English will construct DetP first, and then NP, attaching the latter under the former. A language such as Yoruba would construct NP first, and DetP second, again conceivably attaching NP under DetP by a bottom–up parse. Alternatively, DetP might be attached under NP in this language, by a top–down parse. The former solution for Yoruba is unsatisfactory in that it imposes a left-branching (right-MNC) structure within DetP, $_{DetP}[_{NP}[N \ldots] \text{ Det}]$, on an otherwise right-branching (left-MNC) language. It also undermines any correlation between order and heads, since N precedes its sisters within NP, while Det follows within DetP. (Recall section 11.2.1.) These problems are compounded in languages such as Urhobo (Keenan, 1985: 145) in which Det follows N, as in Yoruba, but precedes sisters of N such as relative clauses, that is N Det s̄, forcing a regular discontinuity between N and s̄ as daughters of NP (in contrast to Yoruba which has N s̄ Det):

(17)   Urhobo
oshale na s̄ [l-lye   na teye o]
man   the that-woman the hit him
'the man that the woman hit'

(18)   Yoruba
isu s̄ [ti mo ra lana]   naa
yam REL I buy yesterday that
'that yam which I bought yesterday'

The second solution for Yoruba (and Urhobo), embedding DetP under NP, is unsatisfactory since it amounts to the claim that a difference in ordering results in a different constituent status for the whole phrase, DetP in English, NP in Yoruba and Urhobo. But we should not be forced by a minor cross-linguistic difference in surface ordering to the assumption of different constituent structures, for reasons discussed in section 11.3.7.

None of these problems arise if we assume a flatter structure for NP in all languages, with different MNCCs performing the task of actually constructing this node, depending on which item comes first. More generally, there is an explanatory intuition here that has a lot of support, I believe: where there are alternative MNCCs for a given M, we predict ordering variation and other alternations, including deletions and the omissibility of all but one MNCC, precisely because these different MNCCs are performing the same parsing function. This intuition is not naturally capturable within a theory in which there is only one head per M, and the kind of data that it predicts is either embarrassing for the heads theory (recall the NP deletion facts in German, sections 11.3.4 and 11.3.7), or results in descriptive complications and a loss of generalizations, as in the examples we have just considered.

We can extend this intuition and its predictions to phrasal categories constructed by additional parsing principles, such as Grandmother Node Construction. For example, if VP can be constructed by non-Nominative case-marked NPs on the basis of GNC, as well as by V (through MNC), then it would be possible for languages that are otherwise left-MNC (for instance prepositional within PP or Det-initial in NP) to be verb-final within the VP, since VP will be constructed early by other VP-unique daughters. I believe that this is (in part) what explains the basic positioning of case-marked pronouns on the left periphery of VP in German (for example, $_{VP}$[ihm das Buch gab] 'him the book gave', that is 'gave him the book'),[3] and the retention of surface case marking on full NPs. German is fundamentally a left-MNC language, though the position of its verb makes it look, deceptively, like a right-MNC language such as Japanese. The deception is removed in the present theory by observing that the VP is constructed early by appropriate case-marked NPs. Conversely, when case is lost, as in the history of English, the verb must shift to the left of VP where it can replace case-marked NPs as the constructor of VP. The other apparently right MNCC of German, the Aux or V_f, does not actually construct S on a right periphery in that language either, since S is already constructed on a left periphery in both main and subordinate clauses: by Aux/V_f in first or second position in main clauses (Hawkins, 1986: 161–213); and by an obligatory complementizer constructing a right-sister S in subordinate clauses.

This approach provides a new explanation for the robust typological correlation between SOV order and surface case marking. Grammatical subjects with, for instance, Nominative case marking will construct S, and non-Nominative case marking on VP-dominated ICs then constructs VP, well in advance of the verb, and so provides good EIC ratios for the S domain. We also make the diachronic prediction that the ICs that are postposed to the right of V in the history of languages such as English will be, first, the non-case-marked ICs such as PP; then full NPs will be postposed as their case marking is lost, at the same time that case-marked pronouns are retained pre-verbally, giving a Pro–V/V–NP co-occurrence (more precisely a co-occurrence of Pro–V with both NP–V and V–NP, the latter being preferred initially with heavier, and then with increasingly shorter NPs); finally $_{VP}$[V ...] may be grammaticalized everywhere. In this way, good EIC ratios for the S domain are preserved at each diachronic stage. Clear evidence for exactly this sequence is provided in Bean (1983: 115, 139).

What these examples show is that alternative constructing categories can occur in the position predicted for that language type. Consider an example now from right-MNC languages. Assume the existence of a syntactic category of subordinate clause (as opposed to a 'root' or main clause in the sense of Emonds 1976), subsuming relative clauses *inter alia*, and abbreviated S_s. Subordinate status can be uniquely indicated by at least two major kinds of daughters: a complementizer constructing S_s through MNC; and special morphological marking on the verb, such as a participial affix constructing S_s by GNC. It is no accident that exactly these two types of phrasal node constructing categories are productively attested in right-MNC languages, in complementary distribution, and both on the right periphery of S_s; compare Lehmann (1984: 49–72). The complementizer is illustrated in Lahu, the participle in Dravidian languages such as Telugu:

(19) Lahu
      [và?-ó+qō thà? cɔ̃   tā ve] yâ+mî+ma
      pig's-head ACC cook PRF COMP woman
      'the woman who has cooked the pig's head'

(20) Telugu
      [mīri nāku ic-cin-a]   pustukamu
      you me   give-PRET-PART book-NOM
      'the book that you gave me'

Within an individual grammar, the existence of alternative PNCCs means that the task of constructing the common M can be distributed among the alternatives. S can be constructed either by Aux or by V_f in English, for instance, by *will* in $_S$[... will ...$_{VP}$[sing in the garden]], and by *sings* in $_S$[... $_{VP}$[sings in the garden]].[4] In negative sentences, S construction by Aux alone has been grammaticalized: *will not sing in the garden*; **not sings in the garden*. If no Aux is otherwise available, a dummy Aux *do* constructs S: *does not sing in the garden*. This account predicts deletion and omissibility possibilities. At least one of

Aux and V_f must always be present for the construction of S in English: *John sings*; *John will*; *John does*; and so on. Similarly, one of the alternative MNCCs for the German NP must always be retained as discussed above.

In all of these examples, categories that are distinct, yet functionally similar from the point of view of higher node construction, exhibit similar behaviour with regard to ordering, and grammars may vary in the extent to which they actually possess the alternatives, and in the manner in which they distribute them among different syntactic environments. Similar positioning and a possible complementarity in distribution are consequences of the fact that these different constructing categories construct the same M, as we see it. Such facts are not naturally explainable by a theory in which there is just one head for a given M, and each such head projects its category status to its M and is obligatorily present. Predictions of complementary distribution and alternative omissibility cannot be made in this model since the Ms that are identical in our theory are distinct in the heads theory (NP versus DetP, or CompP versus S_s for (19) and (20)), and also because not all our constructing categories are heads in any theory (for example, non-Nominative case-marked NPs). And the similar positioning of alternative constructing categories cannot be explained by arguing that these categories are simply heads of different Ms, because head ordering does not, in general, exhibit clear correlations with word order, not all of these categories will be heads, as we have seen, and because of the kinds of technical problems inherent in accounting for variants such as DetN versus NDet within the heads theory considered earlier.

11.5 Mother Node Construction and the correlations with heads

Even though word-order universals do not support a head of phrase generalization there are many fundamental properties of grammar that have been argued to correlate with it and to be definable in terms of it. Hudson (1987: 111) writes: 'The big attraction of the notion "head", for those of us who believe in it, is precisely that it integrates a wide range of different phenomena.' These phenomena include the following:

1 The **obligatory** constituent – the head is the category that has to be present.
2 The **distributionally equivalent** constituent – the head is the category whose distribution is similar to that of the mother.

3 The **morphosyntactic locus** – the head is the constituent on which any inflections that are relevant to the mother are located.

4 The **subcategorizand** – the head subcategorizes for its sisters.

5 The **governor** – the head determines the morphosyntactic form of its sisters.

6 The **semantic functor** – the meaning of the head has the status of a functor in relation to an argument category.

Hudson argues, in contrast to Zwicky (1985) before him, that these properties do, in fact, correlate, and that they provide support for the existence and utility of the head of phrase generalization.

It seems to me that none of these properties provides compelling evidence for heads. Property (6) certainly does not, and properties (1–5) may appear to, but are more naturally analysable and explainable as consequences of MNC and related construction principles. As I see it, head categories are MNCCs in parsing, by definition, since they construct their mother nodes; but not all MNCCs (or PNCCs) need be heads. That is, the set of heads is properly included in the set of constructing categories within a parser. We therefore need to establish what the significant generalizations are in this area: do properties 1–5 correlate with heads, or with the larger set of constructing categories that contains heads? I shall argue for the latter. Because of space limitations, my discussion will be deliberately brief.

11.5.1 Construction properties

Consider properties 1–3, obligatoriness, distributional equivalence and morphosyntactic locus, which I shall refer to as 'construction properties'. Assume the Axiom of Existence in (13) (for each phrasal mother node M there exists at least one daughter category C that can construct M on each occasion of use). It follows that obligatoriness is a necessary requirement for category construction, but not necessarily for heads. If there is no daughter MNCC for M, then M will not be recognisable and constructable, and the axiom will not be fulfilled. Hence, obligatoriness follows from the need to recognize what constituent is actually being parsed. Non-MNCCs do not provide this information, and alternative MNCCs are not all needed at the same time, even if each is analysable as a head within some grammatical model.

Immediately we see why there is controversy over Det and N. Traditionally N has been regarded as the head; Hudson (1987) argues for Det instead; and both categories are analysed as heads, of NP and DetP respectively, in Radford (this volume). But empirically sometimes Det can stand alone, and sometimes just N, in phrases of this type, as we saw in the German data of sections 11.3.4 and 11.3.7. And this is exactly what MNC predicts: at least one MNCC (more generally at least one phrasal constructing category) must be obligatorily present in each M. Hence, the reason for the controversy over Det and N is that both can be MNCCs.

Distributional equivalence is closely related to obligatoriness and is also a consequence of the Axiom of Existence. MNCC and M share the same distribution precisely because the MNCC constructs M and may be the only daughter of M that is present, being obligatory. The distributional equivalence of MNCC and M follows straightforwardly from the construction potential of the former, therefore.

The morphosyntactic locus of inflections relevant to the mother is also related to obligatoriness, and is functionally motivated. It would be counter-productive to position these inflections on a daughter that was regularly omissible since the grammatical information carried by inflections would then be lost. By positioning these affixes on the obligatory constituent, their regular retention is guaranteed.

Once again, problems arise for the heads theory whenever there is a plurality of MNCCs. Zwicky and Hudson disagree in their analysis of Det and N, and the following quote from Hudson (1987: 122) reveals the arbitrariness that is inherent in assigning either one to the category of head: 'the few morphosyntactic markers that there are in the English NP ... seem to be distributed fairly equally between Det and N, so I shall reverse Zwicky's decision by taking Det as the morphosyntactic locus'! The MNC theory, on the other hand, makes a plurality of categories available as morphosyntactic loci, N, Det and even Adj (by Agreement Projection; see Hawkins, forthcoming). Inflections may be marked on just one, or on all of them, or may be distributed between them, presumably with consequences for omission possibilities in specific instances depending on how the distribution is made. But in general this theory predicts that the morphosyntactic features of NP will not be limited to just N or to Det alone, and this is correct.

Morphosyntactic categories and their positioning are correlates of construction categories, therefore, rather than heads. This argument is supported by the kinds of data discussed in section 11.4.2 and involving parsing principles such as Grandmother Node Construction and Agreement Projection. Here it is crucially the morphology that indicates which phrasal node should be constructed above the mother node and to which the mother should be attached. Recall finite lexical verbs, V_f, in English. The V constructs VP by MNC; the morphology of finiteness constructs S by Grandmother Node Construction to which VP is attached. An adjective agreeing with a noun in German will construct AdjP by MNC, but also NP, the mother of the noun, by Agreement Projection from this noun. And a verb with subject agreement will construct VP (by MNC) and S, the mother of the subject, by Agreement Projection from the subject. In all these examples, the morphology of finiteness and agreement constructs higher constituent structure to which mother nodes (constructed by MNC) can be attached. As a result the morphology plays a vital role in indicating how mother nodes are attached to their mothers and contract sisterhood relations within these grandmothers. These morphosyntactic categories are therefore construction properties in the broadest sense, not just head properties.

11.5.2 *Construction domain properties*

Properties (4) and (5), involving subcategorization and government, are generally considered to involve a relationship of co-constituency between ICs. Specifically, the head is claimed to subcategorize for and govern (through 'c-command'; see Reinhart, 1983) its sister categories. Except that it does not! One NP that is productively governed and subcategorized for is the grammatical subject, and the category that does the subcategorizing and governing is a lexical verb. But in all languages that have a VP, the lexical V will not c-command any ICs outside the domination of VP. Hence, various technical manipulations are required in the relevant grammatical models in order to extend subcategorization and government to subjects. For a language such as English, government of a subject by, say, Aux/Infl may get around the difficulties. But in ergative languages, the case of the syntactic subject is intimately dependent upon the transitive or intransitive nature of the lexical verb, that is, on a VP-internal constituent, and this exposes the need for a more general solution to this problem. The proposal in Hawkins (forthcoming) is that a verb may assign case and subcategorization requirements within its 'construction domain', defined as the set of nodes dominated by the highest phrasal node constructed by the category in question. Since a verb, if finite, can construct S, by GNC, in addition to VP (through MNC), the construction domain for V_f is the whole S. Case assignment and subcategorization are therefore defined within construction domains, not c-command domains. This accounts naturally for both subjects and non-subjects, and makes an interesting prediction: only those verbs will subcategorize for and govern a subject that can construct S by some construction principle, for example, by GNC, on the basis of the finiteness of the verb, or else by agreement with the subject, on account of Agreement Projection.

Properties (4) and (5) do not support a head–sister relation, therefore, because the relevant constituents are not always sisters. Instead, these properties are most naturally explainable in terms of the capacity of the verb to define a construction domain within which the syntactic, semantic and morphological co-occurrence requirements of that verb can hold. This account, in effect, extends the notion of c-command so as to avoid the technical awkwardness posed by subjects. It also embodies the functionally motivated claim that syntactic dependencies of this sort will be limited so as to apply within, rather than outside, the highest node actually constructed by the category that defines the dependencies, that is, within nodes that will inevitably be constructed on every occasion of use and to which the dependents can be attached. If dependents could be attached outside construction domains, there would be no way to guarantee that the desired containing category would actually be present on all occasions of use, without additional stipulations and co-occurrence requirements being made. Limiting dependencies to construction domains means that the attachment site is necessarily, and automatically, present.

The status of subcategorization (and government) within the NP also fits with this account. Zwicky and Hudson both argue that Det is the subcategorizand, because of lexical differences between determiners such as *each* (which requires a singular count noun), *many* (which requires a plural) and *much* (which requires a mass noun). But one could argue equally plausibly that N is the subcategorizand here. Just as all transitive verbs are subcategorized for a direct-object NP, so all singular count nouns could subcategorize for certain classes of determiners only (*a* and *each* in English) and so on. It might be objected that it is simpler to state such subcategorizations on the determiner, since the number of relevant subcategorizing determiners is smaller than the number of subcategorizing nouns, and hence fewer statements would be needed in the lexicon overall. But the force of this simplicity argument is weakened when it is considered that every single transitive verb will be listed in the lexicon as subcategorizing for a direct-object NP. The most plausible resolution of the NP issue, therefore, is to say that subcategorization can work in both directions, from Det to N and from N to Det. It does so, moreover, because the construction domains of both Det and N are identical in our account: each constructs NP, hence each can in principle subcategorize for other ICs within its domain. Any priority for Det in this regard is simply a matter of economy, and does not follow from any principled considerations involving its putative head of phrase status.[5]

Properties (4) and (5) are therefore construction domain properties, not head of phrase properties.

11.5.3 *Semantic functors*

I would argue that semantic functors are not always heads. They are not correlated with MNCCs either, and there is no reason why they should be.

A resolution of this issue is complicated by the unclarity in most of the logical literature over which categories are semantic arguments or functors respectively. Zwicky (1985: 4) comments on this as follows: 'With a certain amount of formal ingenuity, a Montague-style semantics that treats Det as a functor on the argument N can be redone as a system treating N as a functor on the argument Det.' One serious attempt to come up with independent criteria for function and argument categories is Keenan (1979), and if we follow his reasoning it is clear that N is the argument within Adj–N and Relative Clause–N pairs, with Adj and Rel the functors, while V is the functor and NP the argument within VP. Hence, if V is both the functor and the head within the VP, then whether one regards N or Det as the head of its phrasal category, Adj and Rel will be functors and not heads, and there will be no general correlation between functors and heads (see Hawkins, 1984).

Nor is there any reason why there should be. Head is a proposed universal of syntax, and there is no necessary isomorphism between syntax and semantics in this particular respect, as far as I am aware. More importantly for our purposes, there is no *a priori* reason why there should be a correlation between semantic functors and MNCCs. MNCCs exist in order to give the listener on-line cues about the groupings of words into syntactic constituents. It is not required that these categories should simultaneously be of one semantic type versus another. Which daughters are arguments and which are functors will be determined quite independently by a semantic theory that maps the categories of the syntax onto their associated logical structures.

11.6 Conclusions

I began this chapter by asking how 'heads' are to be defined, and whether there are clear linguistic generalizations, such as word order, that support the definition. I have argued that the heads concept misses significant generalizations, and that word order does not support it. In its stead I have proposed a parsing theory comprising Mother Node Construction and related parsing principles, which provides a more adequate explanation for the proposed heads phenomena. This principle, operating in conjunction with Early Immediate Constituents, also provides a more adequate explanation for word order. These considerations suggest that the notion of head should be dispensed with. There may be other areas of grammar or other considerations that suggest otherwise. But the facts of this chapter do not support it.

The apparent plausibility of the head of phrase generalization derives from the fact that the set of head categories is properly included in the set of categories that construct phrasal nodes, PNCCs. The two theories differ over category constancy, however, and over the number of categories that can actually construct one and the same phrase (see sections 11.3.7 and 11.3.8). These differences were examined in relation to word order as a linguistic regularity and in relation to the defining properties of heads.

Word-order universals were shown to provide systematic counter-examples to consistent head ordering (section 11.2.1), and to support MNC and EIC in areas where the two theories differ. MNC and EIC can explain cross-categorial universals and numerous re-arrangement (and free word order) phenomena (section 11.2.2). These principles also motivate and explain the existence of a two-way typological parameter (between left-MNC and right-MNC languages), and correctly predict their equal frequency (section 11.4.1). The heads theory is compatible with additional types and has nothing to say about frequency. MNC and EIC also make ordering predictions for alternative MNCCs of one and the same phrasal mother, that is, precisely the categories that are without parallel in the heads theory (section 11.4.2). The predicted alternations are even richer when additional construction principles, such as GNC, are considered. Many of these alternations are either not predicted by the heads theory or are embarrassing for it.

The defining properties of heads were broken down (in section 11.5) into three categories: construction properties, construction domain properties, and semantic functors. Obligatoriness, distributional equivalence and morphosyntactic locus were argued to be construction properties, not heads properties, and to follow from the Axiom of Existence (13). These criteria fail as heads criteria precisely when there are alternative MNCCs or PNCCs. The notion of a construction domain was proposed for syntactic relations such as subcategorization and government. A constructing category can define such relations within the highest node that it constructs. The result is permitted syntactic relations between categories that are not naturally explainable as head–sister relations. Semantic functor status was argued to correlate neither with heads, nor with MNCCs.

Finally, in addition to these specific arguments, I would argue that the parsing theory proposed here is more explanatory than the heads theory. The head of phrase generalization is a stipulation about the form of grammars. It does not follow from anything else that I am aware of, and hence would be a plausible candidate for an ultimately innate principle of grammar. The grammatical consequences of MNC and GNC, such as unique MNCC–M pairings, retention of at least one MNCC under deletion, that is, obligatoriness, and so on, do follow from something else: namely, they follow from the primitives of a theory of language processing, many of which are again plausibly innate and hard-wired, and which guarantee that syntactic structure will be rapidly recognizable in real time, along the lines of Fodor's (1983) modularity thesis. Thus, where the grammatical properties of heads and MNCCs agree, they follow from independent principles of performance that are needed anyway. Where they do not agree, the MNCC properties are independently motivated, and they appear to have greater descriptive and explanatory adequacy.

The kinds of constituent structures I have argued for in this chapter are much flatter and more traditional than those proposed within theories built around heads (see sections 11.3.4, 11.3.7 and 11.4.2). The PS-rules of individual grammars are, none the less, heavily constrained, not by category constancy between head and mother, but by the Axioms of Existence and Uniqueness for phrasal nodes, requiring the constructability of a mother by at least one daughter (section 11.3.5). The syntactic domains for various dependencies are now defined in terms of construction domains, an extension of the c-command concept that provides a simple solution to problems involving subcategorization and government of subjects by lexical verbs within VP. I conclude that many fundamental properties of syntax, including word order, and numerous properties associated with the head of phrase generalization, actually follow from more general principles of performance. These principles are functionally motivated, but also ultimately innate and hard-wired within the human capacity to use language rapidly and efficiently in real time. Such principles have shaped the grammars of all languages far more fundamentally, I believe, than current theorizing typically recognizes, and in ways that I hope to have made a little more plausible through the examples in this chapter.

NOTES

1. This chapter is a revised version of a paper that was originally written for the Talking Heads Round Table in March 1991. The paper was presented for me at that meeting by Norman Fraser, and I am most grateful to him for having presented it on my behalf and for having relayed to me, in considerable detail, the many discussion points that arose in response. In some ways I am glad I was not there, because the paper seems to have elicited the kind of reaction one might expect if one were to show up at the Vatican and argue against the existence of God! Heads are a very central part of current linguistic thinking, and are clearly not to be tampered with lightly. The feedback was extremely useful, however, and I have tried to respond to many of the points that were made. I am also grateful to the following individuals for their written comments; Greville Corbett, Dick Hudson, Jim Miller and Matthew Dryer, and to two anonymous referees (both apparently not members of the linguistic Vatican!). None of these individuals necessarily agrees with the original draft and with the changes I have made, but I hope to have given them something else to think about in this revision.

2. The corresponding noun-phrase prediction for right-MNC languages is more complex, ultimately because of the left-to-right nature of syntactic parsing. In a left-MNC language, either Det or N will be the first element of NP encountered in the parse string, and hence will construct that NP immediately. But in a right-MNC language, which is parsed bottom–up, EIC will define a comparable preference for a right-peripheral MNCC, but any additional MNCC will then, of necessity, occur to its left and will be encountered first in the left-to-right parse, and so will construct the NP first. This leads us to predict that alternative MNCCs will be adjacent and rightmost within their phrasal categories, relative to non-MNCC daughters such as genitives and relative clauses. Empirically, genitives typically do precede both Det and N in OV and postpositional languages, though relative clauses can both precede and follow, for reasons discussed in section 11.2.2 involving temporary ambiguity avoidance and garden paths. More date and analysis are needed to establish whether MNCCs are right-peripheral and adjacent

relative to other *non-branching* categories that are not MNCCs, such as single-word adjectives that do not exhibit agreement with the noun.

3. The other part of the explanation for the leftward positioning of pronouns within the German VP involves their weight: they are all single-word ICs that are shorter than full NPs and PPs on aggregate. Within the VP, the positioning of pronouns is motivated by EIC alone, therefore. These pronouns also carry (non-Nominative) case and so provide recognition of the VP on its left periphery, and hence optimal ratios for the s domain, as discussed in the main text.

4. A grammatical subject and various adverbials may occur in the positions marked by '...' here. These items are, with the exception of Nominative-marked pronouns, incapable of actually constructing s, however, and hence this task typically falls to Aux and V_f, with additional s-dominated material being incorporated under s by Immediate Constituent Attachment (compare Hawkins, 1990, forthcoming).

5. Notice an important difference between the NP and the VP in this regard. Both v and non-Nominative case-marked NPs may construct VP (section 11.4.2), but only the verb can subcategorize for and govern its accompanying NPs. Not all constructing categories may subcategorize for and govern other constituents within their construction domains, therefore. The reason for this has already been given in section 11.3.7: no NP can subcategorize for and govern a verb, since one and the same NP type is distributed among too many predicate frames and does not render its predicate predictable. To this we can now add a second consideration: a (finite) verb can construct an s, by GNC, in addition to a VP, by MNC; hence the construction domain for a verb can contain all the entities (including subjects) that stand in a relationship of co-occurrence. But a non-Nominative case-marked noun, or determiner, or pronoun will construct NP, by MNC, and VP, by GNC, but not s since nothing now requires and guarantees the construction of this node. Hence, the highest node constructed by VP-dominated NPs will be VP, which excludes subjects, and does not contain all the entities that stand in a relationship of subcategorization and government with the verb. What this means is that a constructing category will subcategorize for and govern other constituents just in case (a) its capacity to define co-occurrence restrictions is independently motivated, and (b) its construction domain is large enough to subsume all the entities that stand in the relevant co-occurrence relationship. Both Det and N appear to satisfy these criteria within NP; only the verb does so within VP and s, however.

12 Do *we have heads in our minds?*

RICHARD HUDSON

12.1 Heads without mentalism

The main point of this chapter is that heads must be among the categories used in the mental representations that ordinary people construct when they hear and utter sentences.[1] In other words, the category 'head' and the associated concept 'dependent' are psychologically real; and they are real not only in grammars but also in sentence structure. However, we start with some non-psychological considerations about heads.

12.1.1 *Heads in grammars and in sentence structure: a survey of theories*

The distinction between grammars and sentence structure is an important one, because it is possible to accept the need for heads in the grammar without recognizing them in sentence structure. As Arnold Zwicky pointed out (1988), this possibility is exploited in Generalized Phrase Structure Grammar (GPSG), where the head daughter is represented in the relevant phrase-structure rule as simply 'H' (Gazdar *et al.*, 1985: 51), but this is just a conventional abbreviation which is replaced, in the corresponding phrase marker, by all the 'head features' of the mother node. But these 'head features' are just ordinary features which do not in themselves show explicitly that the head is the head; the head is different from the other daughters only in that its features are the same as those of the mother.

To take a very simple example, suppose the structure of a noun phrase could be defined by the following rule:

(1) $[+\text{N}, -\text{V}] \rightarrow \text{Det}, [+\text{N}, -\text{V}]$

By the convention just mentioned, this can be abbreviated to (2):

(2) $[+\text{N}, -\text{V}] \rightarrow \text{Det}, \text{H}$

This can be fleshed out into (1) by the Head Feature Convention. But of these two rules, it is (1), not (2), that has to be matched by the features of any structure; so the structure of a noun phrase, according to this grammar, is (3), not (4).

(3)   [+N, −V]   (4)   [+N, −V]

     Det   [+N, −V]   Det   H

The GPSG treatment of heads is typical of the theories that are based closely on X-bar theory, including Government–Binding (GB) theory; however important the notion 'head' is in these theories, it is not a primitive category in sentence structure. Just like the other grammatical functions, it is defined configurationally; the head of a construction is the daughter constituent that has the same features (excluding bar-level) as the mother.

The same can also be said of Categorial Grammar (CG), though this is often considered to be a branch of dependency theory (and as such might be expected to show head–dependent relations explicitly). Here the distinction between functors and arguments is explicit in the names of grammatical categories; for example, a determiner might be defined as a functor whose argument is a noun and whose function (that is, 'output') is a noun phrase: NP/N. It is natural to identify functors with heads and arguments with dependents (except in the case of adjuncts, where the relation is reversed; see Vennemann, 1977; Hudson, 1987). Therefore the category name of a word does show whether or not it is the head of some word; for example, if a word is 'NP/N' (that is, a determiner) then it must be the head of a noun.

But although a CG tells us directly whether or not some word is a head, and also what kind of other word it is the head of, a CG sentence structure does not show which particular words are heads of which. For example, the analysis of *the book* would look like this:

(5)   the book
       NP/N   N
          NP

Once again, it is possible to work out that *the* is the head of *book*, on the basis of their respective category names, but this information is not available directly.

Another example of a theory in which heads are not marked as such in sentence structure, although they are picked out in the grammar rules, is Lexical-Functional Grammar (LFG). This is all the more surprising in LFG because other grammatical functions are treated as primitives; for example, 'subject' (abbreviated to 'SUBJ') is one of the labels found in the functional structure (f-structure) generated for a clause. As in GPSG, the head of a construction is distinguished from other constituents by the notation for phrase-structure rules, which generate constituent structures (c-structures). Unlike all other major constituents, it is paired with the equation in (6) (Bresnan, 1982a: 297):

(6) $\downarrow = \uparrow$

This means that the f-structure element which corresponds to the mother constituent (indicated by the 'up' arrow) is the same as the f-structure representation of this daughter constituent (indicated by the 'down' arrow). The point to note, however, is that the equation is a condition that is satisfied by a compatible c-structure and f-structure, but it does not appear in either of them.

For example, the rule in (7), quoted from Kaplan and Bresnan (1982: 184), shows that the VP and the S are not distinguished in the f-structure:

(7)   S $\rightarrow$ NP   VP

         $(\uparrow$ SUBJ$) = \downarrow$ $\uparrow = \downarrow$

This generates a conventional c-structure, in which S dominates NP and VP, and in which there is no indication that VP is the head daughter. The equation merely controls the relation between this c-structure and the f-structure, guaranteeing in effect that the VP is ignored in the f-structure. Moreover, there is no LFG principle that requires every category to have a head marked in this way; for example, the rules for NP and VP recognize no head at all.

In the theories surveyed so far, then, heads are not primitives in sentence structures. This is not true of all contemporary syntactic theories. Most obviously, it is untrue of all versions of dependency theory (as found in the work of linguists like Anderson, Heringer, Mel'čuk, Miller, Sgall and Starosta, and also in my own work). In most of this work the structure of a sentence is shown as a stemma, the tree-like diagramming system invented by Tesnière (1959), in which the head–dependent relation is made explicit by a vertical or sloping line on which the head is higher than the dependent. In my own work I use arrows for the same purpose, with the arrow pointing from the head to the dependent. The diagrams in (8) and (9) are therefore equivalent.

(8)  (9)

in London   in London

I know of one theory that treats 'head' as a primitive category but which in other respects is not a version of dependency theory: Head-driven Phrase Structure Grammar (HPSG). This theory is a blend of features from most of the others: GPSG, LFG, CG and GB (Pollard and Sag, 1987: 1), but as its name implies, it gives unusual prominence to the notion 'head' (see Borsley, this volume). One example of this is that it provides a uniquely labelled slot in the structure of any (non-coordinated) construction for the head daughter (Pollard and Sag, 1987: 56). This slot is labelled 'HEAD-DTR'. The example given by Pollard and Sag is *Bagels, John likes*, in which the head of the whole sentence is *John likes*, whose head in turn is *likes*. Their partial structure for this sentence, which I have simplified further, is given in (10).

(10)

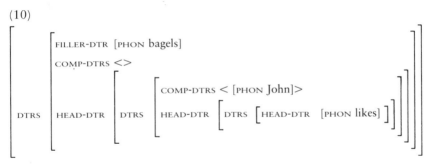

In conclusion, then, most current theories of syntax do **not** recognize 'head' as a basic analytical category in sentence structure, whatever other status they may accord it – as a basic category in grammar rules, or as a configurationally defined functional category. The only exceptions are HPSG and the various versions of dependency grammar.

12.1.2 *Some non-psychological arguments for heads*

I should like to give a brief survey of some of the reasons why grammarians invoke the notion 'head', as background to the later discussion of why this notion is important in understanding how we process language as speakers and hearers.

In the context of a grammar based on constituent structure, the main argument for recognizing heads is that this allows us to capture a significant generalization about feature structures: the head daughter carries virtually the same features as the mother. However, we must note that this argument for heads rests firmly on the assumption that syntactic structure is based on constituency. In a dependency analysis the mother phrase is redundant and therefore not recognized explicitly; consequently, it has no features (or anything else) and the question of whether its features are the same as those of the head word does not arise.

To find an argument for heads which is neutral according to whether we assume constituent structure or dependency structure, we turn to generalizations about word order – generalizations which have apparently been noticed by grammarians since at least as long ago as the Arabic grammarians of the eighth to tenth centuries in Basra and Kufa.[2] As is well known, there are some languages which tend to locate heads before their dependents, and others which tend to favour the reverse order. Sometimes the tendency is close to absolute, but in some languages there is a more or less considerable range of exceptions. I do not know whether every language has a basic head-ordering pattern, but it seems fairly clear that even English is basically a head-first language, with exceptions (notably: subjects, attributive adjectives and nouns, adverbs whose heads are adjectives or adverbs, and some adverbs (for example, NEVER[3]) whose heads are verbs). These head-ordering patterns have been used to very good effect in recent typological work, especially by Hawkins (1983, 1990).[4]

It is important to note that these generalizations collapse the distinction between complements and adjuncts (as also that between subjects and complements, if such is made). This is why the notion 'head' (or its converse, 'dependent') cannot be replaced in the generalizations by 'functor', because an adjunct is the functor, not the argument, of its head. Nor can the generalizations be expressed in terms of the current GB categories 'specifier', 'complement' and 'adjunct', because there is no higher-level relation which embraces all these categories.[5] The best that can be done is to recognize a separate word-order parameter for each of these three relations (Radford, 1988: 273–4). In each case, the parameter is called the 'X-first/X-last parameter'; but, rather misleadingly, when the parameter involves the order of complements and their heads, X = 'head', whereas for the other two, X = 'specifier' or 'adjunct'; indeed, the complement-related parameter is often called just the 'head-parameter'. This makes it look as though GB theory recognizes the role of heads in word order, but of course this is not so.

Indeed, the GB approach is an interesting addition to the typological literature because it suggests that the ordering for specifiers, complements and adjuncts involves three quite separate parameters, that the position of adjuncts relative to their heads has nothing to do with that of complements, and neither is related to the positioning of specifiers. In some cases this separation may be justified; for example, in English specifiers[6] are claimed to precede their heads whereas complements follow their heads (though the uncertainty over what counts as a specifier casts considerable doubt on this claim). But we should also expect to find languages in which all adjuncts consistently follow their heads and all complements consistently precede theirs. I have never heard of any such language, but it is an interesting prediction.

These word-order facts are not, of course, the only justification for recognizing heads. The whole point of the categories 'head' and 'dependent' (as indeed of any other analytical category) is that they allow us to link a range of different facts. The relation between a dependent and its head is relevant not only to their respective positions in linear order, but also to a host of other matters – government, subcategorization, hyponymy, agreement,[7] etc. In relation to Zwicky's analysis of head-like properties (this volume), I agree in including the following properties among the defining characteristics of (true) heads – that is, his feature 'H': morphosyntactic locus, word rank and category determinant. My only disagreement is in wanting to add 'government trigger' to this list (for lack of evidence that it is one of his 'F' characteristics).

The reason why 'head' is such a vital category in syntax is that it brings together all these different properties. In other words, when we refer to 'head' in a government rule we are referring to precisely the same category as when we refer to it in a word-order rule. Its justification is therefore precisely like that of a basic word class such as 'noun', which has the same extension in all the rules where it is mentioned. Any challenge to the need for heads in syntactic analysis must therefore show that these characteristics do not bundle together. It is not enough to show that just one type of generalization which has been claimed to relate to heads can be expressed at least as well without mentioning heads; so even if Hawkins' arguments against head-based word-order rules (this volume) were compelling, they would leave the notion intact for other uses.

12.1.3 Head of a phrase or head of a word?

Let us assume, then, that grammatical rules must be able to distinguish the head of a phrase from the other, dependent, parts of the phrase. This assumption is now widely, though not universally, accepted, and counts as a very clear example of convergence among theories during the last two decades. I take it that the reason for this convergence is simply that this is the way the facts of language are: at least some of them are naturally organized in terms of what we call heads.

Behind this agreement, however, there is profound disagreement about the status of heads. In particular, it makes a great difference whether we assume constituent structure or dependency structure as the basis for syntactic analysis. This is the question I should like to address briefly here. I shall argue that the notion 'head' makes much more sense in the context of a dependency grammar.

Let us start with the more familiar approach, constituent structure. According to this theory the basic relation in syntax is the part–whole relation between a mother phrase and its daughter constituents. The notion 'head' is somewhat marginal in a number of senses. First, it is marginal in that it was ignored completely during the first two decades of transformational grammar (which is, of course, based on a phrase-structure grammar). Second, 'head' may or may not be treated as a basic category (it is so treated in HPSG, but not in GB or LFG; its status in GPSG is somewhat ambiguous). A third kind of marginality lies in the fact that in some theories (for example, LFG) not every phrase has a head. The discussion often refers to Bloomfield's distinction between endocentric and exocentric constructions (1933), where exocentric constructions have no head (meaning a daughter with the same distribution as the whole). Oddly enough, one of Bloomfield's examples of an exocentric construction is the prepositional phrase, but this is now one of the classic 'best examples' of a head–complement structure![8]

As can be seen, constituent structure does not impose any particular notions about heads. In fact, it would be fair to describe 'head' as an optional extra. If there are any constraints on heads, they must be imposed by stipulation within the theory.

We can ask two further questions about heads. First, can a phrase have more than one head? Bloomfield said that endocentric constructions could have more than one head, the obvious example being co-ordination: the phrase *the boy and the girl* has two heads, namely each of the conjoined noun phrases. This assumption is explicitly adopted in GPSG (Sag *et al.*, 1985). But with this model to build on, why should we not recognize more than one head in some other structures, such as the combination of a complementizer with a clause (Warner, 1989)? And secondly, how similar are the categories of the mother and its head daughter? According to x-bar theory, the mother and the head daughter must have the same feature structure but different bar levels (except for adjunct structures). In HPSG they share only some of their features – the HEAD features, but not the SUBCAT features – but for GPSG even the bar levels are normally the same (Gazdar *et al.*, 1985: 52).

Once again we find considerable disagreement over basic principles concerning heads. This is because virtually any assumptions about heads are compatible with the basic assumptions of constituent structure. It is instructive to ask the same five questions about dependency-based theories, where we shall see that assuming word–word dependencies forces a very wide range of answers.

1 *Is it possible to do syntax without ever mentioning heads?* No, 'head' is the name for one end of the dependency relations which are taken as fundamental. We may not call this the 'head' – we may prefer a term like 'controller' (Matthews, 1981: 79) or 'regent' (Zwicky, 1985) but the category is still the same.

2 *How should one distinguish heads from dependents?* Whatever notation one uses for showing dependencies must, by definition, show which end of the dependency is the head. I mentioned two notations in (8) and (9) above, but many more are imaginable. In all of them, the notion 'head' is a basic category which is explicit not only in sentence structures but also in whatever rules generate these.

3 *Does every phrase have a head?* Yes – there are no exocentric constructions. This is because the only way in which one can capture the notion 'phrase' in a dependency structure is via the dependencies: a phrase is a word plus the phrases of all the words dependent on it. By definition, then, a string of words counts as a phrase only if there is a word which could be called its 'head' if we were using constituent structure. For example, take *He lives in London*, with the dependency analysis shown in (11).

(11)

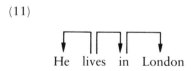

He lives in London

We can identify two phrases: one consisting of *in* plus its dependent, *London*, and the other consisting of the whole sentence, that is, *lives* plus its dependents *he* and *in*, plus the rest of the latter's phrase. These phrases are defined by the dependency structure, but they are derivative (just as dependency structures are in X-bar constituent structures), and play no part in the grammar.

4 *Can a phrase have more than one head?* No, this is ruled out in principle by our definition of 'phrase'. According to my own version of dependency theory, Word Grammar, a *word* may have more than one head; for example, when two verbs share a subject noun through raising or control this noun has both of the verbs as its head, so in *He kept talking* the noun *he* is the subject of both the verbs, and therefore has two heads (Hudson, 1990: 113–20):

(12)

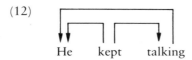

He   kept   talking

But this is different from a phrase having two heads; according to this analysis *he* belongs to two different phrases, one headed by *kept* and the other headed by *talking*. Each of these phrases has just a single head.

5 *How similar are the categories of the mother and its head daughter?* This question does not arise, because there are no mothers in dependency structure. The nearest one can get to a mother node is the derivative notion of 'phrase' as just defined, but since these are never referred to in rules or principles of grammar there is no way in which they could possibly have a classification distinct from that of their head word.

We could put this answer slightly differently in order to bring dependency theory into line with constituency theory. In the latter, every dependent (that is, every complement, subject or adjunct) is a complete ('maximal') phrase, whose internal structure is centred on its head; that is, the dependent is a phrase, and this is distinct from the word which is that phrase's head daughter. In dependency theory, one word – the head of the phrase – fulfils both of these functions: like the mother node, it carries the external relations, but it also carries the phrase-internal relations, like the head daughter. This being so we might answer our question by saying that the similarity between the mother node and its head daughter is total, to the point where the two nodes cannot be distinguished from one another.

The general conclusion, then, is clear: 'head' is intimately related to the rest of dependency theory, but only loosely connected with constituency theory, and certainly not predictable from it. This is why any study of heads has to take a position on the choice between these two theories. It is true that we can study the various properties which converge on heads without making this choice; this is why there is broad consensus that heads are important in grammar. But if we want to understand why these properties do converge in this way, and what limits we can expect to variation among languages, then we must embed the discussion in one or the other of these theories. My claim is that this investigation will be much more fruitful if we choose dependency theory.

One practical consequence of this theoretical split is that there is a serious problem of terminology. According to constituency theory, a word is the head of its mother phrase, but for dependency theory it is the head of the words that depend on it. For example, consider the sentence *He lives in London*. If we ask 'What is *in* the head of?', we get two quite different answers according to whether we are assuming constituency or dependency theory: it is the head of *in London* in the first case, and of *London* in the second. Conversely, if we ask 'What is the head of *in London*?', the constituency answer is *in*, while the dependency answer is (speaking rather loosely) *lives*. I am not aware of any cases where this potential confusion has actually caused problems, so for the time being I merely draw attention to it.

12.2 Heads in the mind of the hearer

I now leave the familiar terrain in which we can argue for heads on the grounds of grammatical generalizations which they allow us to express, in order to explore the psychological reality of heads as constructs in the mind of the hearer. Do we recognize heads as such in the mental representations that we construct for sentences that we hear? I shall argue that we do, and in particular I shall argue that we have heads in my sense, that is, direct head–dependent relations between words. This is not the same as arguing that we recognize the heads of phrases (though no doubt we do this too).

12.2.1 *Evidence against empty categories as mediators*

How do we represent to ourselves the relation between a word and its head – for example, the relation between *Mary* and its head *met* in

Ann met Mary? I shall contrast two answers, each stemming from a different theory of syntax.

  A. The relation is represented directly, as a dependency relation between these two words. This can be represented as follows:

(13)

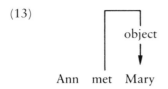

Ann   met   Mary

  B. The relation is not represented directly, but is implied by other relations: the sister–sister relation, the word order and the relation between the features on the first word and those on the mother node. To show this we use a phrase marker:

(14)

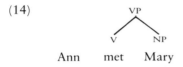

Ann   met   Mary

   Theory A includes dependency theory or Relational Grammar, and may possibly include monostratal constituency theories that recognize grammatical relations as basic (notably Functional Grammar and Systemic Grammar); I think it includes LFG in the new version described by Kaplan and Zaenen (1989). Theory B is any version of constituency theory which derives grammatical relations from surface constituency relations; it is most obviously manifested in GB, and to simplify the discussion I shall identify theory A with a version of dependency grammar (such as my own Word Grammar), and theory B with GB.
   The crucial difference between the two theories is in the way in which the verb–object relation is represented in these structures: directly, as in A, or indirectly via word-order and dominance relations as in B. These differences are matters of competence, not performance, because they concern the mental structures that we construct, rather than the ways in which we construct them. Crucially, theory B says that an element cannot be represented as an object without being represented in the sentence structure next to (and after) its head verb; but theory A allows the normal word-order facts to be separated, under exceptional circumstances, from the relation. These are questions about competence: how do we represent the relations mentally?

The difference between the theories becomes clear in the treatment of extraction, because they make very different predictions about the structures by which we represent such sentences to ourselves. Take an example like (15).

(15)　　Mary Ann met.

According to dependency theory, the structure that has to be built by the hearer is as in (16). According to Word Grammar there is, in fact, a second dependency link between *Mary* and *met*, which corresponds to the 'Comp' link in other theories. This is not relevant here, so I omit it.

(16)

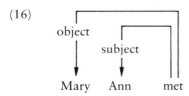

We now contrast this with theory B. According to this theory the object of a verb is, by definition, the NP just after it in the same V'. Therefore the only way to show that an extracted NP is the object of a following verb is to link it to an imaginary NP after the verb – that is, to recognize an empty NP, to which the extracted NP is linked by co-indexing. I shall show co-indexing both by indices and by an extended 'equals' sign, for reasons which will become apparent below.

(17)

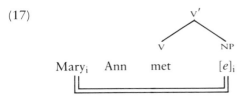

This difference has empirical consequences (Pickering and Barry, 1991). The structures required by B lead to self-embedding for sentences which according to A have no self-embedding; so according to B these sentences should be very difficult to process, but not according to A. These predictions are very easy to test empirically.

We start with sentences like those in (18).

(18)　　a. Who did the dog chase which the farmer bought from the man who used to live next door?
　　　　b. Who did the dog which the farmer bought from the man who used to live next door chase?

Why are sentences like (18a) so much easier to process than those like (18b)? Clearly, the answer must have something to do with the different loads they place on working memory (Frazier and Rayner, 1988), and specifically it must concern the load as it exists after *the dog* has been processed. In some sense, *the dog* places less burden (or perhaps no burden at all) on working memory once it is attached to *chase* (as subject), but until then it counts as a burden; so this load combines with that of the relative clause in (18b) but not in (18a).

Both dependency and constituency analyses allow an account of the load on working memory. The former allows us to count the number of active dependencies, where a dependency is active if either the head or the dependent is still awaited. The latter provides active constituents – that is, constituents which are known to need some further element. The crucial difference between the theories involves the point at which a dependency or constituent ceases to be active, and therefore stops contributing to the burden on working memory.

An active dependency is satisfied as soon as the word concerned is encountered. For example, take the simple sentence (19a), with the partial dependency analysis shown in (19b).

(19)   a. What did the boy give the girl?

    b.
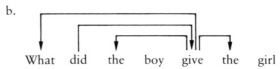

        What   did   the   boy   give   the   girl

According to this analysis there are three active dependencies after *boy* has been processed, but all of them are immediately satisfied by *give*.

In contrast, an active constituent must presumably remain active until its last element is found, and until its elements have been assigned a grammatical function. In particular, if it contains a displaced element (like the extractee *what*), then it remains active until this has a grammatical function. In GB, and more generally in theories which treat grammatical functions as derived from configurations, this means that the constituent remains active until the extractee's empty category is encountered (as shown by the extended 'equals' sign in (20)).

(20)   What did the boy give the girl [e]?
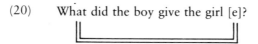

This means that in (19a), the load of *what* persists until the very end of the sentence, rather than ending when its head, *give*, is heard.

As is well known, we cannot cope, as hearers, with many active extractees at the same time. The sentences in (21) illustrate the rapid increase in processing difficulty.

(21)   a. Who did the dog chase?
           b. Who did the dog which the farmer owned chase?
           c. Who did the dog which the farmer who the cat licked owned chase?

It is generally agreed that sentences like (21c) are beyond us, but even (21b) is demanding (much more demanding than the corresponding extraposed sentence, as we saw above in discussing (18)). The difficulty is easy to explain in dependency terms. In (21b) *who* depends on *chase*, while *which* depends on *owned*; so after *which* there are two active extractee dependencies. And in (21c), there are three of them after the second *who*. It seems that this is more than we can accommodate in our working memories (though as we saw in (19), it is quite easy to handle three active dependencies if these are not all extractees). Similar explanations are, of course, possible in constituency terms as well; for example, in (21c) we can blame the breakdown on the existence of three active sentences between *who* and *licked*.

Having established that memory-overload can be quantified in these ways, we now return to Pickering and Barry's argument, which involves examples like the following:

(22)   John found the box in which I put the tray.

The dependency analysis links *in which* directly to *put*, but the GB analysis has to assume an empty category. For the moment I shall simply assume that this is located in the normal position for a prepositional phrase, after the object.

(23)

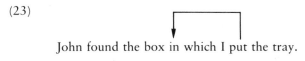

     John found the box in which I put the tray.

(24)   John found the box in which I put the tray [e].

The exact position of the empty element is critical to the following argument. Why can we not assume that, in at least some cases, the object could have undergone 'Heavy NP Shift' as in (25)?

(25)   I put in it the tray for the coffee-cups.

On this assumption the empty element in (24) could precede the object. One reason for believing this not to be true is that in such cases extraction out of the preposition phrase is not permitted:

(26)   a. John found the box which I put the tray for the coffee-cups in [*e*].
        b. *John found the box which I put in [*e*] the tray for the coffee-cups.

It is unlikely that the whole prepositional phrase would have been extracted from a position out of which partial extraction is banned.

Another piece of evidence is that verbs such as WANT do not allow Heavy NP Shift.

(27)   a. I want the tray for the coffee-cups to be ready.
        b. *I want to be ready the tray for the coffee-cups.

(28)   a. I want the tray for the coffee-cups in this box.
        b. *I want in this box the tray for the coffee-cups.

If we find in crucial examples that WANT is possible, then we can be fairly sure that the empty element follows the object.

It seems reasonable, then, to assume the structures in (23) and (24) for *John found the box in which I put the tray*. The critical difference between them is that the dependency needs of *in which* (that is, its need for a head) are satisfied as soon as *put* has been processed, whereas the constituent structure is incomplete until after *the tray*.

Our thought-experiment now proceeds by making the object, *the tray*, longer and more complex.

(29)   John found the box in which I put the tray on which Mary placed the dish.

The two theories now make very different predictions indeed. According to dependency theory the structure is (30).

(30)

... in which I put the tray on which Mary placed the dish.

But according to GB it is (31), in which the dependencies are nested.

(31)   ...in which I put the tray on which Mary placed the dish [*e*] [*e*].

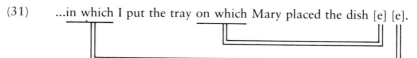

Just to be sure that we have the empty elements in the right place, we can replace the verbs by WANT.

(32)   John found the box in which I wanted the tray on which Mary
          wanted the dish.

This change appears to make no difference to the acceptability of the
examples; so since we can be sure that the empty elements must
follow the object of WANT, this confirms the analysis in (31).

The point of this example, of course, is that if the structure is as
shown in (31), the sentence would be at least as hard to process as
(21b), *Who did the dog which the farmer owned chase?*, because in
both cases there are two simultaneously unplaced extractees; and
indeed it should be harder than (21b) because there is one more
sentence which remains active until the end, as in the unprocessable
(21c). The diagram below shows how many constituents are still
active after the second *which*.

(33)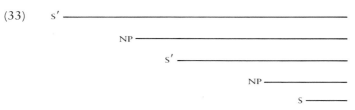

          John found the box in which I put the tray on which

But speakers seem to agree that this is not so. This sentence is, in fact,
easy to process, as predicted by the dependency structure: after the
second *which*, there is precisely one active dependency, as shown in
(34).[9]

(34)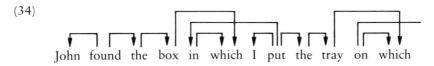

          John found the box in which I put the tray on which

Indeed, the number of relative clauses inside the object can increase
still more without leading to any serious problems. The following
example is taken from Pickering and Barry (1991: 244).

(35)   Jane opened the cupboard in which Bill left the box from which Sue
          took the tray upon which John placed the saucer on which Mary put
          the cup into which I poured the tea.

The GB analysis of this sentence contains no fewer than five nested
dependencies (to say nothing of a vast number of incomplete constituents), but the dependency analysis contains none.

I should like to stress that the point at issue is what structures hearers build in their heads rather than the processes by which they build them; in other words, it is primarily a matter of competence. Performance is relevant only as a clue to the mental structures. Chomsky used the complexity of self-embedding examples long ago as evidence in support of his theory of structures (Miller and Chomsky, 1963); and I am now following Pickering and Barry in reversing the argument: using the simplicity of examples like (29) and (35) as evidence for a very different theory of structures.

It is possible to object to this argument along the following lines (as pointed out to me by Arnold Zwicky). Processing strategies may be much less closely tied to the structures generated than I have assumed. In particular, it is possible to make use of information from the lexicon as soon as it is available, so given the words *in which I put*, the processor can make use of the fact that PUT requires a place expression as complement in order to link *in which* directly to it, without waiting (as I have claimed) for the empty category which sanctions this link in the full structure.

This objection can be answered in two ways. First, the question we are discussing is how the structure of a sentence is represented mentally, so if it is indeed possible to link two words mentally without using the usual constituent structure, we must conclude that the latter is just a clue to a deeper level of structural representation, precisely as claimed by dependency theory. But secondly, I doubt if lexical information is in fact used in this way, because if it is we should have no problem with sentences like (36).

(36)   Which prize shall we present the student who gets the most right solutions to the syntax questions in this year's exams with.

As soon as we encounter *present* we know we can expect *with*, so the fact that this is delayed for so long should be no problem; and yet (so far as I can tell) it does in fact make the sentence hard to process.

Without going into the details, I think it is possible to base a similar argument on sentences like (37).

(37)   Which prize shall we give every student capable of answering all the questions on syntax which we've set over the last ten years in our end-of-year exams.

The dependency analysis links *which prize* directly to *give*, and therefore does not interfere with the processing of the direct object; accordingly, it should be possible for the latter to grow without limit – as indeed seems to be the case.

According to the GB analysis, however, it must be linked to an empty element following the whole of the direct object, and should therefore be very hard to process.[10] Furthermore, the GB analysis of (37) is very similar to the one needed for a sentence with a dangling preposition, such as (38), which is indeed hard to process.

(38)   Which student shall we give the prize that's just been set up by that bequest that we had so much difficulty in sorting out legally to?

In this sentence the extractee *which student* depends on the dangling *to*, and the sentence is extremely difficult to process (as predicted by the dependency analysis); but according to GB it should be about the same as (37), where the empty element is in the same position. So once again the dependency analysis leads to better predictions than does the GB analysis.

12.2.2 *Evidence against higher nodes as mediators*

According to dependency theory, dependency relations between words are just that: relations between one word and another. Constituency-based theory accepts the reality of most of these relations (which go by names like 'subject', 'complement' and 'adjunct') but claims that they are mediated by the relation between the words concerned and their 'mothers', the phrases of which they are parts. What this means for hearers is that they must build structures in which certain mother–daughter relations are present. Precisely which mother–daughter relations are needed in order to express a particular dependency varies from theory to theory, but I shall take GB once again as my example, because it presents the clearest contrast with dependency theory.

I shall consider two overlapping areas of grammar: adjuncts and pre-head dependents. In both cases I shall suggest that the extra phrasal nodes which GB assumes are psychologically implausible.

We start with adjuncts. What is the structure of (39)?

(39)   I saw her yesterday at UCL.

The dependency analysis is, of course, totally flat, as each of the dependent elements is linked directly to the common head, *saw*:

(40)

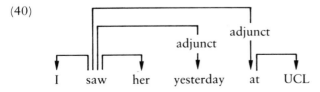

I	saw	her	yesterday	at	UCL

All the dependencies can be classified more precisely as 'subject' and so on, but since we are only concerned with adjuncts I have only labelled these. We can contrast this analysis with a GB-style one (more accurately, one in the spirit of the Extended Standard Theory, but the differences are not relevant to my main point):

(41)

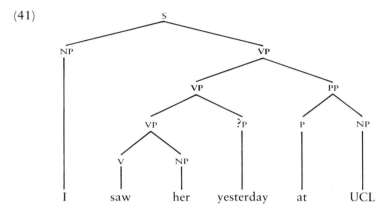

The main point of difference on which I want to focus is the treatment of adjuncts, which in this analysis each require an additional mother node – the two highlighted VP nodes.

Adjuncts do not pose any special processing problems in the dependency analysis, but they do in the GB analysis because of these extra mother nodes. The problem is that processing is non-monotonic: what happens later forces the hearer to undo part of the analysis arrived at so far. Take the example above. At the point where the hearer has heard just the first three words, *I saw her*, there is no reason to assume more than one VP node, so the structure is like this:

(42)

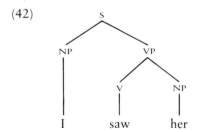

But each time an extra VP node is added, the relations between V and S are changed: at first they are separated by just one VP, then by two and finally by three. Similarly, at first the sister of *I* is also the mother of *saw*, but eventually it is the great-grandmother of *saw*. These revisions in the shape of the tree ought to be problematic for a hearer, in much the same way as standard 'garden-path' sentences; but of course they are not.

It is important to notice that the uncertainty introduced by adjuncts is not like more familiar kinds of ambiguity which could in principle be accommodated by a processor which considered all possible readings simultaneously. Each extra adjunct requires a different structural relation between the verb and the sentence, so how many such structures should we consider when we encounter a verb? However high we set the number, it is always possible to add one more adjunct, which should make a critical difference to the functioning of the system (but does not); and if we consider a reasonable number of alternatives (say, five), this must add enormously (and disproportionately) to the complexity of processing.

I take it that an advocate of GB would react by saying that the extra nodes related to adjuncts do not count, in some sense; in other words, they can be freely added without cost or backtracking. This is intuitively correct – but theoretically odd, because if they do not count, why have them?

We know one reason why they are needed in GB: in order to allow us to distinguish adjuncts from complements without treating these relations as basic. But that is a poor justification at best, because it is an admission of defeat: the only way to distinguish these grammatical relations is by means of a structural trick which is in other respects problematic.

One other possible justification for the higher nodes added to adjuncts is a semantic one: that each such node corresponds to a different element in the semantics. In (41), for example, we have the following phrases:

(43) a. saw her
      b. saw her yesterday
      c. saw her yesterday at UCL
      d. I saw her yesterday at UCL

Each of these could serve as the antecedent for some anaphoric word or process:

(44) a. I *saw her* yesterday at UCL, and I did the day before in the library as well.
      b. I *saw her yesterday* at UCL, and I did in the library as well.
      c. I *saw her yesterday at UCL*, and Bill did as well.
      d. *I saw her yesterday at UCL*, but I regretted it.

If these were the only ways in which these words could be grouped semantically, the argument would be persuasive. But what about an example like (45)?

(45)   I saw her yesterday at UCL, and the same happened the day before.

Here *the same* needs an antecedent to provide the meaning 'I saw her at UCL', but this is not one of the phrases listed in (43). Notice that it does include *I* but does not include *yesterday*. Similarly we can say (46).

(46)   I saw her yesterday at UCL, and Fred did the day before.

Here I assume that the second clause means 'Fred saw her the day before at UCL'. This meaning is easier to see if you put contrastive stress on *yesterday*, which shows that the semantic groupings of the words in a sentence can conflict with the order of words.

My conclusion, then, is that the extra nodes added with adjuncts cannot be justified independently by their contribution to the semantics. We know that we need a rather flexible and rich system for grouping words together in the semantics, so once we have such a system it will make these extra nodes redundant. I have suggested the beginning of such a system in Hudson (1990: 146–51).

The second area of grammar that is relevant to this discussion is pre-head dependents, or 'pre-dependents', and the question is why complex subjects are so much harder to process than equally complex initial adjuncts. Once again the conclusion will be that all that matters is the relation between each of these pre-dependents and the next verb; all the paraphernalia of dominating mother nodes that we find in theories like GB just gets in the way.

The data to be explained are taken from work by Frazier and Rayner (1988). They found that people took longer to read sentences containing complex subjects like (47a) than similar sentences with the complexity shifted to the end of the sentence (47b).

(47)   a. That both of the Siamese twins survived the operation is remarkable.
        b. It is remarkable that both of the Siamese twins survived the operation.

But when they compared pairs of sentences in which a complex adjunct clause varied between initial and final position, such as (48), they found no difference in reading speed.

(48)   a. Because the girls tickled the cat, Mary was laughing. [*sic*]
        b. Mary was laughing because the girls tickled the cat.

Why should subjects and adjuncts be so different?

As Frazier and Rayner point out, their data show that it is not left-branching (that is, head-final order) *per se* that makes for complexity, contrary to what has been widely believed since Yngve's (1960) discussion. This is a comforting conclusion given that at least as many languages in the world seem to be head-final as head-initial. Consequently, it is not the ease of processing of initial adjuncts that needs an explanation, but rather the difficulty of subjects.

Frazier and Rayner's explanation refers to the number of new higher nodes above the subject (the 'Local Non-Terminal Count'), in which a clausal node counts for 1.5 but other nodes count for just 1. This gives a measure of the complexity of processing at any given point in a sentence, and does indeed explain why ordinary extraposition reduces complexity, or rather spreads it more evenly instead of starting a sentence with a peak of complexity. But it does not explain why complex subjects are so much harder to process than equally complex initial adjuncts,[11] because the same number of new higher nodes seems to be needed in both cases. This is especially true if one accepts the widely held belief that clausal subjects are topics, and therefore not, in fact, in subject position. However, I shall not try to demonstrate the point because there are too many uncertainties about the structures concerned.

Let me offer a different, and much simpler, explanation for the difference between clausal subjects and adjuncts. My explanation makes no reference at all to higher nodes, because I assume there are none. Instead, I shall refer to the degree of uncertainty about the relation between the initial clause and the root of the whole sentence. Suppose I hear a sentence starting with the word *because*, as in (48a). I can immediately build the following structure, in which the dotted lines connect words to their meanings.

(49)

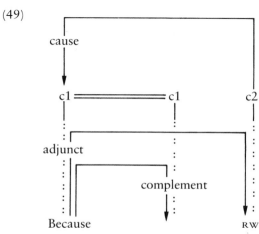

I can reconstruct not only the word's syntactic relation (adjunct) to the anticipated sentence root (RW, for 'root word'), but also its semantic relation to RW ('cause'). And although I do not know whether the complement of *because* will be OF (*because of ...*) or a tensed verb (for example, *because he came*), I do know that this word's referent is the cause of RW's sense. All this information provides a clear framework within which the rest of the processing can continue, and (presumably) it therefore makes few demands on my working memory.

Now suppose, in contrast, that I hear a sentence beginning with *That*, as in (47a) (*That both of the Siamese twins ...*). We can assume that it is pronounced in such a way as to distinguish it from the demonstrative THAT, so I know that it is the complementizer. But what else can I be sure of? I can presumably rule out the possibility of it being an adjunct, but it could still be either the subject or the object of the root word, RW, as in (50).

(50)   a. That both of the Siamese twins survived the operation is surprising.
       b. That both of the Siamese twins survived the operation I didn't know.

And as long as I do not know what RW is, I cannot even guess the semantic role of the clause to be introduced.

My state of knowledge after processing just *That*, then, is as in (51).

(51)

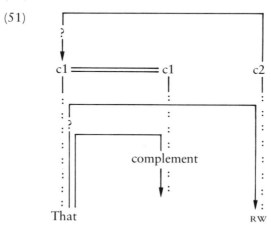

I have to cope with much more uncertainty here, and it seems reasonable to assume that the questions about syntactic and semantic relations take up a significant amount of working memory. I suggest that this is why complex subjects are hard to process, and that it has nothing to do with the number of mother nodes above them.

The main point to notice is that the explanation rested entirely on the assumption that the hearer's task is to reconstruct the syntactic and semantic relations between each word and its head word. The building of higher nodes seems quite irrelevant to this task, and played no part in the explanation.

12.3 Conclusion

I have argued that the relations between words and their heads are central to the tasks of both the grammarian and the hearer or reader. Phrase markers, even phrase markers in which the heads of phrases are marked, are just a clumsily indirect way of showing these relations. Heads are not just an add-on extra, which can be clipped onto a grammatical theory based on other principles. A grammar without heads is as misguided as a portrait-painting showing everything from the shoulders down.

NOTES

1. I should like to acknowledge helpful comments from Bob Borsley, Grev Corbett, Jim Miller and Nigel Vincent, and from all the other participants at the Talking Heads Round Table.
2. According to Owens (1988) the Arabic grammarians recognized two categories which he translates as 'governors' and 'governed'. This relation is primarily based on inflectional selection, but Owens compares the theory and practice of the Arabic grammarians with modern dependency theory (as defined in particular by Robinson, 1970), and shows that they made the same generalizations about governors as we make about heads. Most interestingly, 'in Arabic theory it was held that the unmarked sequence was governor–governed' (Owens, 1988: 53). Owens cites no fewer than ten separate Arabic works for this observation.
3. Capitalized names are reserved in Word Grammar for lexemes, leaving italics for inflected forms or for words in sentences or utterances.
4. Hawkins was arguing that languages display 'Cross-category harmony' based on head–dependent ordering as recently as Hawkins (1990). His contribution to this volume is important because it directly contradicts his earlier work. However, my view is that he is unduly optimistic about the possibility of predicting word order on the basis of recognition clues. For example, the word VERY could be the first word of an adjective

phrase (for example, *Very tall he was*), an adverb phrase (*Very often he comes home late*) or a prepositional phrase (*Very far beyond the Senate House lies the Library*) as well as a noun phrase; and even an adjective is a poor signal for a noun phrase, though an excellent signal for an adjective phrase, given that it may be used either predicatively or attributively. It is important to test the information carried by different kinds of words when they are in a minimal context, such as the start of a sentence; otherwise their content is easily confused with that of the preceding context. I also think that Hawkins is too pessimistic about the relevance of head–dependent relations. Even if the order of nouns and their attributive adjectives is completely unrelated to the order of elements in other constructions, there are surely enough statistical relations among other constructions to justify generalizations in terms of head–dependent ordering.

5. Given the ease with which functional categories are referred to in GB principles and rules, it would be surprising if the notion 'head' could not be defined configurationally. This would permit the same generalizations that are allowed in dependency theory; for example, a head-final language would have the order: 'X–head'. Disjunctive definitions are tolerated in GB (compare the standard definitions for relations like 'proper government'), so head could, if need be, have a different definition for each of the three main types of dependent. Having said all of this, the fact remains that (so far as I know) this kind of generalization has not been suggested in GB.

6. In an X-bar analysis, the specifier of X is the sister of X' and therefore the daughter of the maximum projection of X, XP. This much is agreed, but it is only an agreement on terminology. It remains to be seen whether all the elements that are defined in this way have anything else in common. If 'specifier' did identify a genuine grammatical category, as 'subject', 'complement', 'modifier/adjunct' and 'head' clearly do, then we should expect other criteria to converge with the configurational definition, thereby supporting the latter. This appears not to be the case, as witness the fact that for some linguists, the typical specifier is a subject, whereas for others it is a degree expression. Moreover, there is considerable uncertainty over the identity of the specifier of vp; for many (such as Chomsky, 1986a: 3) it is the subject, but for Radford (1988: 227) it is the aspectual auxiliary, while for Haegeman (1991: 82) it is the 'floated' quantifier *all*!

7. Agreement is relevant in that genuine agreement generally involves a dependent and its head. (Consequently, we must assume, for example, that since a reflexive pronoun does not depend on its antecedent, nor vice versa, the link between them is one of semantic binding rather than syntactic agreement.) As I argued in Hudson (1987), however, agreement does **not** tell us which of the linked elements is the head and which the dependent, in spite of the widely held assumption that the dependent

always agrees with the head. Rather, I claim that the relevant generalization is much simpler than this: the element which determines the agreement is the one which is a noun, because this is generally the one whose semantics and syntax fix the values concerned. For example, in *They are coming*, the plurality of the subject is fixed by its meaning, so it determines the number of the verb, rather than vice versa. All the grammar need say is that the two elements agree, without saying which follows which.

8. Among theories which recognize heads as basic, the only one that I know of which treats prepositional phrases as headless is Lexicase (Starosta, 1988). One could perhaps also mention Relational Grammar in this context, since its treatment of predicates is tantamount to calling them heads of their clauses, but prepositions are treated as mere markers of relations, with a status similar to that of case inflections.

9. The details of this dependency structure are all explained in Hudson (1990). The 'pied-piping' of prepositions requires complex dependency structures, commensurate with the difficulty of processing them, and also requires a special grammatical relation which I call 'projection' (1990: 367–78).

10. The example is chosen to exclude both Heavy NP Shift and Extraposition. The former is impossible because it never applies to an indirect object (cf. *I gave chocolates all my friends*). The latter is ruled out by the fact that the first modifier of the direct object is a postmodifying adjective, *capable*; these are never allowed to extrapose (cf. *I admire every linguist a lot capable of keeping up with the literature*). Consequently, the only possible structure for the example is '...-give–NP– [ ]'.

11. According to the figures given by Frazier and Rayner (1988: 252), sentences with initial adjunct clauses were read about as fast as those with extraposed subject clauses – about 35 msec. per character – and much faster than those with unextraposed subject clauses, which took nearly 42 msec. per character.

13 *Heads, bases and functors*

ARNOLD M. ZWICKY

13.1 Introduction

This chapter argues that when syntacticians refer to heads, they are referring to one of at least three distinct notions, all of which have a place in the theory of syntax.[1] It can thus be seen as a working out and refinement of the syntactic portions of Zwicky (1985), especially in response to the discussion by Hudson (1987).

My 1985 paper examined several situations in which the assignment of head or dependent status to some participant in a syntactic construction is unclear; for them, tests that pick out the head in straightforward cases like verb or preposition plus object (*see penguins, about penguins*) do not always make a unique assignment. Hudson (1987) attempted to show that a unique head could be picked out anyway, but at the cost of abandoning some tests and re-interpreting others. Still other syntacticians (for instance, Fenchel, 1989; Warner, 1989; Radford, this volume) have proposed that various problematic cases involve the assignment of head status to more than one participant in a construction, but again at a cost (complications in other parts of the description or other parts of the theory). With these latter authors, I propose to 'have it both ways', but not by assigning multiple head status, a step I reserve (see section 13.8) for quite a different set of phenomena.

Instead, what I want to say about heads is rather like what most syntacticians now say about subjects. Over a considerable period of time, the literature on subjects has gradually disentangled a number of notions that coincide in prototypical instances of subjects, among them nominative marking, sentence topic, reference to the agent in an event and the 'grammatical relation' now simply labelled *subject*. All of these notions are relevant in some way to statements of grammatical generalizations, and they are related to one another by default associations (for instance, the grammatical relation subject is by default expressed by nominative marking).

I am proposing here to disentangle at least three notions that coincide in prototypical instances of heads: the semantic *functor* (F); the *base* (B), which is the required participant in a combination (in the sense that omitting it yields some sort of ellipsis); and the *head* (H), roughly as in the Head Feature Convention of Generalized Phrase Structure Grammar (GPSG). Each of these is central to a combination, but in different ways: F is internally central, both semantically and for the purposes of lexical subcategorization; B is central in the same two ways, but for the purposes of semantic interpretation and lexical subcategorization with respect to elements external to its construct; and H is central with respect to the location of agreement or government morphology with respect to elements outside its construct. All of these notions are thus relevant to statements of grammatical generalizations. They are also related by default associations; the default is for H to coincide with B (though this association is broken in the constructions that are the major focus of this chapter), and for H to coincide with F (though this association is broken for modification constructions).

This is an essay in the foundations of syntax. It advances no particular theory of syntax, old or new, but instead concerns itself with pre-theoretical observations and metatheoretical strategies. Pre-theoretical observations lead to claims about what concepts an adequate theory must incorporate and what sorts of propositions such a theory must be able to articulate, and so serve as boundary conditions on theories. Metatheoretical strategies are proposals about how theories should be constructed, given such boundary conditions. It follows that neither conceptual economy nor formalism will be my concerns in this chapter – which is not to say that these are unworthy or irrelevant topics, only that I am taking up issues that are to some extent antecedent to them.

An adequate theoretical framework for syntax will include a considerable conceptual apparatus, one part of which has to do with syntactically relevant properties of expressions and their parts, for instance, the category they belong to (Noun, Verb, etc.) and their rank (Word, Phrase and Clause, at least), another part of which – the part I am concerned with in this chapter – has to do with syntactically relevant relations between parts of expressions. Two of these relations, inclusion and ordering, serve as the basis for constituent-structure theories; given this much conceptual apparatus, we can make descriptive statements like those in (1). My interest here is with two further sets of relations, which serve as the basis for dependency and 'relational' theories; descriptive statements like those in (2) are couched in terms of relations of this sort.

(1)   a. The Clause *penguins fly* includes the Noun Phrase *penguins* and the Verb Phrase *fly*.

        b. In this Clause, the Phrase *penguins* precedes the Phrase *fly*.

(2)   a. In this Clause, the Phrase *penguins* is a Dependent-of, in particular an Argument-of, the Phrase *fly*.

        b. In this Clause, the Phrase *penguins* is a Subject-of and an Absolute-of the Phrase *fly*.

13.2   Conceptual apparatus: dependency relations and functions

One specific issue I will be examining has to do with the relation, or relations, holding in a hypotactic syntactic construction between a central element, the *head*, and its satellite elements, its *dependents*. In a set of syntactically related constituents, which one or ones should be picked out as having a special central status? For what purposes – that is to say, to capture what sorts of generalizations? And on what grounds?

Here we are concerned with a theory of *dependency relations*, the central notions of which are the cross-cutting contrasts between Head-of and Dependent-of, on the one hand, and Functor-on and Functee-of (I apologize for the barbarous terminology, but all the good terms seem to be taken), on the other.[2] The four dependency relations so defined are charted in (3), where the arrows connect converse relations.[3]

(3)

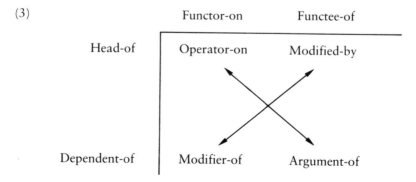

Functor-on   Functee-of

Head-of   Operator-on   Modified-by

Dependent-of   Modifier-of   Argument-of

In what follows it will sometimes be convenient to refer to a single term in a dependency relation, that is, to a subexpression serving as Head, Dependent, Functor, Functee, Operator, Modifier, Modified or Argument. For this I will use the label *dependency function*.[4] For each dependency relation there is a dependency function, which is a property possessed by a subexpression that bears the dependency relation to some other subexpression within its sentence.

13.2.1 *Modifier versus Argument*

The intuition behind the distinction between Modifier and Argument is that these functions typically differ semantically, syntactically and morphologically. Semantically, Modifiers are functors, while Arguments are (semantic) arguments.

Syntactically, Modifiers are optional, while Arguments are obligatory within their constructions; several instances of the same type of Modifier can co-occur in a flat structure, while only one instance of any given type of Argument is allowed per construction; and a Modifier construction will be associated with a *lexical subcategory* of the Modifier (a class of lexemes eligible to serve in that function in the construction), the corresponding Head category being lexically unrestricted, while an Argument construction will have a lexically unrestricted Argument category but a lexical subcategory for the corresponding head.[5]

Morphologically, Modifiers agree with their Heads and govern morphosyntactic properties of these Heads, while Arguments trigger agreement on their Heads and have morphosyntactic properties governed by their Heads. These morphological characteristics follow from the fact that Modifiers are Functors, given the generalization, originally due to Keenan (1974), that within a Functor–Functee construction, the Functor is the target for agreement triggered by the Functee (so that Operators agree with their Arguments, as when verbs agree with their Subjects and Direct Objects, and Modifiers agree with the Modifieds, as when adjectives agree with their companion nominals). Others, including Zwicky (1985), have extended this generalization to cover government: within such a construction, the Functor is a trigger for government with the Functee as target (so that Operators govern their arguments, as when verbs govern case forms on their Subjects and Direct Objects, and – much more rarely – Modifiers govern their Modifieds, as in the Arabic 'construct state'

examples mentioned by Vincent (this volume), where a Modifier
Noun, in base form, governs the construct form on the preceding
Modifier Noun). I will refer to this generalization about how syntax
mediates between semantics and morphological form as 'the extended
Keenan generalization'. As a slogan: Functors are agreement targets
and government triggers.

The characteristic differences between Modifiers and Arguments
can then be summarized as in (4):[6]

(4)		*Modifier*	*Argument*
	Semantics	semantic functor	semantic argument
	Syntax	optional	obligatory
		iterable	unique
		lexically subcategorized	lexically unrestricted
	Morphology	agreement target	agreement trigger
		government trigger	government target

Note that agreement and government achieve marking of syntactic
relations by two different principles. Agreement is a kind of sharing
of properties between items that stand in some syntactic relation,
while government merely marks the presence of this syntactic relation, via a property of the Dependent. However, the presence of a
syntactic relation could also be indicated on the Head, via a mark of
the lexical subcategory to which the Head belongs, as when the
relation between a Verb and its Direct Object is marked not by
government of some case (accusative or other) on the Direct Object,
but rather by a transitivity marker on the Verb (like Tok Pisin -*im*, as
in *i tokim ol* '(s)he says to them'). This is one way in which languages
(or constructions within one language) can choose to mark either
Dependent or Head (see Nichols, 1986), though the marks are
different in character.

13.2.2 Head versus Dependent

The intuition behind the distinction between Head and Dependent is
that these functions, too, differ in all three ways.

Semantically, the Head is the characterizing participant in a
construction; intuitively, the meaning of a construct is a subtype of
the meaning of the Head (*red apple* denotes a subtype of apple, *make
a box* a subtype of *make*), while the Dependent plays a contributory
role in the semantics, restricting the meaning of the Head in one way
or another. This is the 'kind of' property of McGlashan (this volume).

With respect to its internal syntax, the Head is the *required* element in a construction, even an Argument + Head construction, 'required' in the special sense that without this element the construct is elliptical; the Verb Phrase *turkey* in *I ate chicken, and Kim turkey* is missing its Head Verb, and is grammatical but elliptical. A Dependent is syntactically 'accessory', in the sense that without a Dependent a construct is simply of a different type; the Verb Phrase *walked* in *Kim walked* lacks a Dependent, but is simply an intransitive, rather than an elliptical transitive. And the Head is the participant in the construction that is typically specified as of Word rank in the rule describing the construction, while a Dependent is typically specified as of Phrase rank (as in the rules describing Verb Phrase comprising Verb Word and Noun Phrase, and Noun Phrase comprising Noun Word and Adjective Phrase).

With respect to both its internal and its external syntax, the Head is the syntactic *category determinant*. It determines the syntactic category of the construct as a whole; that is, it is the constituent with which the construct as a whole shares its syntactic category (though not necessarily its rank), while the category of the Dependent has no direct reflection in the category of the construct.

With specific reference to its external syntax, the Head is the determinant in a somewhat different sense: the distribution of the construct as a whole is predictable from properties of the Head, the properties of a Dependent being irrelevant or 'transparent' in the matter, so that the Head determines what is in effect the lexical subcategory of the construct as a whole. The Head as *external representative*, or 'external determinant', is the element in a construction that serves as the trigger or the target for external lexical subcategorization (whichever is relevant for the type of Head in question), with respect to partners of the construct as a whole, and as the trigger for government or agreement (again, whichever is relevant for the type of Head in question). For external purposes, *demonstrate that the earth is flat* has a distribution predictable from the properties of *demonstrate*, with the Argument *that the earth is flat* transparent for these purposes, and *very red tomatoes* has a distribution predictable from the properties of *tomatoes*, with the Modifier *very red* transparent for these purposes. This is the 'distributional equivalence' criterion for headship of Zwicky (1985), which was based on Bloomfield's (1933: 194) formulation in terms of 'same form class'. In order to apply it, morphology must be ignored, whether this morphology indicates syntactic relations outside the combination in question or whether it indicates syntactic relations between the participants in the combination; the point is to distinguish the selection of lexical subcategories from the selection of inflectional forms.

These closely linked characteristics – being the category determinant and the external representative – play a central role in the work of Harris (1946, 1951) that serves as the immediate antecedent of the 'X-bar syntax' in a variety of generative frameworks, including all of the last decade's versions of GB (Pullum, 1985; Kornai and Pullum, 1990). Morphologically, the Head is the *morphosyntactic locus*, the element that exhibits the morphosyntactic properties that belong to the construct as a whole, including those determined in agreement and government; thus, the Head Verb *eats* in the Verb Phrase *eats fish* in *Kim eats fish* exhibits in its suffix the present-tense property of the Verb Phrase as well as the third person and singular number properties that belong to this Phrase. The Head Feature Convention of GPSG (Gazdar *et al.*, 1985) packages the morphosyntactic locus characteristic together with the syntactic determinant characteristic, treating them both as a kind of feature-sharing between construct and constituent.

The characteristic differences between Heads and Dependents are summarized in (5):[7]

(5)

		Head	*Dependent*
	Semantics	characterizing	contributory
	Syntax	required	accessory
		Word rank	Phrase rank
		category determinant	non-determinant
		external representative	externally transparent
	Morphology	morphosyntactic locus	morphosyntactically irrelevant

13.3   Conceptual background: syntactic relations and functions

Another issue has to do with the relationship between dependency relations and the specific relations usually called 'grammatical relations': Subject, Direct Object, Adjectival, Predicator, etc. In what follows I will use the label *syntactic relation* for these two-place relations and the label *syntactic function* for one term in such a relation, so that in the clause *penguins fly* the ordered expression-pair (*penguins*, *fly*) belongs to the Subject-of syntactic relation, the expression *penguins* has the Subject syntactic function and the expression *fly* has the Predicator syntactic function.

I opt for the modifier 'syntactic' rather than 'grammatical' to emphasize that these notions are grounded specifically in syntax, whatever associations they might have with other aspects of a grammar (in particular, with semantics or morphology). This is not merely a terminological quibble. The substantive point is that the inventory of syntactic relations – in one language, or in a theoretical framework for all languages – is determined in the first instance by the needs of *syntax*. We posit these theoretical entities because some generalizations about the syntax of individual languages cannot be stated properly without them; if we must frame generalizations entirely in terms of syntactic categories, syntactic constituent structure and linear precedence – even if we can also refer to the categories of inflectional morphology, phonological properties of constituents, semantic content and pragmatic function – we will miss some generalizations.

A particularly simple approach to syntactic functions/relations would treat them as subordinate to the four main dependency functions/relations. There would then be a single hierarchy – actually, as in (3) above, a number of cross-cutting splits – embracing both types of entities.

Thus, the dependency function Argument would split into syntactic functions like Nuclear versus Oblique and Internal versus External, at a rather high level; at a somewhat lower level, Nuclear would split into Subject, Absolute, Direct Object and Ergate,[8] and Internal into Direct Object, Indirect Object and others. The dependency function Operator would split into syntactic functions like Predicator and Locator. And the dependency function Modifier would split into syntactic functions like Adjectival (Modifier-of-N) and Adverbial (Modifier-of-non-N); in turn, Adjectival and Adverbial would split into various subtypes.

These particular splits are summarized in (6), which is intended to be illustrative rather than definitive; it is not my purpose here to provide a detailed theory of syntactic functions. A somewhat different way of splitting dependency functions and syntactic functions, without cross-cutting, has been proposed by Hudson in various recent papers (see especially Hudson, 1988: 312).[9]

(6)   Argument: Nuclear versus Oblique; External versus Internal
           Nuclear: Subject, Absolute, Direct Object, Ergate
           Internal: Direct Object, Indirect Object, Oblique Object, Predicative, Complement, etc.

Operator: Predicator versus Locator
Modifier: Adjectival versus Adverbial
  Adverbial: Degree Adverbial (Modifier-of-A), Sentence Adverbial
  (Modifier-of-S), etc.

13.4   Local determination of Word properties

In the approach I am taking here, which unites aspects of constituency and dependency frameworks, both dependency relations and syntactic relations are specified in the rules for particular syntactic constructions. (It is not my concern here whether some or all of these relations can be predicted from universal principles and/or parameter settings for a particular language.) In this regard they are like the relations of inclusion or linear precedence.

Phrase-structure syntax frameworks provide a way of taking the relations of inclusion and linear precedence, as specified in a particular rule for the participant constituents in that rule, and systematically determining such relations for subconstituents, ultimately for individual syntactic words within an expression. From the fact (determinable from one rule) that the Clause *purple penguins fly hesitantly* includes a Noun Phrase *purple penguins* and a Verb Phrase *fly hesitantly*, in that order, and the fact (determinable from a second rule or rules) that the Noun Phrase *purple penguins* includes an Adjective Word *purple* and a Noun Word *penguins*, in that order, and the fact (determinable from a third rule or rules) that the Verb Phrase *fly hesitantly* includes a Verb Word *fly* and an Adverb Word *hesitantly*, we can determine that the Clause *purple penguins fly hesitantly* includes the Noun Word *penguin*, that in this expression the Adjective Word *purple* precedes the Verb Word *fly* and so on. These predictions follow via general principles of relational inheritance: if X includes Y and Y includes Z, then X includes Z; and if X precedes Y, X includes X_1, and Y includes Y_1, then X_1 precedes Y_1.

What is important here is that the relevant properties of and relations between words can be *locally determined*, predicted from the properties of and relations between the constituents that participate in particular local rules. In a strictly word-based framework, there must be a converse mechanism, for predicting properties of and relations between larger expressions, ultimately from those specified in rules that concern individual words. It is not my purpose here to argue for a constituent-based framework over a word-based one. But there is no way to talk about these matters without choosing one sort of framework, so I have chosen the one I believe to be better supported. I should add that this choice has nothing to do with a top–down versus bottom–up versus pure-licensing view of the way syntactic rules are applied in determining whether a particular expression is licensed by a grammar; both word-based and constituent-based frameworks can be viewed in all of these, and presumably many other, ways.

In any event, there are general principles that allow local determination of dependency relations and syntactic relations between individual words, given the relations that are specified between immediate constituents in particular syntactic rules. First, I assume that any multi-word expression has immediate constituents each of which bears a dependency relation and a syntactic relation to at least one other immediate constituent of it; there are no constituents that are simply 'thrown in'. Next I define what it is to be a *Head-within* a constituent: in a construct X, any immediate constituent X_1 of X that is Head-of some other immediate constituent of X is Head-within X; and if X_2 is Head-within X_1 and X_1 is Head-within X, then X_2 is Head-within X. Then the principle of relational inheritance is that a Head-within a construct bears all the dependency relations and syntactic relations of the construct itself.

13.5 Dissociations

The world of syntactic functions is systematically related to the world of syntactic categories, via default associations between the two: Noun with Nuclear Argument, Verb with Predicator, Adposition with Locator, Adjective with Adjectival, Adverb with Adverbial and so on. These associations can be viewed in constituent-structure terms, as relating syntactic functions to categories like Noun Phrase, or in terms of word properties, as relating syntactic functions to categories like Noun Word.

But, as is well known, there are dissociations between syntactic functions and syntactic categories. In certain circumstances, Clauses can serve as Nuclear Arguments (*That people are refusing to fly means we shouldn't invest in airline stocks*), PPs as Subjects (*Under the bed is a poor place to hide*), bare NPs as Adverbials (*Be here Tuesday*), NPs as Determiners (*a thousand clowns*) and so on.

There are also phenomena that suggest that dependency functions and syntactic functions are dissociable from one another, that the latter are not simply subtypes of the former as in hierarchical frameworks. One well-known class of such phenomena involves Arguments that clearly have the syntactic functions (and often the syntactic categories as well) normally associated with Modifiers, as in the locational Dependent of verbs like *reside* in *I reside near Stanford* or the manner Dependent of verbs like *word* in *We worded our response carefully*. These are Arguments on the syntactic tests in (4), since they are obligatory, unique and lexically unrestricted. Yet what fills these slots in the construction at issue is not any standard sort of Argument syntactic function but, rather, specific types of Adverbial – which is to say, on the hierarchical view, a subtype of Modifier.

The natural suggestion to make is that the associations between syntactic functions and dependency functions that are assumed in the hierarchical view are, like the standard associations between syntactic functions and syntactic categories, only defaults, which can be overridden by stipulations for particular constructions in particular languages. Adopting this suggestion means giving up the hierarchical view and treating dependency functions and syntactic functions as two independent, though intimately related, systems. We then say that English has a construction in which a Verb Head (like *word*) is licensed with three Arguments: a Subject, a Direct Object and an Adverbial (of a specific type). Adverbials are by default Modifiers, but here we have Adverbials stipulated to be Arguments.

In examples like these, there is in a sense conflicting evidence as to whether some constituent is a Modifier or an Argument. Internally, constituents like *carefully* or *with great care* are typical Modifiers, and they have modificational semantics, but in their external syntax in construction with Heads like *word* they act like Arguments.

13.6 Splits

Modifiers and Arguments are both Dependents, so that examples like *phrase my response with malice* present no particular difficulty in assigning Head versus Dependent status. But there are other examples that do, and it is these that I am primarily concerned with in this chapter.

In a number of different places in the grammars of many, quite probably all, languages, there are elements of Word rank that are Dependents on some tests, but Heads on others: for instance, English auxiliaries like *is* in *is going*, *has* in *has gone* and *must* in *must go*. More specifically, these elements seem to be Modifiers (Adverbials or Adjectivals) serving as Operators; the English auxiliaries, for instance, have the semantics of (Adverbial) Modifiers but exhibit tense, person and number inflection the way Operator Verbs do.

The split of the morphosyntactic locus characteristic of Heads from some of the other characteristics has been stressed in Nichols' (1986 and elsewhere) very important work on what she calls 'head-marking' versus 'dependent-marking', though in fact her assignments of Head versus Dependent status on non-morphological grounds are still problematic; in particular, she treats auxiliaries as Heads without comment.

In the generative, especially GB, literature, these elements are sometimes given a special status by being labelled Specifiers,[10] a label I will adopt here (but without adopting any attendant assumptions of GB syntax). As I observe below, some recent GB work takes these elements (in particular, auxiliaries, infinitival *to* and determiners) to be Heads. In contrast, in the Categorial Grammar literature, as in Bouma (1988, citing work by Bach), Specifiers are treated as special types of Modifiers, because of their semantics.

In general, a Specifier serves as a marker of grammatical categories – aspect, tense, modality, case, definiteness, subordination, degree, etc. – on the constituent with which it combines (the Specified). While individual Specifiers might have additional lexical content, they all are to some degree 'particle words', occurring in alternation with, or in combination with, inflectional expression of these grammatical categories on their Specifieds. Specifiers are thus the syntactic analogues of inflectional morphology (the *to* of *to sing* being parallel to the *-ing* of *singing*), while Arguments are the syntactic analogues of category-changing derivational morphology (the *people* of *people sing* being parallel to the *-er* of *singer*) and Modifiers are the syntactic analogues of category-preserving derivational morphology (the *rather* of *rather blue* being parallel to the *-ish* of *bluish*).

Here is the array of the characteristics that make them theoretically problematic (with short code names for each of the relevant characteristics):

(7)   *Dependent characteristics:*
          Semantics: they are contributory (like Modifiers and Arguments)
                ¬CLS: they are not classifying
          specifically like Modifiers [Functors]:
                FTR: they are semantic functors
          Internal syntax: they are accessory (like Modifiers and Arguments)
          specifically like Modifiers [Functors]:
                ¬REQ: they are not required
          specifically   like   Arguments   (Functees]   (and   Operators

[Functors]):
   UNQ: they are unique
specifically like Modifiers [Functors] (and Operators [Functors]):
   LEX: they are lexically subcategorized
External syntax: like Modifiers and Arguments
   ¬REP: they are not external representatives
Head characteristics: like Operators [Functors] and Modifieds [Functees]
  Internal syntax:
   WRD: they are of Word rather than Phrase rank
  Internal/external syntax:
   CAT: they are category determinants
  Morphology:
   LOC: they are morphosyntactic loci
Characteristics that go both ways:
  Morphology: like Operators and Modifiers [both Functors]
   AGR: they are agreement targets
   GOV: they are government triggers

Let me go through these characteristics for one class of Specifiers, the English auxiliaries, in combination with Specifieds that have the syntactic category Verb Phrase and the syntactic function Complement.

First, on the Dependent side of the ledger: the auxiliaries have contributory rather than classifying semantics (¬CLS); the meaning of *will sing* is a subtype of the meaning of *sing*. In fact, semantically they act like Modifiers (Adverbials, in particular) rather than Arguments; they are semantic functors (FTR).

Auxiliaries are not required (¬REQ); for the most part, English clauses do not have to have an auxiliary to be well formed (though there are special clause types, like the inverted type in *Do you love me?*, that do). They are unique (UNQ); sequences of auxiliaries, as in *must have been being praised*, have hierarchial rather than flat structure, with only one auxiliary per constituent. They are lexically subcategorized (LEX); there is a small class of auxiliaries, and though there is a semantic core to the class, membership in the class is somewhat unpredictable, while there is no such lexical restriction for their Complements. Finally, they are not external representatives (¬REP); the distribution of a Verb Phrase like *must rain a lot in Seattle* or *is raining here* is predictable not from the properties of modal *must* or progressive *be*, but from the properties of their Complements, both of which have the weather verb *rain* as their Head.

On the Head side of the ledger: in the rules introducing them (VP →
V + VP, in a standard formulation) the auxiliaries are of Word rather
than Phrase rank (WRD). As for category determination (CAT) in this
case, we cannot tell, since both constituents and the construct have
the category Verb. But they are morphosyntactic loci (LOC); the
auxiliary in *It was becoming a dark and stormy night*, not its
Complement *becoming*, shows the morphological indications of
tense, person and number. In English we cannot really tell whether
auxiliaries are agreement targets (AGR) or not, since Verbs do not
show any morphological reflexes of agreement with their Complements. But they are certainly government triggers (GOV), since each
auxiliary requires a particular verb form on its Complement: the
modals require a base form, progressive BE requires a present
participle form, perfective HAVE and passive BE require a past
participle form and so on.[11]

For combinations of auxiliary Verb with a Complement Verb
Phrase, then, the characteristics of the Head are split between
Specifier and Specified. It will be clear from (7) that the characteristics
of the Functor are also split between Specifier and Specified. This is a
fresh array of characteristics.

13.6.1 *Instances of the split*

This particular array arises in at least four different situations in one
language or another. All of these have figured in the recent literature
that has concerned itself with properties of Heads (notably, Zwicky,
1985; Hudson, 1987; and nearly all the other chapters in this
volume).

First, as already discussed, there are some instances of certain
('auxiliary') Verbs in combination with a Complement Verb Phrase,
though most instances of Verbs taking Complement Verb Phrases (as
in *start raining* or *expect to go*) are unproblematically Heads.

Second, there are some instances of a determiner in combination
with its companion nominal constituent, as in English *those penguins,
three iguanas, each kangaroo* and *you guys*. These have some
properties of clear Modifiers, like *numerous* in *numerous difficulties*,
and some properties of clear (Operator) Heads, like *pile* in *a pile of
potatoes*. They fit the profile of Specifiers in (7) perfectly, except
perhaps for the category-determinant (CAT) property.

As many have noticed in the past decade, the resulting rule for
determiners is quite parallel to the one for auxiliaries. There are, of
course, two ways the rules could be framed so as to be parallel. On

the one hand, we could take the rule VP → V + VP (where different subtypes of Specifier Vs govern different Specified VPs) to be the model for the analysis of determiners. This entails treating the determiners in question as a special kind of Noun in combination with a Complement Noun Phrase, as was (apparently) first suggested by Hudson (1987: section 6); see also Zwicky (forthcoming). The relevant NP rule is then NP → N + NP, where different subtypes of Specifier Ns govern different Specified NPs.

Or we could posit (as in Abney, 1987; Hoeksema, 1988; and a number of other works, including several in this volume) a rule DP → D + NP and take it as the model for the analysis of auxiliaries, in which case the relevant VP rule is XP → X + VP, for some appropriate X that carries tense and agreement information in finite clauses lacking an overt auxiliary.[12] If we take X to be I, then the rule DP → D + NP will be parallel to IP → I + VP; indeed, Grimshaw (in recent, still unpublished, work reported on at the 1991 West Coast Conference on Formal Linguistics) extends these proportions so that N:V :: D:I :: P:C, where P is Adposition and C is Complementizer. I now turn to cases of P and C.

The third collection of problematic cases comprises some instances of ('grammatically used') Adpositions in combination with a Direct Object Noun Phrase, like the uses of *to*, *of* and *by* in *give money to Pat* and *the discovery of flying pigs by Chris*. Ordinary Adpositions, as in *send books to China* or *eating sushi with your friends*, are unproblematically Heads.

Grammatically used Adpositions show fairly clearly the split between the two 'determinant' characteristics in Specifier–Specified combinations; the Specifier is the category determinant (CAT) while the Specified is the external representative (REP). Concerning the Specifier as CAT: it is clear in many languages that the syntactic category of an Adposition in combination with its Object Noun Phrase is Adposition, not Noun; dative *to Pat*, ergative *by Chris* and so on in English are PPs, not NPs, on every relevant test I know of. (In particular, these Prepositions can be stranded, as in *Who did you give it to?*) On the Specified as REP: in general, grammatically used Adpositions serve as syntactically transparent 'flags' of the relationship between these Noun Phrases and some external Operator; in particular, in some languages Verbs show agreement with Adpositionally marked Objects of various sorts (Zwicky, forthcoming, citing Seiter, 1983, on Niuean; Davies, 1986, with respect to Jake, 1980, on Tigre; and Durie, 1988, on Acehnese).

The fourth collection of problematic cases comprises some instances of a subordinator (a 'complementizer') in combination with its clause (which we might want to treat as instances of a special kind of Adposition in combination with a Direct Object Clause). In English, complementizer *that* (as in *that pigs can't fly* or *that you be the leader*) belongs here, while ordinary adverbial subordinators (as in *after you're gone* and *while we were singing*) are unproblematically Heads. The clause is certainly the Specified in such combinations; in particular, it is the external representative. Whether the complementizer is the category determinant or not depends on what categories are to be assigned to the two constituents and the construct in question; the rule CP → C+XP (for some appropriate X; IP is the choice in current GB work) achieves the desired result, though it is not the only imaginable way. But where we can tell, the complementizer has Specifier characteristics; it is a semantic function (FTR) and is lexically restricted (LEX), and in several languages (see Hoeksema, 1986, on Dutch; Rizzi, 1990: 55–7, with references on Kinande, Bavarian and French, among other languages) there is evidence indicating that complementizers of this sort can be agreement targets, exhibiting agreement with the Subject of the Specified clause (AGR).

(Some instances of a 'degree' Adposition in combination with a measure or extent phrase, as in English *over thirty students* and *about as many people as we expected* or in similar Russian expressions with case-governing prepositions (see Babby, 1988), might belong here as well.)

13.6.2 *The analysis of Specifiers*

What are we to make of these splits? No assignment of otherwise motivated syntactic categories, Functor–Functee status, Head–Dependent status or specific syntactic functions will yield the right split of characteristics for Specifier and Specified.

Nor will it do merely to add Specifier and Specified as new dependency functions on a footing with Operator, Modified, Modifier and Argument in (3), as in (8). Whether we do this by positing some third item, say Companion, in addition to Head and Dependent (8a), or by treating Head as a three-valued feature, along the lines of (8b), or by breaking Head and Dependent (like the phonological features High and Low) into cross-cutting binary features (8c), the right arrays of characteristics will not fall out.

(8)

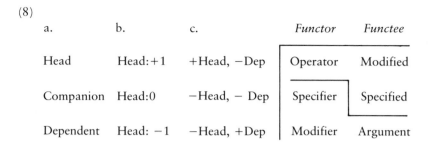

	a.	b.	c.	*Functor*	*Functee*
	Head	Head: +1	+Head, −Dep	Operator	Modified
	Companion	Head: 0	−Head, − Dep	Specifier	Specified
	Dependent	Head: −1	−Head, +Dep	Modifier	Argument

Instead, we can preserve the essentially binary oppositions Functor–Functee (F versus non-F) and Head–Dependent (H versus non-H) in (3), while adding a third one at the top level of dependency functions. This third binary opposition, B (for base) versus non-B, picks out Specified versus Specifier as well as Operator versus Argument and Modified versus Modifier; that is, it picks out the three dependency functions in the upper right of (8), versus the three in the lower left.

Different dependency functions at the bottom level are then obtained by assigning B either to the H element in the 'square of opposition' in (3) or to the non-H element. The four possible assignments are enumerated in (9) and (10).

(9)   H   + non-H
    a. Operator = Base: Operator + Argument
                    F B
    b. Modified = Base: Modified + Modifier
                  B   F

(10)   a. Argument = Base: Specifier + Specified
                  F   B
    b. Modifier = Base: Specifier + Specified
                      F B

Let me emphasize that H, B and F in the charts in (9) and (10) are still dependency functions, that is, they are still to be thought of as inherently relational in character. Saying that some constituent is an H in a construction is just a shorthand way of saying that it bears the H function to a co-constituent in that construction; and similarly for B and F.

Now that there is no longer a single notion of 'head', the scheme for local determination of Word properties, sketched in section 13.4 above, must be replaced by separate schemes for H, B and F, and for their associated syntactic relations. When this is done, all the syntactically relevant relations between Words in an expression will be predictable from relations specified in rules stated over constituents.

13.6.3 Another sort of Specifier

In the unproblematic Operator + Argument (9a) and Modified + Modifier (9b) combinations, B coincides with H; indeed, in Operator + Argument combinations, which are in a sense the prototypical combinations of head and dependent, H, F and B coincide in a single element, the Operator. The Specifier + Specified combinations in (10) are problematic in that B is assigned to a non-H element. In the ones we have been considering, schematized in (10a), the H element is still the F.

There remains the logical possibility of a different sort of Specifier + Specified combination, in which F is assigned to a non-H element, as in (10b). In the Specifier + Specified combination of (10a), the Specifier is the F and thus is the agreement target and government trigger. In (10b), the Specified is the F, and so should be the agreement target and government trigger. Both patterns can be illustrated from possessive constructions in the world's languages. I assume that in both patterns possessors are Specifiers and possesseds are Specifieds.

In the (10a) pattern, a possessor falls in with garden-variety determiners, and consequently shows agreement with the possessed nominal; pronominal possessors in many European languages are of this type. In the (10b) pattern, a possessor falls in with Subjects (Ergates, in particular) so that it can show a governed case (like the English genitive in 's), while the possessed nominal can show agreement (as in Turkish).

13.7 Property correlates of F, H and B

None of this would be more than cleverness in chart-making if F, H and B lacked consistent correlates in properties of subexpressions. In fact, each has a primary 'property correlate', plus one or more subsidiary property correlates, as follows:

(11) a. F: semantic functor (FTR)
         agreement target (AGR)
         government trigger (GOV)
         lexically subcategorized (LEX)
      b. H: morphosyntactic locus (LOC)
         Word rank (WRD)

> category determinant (CAT)
> c. B: external representative (REP)
>   required (REQ)
>   classifying (CLS)

This assignment of correlates, together with the interpretation of the eight different assortments of H, B and F into dependency functions, in (9) and (10), correctly sorts out the characteristics of these eight types of participants in syntactic constructions.

The characteristics not yet accounted for are uniqueness (UNQ) and (within ¬REQ constituents) optionality (OPT). As for OPT: all B dependency functions (Operator in (9a), Modified in (9b), Specified in (10)) are obligatory, as in the non-B dependency function Argument in (9a); all other non-B dependency functions are optional. As for UNQ: any dependency function that is H or B or non-F is unique; only Modifiers in (9b) are iterable.

13.8 Multiply headed hypotaxis

Although the dependency functions that are both H and F, Operators and Specifiers, are unique, there are reasons for wanting to say that in certain constructions both constituents in a construction can be H, so that these constructions will appear to be to some extent paratactic.

The cases I have in mind are (a) contracted *wanna, gonna* etc., on the analysis suggested by Frantz (1979), where the contraction is dependent on 'relation sharing' between the main verb *want* and the infinitival verb *to*; and (b) American English quasi-serial *go get, come see*, etc., on the analysis suggested by Pullum (1990), which also involves relation sharing. My proposal is that these are variant forms of, respectively, (a) the ordinary Verb + Complement construction of *want to sing* (where *want* is H, F and B and *to sing* is none of these), and (b) the auxiliary Verb + Complement construction of *will sing* (where *will* is H and F while *sing* is B). In these variant forms both the Verb and the Complement are H.

Being H means that both constituents are morphosyntactic loci with respect to agreement with or government by external material; both constituents will have morphosyntactic features that are determined from outside their construct. But there is also government within the construct: a Verb like *want* governs a 'marked infinitive' Complement, with *to*, and a Verb like *will* governs a base-form ('unmarked infinitive') Complement. The result is a double set of morphosyntactic features on the H Word of the Complement; in *I wanna go*, the infinitive marker *to* will have both a set of −Finite features (imposed by government by *want*) and a set of +Finite features (imposed by agreement with *I*), and in *I go sing a lot, sing* will have both a set of −Finite features (imposed by government by *go*) and a set of +Finite features (imposed by agreement with *I*).

Multiple sources of morphosyntactic features are quite common, of course (Zwicky, 1986). Sometimes the features are separately realized in the morphology of the language (as when Verbs show agreement with both Subject and Direct Object), but quite often one source of features receives morphological realization while another is, so far as the morphology is concerned, suppressed. In the case of *wanna* contraction, the features imposed by the main verb always 'win'. In the case of the quasi-serial construction, speakers differ as to whether the main verb's requirements, of the base form, wins (allowing things like *I have come visit them*) or whether an external determinant's requirement wins (for perfective *have* as the external determinant, allowing things like *I have come visited them*), or whether the construction is possible only if both requirements can be satisfied (so that neither **I have come visit them* nor **I have come visited them* is acceptable, but *I have often come put water on their plants* is; see Pullum, 1990, for further details).

I should point out that the 'double H' analysis for *wanna* contraction and the quasi-serials is independent of the treatment of co-ordination. It is true that the standard GPSG approach to co-ordination treats every conjunct as a Head, that is, as H (in my terms here, it should also treat every conjunct as B) but this line of analysis could be abandoned (as I believe it should be) without any consequences for an analysis of some hypotactic constructions as having two H constituents.

13.9 References to H and to B

It has often been suggested that there are generalizations about the grammars of particular languages that make crucial reference to the distinction between Head and Dependent, H and non-H. In English, for example, many syntacticians have noted the powerful generalization that in Phrase constructs, the H constituent precedes all of its Arguments – a generalization that runs across VPs (including those with auxiliary Hs), PPs (including those with grammatically used P Hs), AdjPs and AdvPs, as in Pollard and Sag (1987). On the other hand, the H constituent is also the one of Word rank, so that (as many have observed) the generalization could be stated instead in terms of rank (with 'lexical' categories preceding phrasal categories).

The dependency function B seems frequently to play a role in the statement of the syntactic rules of particular languages. In English, for instance, rules that are standardly framed with references to 'the main verb' (see Levin, 1986) involve reference to the B Verb Word. Thus, the gapping construction of English (as in *I will order the salmon, and Terry the steak*) has as one of its defining characteristics that it is missing material that contains the B Verb Word (the 'main verb'). In contrast, the VP ellipsis construction (as in *You must have been singing, and they must, too*) has as one of its defining characteristics that a non-B H Verb Word remains. The pseudo-gapping construction (as in *I can finish my salmon before you can your steak*) involves both of these conditions.

The dependency function B also plays the central role in one instance of 'direct reference to heads' (Zwicky, 1988). What is at issue here is a condition that for some speakers of English requires that in genitive plural NPs the mark of plurality within the NP must be located on the same syntactic Word as the genitive mark. Genitive case is marked on the final Word of an NP (*the student I was talking to's ideas*), while plurality is marked on the 'head' (actually B) Word within the NP (*the students I was talking to*), and when these two do not coincide the result is ungrammatical for some speakers: *the students I was speaking to's ideas*.

It may well be that most of the references to 'heads' in the grammars of particular languages are to be reformulated as references to the B participant, and ultimately the B Word, in some construction.

13.10 Concluding remarks

I have already remarked on the importance of Nichols' work on what is, in my terms, the dissociation of the morphosyntactic locus characteristic (now labelled H) from other characteristics of 'heads'. There are antecedents for other aspects of my proposals.

In particular, analyses with something of the flavour of (9) and (10) are to be found in Warner (1989), with special reference to complementizers and co-ordinating conjunctions, and Fenchel (1989), with special reference to determiners. Both Warner and Fenchel propose that these constructions have *two* heads and attempt to sort the syntactic features into two sets in such a way that the conventions of GPSG, in particular the Head Feature Convention (HFC) and the Control Agreement Principle (CAP), will distribute them properly between the two participants in a Specifier + Specified combination. In a similar vein, Hoeksema (1986) on agreement of complementizers with Subjects in Dutch and Zwicky (forthcoming) on agreement of verbs with Adpositionally marked Arguments both propose to use the HFC and CAP to move features from a Specified to a Specifier to the construct embracing them both, so that these features can 'communicate' outside the construct.

My proposal here (also aired in Zwicky, 1990a, 1990b) is that such combinations do indeed have two central constituents in them, but that these two are of different type and that the difference should be available in a universal framework for syntax – available in the sense that within certain limits the individual constructions of particular languages are free to impose values for the features H, F and B on their constituents.

Somewhat different sorts of antecedents are to be found in Simpson (1983: section 2.5), who distinguishes between 'phrase structure heads' and 'functional heads' (adopting the distinction between 'categorial' and 'functional' properties in Lexical Functional Grammar, as in Bresnan, 1982b), and in Wandruszka (1989), who distinguishes between 'heads on the classemic level' and 'heads on the lexemic level', both of which I take to be roughly the distinction between H on the one hand and F/B on the other. An appreciation that there is some sense in which both parts of a Specifier + Specified construction contribute to the characteristics of their construct is to be found in Abney (1987) and much other recent GB work.

All of these writers thus distinguish what Nichols (1986: 57) takes to be concurrent defining characteristics of 'heads' across various theoretical frameworks, the F characteristics of government trigger (GOV) and lexical subcategorizand (LEX) and the H characteristic of category determinant (DET):

Linguists of divergent theoretical persuasions are in almost complete agreement as to what is the head and what is the non-head in a given construction; cf. Tesnière 1959, Garde 1977, Mel'čuk 1979b, 1981, Bresnan 1982[c] (passim), Marantz 1984. Briefly, the head is the word which governs, or is subcategorized for – or otherwise determines the possibility of occurrence of – the other word. It determines the category of the phrase.

Still another type of related proposal is to be found in Carlson (1983) and Pollard and Sag (forthcoming), where certain sorts of 'grammatical words' or 'particle words' are distinguished as *markers*. But these are neither Hs (at least on the morphosyntactic-locus and category-determinant criteria) nor Bs (on the external-representative criterion); they would appear to make a special class of F elements.

Undoubtedly, there are many earlier, perhaps even ancient, intimations that such constructions divide up, between their two constituents, various 'central' characteristics that, for other constructions, coincide in a single constituent. What I hope to have provided here is a reasonably full account of the characteristics in question, the extent to which they vary together and the extent to which they can vary independently. The central claim is that an adequate account of dependency functions requires that we recognize at least three relevant primitive functions, H, F and B.

NOTES

1. My thanks to Joyce Powers for comments on a much earlier version of this chapter and to David Dowty for pointing out the Wandruszka reference to me; and for their comments on intermediate versions, my thanks to members of the audience (especially Joan Bresnan and Peter Sells) at my 26 January 1990 presentation at Stanford's Center for the Study of Language and Information and to participants in the Talking Heads Round Table at the University of Surrey, 21–2 March 1991. The version of 31 March 1991 was finished at the Center for Advanced Study in the Behavioral Sciences, Stanford, California; my thanks to the Center for its hospitality and to the Ohio State University for sabbatical-year support (and for the assistance of Alex Schott in preparing the final manuscript, of 26 October 1991).

2. The names of dependency relations/functions and syntactic relations/functions will have initial capitalization. The choice of particular names is essentially arbitrary; nothing could possibly hinge on whether *Predicator* or *Verbal* or something else is selected as the name of a particular syntactic function, so long as the same name is chosen for corresponding functions in different languages. Some names are resonant with historical associations, of course – a fact that has both positive and negative consequences.

3. Modifier-of is also known as Adjunct-of, and Argument-of as Complement-of. I will not use 'Adjunct' at all in what follows, so that the reader is free to treat it as a synonym for 'Modifier'. I will, however, be using 'Complement' in a special sense, to refer to a specific syntactic function.

4. With *function* here understood as referring not to functions in the mathematical sense, which are special types of relations, but rather to the functions in the sense 'uses, roles', which are, speaking mathematically, properties.

5. See Pollard and Sag (1987: especially section 5.6) for further discussion of the Argument/Modifier distinction.

6. There is, of course, no claim here that all of these properties will be manifested for every Modifier and every Argument, or even somewhere or another in each language. The properties are nevertheless intended to

be universal, in the sense that if there is relevant evidence within a language then Modifiers and Arguments are distinguished as in (4).

7. As with (4), these distinctions are intended to be universal, in that if there is relevant evidence on the matter in a language, Heads and Dependents will be distinguished as in (5).

8. I reserve the names *absolutive* and *ergative* for morphological cases, parallel to *nominative* and *accusative*. Absolute and Ergate are the syntactic functions marked by absolutive and ergative case, respectively.

9. There is no necessary claim here that all syntactic functions, even all of the ones listed in (6), play a role in every language. Instead, different languages can make use of different assortments of functions from a universally characterized list, much as different languages make use of different assortments of phonological feature distinctions from a universally characterized list.

10. The companion constituent to a Specifier is usually labelled Head, and in much of this literature it is assumed that all endocentric constructions (even subject–predicate constructions) are Specifier + Head, so that the problematic characteristics of what I am calling Specifiers are obscured.

11. The observation that this is in fact government seems to have been made first by Pullum and Wilson (1977).

12. In recent GB work, following Pollock's (1989) positing of the categories T (tense), TP, Agr (agreement), and AgrP, an assortment of grammatical categories are segmentalized as formatives, each with its own Specifier + Specified rule.

References

Abney, Stephen P. (1986). Functional elements and licensing. Paper presented at GLOW 1986, Gerona, Spain.

— (1987). The English noun phrase in its sentential aspect. PhD thesis, Massachusetts Institute of Technology.

Ajdukiewicz, Kazimierz (1935). Die syntaktische Konnexität. *Studia Philosophica* **1**: 1–27.

Anderson, John M. (1971). *The grammar of case: towards a localistic theory*. Cambridge: Cambridge University Press.

— (1976). *On serialization in English syntax* (Ludwigsburg Studies in Language and Linguistics 1). Ludwigsburg: Strauch.

— (1977). *On case grammar: prolegomena to a theory of grammatical relations*. London: Croom Helm.

— (1979). Serialization, dependency and the syntax of possessives in Moru. *Studia Linguistica* **33**: 1–23.

— (1986). Suprasegmental dependencies. In Jacques Durand (ed.) *Dependency and non-linear phonology*. London: Croom Helm. 55–133.

— (1989a). Reflections on notional grammar. In Doug Arnold, Martin Atkinson, Jacques Durand, Claire Grover and Louisa Sadler (eds.) *Essays on grammatical theory and universal grammar*. Oxford: Clarendon Press. 13–36.

— (1989b). *Structural analogy in language*. Ann Arbor: Karoma.

Anderson, John M. and Jacques Durand (1986). Dependency phonology. In Jacques Durand (ed.) *Dependency and non-linear phonology*. London: Croom Helm. 1–54.

Anderson, Richard C. and Antony Ortony (1975). On putting apples into bottles – a problem of polysemy. *Cognitive Psychology* **7**: 167–80.

Andry, François, Norman M. Fraser, Scott McGlashan, Simon Thornton and Nick J. Youd (forthcoming). Making DATR work for speech: lexicon compilation in Sundial. *Computational Linguistics* 18(3).

Antinucci, Francesco, Alessandro Duranti and Lucyna Gebert (1979). Relative clause structure, relative clause perception, and the change from sov to svo. *Cognition* **7**: 145–76.

318   *References*

Austin, Peter (ed.) (1988). *Complex sentence constructions in Australian languages*. Amsterdam and Philadelphia: John Benjamins.

Babby, Leonard H. (1985). Noun phrase internal case agreement. *Russian Linguistics* 9: 1–15.

——— (1987). Case, prequantifiers, and discontinuous agreement in Russian. *Natural Language and Linguistic Theory* 5: 91–138.

——— (1988). Noun phrase internal case agreement in Russian. In Michael Barlow and Charles Ferguson (eds.) *Agreement in natural language: approaches, theories, descriptions*. Stanford: Center for the Study of Language and Information. 287–304.

Baker, Mark C. (1988). *Incorporation: a theory of grammatical function changing*. Chicago and London: University of Chicago Press.

Baker, Mark C. and Kenneth L. Hale (1990). Relativized minimality and pronoun incorporation. *Linguistic Inquiry* 21: 289–97.

Baltin, Mark R. (1989). Heads and projections. In Mark R. Baltin and Antony S. Kroch (eds.) *Alternative conceptions of phrase structure*. Chicago: University of Chicago Press. 1–16.

Barwise, Jon and John Perry (1983). *Situations and attitudes*. Cambridge, Mass.: MIT Press.

Battye, Adrian and Ian Roberts (eds.) (forthcoming). *Papers from the first conference on diachronic generative syntax*. New York: Oxford University Press.

Bauer, Laurie (1990). Be-heading the word. *Journal of Linguistics* 26: 1–31.

Bean, Marian C. (1983). *The development of word order patterns in Old English*. London: Croom Helm.

Bloomfield, Leonard (1933). *Language*. New York: Holt, Rinehart, Winston, and London: Allen and Unwin.

Bogusławski, Andrzej (1966). *Semantyczne pojęcie liczebnika i jego morfologija w języku rosyjskim* (Monografie Slawistyczne 10). Wrocław: PAN.

Börjars, Kersti (1987). Raising constructions in Swedish. Master's thesis, University of Manchester.

Borsley, Robert D. (1986). Prepositional complementizers in Welsh. *Journal of Linguistics* 22: 67–84.

——— (1987). Subjects and complements in HPSG. Technical report, Center for the Study of Language and Information, Stanford. CSLI report no. 107.

——— (1990). A category-driven computational grammar of English. Technical report, IBM UK Scientific Centre, Winchester. IBM UKSC report no. 223.

——— (forthcoming). Subjects, specifiers and complements in HPSG. In Carl Pollard and Ivan Sag (eds.) *Readings in head-driven phrase structure grammar*. Stanford: Center for the Study of Language and Information.

Bouma, Gosse (1988). Modifiers and specifiers in Categorial Unification Grammar. *Linguistics* **26**: 21–46.

Bowe, Heather J. (1990). *Categories, constituents and constituent order in Pitjantjatjara*. London: Routledge and Kegan Paul.

Brame, Michael K. (1978). *Base generated syntax*. Seattle: Noit Amrofer.

Bresnan, Joan (1974). The position of certain clause principles in phrase structure. *Linguistic Inquiry* **5**: 614–19.

(1982a). Control and complementation. In Joan W. Bresnan (ed.) *The mental representation of grammatical relations*. Cambridge, Mass.: MIT Press. 282–390.

(1982b). Control and complementation. *Linguistic Inquiry* **13**: 343–434.

(ed.) (1982c). *The mental representation of grammatical relations*. Cambridge, Mass.: MIT Press.

Bybee, Joan and William Pagliuca (1985). The evolution of future meaning. In Anna Giacalone Ramat, Onofrio Carruba and Giuliano Bernini (eds.) *Proceedings of the Seventh International Conference on Historical Linguistics*. Amsterdam and Philadelphia: John Benjamins. 108–22.

Calabrese, Andrea (1992). The lack of infinitival clauses in Salentino: a synchronic analysis. In C. Laeufer and T. A. Morgan (eds.) *Theoretical analyses in Romance linguistics*. Amsterdam and Philadelphia: John Benjamins. 267–94.

(forthcoming). The sentential complementation of Salentino: a study of a language without infinitival clauses. In Adriana Belleti (ed.) *Studies in Italian dialect syntax*. Turin: Rosenberg and Sellier.

Calder, Jo, Ewan Klein, Marc Moens and Henk Zeevat (1987). Problems of dialogue parsing. Technical report, Centre for Cognitive Science, University of Edinburgh. Research paper EUCCS/RP-1.

Cann, Ronnie (1989) Splitting heads. Unpublished manuscript, Department of Linguistics, University of Edinburgh.

Cann, Ronnie and Mary E. Tait (1989). Free relatives revisited. Paper presented at the spring meeting of the Linguistics Association of Great Britain, Queen's University, Belfast.

Carlson, Greg N. (1983). Marking constituents. In Frank Henry and Barry Richards (eds.) *Linguistic categories: auxiliaries and related puzzles*. Dordrecht: D. Reidel. 69–98.

Chomsky, Noam (1965). *Aspects of the theory of syntax*. Cambridge, Mass.: MIT Press.

(1970). Remarks on nominalization. In Roderick A. Jacobs and Peter S. Rosenbaum (eds.) *Readings in English transfomational grammar*. Waltham, Mass.: Ginn. 184–221.

(1981). *Lectures on government and binding*. Dordrecht: Foris.

(1986a). *Barriers*. Cambridge, Mass.: MIT Press.

(1986b). *Knowledge of language*. New York: Praeger Press.

(1989). Some notes on economy of derivation and representation. In

I. Laka and A. Mahajan (eds.) *Functional heads and clause structure* (MIT Working Papers in Linguistics 10). 43–74.

Clancy, P. M., H. Lee and M. Zoh (1986). Processing strategies in the acquisition of relative clauses: Universal principles and language-specific realizations. *Cognition* **14**: 225–62.

Clark, Herb H. (1983). Making sense of nonce sense. In Giovanni B. Flores d'Arcais and Robert J. Jarvella (eds.) *The process of language understanding*. Chichester: John Wiley. 297–331.

Clements, Clancy J. (1989). Lexical category hierarchy and syntactic headedness in compounds. In *Proceedings of ESCOL '89*. 46–57.

Cohen, Benjamin and Gregory L. Murphy (1984). Models of concepts. *Cognitive Science* **8**: 27–58.

Comrie, Bernard (1981). *The languages of the Soviet Union*. Cambridge: Cambridge University Press.

   (1987). Grammatical relations, semantic roles and topic–comment structure in a New Guinea Highland language: Harway. In Ross Steel and Terry Threadgold (eds.) *Language topics: essays in honour of Michael Halliday*, vol. I. Amsterdam: John Benjamins. 355–66.

   (1988). Haruai verb structure and language classification in the Upper Yuat. *Language and Linguistics in Melanesia* **17**: 140–60.

   (1989). Haruai attributes and processing explanations for word order. In F. J. Heyvaert and F. Steurs (eds.) *Worlds behind words: essays in honour of Prof. Dr. F. G. Droste on the occasion of his sixtieth birthday*, vol. VI of *Symbolae Facultatis Litterarum et Philosophiae Lovaniensis, Series C Linguistica*. Leuven: Leuven University Press. 209–15.

Corbett, Greville G. (1978a). Apposition involving *dva*, *tri*, *četyre* in Russian – a solution to Worth's riddle. *Quinquereme – New Studies in Modern Languages* **1**: 258–64.

   (1978b). Problems in the syntax of Slavonic numerals. *Slavonic and East European Review* **56**: 1–12.

   (1978c). Universals in the syntax of cardinal numerals. *Lingua* **46**: 355–68.

   (1981). Syntactic features. *Journal of Linguistics* **17**: 55–76.

   (1983). *Hierarchies, targets and controllers: agreement patterns in Slavic*. London: Croom Helm.

Croft, William A. (1990). *Typology and universals*. Cambridge: Cambridge University Press.

Cruse, D. A. (1986). *Lexical semantics*. Cambridge: Cambridge University Press.

Dahl, Östen (1980). Some arguments for higher nodes in syntax: a reply to Hudson's 'Constituency and dependency'. *Linguistics* **18**: 485–8.

Davies, William D. (1986). *Choctaw verb agreement and universal grammar*. Dordrecht: D. Reidel.

Dayley, Jon P. (1985). *A Tzutujil grammar* (University of California Publications in Linguistics 107). Berkeley, Los Angeles: University of

California Press.

Dench, Alan and Nicholas Evans (1988). Multiple case-marking in Australian languages. *Australian Journal of Linguistics* 8: 1–47.

Dingwall, William O. (1969). Government, concord and feature-change rules. *Glossa* 3: 210–40.

Dixon, R. M. W. (1979). Ergativity. *Language* 55: 59–138.

Dryer, Matthew S. (1988). Object–verb and adjective–noun order: dispelling a myth. *Lingua* 74: 185–217.

(1991). SVO languages and the OV:VO typology. *Journal of Linguistics* 27: 443–82.

(1992). The Greenbergian word order correlations. *Language* 68: 81–138.

Durie, Mark (1988). The so-called passive of Acehnese. *Language* 64: 104–13.

Emonds, Joseph E. (1976). *A transformational approach to English syntax: root, structure-preserving, and local transformations.* New York: Academic Press.

(1985). *A unified theory of syntactic categories.* Dordrecht: Foris.

Evans, Nicholas (1988). Odd topic marking in Kayardild. In Peter Austin (ed.) *Complex sentence constructions in Australian languages.* Amsterdam and Philadelphia: John Benjamins.

Fassi Fehri, A. (1990). Issues in the structure of Arabic clauses and words. Unpublished paper, University of Rabat.

Fenchel, Klaus (1989). Nominal hydras. A GPSG approach to agreement in the German NP. In Caroline Wiltshire, Randolf Graczyk and Bradley Music (eds.) *Papers from the twenty-fifth regional meeting of the Chicago Linguistic Society, Part 1.* Chicago: Chicago Linguistic Society. 133–44.

Fenstad, Jens Erik, Per-Kristian Halvorsen, Tore Langholm and Johan van Bethem (1987). *Situations, language and logic.* Dordrecht: D. Reidel.

Fillmore, Charles J. (1982). Towards a descriptive framework for spatial deixis. In Robert J. Jarvella and Wolfgang Klein (eds.) *Speech, place and action: studies in deixis and related topics.* Chichester: John Wiley. 31–59.

Fischer, Wolfdietrich and Otto Jastrow (1977). *Lehrgang für die Arabische Schriftsprache der Gegenwart,* vol I. Wiesbaden: Dr Ludwig Reichert.

Fleischman, Suzanne (1983). From pragmatics to grammar: diachronic reflections on complex pasts and futures in Romance. *Lingua* 60: 183–214.

Flynn, Michael (1983). A categorial theory of structure building. In Gerald Gazdar, Geoffrey K. Pullum and Ewan Klein (eds.) *Order, concord and constituency.* Dordrecht: Foris. 139–74.

Fodor, Jerry A. (1983). *The modularity of mind.* Cambridge, Mass.: MIT Press.

Franks, Bradley (1989). Concept combination: towards an account of privatives. In George Dunbar, Bradley Franks and Terry Myers (eds.)

Papers from the 1989 Edinburgh round table on the mental lexicon (Edinburgh Working Papers in Cognitive Science 4). Edinburgh: Centre for Cognitive Science, University of Edinburgh. 85–109.

Franks, Bradley, Terry F. Myers and Scott McGlashan (1988). Defeasibility in concept combination: a criterial approach. *Proceedings of the Tenth Annual Conference of the Cognitive Science Society.* 644–50.

Frantz, Donald G. (1979). A new idea of *to*-contraction. *Canadian Journal of Linguistics* 24: 137–41.

Frazier, Lyn (1978). On comprehending sentences: syntactic parsing strategies. PhD thesis, University of Connecticut.

  (1985). Syntactic complexity. In David Dowty, Lauri Kartunnen and Arnold Zwicky (eds.) *Natural language parsing: psychological, computational, and theoretical perspectives.* Cambridge: Cambridge University Press. 129–89.

Frazier, Lyn and Keith Rayner (1988). Parameterizing the language processing system: left- vs. right-branching within and across languages. In John Hawkins (ed.) *Explaining language universals.* Oxford: Basil Blackwell. 247–79.

Fukui, N. (1986). A theory of category projection and its application. PhD thesis, Massachusetts Institute of Technology.

Fukui, N. and Margaret Speas (1986). Specifiers and projection. In *MIT Working Papers in Linguistics 8.* 128–72.

Gabelentz, Georg von der (1891). *Die Sprachwissenschaft: ihre Aufgaben, Methoden und bisherigen Ergebnisse.* Leipzig: Weigel Nachf.

Gaifman, Haim (1965). Dependency systems and phrase structure systems. *Information and Control* 8: 304–37.

Gallis, Arne (1947). Tallordenes syntaks i russisk. In *Festskrift til Professor Olaf Broch på hans 80-årsdag fra venner og elever.* Oslo: Norske Videnskaps Akademi i Oslo. 63–75.

Garde, Paul (1977). Ordre linéaire et dépendance syntaxique: contribution à une typologie. *Bulletin de la Société de Linguistique* 72: 1–26.

Gazdar, Gerald (1987). Linguistic applications of default inheritance mechanisms. In Peter Whitelock, Mary McGee Wood, Harold L. Somers, Rod L. Johnson and Paul Bennett (eds.) *Linguistic theory and computer applications.* New York: Academic Press. 37–67.

Gazdar, Gerald and Geoffrey K. Pullum (1981). Subcategorization, constituent order and the notion 'head'. In Michael Moortgat, Harry van der Hulst and Teun Hoekstra (eds.) *The scope of lexical rules.* Dordrecht: Foris. 107–23.

Gazdar, Gerald, Geoffrey K. Pullum and Ivan Sag (1982). Auxiliaries and related phenomena in a restrictive theory of grammar. *Languages* 58: 591–638.

Gazdar, Gerald, Ewan Klein, Geoffrey K. Pullum and Ivan Sag (1985). *Generalized phrase structure grammar.* Oxford: Basil Blackwell.

Gentner, Dedre (1981). Some interesting differences between nouns and verbs. *Cognition and Brain Theory* 4: 161–78.

Giorgi, Alessandra and Giuseppe Longobardi (1987). Typology and noun phrases. *Rivista di Linguistica* 1: 115–60.

(1991). *The syntax of Noun Phrases*. Cambridge: Cambridge University Press.

Greenberg, Joseph H. (1966). Some universals of grammar with particular reference to the order of meaningful elements. In Joseph H. Greenberg (ed.) *Universals of language*, 2nd edn. Cambridge, Mass.: MIT Press. 73–113.

Grosu, Alexander (1988). On the distribution of genitive phrases in Rumanian. *Linguistics* 26: 931–49.

Haegeman, Liliane (1991). *Introduction to Government and Binding theory*. Oxford: Basil Blackwell.

Hagman, Roy S. (1974). *Nama Hottentot grammar*. Indiana: University Microfilms.

Haider, Hubert (1986). Who is afraid of typology? *Folia Linguistica* 20: 109–46.

Hale, Kenneth L. (1976). Person marking in Walbiri. In Stephen Anderson and Paul Kiparsky (eds.) *A festschrift for Morris Halle*. New York: Holt, Rinehart, Winston. 305–54.

(1983). Warlpiri and the grammar of non-configurational languages. *Natural Language and Linguistic Theory* 1: 5–47.

Hampton, James A. (1987). Inheritance of attributes in natural concept conjunctions. *Memory and Cognition* 15: 55–71.

Harris, Martin (1991). Demonstrative adjectives and pronouns in a Devonshire dialect. In Peter Trudgill and J. K. Chambers (eds.) *Dialects of English: studies in grammatical variation*. London: Longman. 20–8.

Harris, Zellig S. (1946). From morpheme to utterance. *Language* 22: 161–83.

(1951). *Methods in structural linguistics*. Chicago: University of Chicago Press.

Hawkins, John A. (1982). Notes on cross category harmony, X-bar and the predictions of markedness. *Journal of Linguistics* 18: 1–35.

(1983). *Word order universals*. New York: Academic Press.

(1984). Modifier–head or function–argument relations in phrase structure? *Lingua* 63: 107–38.

(1986). *A comparative typology of English and German: unifying the contrasts*. London: Routledge (Croom Helm), and Austin: University of Texas Press.

(1988). On explaining some left–right asymmetries in syntactics and morphological universals. In Michael Hammond, Edith Moravcsik and Jessica Wirth (eds.) *Studies in syntactic typology*. Amsterdam: John Benjamins. 321–57.

(1990). A parsing theory of word order universals. *Linguistic Inquiry* 21: 223–61.

(1992a). Innateness and function in language universals. In John A.

Hawkins and Murray Gell-Mann (eds.) *The evolution of human languages*. Redwood City, Calif.: Addison-Wesley.

(1992b). Syntactic weight versus information structure in word order variation. In Joachim Jacobs (ed.) *Informationsstruktur und Grammatik. Linguistische Berichte, Sonderheft 4*. 196–219.

(forthcoming). *A performance theory of order and constituency*. Cambridge: Cambridge University Press.

Hawkins, John A. and Anne Cutler (1988). Psycholinguistic factors in morphological asymmetry. In John A. Hawkins (ed.) *Explaining language universals*. Oxford: Basil Blackwell. 280–317.

Hawkins, John A. and Gary Gilligan (1988). Prefixing and suffixing universals in relation to basic word order. *Lingua* **74**: 219–59.

Hays, David G. (1964). Dependency theory: a formalism and some observations. *Language* **40**: 511–25.

Heath, Jeffrey (1980). *Nunggubuyu myths and ethnographic texts*. Canberra: Australian Institute of Aboriginal Studies.

(1984). *Functional grammar of Nunggubuyu*. Canberra. Australian Institute of Aboriginal Studies.

(1986). Syntactic and lexical aspects of non-configurationality in Nunggubuyu (Australia). *Natural Language and Linguistic Theory* **4**: 375–408.

Heine, Berndt and Mechtild Reh (1984). *Grammaticalization and reanalysis in African languages*. Hamburg: Helmut Buske.

Heine, Berndt and Elizabeth Traugott (eds.) (1991). *Approaches to grammaticalization*, Vols. I and II. Amsterdam and Philadelphia: John Benjamins.

Heine, Berndt, Ulrike Claudi and Frederike Hünnemeyer (1991). *Grammaticalization: a conceptual framework*. Chicago and London: University of Chicago Press.

Hellan, Lars (1986). The headedness of NPs in Norwegian. In Pieter Muysken and Henk van Riemsdijk (eds.) *Features and projections*. Dordrecht: Foris. 89–122.

Hjelmslev, Louis (1939). La notion de rection. *Acta Linguistica* **1**: 10–23.

Hockett, Charles A. (1958). *A course in modern linguistics*. New York: Macmillan.

Hoeksema, Jack (1986). Some theoretical consequences of Dutch complementizer agreement. In Henry Thompson, Kenneth Whistler, Vicki Edge, Jeri J. Jaeger, Ronya Javkin, Miriam Petruck, Christopher Smeall and Robert D. Van Valin (eds.) *Proceedings of the twelfth annual meeting of the Berkeley Linguistics Society*. Berkeley, Calif.: Berkeley Linguistics Society. 147–58.

(1988). Head-types in morpho-syntax. In Geert Booij and Jaap van Marle (eds.) *Yearbook of Morphology*, Vol. I. 123–37.

Hoekstra, Teun (1984). *Transitivity: grammatical relations in Government–Binding theory*. Dordrecht: Foris.

Hogg, Richard M. (1977). *English quantifier systems.* Amsterdam: North Holland.

Hoodfar, Katayoon (1983). Gapping and the phrase structure of Persian. MA thesis, University of Manchester.

Hopper, Paul and Elizabeth Traugott (forthcoming). *Grammaticalization.* Cambridge: Cambridge University Press.

Horrocks, Geoffrey and Melita Stavrou (1987). Bounding theory and Greek syntax: evidence for wh-movement in NP. *Journal of Linguistics* 23: 79–108.

Huddleston, Rodney (1984). *Introduction to the grammar of English.* Cambridge: Cambridge University Press.

Hudson, Richard A. (1976). *Arguments for a non-transformational grammar.* Chicago: University of Chicago Press.

(1980a). Constituency and dependency. *Linguistics* 18: 179–98.

(1980b). A second attack on constituency: a reply to Dahl. *Linguistics* 18: 489–504.

(1984). *Word grammar.* Oxford: Basil Blackwell.

(1987). Zwicky on heads. *Journal of Linguistics* 23: 109–32.

(1988). Coordination and grammatical relations. *Journal of Linguistics* 24: 303–42.

(1990). *English Word Grammar.* Oxford: Basil Blackwell.

Hurford, James R. (1987). *Language and number: the emergence of a cognitive system.* Oxford: Basil Blackwell.

Iatridou, Sabine (1990). About Agr(P). *Linguistic Inquiry* 21: 551–77.

Ihalainen, O. (1991). Periphrastic *do* in affirmative sentences in the dialect of East Somerset. In Peter Trudgill and J. K. Chambers (eds.) *Dialects of English: studies in grammatical variation.* London: Longman. 148–60.

Iomdin, L. L. (1979). Fragment modeli russkogo poverxnostnogo sintaksisa: opredelitel'nye konstrukcii. *Južnoslovenski filog* 25: 19–54.

(1990). *Avtomatičeskaja obrabotka teksta na estestvennome jazyke: model' soglasovanija.* Moscow: Nauka.

Iordanskij, A. M. (1958). Istorija upotreblenija soglasovannyx opredelenij pri sočetanijax čislitel'nyx dva, tri, četyre s imenami suščestvitel'nymi v russkom jazyke. *Učenye zapiski Vladimirskogo gosudarstvennogo pedagogičeskogo instituta* 4: 54–82.

Isačenko, A. V. (1962). *Die russische Sprache der Gegenwart,* vol. I: *Formenlehre.* Halle (Saale): Max Niemeyer.

Jackendoff, Ray S. (1972). *Semantic interpretation in generative grammar.* Cambridge, Mass.: MIT Press.

(1973). The base rules for prepositional phrases. In Stephen Anderson and Paul Kiparsky (eds.) *A festschrift for Morris Halle.* New York: Holt, Rinehart, Winston. 345–56.

(1977a). Constraints on phrase structure rules. In Peter Culicover, Thomas Wasow and Adrian Akmajian (eds.) *Formal syntax.* London and New York: Academic Press. 249–83.

(1977b). $\overline{X}$ *syntax: a study of phrase structure.* Cambridge, Mass.: MIT

Press.

(1990). *Semantic structures*. Cambridge, Mass.: MIT Press.

Jacobs, Roderick A. and Peter S. Rosenbaum (1968). *English transformational grammar*. London: Ginn.

Jake, Janice (1980). Object verb agreement in Tigre. In Charles W. Kisseberth, Braj B. Kachru and Jerry L. Morgan (eds.) *Studies in the Linguistic Sciences* 10.1 Urbana, Ill.: Department of Linguistics, University of Illinois. 71–84.

Jespersen, Otto (1924). *The philosophy of grammar*. London: Allen and Unwin.

Jones, M. A. (forthcoming). *Sardinian syntax*. London: Routledge.

Kamp, J. A. W. (1975). Two theories about adjectives. In Edward L. Keenan (ed.) *Formal semantics of natural language*. Cambridge: Cambridge University Press. 123–55.

Kaplan, Ronald and Joan Bresnan (1982). Lexical-Functional Grammar: a formal system for grammatical representation. In Joan W. Bresnan (ed.) *The mental representation of grammatical relations*. Cambridge, Mass.: MIT Press. 173–281.

Kaplan, Ronald and Annie Zaenen (1989). Long-distance dependencies, constituent structure and functional uncertainty. In Mark Baltin and Anthony Kroch (eds.) *Alternative conceptions of phrase structure*. Chicago: University of Chicago Press. 17–42.

Keenan, Edward L. (1974). The functional principle: generalizing the notion of 'subject of'. In Michael W. Galy, Robert A. Fox and Antony Bruck (eds.) *Papers from the tenth regional meeting of the Chicago Linguistic Society*. Chicago: Chicago Linguistic Society. 298–309.

(1976). Towards a universal definition of subject. In Charles N. Li (ed.) *Subject and topic*. New York: Academic Press. 303–33.

(1979). On surface form and logical form. *Studies in the Linguistic Sciences* 8: 163–203. Reprinted in Edward L. Keenan (1987). *Universal grammar: fifteen essays*. London: Croom Helm. 375–428.

(1985). Relative clauses. In Timothy Shopen (ed.) *Language typology and syntactic description*, Vol. II: *Complex constructions*. Cambridge: Cambridge University Press. 141–70.

Keenan, Edward L. and L. Faltz (1985). *Boolean semantics*. Dordrecht: D. Reidel.

Kenesei, István (1991). Functional categories in Finno-Ugric. In Nigel Vincent and Kersti Börjars (eds.) *EUROTYP Working Papers III.3*. Strasbourg: European Science Foundation.

Kibrik, A. E. (1977). O sootnošenii ponjatija sintaksičeskogo podčinenija s ponjatijami soglasovanija, upravlenija i primykanija. In V. A. Zvegincev (ed.) *Problemy teoretičeskoj i èksperimental'noj lingvistiki: Sbornik statej* (Publikacii otdelenija strukturnoj i prikladnoj lingvistiki 8). Moscow: MGU. 161–79.

Kiparsky, Paul (1982). From clitic phonology to lexical phonology. In Harry van der Hulst and Norval Smith (eds.) *The structure of phonological representations*. Dordrecht: Foris. 131–75.

Kornai, András and Geoffrey K. Pullum (1990). The X-bar theory of phrase structure. *Language* **66**: 24–50.

Lakoff, George (1987). *Women, fire, and dangerous things: what categories reveal about the mind*. Chicago: University of Chicago Press.

Laughren, Margaret (1989). The configurationality parameter in Warlpiri. In Laszlo Maracz and Pieter Muysken (eds.) *Configurationality*. Dordrecht: Foris. 319–53.

Lehmann, Christian (1982). Universal and typological aspects of agreement. In Hansjakob Seiler and Franz-Josef Stachowiak (eds.) *Apprehension: das Sprachliche Erfassen von Gegenständen*, vol. II: *Die Techniken und ihr Zusammenhang in Einzelsprachen*. Tübingen: Gunter Narr. 201–67.

(1984). *Der Relativsatz*. Tübingen: Gunter Narr.

Levin, Nancy S. (1986). *Main-verb ellipsis in spoken English*. New York: Garland.

Lichtenberk, Frantisek (1991). On the gradualness of grammaticalization. In Berndt Heine and Elizabeth Traugott (eds.) *Approaches to grammaticalization*, Vol. I. Amsterdam and Philadelphia: John Benjamins. 37–80.

Lieber, Rochelle (1982). *On the organization of the lexicon*. Bloomington: Indiana University Linguistics Club.

Lightfoot, David W. (1990). Old heads and new heads. In Joan Mascarò and Marina Nespor (eds.) *Grammar in progress*. Dordrecht: Foris. 317–22.

Link, Godehard (1987). Generalized quantifiers and plurals. In Peter Gardenförs (ed.) *Generalized quantifiers*. Dordrecht: D. Reidel. 151–80.

Löbel, Elisabeth (1989). Q as a functional category. In Christa Bhatt, Elisabeth Löbel and Claudia Schmitt (eds.) *Syntactic phrase structure phenomena*. Amsterdam and Philadelphia: Benjamins. 133–58.

Loebner, Sebastian (1987). Natural language and generalized quantifier theory. In Peter Gardenförs (ed.) *Generalized quantifiers*. Dordrecht: D. Reidel. 181–201.

Lord, Carol (1976). Evidence for syntactic reanalysis: from verb to complementizer in Kaw. In Sanford B. Steever, Carol A. Walker and Saliko S. Mufwene (eds.) *Papers from the parasession on diachronic syntax*. Chicago: Chicago Linguistic Society. 179–91.

Lyons, Christopher (1991). Some thoughts on the DP hypothesis. Unpublished paper, Department of Modern Languages, University of Salford.

Lyons, John (1968). *Introduction to theoretical linguistics*. Cambridge: Cambridge University Press.

(1977). *Semantics*, vols. I and II. Cambridge: Cambridge University Press.

Marantz, Alec P. (1984). *On the nature of grammatical relations*. Cambridge, Mass.: MIT Press.

Matthews, Peter H. (1981). *Syntax*. Cambridge: Cambridge University Press.

McCawley, James D. (1988). *The syntactic phenomena of English*. Chicago:

University of Chicago Press.

Meillet, Antoine (1912). L'évolution des formes grammaticales. *Scientia* **12**: 384–400.

Meillet, Antoine and J. Vendryes (1948). *Traité de grammaire comparée des langues classiques.* Paris: Champion.

Mel'čuk, Igor A. (1979a). Lexical, or syntactic, zero in natural language. In Christine Chiarello, John Kingston, Eve. E. Sweetser, James Collins, Haruko Kawasaki, John Manley-Buser, Dorothy W. Marschak, Catherine O'Conner, David Shaul, Marta Tobey, Henry Thompson and Katherine Turner (eds.) *Proceedings of the fifth annual meeting of the Berkeley Linguistics Society.* Berkeley, Calif.: Berkeley Linguistic Society. 224–60.

(1979b). *Studies in dependency syntax.* Ann Arbor: Karoma.

(1981). Types de dépendance syntagmatique entre les mot-formes d'une phrase. *Bulletin de la Société de Linguistique* **76**: 1–59.

(1985). *Poverxnostnyj sintaksis russkix čislovyx vyraženij, Wiener Slawistischer Almanach: Sonderband XVI.* Vienna: Institut für Slawistik der Universität Wien.

(1988). *Dependency syntax: theory and practice.* Albany: SUNY Press.

Merlan, Francesca (1982). *Mangarayi* (Lingua Descriptive Series 4). Amsterdam: North Holland.

Miller, George and Noam Chomsky (1963). Finitary models of language users. In R. Duncan Luce, Robert R. Bush and Eugene Galanter (eds.) *Handbook of mathematical psychology,* vol. II. New York: Wiley. 419–92.

Miller, Jim (1985). *Semantics and syntax.* Cambridge: Cambridge University Press.

(1988). A verb-dependency account of numerals in Russian. Unpublished paper, Department of Linguistics, University of Edinburgh.

(1989). Dependency relations and constituent structure in spoken language: numerals, demonstratives and adjectives in Russian. Unpublished paper, Department of Linguistics, University of Edinburgh.

Mithun, Marianne (1984). The evolution of noun-incorporation. *Language* **60**: 847–95.

Murphy, Gregory L. (1988). Comprehending complex concepts. *Cognitive Science* **12**: 529–62.

Murphy, Gregory L. and Douglas L. Medin (1985). The role of theories in conceptual coherence. *Psychological Review* **92**: 289–316.

Muysken, Pieter (1982). Parameterizing the notion 'head'. *Journal of Linguistic Research* **2**: 27–75.

Neidle, Carol (1988). *The role of case in Russian syntax* (Studies in Natural Language and Linguistic Theory). Dordrecht: Kluwer.

Nichols, Johanna (1985a). The directionality of agreement. In Mary Niepokuj, Mary Van Clay, Vassiliki Nikiforidou and Deborah Feder (eds.) *Proceedings of the eleventh annual meeting of the Berkeley Linguistics Society.* Berkeley, Calif.: Berkeley Linguistics Society. 273–86.

(1985b). The grammatical marking of theme in literary Russian. In Michael S. Flier and Richard D. Brecht (eds.) *Issues in Russian morphosyntax*. Columbus: Slavica. 170–86.

(1986). Head-marking and dependent-marking grammar. *Language* 62: 56–119.

(forthcoming a). Chechen. In D.M. Job and R. Smeets (eds.) *The indigenous languages of the Caucasus: Northeast Caucasian*. Delmar, N.Y.: Caravan Books.

(forthcoming b). Ingush. In D.M. Job and R. Smeets (eds.) *The indigenous languages of the Caucasus: Northeast Caucasian*. Delmar, N.Y.: Caravan Books.

Noonan, Michael (1985). Complementation. In Timothy Shopen (ed.) *Language typology and syntactic description*, vol. II: *Complex constructions*. Cambridge: Cambridge University Press. 42–140.

Obenauer, Hans-Georg (1976). *Etudes de syntaxe interrogative du français*. Tübingen: Niemeyer.

Olsen, Susan (1989). AGR(eement) in the German noun-phrase. In Christa Bhatt, Elisabeth Löbel and Claudia Schmitt (eds.) *Syntactic phrase structure phenomena*. Amsterdam and Philadelphia: John Benjamins. 39–49.

Owens, Jonathan (1988). *The foundations of grammar: an introduction to mediaeval Arabic grammatical theory*. Amsterdam: John Benjamins.

Philippaki-Warburton, Irene and Georgia Catismali (1990). On the theory of control and raising in Ancient Greek: implications for the definition of subject. Unpublished paper, University of Reading.

Pickering, Martin and Guy Barry (1991). Sentence processing without empty categories. *Language and Cognitive Processes* 6: 229–59.

Pollard, Carl and Ivan Sag (1987). *Information-based syntax and semantics*, vol. I: *Fundamentals*. Stanford: Center for the Study of Language and Information.

(forthcoming). *Head-driven phrase structure grammar*. Stanford: Center for the Study of Language and Information.

Pollock, Jean-Yves (1989). Verb movement, universal grammar, and the structure of IP. *Linguistic Inquiry* 20: 365–424.

Postal, Paul M. (1969). On so-called 'pronouns' in English. In David A. Reibel and Sanford A. Schane (eds.) *Modern studies in English: readings in transformational grammar*. Englewood Cliffs, N.J.: Prentice-Hall. 201–24.

(1974). *On raising*. Cambridge, Mass.: MIT Press.

Pullum, Geoffrey K. (1985). Assuming some version of X-bar theory. In William H. Eilfort, Paul D. Kroeber and Karen L. Peterson (eds.) *Papers from the twenty-first regional meeting of the Chicago Linguistic Society*. Chicago: Chicago Linguistic Society. 323–53.

(1990). Constraints on intransitive quasi-serial verb constructions in modern colloquial English. In Brian D. Joseph and Arnold M. Zwicky (eds.) *When verbs collide: papers from the 1990 Ohio State mini-*

conference on serial verbs (Ohio State University Working Papers in Linguistics 39). 218–39.

(1991). English nominal gerund phrases as noun phrases with verb phrase heads. *Linguistics* **29**: 763–99.

Pullum, Geoffrey K. and Deirdre Wilson (1977). Autonomous syntax and the analysis of auxiliaries. *Language* **53**: 741–88.

Radford, Andrew (1981). *Transformational syntax*. Cambridge: Cambridge University Press.

(1988). *Transformational grammar*. Cambridge: Cambridge University Press.

(1989). The syntax of attributive adjectives in English: abnegating Abney. Paper presented at the Colloquium on Noun Phrase Structure, University of Manchester. Slightly revised version to appear as Radford, forthcoming.

(1990). Profiling proforms. Unpublished paper, Department of Language and Linguistics, University of Essex.

(forthcoming). The syntax of attributive adjectives in English and the problem of inheritance. In John Payne (ed.) *Noun phrase structure: empirical approaches to language typology*. Berlin: Mouton de Gruyter.

Reinhart, Tanya (1983). *Anaphora and semantic interpretation*. London: Routledge (Croom Helm).

Ritter, E. (1988). A head-movement approach to construct-state noun phrases. *Linguistics* **26**: 909–29.

Rivero, Maria-Luisa (1988). The structure of ip and v-movement in the languages of the Balkans. Unpublished paper, University of Ottawa.

Rizzi, Luigi (1986). Null objects in Italian and the theory of *pro*. *Linguistic Inquiry* **17**: 501–57.

(1990). *Relativized minimality*. Cambridge, Mass.: MIT Press.

Roberts, Ian and Nigel Vincent (1991). Towards a typology of complementizer systems. Paper delivered at the Autumn Meeting of the Linguistics Association of Great Britain, University of York.

Robins, R. H. (1979). *A short history of linguistics*, 2nd edn. London: Longman.

Robinson, Jane J. (1970). Dependency structure and transformational rules. *Language* **46**: 259–85.

Rosenbaum, Peter (1967). *The grammar of English predicate complementation*. Cambridge, Mass.: MIT Press.

Sadock, Jerrold M. (1991). *Autolexical syntax*. Chicago and London: University of Chicago Press.

Sag, Ivan, Gerald Gazdar, Thomas Wasow and Steven Weisler (1985). Coordination and how to distinguish categories. *Natural Language and Linguistic Theory* **3**: 117–71.

Scalise, Sergio (1988). Inflection and derivation. *Linguistics* **26**: 561–81.

Schachter, Paul (1985). Parts-of-speech systems. In Timothy Shopen (ed.) *Language typology and syntactic description*, vol. I: *Clause structure*.

Cambridge: Cambridge University Press. 3–61.

Seiter, William J. (1983). Subject–direct object raising in Niuean. In David M. Perlmutter (ed.) *Studies in Relational Grammar*, vol. 1. Chicago: University of Chicago Press. 317–59.

Šeludjakov, Aleksandre (1972). *Iz plemeni Kedra: juganskaja istorija*. Moscow: Sovremennik.

Šerech, J. [Shevelov, G.] (1952). *Probleme der Bildung des Zahlwortes als Redeteil in den Slavischen Sprachen*. Lunds Universitets Årsskrift, N. F. Avd. 1, 48, Lund: Lund University.

Shieber, Stuart M. (1986). *An introduction to unification-based approaches to grammar*. Stanford: Center for the Study of Language and Information.

Simpson, Jane (1983). Aspects of Warlpiri morphology and syntax. PhD thesis, Massachusetts Institute of Technology.

  (1988). Case and complementizer suffixes in Warlpiri. In Peter Austin (ed.) *Complex sentence constructions in Australian languages*. Amsterdam and Philadelphia: John Benjamins. 205–18.

Skorik, P. Ja. (1968). Čukotskij jazyk. In V. V. Vinogradov (ed.) *Mongol'skie, tungusoman'čžurskie i paleoaziatskie jazyki* (Jazyki narodov SSSR 5). Leningrad: Nauka. 248–70.

  (1977). *Grammatika čukotskogo jazyka*, vol. II. Leningrad: Nauka.

Speas, Margaret J. (1990). *Phrase structure in natural languages*. Dordrecht: Kluwer.

Sportiche, Dominique (1988). A theory of floating quantifiers and its corollaries for constituent structure. *Linguistic Inquiry* **19**: 425–49.

Starosta, Stanley (1988). *The case for Lexicase: an outline of lexicase grammatical theory*. London: Pinter.

Stowell, Timothy (1981). Origins of phrase structure. PhD thesis, Massachusetts Institute of Technology.

  (1989). Subjects, specifiers and X-bar theory, In Mark R. Baltin and Anthony S. Kroch (eds.) *Alternative conceptions of phrase structure*. Chicago: University of Chicago Press. 232–62.

Stuurman, Frits (1991). X-bar and X-plain. Seminar paper presented at the Department of Language and Linguistics, University of Essex.

Šukšin, Vasilij (1975). Raskas. *Izbrannye proizvedenija v dvux tomax*, vol. I. Moscow. 83–8.

Suprun, A. E. (1957). K upotrebleniju roditel'nogo i imenitel'nogo padežej množestvennogo čisla prilagatel'nyx v sočetanijax s čislitel'nymi *dva, tri, četyre* v sovremennom russkom jazyke. *Učenye zapiski Kirgizskogo gosudarstvennogo pedagogičeskogo instituta* 3: 72–84. Reprinted with minor changes in Suprun (1959: 61–75).

  (1959). *O russkix čislitel'nyx*. Frunze: Kirghiz State University.

  (1969). *Slavjanskie čislitel'nye (stanovlenie čislitel'nyx kak osoboj časti reči)*. Minsk: Belorussian State University.

Sutcliffe, Edmund F. (1936). *A grammar of the Maltese language*. Oxford: Oxford University Press.

Szabolcsi, Anna (1987). Functional categories in the noun-phrase. In István Kenesei (ed.) *Approaches to Hungarian*, vol. II: *Theories and analyses*. Szeged: JATE. 167–89.

(forthcoming). Is DP analogous to IP or CP? In John Payne (ed.) *Noun phrase structure: empirical approaches to language typology*. Berlin: Mouton de Gruyter.

Tait, Mary E. (1991). The syntactic representation of morphological categories. PhD thesis, University of Edinburgh.

Tait, Mary E. and Ronnie Cann (1990). On empty subjects. In *Proceedings of the Workshop on Parametric Variation*. Edinburgh: Centre for Cognitive Science. University of Edinburgh. 209–27.

Tesnière, Lucien (1959). *Eléments de syntaxe structurale*. Paris: Klincksieck.

Thompson, Sandra A. (1988). A discourse approach to the cross-linguistic category 'adjective'. In John A. Hawkins (ed.) *Explaining language universals*. Oxford: Basil Blackwell. 167–85.

Travis, Lisa (1984). Parameters and effects of word order variation. PhD thesis, Massachusetts Institute of Technology.

(1989). Parameters of phrase structure. In Mark R. Baltin and Anthony S. Kroch (eds.) *Alternative conceptions of phrase structure*. Chicago: University of Chicago Press. 263–79.

Van Valin, Robert D. (1985). Case marking and the structure of the Lakhota clause. In Johanna Nichols and Antony C. Woodbury (eds.) *Grammar inside and outside the clause*. Cambridge: Cambridge University Press. 365–413.

Vennemann, Theo (1974). Theoretical word order studies: results and problems. *Papiere zur Linguistik* 7: 5–25.

(1975). An explanation of drift. In Charles N. Li (ed.) *Word order and word order change*. Austin: University of Texas Press. 269–305.

(1976). Categorial grammar and the order of meaningful elements. In Alphonse Juilland (ed.) *Linguistic studies offered to Joseph Greenberg on the occasion of his sixtieth birthday*. California: Saratoga. 615–34.

(1977). Konstituenz und Dependenz in einigen neueren Grammatiktheorien. *Sprachwissenschaft* 2: 259–301.

(1984). Typology, universals and change of language. In Jacek Fisiak (ed.) *Historical syntax*. Berlin: Mouton. 593–612.

Vennemann, Theo and R. Harlow (1977). Categorial grammar and consistent basic VX serialization. *Theoretical Linguistics* 4: 227–54.

Vincent, Nigel (1980). Syntactic categories old and new. Paper delivered to the Philological Society, London.

(1989). Constituentization. Paper delivered at the ninth International Conference on Historical Linguistics, Rutgers University.

(1992). The Latin supine – a neglected grammatical category. Paper delivered to the Cambridge Philological Society.

(forthcoming a). On the history of complementation in Romance. In Adrian Battye and Ian Roberts (eds.) *Papers from the first conference on diachronic generative syntax*. New York: Oxford University Press.

(forthcoming b). Burzio's generalization, raising and lexical mapping theory. University of Manchester.

Wandruszka, Ulrich (1989). 'Klassemisch' versus 'Lexemisch': zwei Grundtypen sprachlicher Strukturbildung. *Papiere zur Linguistik* **41**: 77–100.

Warner, Anthony R. (1989). Multiple heads and minor categories in generalized phrase-structure grammar. *Linguistics* **27**: 179–205.

Wells, R. S. (1947). Immediate constituents. *Language* **23**: 81–177.

Williams, Edwin (1981). On the notions 'lexically related' and 'head of a word'. *Linguistic Inquiry* **12**: 245–74.

(1982). Another argument that passive is transformational. *Linguistic Inquiry* **13**: 160–3.

Worth, Dean S. (1959). Grammatical and lexical quantification in the syntax of the Russian numeral. *International Journal of Slavic Linguistics and Poetics* **1–2**: 117–32.

Yngve, Victor H. A. (1960). A model and an hypothesis for language structure. *Proceedings of the American Philosophical Society* **104**: 444–66.

Zeevat, Henk (1988). Combining categorial grammar and unification. In Uwe Reyle and Christian Rohrer (eds.) *Natural language parsing and linguistic theories*. Dordrecht: D. Reidel. 202–29.

Zemskaja, E. A. and L. A. Kapanadze (1978). *Russkaja razgovornaja reč': teksty*. Moscow: Nauka.

Žukova, A. N. (1980). *Jazyk palanskix korjakov*. Leningrad: Nauka.

Zwicky, Arnold M. (1985). Heads. *Journal of Linguistics* **21**: 1–29.

(1986). Imposed versus inherent feature specifications, and other multiple feature markings. In *Indiana University Linguistics Club Twentieth Anniversary Volume*. Bloomington: Indiana University Linguistics Club. 85–106.

(1988). Direct reference to heads. *Folia Linguistica* **22**: 397–404.

(1989). What's become of derivations? Defaults and invocations. In *Proceedings of the fifteenth annual meeting of the Berkeley Linguistics Society*. Berkeley, Calif.: Berkeley Linguistics Society. 303–20.

(1990a). Syntactic representations and phonological shapes. In Sharon Inkelas and Draga Zec (eds.) *The phonology–syntax connection*. Chicago: University of Chicago Press. 379–97.

(1990b). What are we talking about when we talk about serial verbs? In Brian D. Joseph and Arnold M. Zwicky (eds.) *When verbs collide: papers from the 1990 Ohio State mini-conference on serial verbs* (Ohio State University Working Papers in Linguistics 39). Columbus, Ohio: Ohio State University, Department of Linguistics.

(forthcoming). Jottings on adpositions, case inflections, government and agreement. In Diane Brentari, Gary Larson and Lynn MacLeod (eds.) *The joy of grammar: a festschrift for James D. McCawley*. Amsterdam: John Benjamins.

Index